RACE, NATION, TRANSLATION

RACE, NATION, TRANSLATION

South African Essays, 1990–2013

Zoë Wicomb

Edited by Andrew van der Vlies

Yale

UNIVERSITY

PRESS

New Haven & London

Published with assistance from the foundation established
in memory of James Wesley Cooper of the Class of 1865, Yale College.

Yale University Press books may be purchased in quantity for educational,
business, or promotional use. For information, please e-mail sales.press@yale.edu
(U.S. office) or sales@yaleup.co.uk (U.K. office).

Set in Electra type by Westchester Publishing Services.
Printed in the United States of America.

Library of Congress Control Number: 2018938165
ISBN 978-0-300-22617-1 (hardcover : alk. paper)

A catalogue record for this book is available from the British Library.

This paper meets the requirements of ANSI/NISO Z39.48-1992
(Permanence of Paper).

10 9 8 7 6 5 4 3 2 1

CONTENTS

Acknowledgments

ZOË WICOMB

My thanks to Andrew van der Vlies: without the gentleness of his nudges and questions, his insightful editing, this project would have vanished.

Thanks to Dorothy Driver, who initiated the collection, is overdue, as well as to others whose support and encouragement in the past have helped me to carry on writing: Derek Attridge, Kai Easton, David Attwell, Meg Samuelson, Sean Jacobs, Desiree Lewis, Patrick Flanery.

Thanks as always to Roger Palmer.

ANDREW VAN DER VLIES

My thanks to Zoë Wicomb: I am grateful for her invitation to collaborate on this editorial project, and for the grace and good humor with which she worked with me to bring it to publication.

Thanks to Roger Palmer for his encouragement and his assistance with images and permissions, Theresa Harney for early research assistance, Rita Barnard for advice and support over many years, and Derek Attridge for prompting me to work on Zoë Wicomb's writing in the first place.

I acknowledge the institutional and financial support of the School of English and Drama at Queen Mary University of London. Thanks to Sarah Miller, Ash Lago, and Mary Pasti at Yale University Press and to copyeditor Otto Bohlmann. Thanks, too, to the press's readers for helpful suggestions.

This project and much else would have been impossible without the support of Patrick Flanery, as ardent an admirer of the author's work as I am.

✦ ✦ ✦

The author and editor acknowledge with gratitude permission to reprint, in edited and in some cases substantially revised form, material by the author published previously, as indicated below.

A version of Chapter 1 was first published in *Critical Fictions: The Politics of Imaginative Writing*, edited by Philomena Mariani (Seattle: Bay Press, 1991), 242–50.

Chapter 2 is revised from the article "Nation, Race, and Ethnicity: Beyond the Legacy of Victims" published in *Current Writing: Text and Reception in Southern Africa* 4, no. 1 (1992), and online on 1 June 2011. It is included here with permission of the journal and reprinted by permission of Taylor & Francis Ltd., copyright © Owned by the editorial board, http://www.tandfonline.com/. See http://dx.doi .org/10.1080/1013929X.1992.9677887.

A version of Chapter 3 first appeared in print under the same title in *Transition* 60 (1993), 27–32. It is included here with permission of the journal and of Indiana University Press.

A version of Chapter 4 was first published in the *Journal of Commonwealth Literature* 30, no. 2 (1995), 1–15. The author exercises her right to republish this revised version with thanks to the publisher, Sage Publications Ltd.

Chapter 5 is revised from the article "To Hear the Variety of Discourses" published in *Current Writing: Text and Reception in Southern Africa*, 2, no. 1 (1990), and online on 1 June 2011. It is included here with permission of the journal and reprinted by permission of Taylor & Francis Ltd., copyright © Owned by the editorial board, http://www.tandfonline.com/. See http://dx.doi.org/10.1080 /1013929X.1990.9677857.

Chapter 6 was first published, in slightly different form, as a chapter in *Gendering the Reader*, edited by Sara Mills (London: Harvester Wheatsheaf, 1994), 99–127; Chapter 4 © 1994 Zoë Wicomb. It is used with permission from Pearson Education Limited.

A version of Chapter 7 was published as "Postcoloniality and Postmodernity: The Case of the Coloured in South Africa" in the conference proceedings of AUETSA 1996, and later under the current title in *Writing South Africa: Literature, Apartheid, and Democracy, 1970–1995*, edited by Derek Attridge and Rosemary Jolly (Cambridge: Cambridge University Press, 1998), 91–107 (http://dx.doi .org/10.1017 /CBO9780511586286.009). The author exercises her right to republish this revised version with thanks to the publisher, Cambridge University Press.

A version of Chapter 8 first appeared in the *New Yorker* magazine on 16 December 2013 (p. 27), in the regular "The Talk of the Town" section, and is included here with permission of the publisher.

Chapter 9 is revised from an article with the same title published in *Social Identities* 4, no. 3 (1998), 363–83, and online on 25 August 2010, available at: http://www.tandfonline.com/. See http://dx.doi.org/10.1080/13504639851672. It is included here with permission of the journal and of Taylor and Francis.

Chapter 10 is revised from the article "Translations in the Yard of Africa" published in the *Journal of Literary Studies* 18, nos. 3–4 (2002), 209–23, and online on 6 July 2007; copyright © JLS/TLW, reprinted by permission of Taylor & Francis Ltd., http://www.tandfonline.com, on behalf of JLS/TLW. See https://doi.org/10.1080/02564710208530301.

A version of Chapter 15 with the same title was published in *Step across This Line: Proceedings of the 3rd AISLI Conference*, edited by Alessandra Contenti, Maria Paola Guarducci, and Paola Splendore (Venice: Cafoscarina, 2004). The text used here is revised from an article, also with the same title, published in the *Journal of Postcolonial Writing* 41, no. 2 (2005), and online on 19 August 2006, available at: http://www.tandfonline.com/. See http://dx.doi.org/10.1080/17449850500252268. It is included here with permission of the journal and of Taylor and Francis.

Chapter 16 is revised from the article "*Slow Man* and the Real: A Lesson in Reading and Writing," published in the *Journal of Literary Studies* 25, no. 4 (2009), 7–24, and online on 19 November 2009; copyright © JLS/TLW, reprinted by permission of Taylor & Francis Ltd., http://www.tandfonline.com, on behalf of JLS/TLW. See http://dx.doi.org/10.1080/02564710903226676.

INTRODUCTION

Zoë Wicomb's South African Essays: Intertextual Ethics, Translative Possibilities, and the Claims of Discursive Variety

Andrew van der Vlies

Zoë Wicomb is one of South Africa's most important writers. Born in 1948, six months after the election victory by an Afrikaner nationalist party committed to racial segregation introduced the term "apartheid" to the world, she was educated in Cape Town, before leaving for the United Kingdom in the early 1970s. With the exception of a brief period in South Africa in the early 1990s, and regular return visits after 1994, she has lived abroad ever since.[1] Despite this absence from the country of her birth, Wicomb has a claim to be one of the most significant authors of late-apartheid and postapartheid South Africa. Her creative oeuvre to date includes the 1987 linked-story collection, *You Can't Get Lost in Cape Town*, the novels *David's Story* (2000), *Playing in the Light* (2006), and *October* (2014), and numerous short stories, including those assembled in *The One That Got Away* (2008). Wicomb was awarded a Donald Windham–Sandy M. Campbell Literature Prize by Yale University in 2013, the prize's inaugural year.

Zoë Wicomb is also among South Africa's most significant literary critics and public intellectuals. She has, over the past quarter century, published a body of insightful essays and delivered key interventions at conferences and colloquia in the country and abroad. It is a selection of these writings—including several hitherto unpublished pieces—that are brought together for the first time in this collection, in which they appear with Americanized spelling and changes made since their initial delivery or publication. They show a thinker returning often to such themes as race, identity, and gender politics in the postcolony, the relationships among textual and visual literacy, print cultures, and orality, the politics of memory and nostalgia and the nature of the archive, the lessons of linguistics and critical theory for reading, writing, and teaching, the fates of genre, the politics of representation, and ethics of intertextuality. Just as Wicomb had been a critic of the apartheid regime and chronicler of its pernicious effects on South Africa's social and cultural life, so her critical work since 1990 offers brave and unstinting critique of the dangers of the hegemonic discourses of a new postapartheid nationalism—one not necessarily black African but occasionally uncompromising in its unwillingness to countenance the subtleties of a culturally, racially, and linguistically heterogeneous country, one whose complexities Wicomb charts so strikingly in her own fiction. In a world once more witness to rising nationalist rhetoric and to rightward populist movements that declare themselves the enemy of diversity and pluralism, Wicomb's essays speak powerfully to many other national and regional contexts in the present.

Several collections of essays by leading authors from South Africa have shown the broader international relevance of engagements by the country's writers with the challenges posed to the arts—and intellectual life in general—by the politics of race, by brands of exclusionary ideology, and by the exigencies of antiauthoritarian struggle. Important examples include Es'kia Mphahlele's *The African Image* (1962) and Lewis Nkosi's *Home and Exile* (1965), each grappling with what it meant for black writers to work in the shadow of apartheid or go into exile.[2] Also significant are Nadine Gordimer's essays and speeches, in particular those from the 1970s and 1980s (many published in the 1988 collection *The Essential Gesture*) that explored with a sense of great urgency the challenges faced by writers working under an oppressive regime.[3] Then there are the contributions made by writers closer in age to Wicomb, the Nobel literature laureate J. M. Coetzee (b. 1940) and the author and public intellectual Njabulo Ndebele (b. 1948), whose interventions are most alike in spirit and range to Wicomb's. To the work of these eminent forerunners we can now add the present collection, Zoë Wicomb's *Race, Nation, Translation: South African Essays, 1990–2013*.

Coetzee has published a number of collections of critical nonfiction: a sophisticated historicizing of the conditions under which European literary traditions came to find purchase in Southern Africa and with what complications and complicities, *White Writing* (1988); reflections on form, voice, genre, and politics in *Doubling the Point* (1992); an examination of the effects of censorship on aesthetics, *Giving Offense* (1996); and three selections of reviews, *Stranger Shores* (2001), *Inner Workings* (2007), and *Late Essays* (2018).[4] Like

Coetzee, Wicomb is a virtuoso close reader; she is as erudite as Coetzee, certainly as au courant with currents of critical opinion—and as likely to give them short shrift. Her interventions are, however, more alert to feminist insights than Coetzee's, perforce sensitive to what it means to theorize from a body always already raced and gendered by the society in which an author writes and speaks.

Ndebele's *South African Literature and Culture: Rediscovery of the Ordinary* (1994), with its much-referenced centerpiece essay (from which the collection took its subtitle), shares with Wicomb's work an impulse to challenge received assumptions about the role of the literary in the dispensation to come. Ndebele's more recent collection, *Fine Lines from the Box* (2007), displays a wariness very like Wicomb's about nationalist and gender politics in the "new" South Africa (in Ndebele's case, in relation to the Mbeki and Zuma administrations in particular).[5] In their insistence on difficulty, on complexity and nuance, Wicomb's critical works echo some of the most important of Ndebele's injunctions that writers embark on what he called, in that central essay of his first collection, a "rediscovery of the ordinary."[6] By this Ndebele meant the everyday ways in which people survived—indeed, made lives for themselves—throughout the oppressive years of apartheid rule. In his analysis, offered during the worst years of state violence against antiapartheid activism (the essay first appeared in a journal in 1986),[7] such a revalorization of the quotidian could enact powerful proto-national possibilities. Instead of merely reflecting the spectacle of apartheid—which would effectively allow the state to act as "author" of their works—black writers might instead insist that the future would make room for the parochial, the quiet, the ordinary.

A similar position is certainly evident in Wicomb's essays, just as it is in Wicomb's body of creative work.[8] Taken together, the oeuvre offers an insistence on exploring the complexity of individual lives not easily aligned with national or racial narratives authorized by whoever might be in power. Carol Sicherman, in her afterword to the Feminist Press edition of *You Can't Get Lost in Cape Town*, calls Wicomb a "post-protest" writer, one "committed to democratic ideals but refusing a single ideological stance."[9] Rita Barnard makes a case for the application to Wicomb's work of Loren Kruger's description of writing from the period of the long transition being termed "post-anti-apartheid" instead of "post-apartheid" writing.[10] We might also think of Edward Said's defense of the role of the intellectual and writer being to present "a kind of countermemory with its own counterdiscourse" to defend against the rise of new orthodoxies.[11] Wicomb's has been one of the preeminent voices of this kind of responsible critique in what I am choosing to call the postapartheid (rather than post-apartheid) era, that is to say, an era that is by now its own period, one that not only comes after

apartheid, or does not come after it in a way that suggests that the problems bequeathed by apartheid have been superseded, but a period that is forever in
apartheid's long shadow.

The analyses, critiques, and interventions contained in this selection of Zoë
Wicomb's most important nonfiction address important cultural and political
movements and events during—and stage readings of significant literary texts
in the midst of—the period from the late 1980s to the present, which is to say,
from the moment at which the transition to a democratic South Africa seemed
(finally) tantalizingly achievable, even if fraught with uncertainty and the very
real prospect of violent disappointment, to a period in which hopes for freedom
and equality for all—in what Archbishop Emeritus Desmond Tutu famously
called the "Rainbow Nation"—have come under severe pressure. Nelson Mandela is dead, his legacy widely and critically debated within the country. South
Africa's fourth (post-1994) president, Jacob Zuma, was for most of his tenure
(which came to an abrupt end as this volume was being readied for press) in-
tractably mired in allegations of corruption and impropriety. The nation waits,
once more, to see how a new president (Cyril Ramaphosa) will grapple with the
country's many problems. Protests over failing infrastructure and lack of delivery of crucial social services routinely flare up. There remains great uncertainty
on university campuses throughout South Africa in the wake of several years of
protests about curricula, access, funding, and employment practices. Building
on a movement to remove a statue of Cecil Rhodes, the mining magnate and
imperialist (also onetime premier of the Cape Colony), on the University of
Cape Town campus in early 2015, the protest movement metamorphosed into a
countrywide push to ensure there would be no increases in tuition fees at the
end of the year, before coalescing in late 2016 as a series of demands for free
higher education for all, for an end to the outsourcing of low-paid jobs on campus, and for a thoroughgoing decolonization of university curricula. Debates
about the role of students, academics, and the state in shaping the direction of
higher education in the country have been polarized and polarizing, but it is
fair to say that little in recent South African history has so publicly galvanized
debates about pedagogy and the politics of representation.

Many commentators have observed that the young people engaging in protest are no longer inclined to wait, as their parents may have been, for the change
that was promised by the antiapartheid struggle, for the fulfillment of what the
African National Congress (A.N.C.) promised in 1994. Wicomb has consistently
anticipated this impatience and the dangers of the disappointment that all recognize is now close to becoming a national structure of feeling in the country.[12]
No amount of symbolic overhaul will make up for economic transformation,

she argues in "Five Afrikaner Texts and the Rehabilitation of Whiteness" (included in this volume as Chapter 9). "In the world beyond texts where whiteness remains bound up with privilege and economic power, it cannot simply be written off," she notes. In Wicomb's most recent novel, *October*, a South African–born Scottish-resident academic responds to her brother saying that she should consider herself "lucky" that she does not live in South Africa, lucky that she is not "here, in this mess," by reflecting on his—and others'—"unreasonable expectations" for change, "given how much of the old South Africa is still in place."[13] Several of the essays in this collection make reference to these conditions, even if only by pointing to and implicitly questioning the work done by myth, that which is removed from the realm of the ordinary, overdetermined through processes of political expediency or vicarious investment (another form of ideological work), in other words by that which might have helped generate the sense that the transition would be easier. We see something of this mode of analysis in Wicomb's unusual reflection in memory of Mandela, first published in the *New Yorker*, with which the first part of this collection closes (Chapter 8). Where she might have remembered the great antiapartheid leader and first president of a democratic nation as a hero, as many chose to do, for his investment in reconciliation, for his global stature, Wicomb wonders instead about the man's hair, about what he said in private over tea. She acknowledges the work of myth but asks us to think too about the body, dwelling on the unknowable and the contradictory. Taking account of such complexity, of the tensions between public and private, and of the discursive construction of positions that might threaten to overwhelm complexity, is at the heart of the Wicomb project, both creative and critical.

How to effect meaningful symbolic overhaul that does not lose sight of the necessity of insisting too on real structural overhaul; how to imagine, in writing, the nature of a heterogeneous plurality respectful of variety of all kinds; how to demonstrate what role critique and pedagogy can play in helping to realize an equal society; what responsibilities writers might have to those whose material experiences will always strain at the possibilities of representation: these are preoccupations of all of the essays in this collection. In the earlier pieces, those dating from the uncertain first years of the transition (that began with the release of Mandela and other A.N.C. leaders from prison in 1990) through (perhaps) to the adoption of the country's new constitution in 1996, Wicomb asks what "culture" will—or *should*—mean in a postapartheid South Africa to come. She wonders how women will serve the new order's cultural and political imagination, and asks what future there might be for the rich oral heritage of the country's many linguistic communities. How do we hear the voice of those disadvantaged under the old regime, and what might their role be under the new? How, indeed, do we hear the variety of discourses without fetishizing difference or continuing to assign each discourse a category too readily bequeathed from a divisive, traumatic past?

Given the focus of many of these earlier essays on the cultural-political field during the transition from late-apartheid to early postapartheid South African society, we have grouped these together in Part 1 of this collection, "Hearing the Variety of Discourses," a heading that echoes the injunction heard in the title of the very earliest of the essays (offered there in the infinitive). For the most part, these are Wicomb's public-political essays, though no neat categorization is possible. "Motherhood and the Surrogate Reader" (Chapter 6 here), for example, purports to read closely a series of advertisements, yet Wicomb has in her sights both gender politics in the new nation *and* the gender politics of reading (and of semiotics) more generally. The collection's second part contains those of Wicomb's essays that deal principally with questions of reading and authorship, here collected under a heading—"Intertextuality and the Postcolonial Author"—that quotes from the title of the essay in which they are staged perhaps most polemically. In these essays, Wicomb responds to individual authors and texts, reflects on the ethics of narrative acts, and contemplates her own identity as writer *and* reader. She confirms herself as a sensitive and illuminating commentator on the work of a range of important South African writers who, like her, have a claim to world literary significance—J. M. Coetzee, Bessie Head, Nadine Gordimer, and Ivan Vladislavić. Again, no easy categorization is possible: close reading and literary analysis are central to many of the earlier essays, too; some of these later essays have an eye on the "scripto-visual" (a term Wicomb deploys with great acuity) in addition to the literary; and readings of literary texts—Wicomb's bravura engagement with Coetzee's 1999 novel, *Disgrace*, comes to mind—frequently also serve broader cultural analysis or diagnosis. Thus while our arrangement has been made to enable readers more easily to find their way to those essays that might be thought to look *outward*, to questions of nation, nationalism, race, and history (in the first part), and to those (in the second part) that mediate concerns with many of the same questions but primarily through attention to *textual* objects, Wicomb's focus on the ethical imperative to read (and reread) well, carefully, thoughtfully, and warily militates against reading *only* in relation to these categories. Similarly, while these essays focus predominantly on South or Southern African texts, they promise payoffs for scholars and students of postcolonial studies, of world literatures in English, and of cultural studies more broadly.

In what follows, I expand on the contexts, personal and political, that frame this important body of criticism. While offering an introduction to the essays (by way of their recurrent concerns), I must issue a caveat: to experience the inventiveness, the clarity and surprise, the erudition and the productive difficulty of Wicomb's critical and theoretical work, there is no substitute for reading and rereading the essays themselves, and preferably as a whole body of work, rather than selectively.

BIOGRAPHY AND THE APARTHEID CONTEXT

The framing context for Zoë Wicomb's work is the historical reality and the afterlife of apartheid rule in South Africa, between 1948 and 1994.[14] Indeed, all of the essays suggest just how inescapable are its lingering political, structural, cultural, and psychological effects. Meaning "separateness" (*apart*-ness) in Afrikaans, the creole language derived largely from seventeenth-century Dutch spoken by the majority of the white minority that ruled until the transition, apartheid was a system of governance that involved the official assigning of every person to a racial group and the social and economic engineering of every aspect of life in accordance with that classification. The Population Registration Act codified the recognition of four such groups: white; black, divided further into separate ethnic groups gradually allocated their own nominally self-governing "homelands" or reservations (land least desirable for white agriculture, in which restricted common title was technically possible); Coloured (spelled and capitalized thus in the Population Registration Act), a complex category most simply glossed for now as mixed-race; and Indian, composed largely of descendants of indentured sugarcane workers and the merchants and professionals who followed them in the late nineteenth and early twentieth centuries from India. Further Acts of Parliament directed which amenities you could use, where you might live and work, whom you might marry, what kind of job you could do, and how your children were educated, all on the basis of your racial classification.

In some measure, of course, apartheid legislation built on colonial- and dominion-era segregation, expanding on the logic of such earlier laws as the 1913 Natives Land Act[15] and stripping away the limited franchise and land-ownership rights that persisted in parts of the country (in particular in the former Cape Colony). Readers should look elsewhere for detailed histories of apartheid, including recent reassessments of its scope and coherence: as Deborah Posel notes, attempts at a summary description bear "the obvious risk of caricature, essentialising and dehistoricising a system of rule that was more internally fractious and fractured, historically fluid and complex, than the formulaic reductions can possibly render."[16] Apartheid had distinct periods too, the 1950s being marked by more cautious attempts at social engineering than took place in the 1960s, a more doctrinaire and ruthless phase made possible by a period of economic growth, a solid parliamentary majority for the National Party, and brutal suppression of activism that saw leading liberation-movement figures either executed, jailed, or exiled.[17] The 1970s saw a decline in the white state's economic strength and a resurgence of political activism, including the rise of Black Consciousness, culminating in the student uprising that began in Soweto on 16 June 1976. This heralded an age of tentative internal reform that would splutter through spasms of heightened restriction, states of "emergency" (and quasi-martial law), misadventures in proxy Cold War conflicts (especially in Angola), toward secret talks in the late 1980s and the beginning of direct negotiations for a new constitutional settlement in the early 1990s.

Wicomb's first book, *You Can't Get Lost in Cape Town*, gives a sense of the effects on ordinary people of apartheid's pervasive and pernicious racial hierarchizing and its attempts to manage interaction between races instrumentally. In "Bowl Like Hole," the first story (or chapter), the reader sees the young protagonist, Frieda Shenton, chastised for sitting under the kitchen table and taunted by her mother with the suggestion that she is behaving "like a tame Griqua."[18] Note the use of the adjective "tame," as if to suggest that to be "Griqua" is somehow other than human. In the book's second chapter, "Jan Klinkies," Truida, the wife of the eponymous Jan (a relation of the Shentons), despite being well educated (it is Truida who had been able to read official documents evicting the family from an area designated for white ownership under the notorious Group Areas Act), is stigmatized by her in-laws on the basis of her extended family's dark complexion, an association "her light skin" does nothing to ameliorate. That there is "something nylonish about her hair" confirms for them Truida's inferiority; the young Frieda is unsurprisingly preoccupied with her own hair's condition, lest it appear similarly "fuzzy."[19] Each of these instances—and many others—evidence the harmful adoption of racial stigmatization by members of a heterogeneous community occupying a notional space between two imagined and impossible points of imagined purity and Manichean opposition: "white" and "black."

Griqua is a loose ethnic identity shared by those descended from autochthonous peoples of the Cape and white settlers. Speaking Dutch and then Afrikaans (as it grew out of a creole "kitchen" Dutch—"Bowl Like Hole" stages the tensions about levels of propriety and the difficulties of language in the kitchen), the Griqua were, Dorothy Driver notes, "what has been called a 'mixed race,' although they were often not physically distinguishable from early South African Dutch settlers, as early documents confirm."[20] Driven to abandon their pastoral lifestyle by the Natives Land Act, they became a peripatetic people, searching for a permanent settlement amid the fissures of a state increasingly unwilling to make room for any group or way of life that did not conform to a notion of racial "purity." Derek Attridge suggests that "we cannot forget, once we are aware of them, Wicomb's own Griqua origins."[21] He notes that she claims birth (in an interview) "in a little, remote Griqua settlement,"[22] Beeswater, which features in a number of the fictions. In *David's Story*, the character David Dirkse shares similar origins, but his attempts to research a reliable history of the Griqua people is frustrated both by the mythmaking of the group's own leaders and by an unnamed female amanuensis (a presence not unlike Wicomb herself) whose skepticism about all totalizing racial categories—not to mention official histories—unsettles David's search for a reliable truth.[23] If *David's Story* "both entertains and mocks the possibility of a Griqua identity," suggests Rita Barnard, Wicomb's second novel, *Playing in the Light*, "exposes the constructedness of racial categories, even as it explores the characteristically coloured experience of passing for white."[24] (An aside: the echo of Toni Morrison's *Playing in the Dark* in Wicomb's title is not accidental and reveals a long-standing conversation with and influence by African American fiction and theory.) Perhaps we cannot forget her assumed Griqua origins, but Wicomb asks her readers always to question any such label, to recall the power relations that remain invested in such categorizations, and never to forget the real human costs of such definitions.

Indeed, *Playing in the Light* makes much of the absurdity of the classificatory laws. Marion Campbell spends a lunch hour in the National Library in Cape Town researching "the laws and confusing racial definitions" and learns that while "1946 franchise laws allowed mixed blood in one parent or grandparent, . . . the new bill of 1950, designed to formalise and fix the categories of coloured and white, conflicted with the earlier one," and "many whites who until then had thought of themselves as European were in the fifties transferred to the newly established separate coloured voters' roll."[25] The 1950 law used as definition for a white person "one who in appearance obviously is, or who is generally accepted as a white person," excluding "a person who, although in appearance obviously a white person, is generally accepted as a coloured person." By 1962, the definition of "white" had changed to "a person who (a) in appearance is obviously a white person and who is not generally accepted as a coloured person; or (b) is generally accepted as a white person and is not in appearance obviously not a white person, but does not include any person who for the purposes of classification under the Act, freely and voluntarily admits that he is by descent a native or coloured person unless it is proved that the admission is not based on fact."[26] Marion is amazed, even amused, at the terminological contortions of these definitions. They nonetheless belie the great costs involved in reclassification, or in deciding to "pass" as "white"—which, she discovers, is precisely what her parents have done, unbeknownst to her, for her whole life.[27]

Although Wicomb's extended family spoke Afrikaans as its first language, she was raised speaking English too, and literature in English provided important models in childhood. Her rural home in Beeswater was near neither school nor public library facilities for "'non-Europeans,'" she explains, citing one apartheid-era epithet for those not classified white. Yet her home housed "two books, *Pride and Prejudice* (barely comprehensible) and an abridged *Oliver Twist*. I still love both. . . . I was transported from the vulgarity of apartheid by books—books opened up different worlds, and brought freedom from an oppressive social order."[28] As a girl, Wicomb was sent to live with an aunt in Cape Town in order to attend a good English-medium school; her parents believed this would give her a better start than that which might ordinarily come to a small-town Afrikaans-speaking woman of color at the height of apartheid. After school, Wicomb subsequently studied at what is now the University of the Western Cape, then a higher-education institution reserved by the apartheid government for the education of coloured students. Here she took a B.A. in English literature in 1968. In a profile in the *Scotsman* in 2005, she is quoted as explaining how "history played a cruel trick on her . . . : the anti-apartheid resistance movement was weak in the late Sixties, when she was a student, and she left the country two years before Steve Biko's Black Consciousness movement flared up on the campuses."[29] That Wicomb might have become an activist inside the country had the political climate not been so stultifying and repressive is a claim she repeats in the interview that closes the present collection. One can only speculate that it is partly on account of her years in exile, and her ongoing insider-outsider perspective, that her critical work on South African literature and culture is so trenchant, allowing it to speak with uncommon force to transnational concerns.

After moving to Britain, Wicomb studied for a single-honors degree in English at the University of Reading during the mid-1970s (B.A. 1979) and worked as a schoolteacher and in adult education, for many years in Nottingham. Moving to Glasgow in 1987, she completed a master's degree in linguistics at the University of Strathclyde in Glasgow (in 1989), before returning briefly to South Africa (1991–94).[30] Since the mid-1990s, she has been principally resident in Glasgow, where she lives with her partner, the artist and academic Roger Palmer.

Until her retirement in 2012, she taught at the University of Strathclyde, where, as professor of creative writing, she tutored several of Scotland's leading younger novelists.

The Scotland to which she and Palmer moved, Wicomb notes in our interview (Part 3 of this book), was often racist and parochial, "not a place where [she] wanted to live." Yet it also offered insights into the effects of cultural imperialism, in its response to the hegemony of England (Scotland had not yet regained its parliament and substantial self-government, and it suffered perhaps disproportionately from austerity under Margaret Thatcher, a point Wicomb makes in her obituary for Mandela), and also in what Wicomb suddenly understood as its role in empire. It was in Scotland, she discovered, that "the roots of our South African Calvinism as well as our education and legal systems lay, and where our non-standard English still resonated." The first short story that she wrote in Scotland, "In the Botanic Gardens," she observes in our interview, "explores some of these aspects." Wicomb frequently has characters in her fiction attest to the impact Scottish missionaries had on the mental and physical landscape of the country. In *David's Story*, David Dirkse finds in Scotland "the names of places" he recognizes from "home: Kelvingrove, Glencoe, Aberdeen, Lyndoch, Sutherland, Fraserburgh, Dundee." These are all South African places named by missionaries and engineers in what would to them have seemed outposts of empire. "There was no danger of feeling lost in Scotland," we read of David's experience, "except that he felt dizzy with the to-ing and fro-ing between rain-sodden place names and the dry, dusty dorps [towns] at home."[31]

There is a sinister aspect to this connection to Scotland, too, which helps us to understand the complexities of racial discourse in South Africa. Wicomb's family might (or might not) have thought of themselves as Griqua, but apartheid classified them as "Coloured." The term continues to be spelled thus, differentiating it from the American usage "colored," but it is now typically not capitalized by those South Africans who self-identify in this way, or indeed in the majority of contemporary critical literature, in order to mark a difference from the term as it was institutionalized by the apartheid regime. Wicomb, too, prefers this lower-case form, while lamenting the term's continued use at all. Sometimes but not always deployed as a synonym for mixed-race, the label in fact named (and names) a heterogeneous community encompassing a wide range of ethnic heritages and histories, including descendants of slaves from the Indian Ocean rim, of black Africans and white Europeans (missionaries, farmers, soldiers, and traders), as well as of aboriginal or autochthonous peoples, those variously called Khoi (or Khoikhoi) and San, speaking languages like !Kun and !Xam. South Africans of mixed-race *and* autochthonous ancestry were thus included under this label, and questions of racial purity remain contentious in the coloured community to the extent to which it constitutes itself thus today.

Many of Wicomb's coloured characters have Scottish names, the McKays and Campbells in *Playing in the Light,* the Pringles in *The One That Got Away,* the Murrays in *October.* We learn that the latter "were of old Scottish stock," that they were "a good old coloured family, evenly mixed, who having attained genetic stability could rely on good hair and healthy dark skin, not pitch-black like Africans, and certainly nothing like sly Slamse from the east, who were not to be trusted."[32] Keen to differentiate his family from Muslim South Africans, particularly from the so-called Cape Malay community alluded to by the deroga-tory term "Slamse" (from I*slam;* members of the Cape's Muslim community are largely descended from slaves from the East Indies freed in the early nine-teenth century), Mercia Murray's father insists on his European ancestry and all the incremental class privileges that this ought, to his mind, to convey. Wicomb draws our attention, through references to what Scotland means for some of her characters, to the way in which Scottish—and other "white"—ancestry served the discourse of comparative racial hierarchy in South Africa, co-opting some in the coloured community into complicity with the racist logic of apart-heid.[33] Thus she makes a point about origins, purity, and self-identification, elaborated in her essays and in interview, through references in her fiction to links between Scotland and South Africa.

If Wicomb's fiction revisits the entangled absurdities and traumas of apart-heid racial classifications, Wicomb's critical work explores the consequences of misguided efforts to look beyond the legacies of such fetishization of difference in the present. We find Wicomb resisting the revisionism she has seen at work in the politics of the coloured community, eliding (for example) the experience of slavery in a drive to claim descent instead from autochthonous communities. At the root of this desire for indigenous roots, she argues, is the continued im-brication of discourses of coloured identity with those of concupiscence and shame. In what is perhaps her best-known critical essay, "Shame and Identity: The Case of the Coloured in South Africa" (Chapter 7 in this collection), she declares as her project an attempt to "find a way of discussing the textual con-struction, ethnographic self-fashioning, and political behavior of coloureds in South Africa, which is to say our condition of postcoloniality, through the con-cept of shame."[34] Shame is significant not least because, as historian Marcia Wright remarks, "At the heart of . . . ambiguity for coloured peoples are the im-plications of their mixed ancestry," in other words the suggestion that their origins lie in miscegenation, which means that "two sorts of prejudice" are at issue: that based on color and against "women in particular as (presumptively) available for sexual liaisons."[35] "Shame and Identity" takes as its starting point Wicomb's unease, perhaps even disgust, with the fact that coloured voters in the Western Cape (which includes Cape Town), constituting a majority there, gave electoral victory in the province to the National Party, the party of apartheid, in the first democratic elections of April 1994. This was a response, in part, she and others speculate, to rhetoric invoking the fear of oppression from a newly enfranchised black majority nationally. Shame is in part responsible, Wicomb argues, shame that leads to and feeds on complicity with ongoing rhetorical discourses of oppression. Metaphor matters, she insists, and a continued reliance on tropes of mixing, provisionality, and hybridity in discussing the state of being coloured is consequently dangerous. She identifies Homi Bhabha's engagement with Nadine Gordimer's depiction of mixed-race characters in her 1991 novel, *My Son's Story*, as a pernicious kind of "postcolonial theorizing" that, in relying on metaphors of the interstitial (the "borderline," the "inbetween"), echoes a "tragic mode where lived experience is displaced by an aesthetics of theory."[36] Although, as we shall see, Wicomb uses the insights of poststructuralist-informed critics like Bhabha elsewhere (always pragmatically), she is ever keen to test language against real embodied experience. She argues for a rejection of the "mythical excess of belonging or exorbitance of coloured identity" in favor of a new emphasis on the lived performance of multiple overlapping identities in what she calls a "larger South African community."[37]

AUTHORITY AND INTERTEXTUALITY

Commitment to the idea of a larger South African community and responsibility to the particular lived realities of individuals are twin lodestars in Wicomb's critical and creative practice. She repeatedly balances an ethics based on respect for the particularity of each individual's otherness with a suspicion of any attempt to co-opt such individuality into a too-easy explanatory narrative, and this in itself must give pause to any reader who tries to make direct connections between the author's life and the experiences of the author's protagonists. Thus while in *You Can't Get Lost in Cape Town* Frieda Shenton shares many biographical features with Wicomb (she travels, as indeed Wicomb did, from her home in Namaqualand to school and university in Cape Town, and thence to exile in the United Kingdom), the differences are what matter. Wicomb has frequently critiqued the ways in which readers of writing by black women from postcolonial contexts are too often tempted to impute autobiographical impulses to all such writing, whether or not cast as memoir; her playful use of metafiction and unreliable narration in this debut deliberately undercut the impression of a straightforwardly realistic *Bildungs-* or *Künstlerroman*. Bharati Mukherjee, reviewing the book in the *New York Times* on its first publication, noted then that the stories were self-reflexive without being arch, that this was not straight-forward life narrative, though also not postmodern writing that might be accused of abandoning the political.[38] For Sue Marais, scholar of the South African short story, the book "subverts the reader's naive expectation of a sense of solidarity and of documentary realism or historically verifiable or substantive evidence by advertising its existence as discourse or story and by foregrounding the fictiveness of all visions/versions of South African reality/identity."[39]

Each subsequent work of fiction has continued to unsettle the presumptions of those discourses that oversimplify the complexities of lived experience, whether narratives of the struggle that subordinate gender liberation to race or more contemporary discourses that seek a return to ideas of ethnic purity and that abhor the in-between. Wicomb's repeated use of narrative unreliability, of metafiction and fragment, always foregrounds the difficulty of representation itself, the ethics involved in telling the stories of others—and particularly those disadvantaged by structures of racism, patriarchy, and exclusionary understand-ings of culture. Thus Frieda grows as a writer through the stories of *You Can't Get Lost in Cape Town* but has repeatedly to weigh the costs of using the story of her upbringing, or indeed stories of those she meets, for her own creative purposes: is she exploiting those whose stories she chooses to tell? In *David's Story*, the unnamed amanuensis struggles against the digressive impulses of the eponymous conflicted struggle-era "hero," who has enlisted her help to bring order to his own explorations of his community's history but who remains trou-bled by the unknown fate of a mysterious female cadre in whose death he may or may not be implicated. The reader apprehends the unsettling possibility of this involvement not through direct statements claiming a truth status, the mode of witnessing favored by the Truth and Reconciliation Commission (T.R.C., 1996–98, some branches running to 2002), which collected accounts of human rights violations during a circumscribed period (1960–94), but rather in "jokes, parables, fictional imaginings, and subtle repetitions and parallels," as if to suggest, Aryn Barley observes, that "silences and sideways glances" have more to reveal than the authorized narratives.[40]

In *Playing in the Light*, numerous of the short stories, and *October*, charac-ters write or muse about the *difficulty* of writing and the ethics of adopting the stories of others. Wicomb's deep skepticism of omniscient narration and of texts that do not reveal their own limitations and inevitable investments is part of this broad philosophical commitment to critiquing authority and authorita-tiveness; indeed, it extends the questioning, naturally, to the act of authorship itself. As Carli Coetzee observes, "Readers of Wicomb's novels (as readers in her novels) are taught that meaning cannot be pinned down, but instead needs to be generated, each time anew."[41] Stéphane Robolin notes that "the unfastening of alternative, dissident stories" in all of Wicomb's work "functions as the resistant alternative to a conservative monopolization of representation."[42] And in Wicomb's own words, a deliberate "chaos on the page" seeks to lay bare "the camouflage of coherence that socio-political structures are about."[43]

In each of her works of fiction, Wicomb has focused on the interconnected nature of South African identities and imaginaries with the world beyond. And if the works' metafiction engages the ethics of representation, its recurrent intertextuality insists on the connection of all narratives that presume any measure of authority to all others, which might complicate such authority (or any pretense at originality). Intertextuality, Wicomb writes in her essay on translation and allusion in Coetzee's novel *Disgrace* (Chapter 10 in this volume), is a strategy that has not surprisingly become "a staple of postcolonial discourse" because of its "translative" or disruptive possibilities.[44] She engages further with postcolonial intertextuality on a theoretical level in other essays in this collection, but it suffices here merely to note that her own fiction is frequently in conversation with other texts, including a range of South African works—from Sarah Gertrude Millin's 1924 *God's Stepchildren* to the work of Bessie Head—and a body of American writing that includes Toni Morrison and Marilynne Robinson's novels each entitled *Home*, with both of which Wicomb's novel *October* is in conversation.[45] Millin's novel, a now notorious treatment of "miscegenation" and coloured identity, is no longer widely read, regarded as racist and eugenicist, but at one time it was perhaps the best-known work of "South African" writing, to be eclipsed only later by Paton's *Cry, the Beloved Country* (1948) and subsequently by Coetzee's *Disgrace*.[46] Head's work attracts Wicomb on account of the way it grapples with race and gender, its frequent staging of scenes of reading, and its complex negotiation of the distance between an author's biography and imagination.[47]

The larger effect of the wide range of allusive and intertextual conversation Wicomb employs is to emphasize her insistence on the hybrid nature of culture more broadly. In other words, no culture is "pure"; all cultures involve layers of quotation and improvisation. When asked in interview about a South African canon and a notional national tradition, Wicomb responded: "What would be the South African tradition? It would, like in any culture, be a mixed bag, with little to hold it together other than geography, precisely because no 'nation' is cohesive, and affiliations of gender, race and class will always woof across such national traditions."[48] *David's Story* draws the reader's attention to the hybrid and syncretic nature of custom, including the several faux-authentic traditions cultivated by a (real-life) leader of the Griqua people, Andrew Le Fleur.[49] The narrator-amanuensis frequently emphasizes the absurdity of claims of purity in relation to cultural practice and markers of ethnic identification, a running concern of the novel and indeed of Wicomb's critical project more broadly. "When you've got 'pure blood'? Isn't it replicating the old identities of apartheid?" Wicomb remarks in interview about what she calls "this business about finding out who you are."[50]

A CONFLICTUAL MODEL OF SOCIETY

A desire to promote and protect the heterogeneous nature of South African society from anything that might replicate if not the old identities of apartheid then its authoritarian impulses to categorize, compartmentalize, hierarchize, and exclude informs the earliest of the essays in Part 1 of this collection. Wicomb's sense of the way in which the broad brushstroke paints over fine detail is frequently in evidence, as when Wicomb warns the A.N.C., not yet in power, against elevating one version of tradition, especially one cast in relation to black African identity, above all others, one that risks being commodified, frozen, rendered spectacle ("Tracing the Path from National to Official Culture," Chapter 1 here), or when she worries (in "Culture Beyond Color?"—Chapter 3—and elsewhere) about how the promotion of English in writing, in political discourse, in official documentation, would further disadvantage marginalized language groups and stifle the growth of culture in those communities. "The search for a literary or cultural theory to suit the South African situation must surely take as a point of departure"—she writes in "To Hear the Variety of Discourses" (Chapter 5)—"a conflictual model of society where a variety of discourses will always render problematic the demands of one in relation to others and where discursive formations admit of cracks and fissures that will not permit monolithic ideological constructs."

The first essay in the collection, "Tracing the Path from National to Official Culture," published in 1991, is a tour-de-force performance that bridges Wicomb's own location, theoretical preoccupations (language, irony, relevance), astute literary analysis, and attention to real material conditions (including sexual violence). Wicomb's point of departure is a series of political discussions and cultural performances held in Glasgow in September 1990 during the city's tenure as European "Capital of Culture."[51] The events, advertised as the "Sechaba Festival of Culture," looked forward to the "new" South Africa, whose dawn was just beginning to seem possible. Yet some of what the organizers cast as intrinsically South African (and the fact that it was done with the apparent cooperation of representatives of the A.N.C.), revealed, Wicomb argues, a tendency to reify tradition without accounting for its shifting, constructed nature, an inclination to seek to occlude the complexities—the messiness—of the country's ethnic, linguistic, and religious heterogeneity. "Cultural renewal cannot be a switch from the old to the new," she writes; it has rather to involve "a continuous process of assessment and criticism" that includes assessing the spaces in which such commentary takes place. A national culture, "an imaginary entity that fires our will to be free," might very easily turn into an "official" version, "an ossification."

In its determination to speak truth to power—even to the liberation movement whose aims Wicomb supported—this essay, like those that follow it here, serves as a companion piece to Albie Sachs's much-cited "Preparing Ourselves for Freedom" (delivered in 1989, widely disseminated by 1991),[52] as well as to Njabulo Ndebele's earlier "The Rediscovery of the Ordinary." It also shows how her analyses are often rendered especially powerful *because* of her position as an expatriate writer, a South African in Britain, able to see clearly what may be occluded to those *in* South Africa, or, in this case, among communities of exiled antiapartheid activists. This essay is exemplary too of Wicomb's method of critical analysis. It demonstrates how close reading can be applied to a range of cultural forms and events. Here, for example, she offers a subtle reading of Ndebele's story "The Prophetess," attending to its ironies and syncretisms and contrasting these with the "uncomplicated step into the past to recover an authentic culture" perpetrated by the Sechaba Festival.

Wicomb's use of literary examples is showcased further in "Nation, Race and Ethnicity: Beyond the Legacy of Victims" (Chapter 2), which thinks about the "new" South Africa as historical and epistemological rupture. Another rupture—or rather eruption—is imagined here too, that of the everyday lived experience of deprivation and destitution that threatens to overwhelm representation itself. "The question," Wicomb notes, "is surely what to do about those real voices that intrude," those of "the beggars beating at our doors for food," for instance, "how not to think of writing in this context as a shameful activity that does little or nothing about redistributing cultural and linguistic capital." Concerns with experience conveyed in nontextual forms, negotiations of strong affective responses to the exigencies of South African life, and the ethic involved in witnessing to the "real": these will continue to preoccupy Wicomb and find expression both in the subjects of her essays and in formal choices in her fiction.

"Culture Beyond Color? A South African Dilemma," the third essay in Part 1, was written for *Transition* magazine and, in the spirit of engaged reportage,

offers a clear-sighted prognosis of the problems that would attend the first decades of South African literary production after the transition to majority
rule. Beginning with a discussion of the draft document of the newly formed
Federation of South African Cultural Organizations (FOSACO), dating from
March 1992 (the essay serves, therefore, as reminder of the ferment of organizing
and planning in the fields of cultural production and policy making in the early
1990s), Wicomb addresses, with her characteristic blend of keen observation and
humor, the question of what *kind* of writing might be expected in whatever was
to follow apartheid. "In the plethora of conferences in Europe and the U.S.A.,"
she notes, "writers are routinely asked whether the removal of apartheid will not
also remove our subject matter and therefore the impetus to write, a question
that perversely casts apartheid as an enabling system." Questioners presume that
there will be a complete change in theme and form, she observes, which is to
presuppose real political and economic change; time has proven correct her
prediction that "we will be disappointed" in wishing for this. Her observation
in this essay that "if the resistance culture was successfully mobilized by a revolutionary call to make the country ungovernable," the legacy of such tactics
would hamper the new government, seems terribly prescient and accurate a
quarter century later, too. The country has remained, as she notes here, "umbilically linked to the matrix of apartheid so that parturition is a slow affair."

   "Culture Beyond Color?" introduces an enduring concern with the links between verbal and visual representation. "It is no accident," Wicomb notes, "that
the most vibrant cultural production among black people is in the visual arts,
where poorly educated artists, in their mining of low culture, depart from the
symbolism of traditional African art." Here we have several key arguments
brought together: that tradition cannot be fetishized; that attention must be paid
to the full range of cultural production in order to account for ongoing structural
inequalities in South Africa; that no straightforward narrative of the country's
"culture" can be produced without accounting for these inequalities or thinking about whose interests the valorization of particular forms serves. How,
Wicomb asks, might "a literary culture be interracial if it conducts its business
in a minority language and its minority dialect of standard English that few
have access to?" The continuing hegemony of English and asymmetries in
levels of access to the institutions of culture, and indeed to the relative cultural
capital ascribed to different media, remain issues of concern in the present,
despite attempts by the postapartheid government to effect structural transformation, including some fifteen Acts of Parliament promulgated between 1998
and 2001 aimed at promoting cultural heterogeneity, establishing new national
arts councils, boards, and resource agencies for a range of heritage programs.

"Then and now," Bhekizizwe Peterson observed recently, "the policies and strategies pursued are marked . . . by the contending, contradictory approaches and differences . . . about whether the state should assume an enabling or interventionist role, and the tensions between the sociocultural and commercial imperatives that inform the production, distribution and consumption of the arts."[53] "Legislation on the arts, the well-meaning documents produced by our cultural organizations," Wicomb argues, will "only lead to shrewd investments by those who already have cultural capital, unless we address the question of literacy, the raw material for producing poetry."

We see some of these questions elaborated differently in the fourth essay in Part 1, "Reading, Writing, and Visual Production in the New South Africa," in which Wicomb takes issue with established theorists of literacy and orality to argue that what they often overlook are practices of "visual literacy" that contribute "to communal cognitive lives." South Africans, she suggests, might well be skeptical of the "gifts of reading and writing": from missionary intervention in the orthographic reduction of autochthonous languages into forms fixed with little sense of their varieties or contexts, to the ongoing valorization of the literary over other kinds of much more widely accessed media, there has in general been a failure adequately "to examine other works that exemplify the literacy/ orality dialectic" operative in the country. As a corrective, she offers a fascinating array of examples of such operations from the work of a number of largely untutored artists, including Tito Zungu, Derrick Nxumalo, Chickenman Mkhize, and Jackson Hlungwani, who emerged in revisionist surveys of contemporary art production in South Africa in the late 1980s.[54] Particularly interested in how these artists use *writing* even as they may not themselves be literate, she tracks relationships among literacy, literariness, vocabularies of representation, and practices of interpretation—whether reading or viewing.

Although similar to the mode of analysis of the first clutch of essays, here Wicomb adds the supporting scaffolding of literary and cultural theory that engages with literacy and the relationship between speech and writing—from Plato, Rousseau, Lévi-Strauss, and McLuhan, to Bloomfield, Finnegan, Havelock, Goody, Sapir, and Street (there is a particularly arresting use of Derrida to counter Ong). We shall also see her cite with great appreciation work by feminist critics like Hazel Carby, Deborah McDowell, Gayatri Spivak, and bell hooks, making clear her sense of shared practice (especially) with African American critics. Like the first essay in this collection, "Reading, Writing, and Visual Production" turns in its final pages to consider the lessons for literary critical analysis of what has been observed about the status of writing (or at least of text) in visual art. Wicomb offers engaging readings of Gcina Mhlope's story "The

Toilet" and Bessie Head's posthumously published *The Cardinals* (a novel to
which Wicomb will return), before, in a manner that takes seriously her own
admonition that scholars pay attention to cultural forms beyond print, turning
to the Xhosa practice of *hlonipha*, in which words are rendered taboo for married women if they contain homophones for names in a husband's extended
family (the women must develop a complex practice of circumlocution).[55]

NEW MODES OF HEARING AND READING

New or newly visible (or audible) practices of representation require new
methods of reading, and it is in the essays included here as Chapters 5 and 6
that Wicomb the critic matches her analytical skills with a dedication to what
she calls an "interventionist" pedagogy, one that is particularly alert to the imbrication of questions of race and gender. The occasion for the development of
the argument in "To Hear the Variety of Discourses" (Chapter 5) is twofold. The
first is an event, the appearance in 1990 at the University of Cape Town of Albie
Sachs, a leading A.N.C. intellectual recently returned from exile, and the spectacle of "traditional" dancers, women with bare breasts and beads and fetishized
as markers of autochthonous "purity," who performed while the crowd waited.
The second is a debate in South Africa in the late 1980s about the relative
values of feminism and womanism for the transition. The analysis focuses, in
Wicomb's words, "on the contradictions inherent in the attempts to negotiate
between race and gender" that emerge from both event and debate, and argues
that any attempt to enunciate a singular response would fall into the trap of refusing to honor the complexity clearly discernible in the variety of black women's
discourse(s). The essay discusses a range of literary texts by authors including
Head and Miriam Tlali, with glances at Toni Morrison.

Chapter 6, "Motherhood and the Surrogate Reader: Race, Gender, and Interpretation," considers the imbrication of discourses of race and gender in ideological constructions of the female citizen-subject of the "new" South Africa
that was imagined in cultural production of the late 1980s and early 1990s (the
essay appeared in print in 1994). Engaging with the legacies of gender having
been regarded as "a distraction from national liberation" by some in the antiapartheid struggle, Wicomb here offers a critique of the simplistic valorization
of tradition in relation to gender and race by reading closely a family planning
advertisement in the April 1989 issue of *True Love*, a popular South African
monthly magazine aimed at black women readers. She is eager to reveal contradictions at play in this periodical's "construction of womanhood" and to consider the wider ramifications of such paradoxes. She also reveals how documents

like this advertisement draw attention to the continuing power of "white minority norms" that are "concerned with demographic survival" and asks what happens when these norms interact with "black norms related to economic survival." The essay shows Wicomb as accomplished semiologist marshaling her considerable knowledge of cultural studies and of linguistics to offer a dual methodological and pedagogic intervention. The essay models a "pragmatic way of reading an image" without the pitfalls or blindnesses ascribed to theorists of relevance or to pragmatists like Trevor Pateman, Victor Burgin, and Judith Williamson; it "extend[s] the application of pragmatics from its usual single utterances or short exchanges to include extended discourse and its participation in ideology" (here Wicomb draws in particular on the insights of theorist Michel Pêcheux). Such use of tools from pragmatics to show how the old persists in the new, might signal a possible "interventionist" pedagogy: "Close reading, put to pedagogical use, has an important interventionist function, and attempts at changing slack reading habits may well be useful. Knowledge of language and its ideological functions and an awareness of how advertising exploits existing discourses could lead to material changes in people's lives: the resisting reader could be moved to resist more actively."

Wicomb's commitment to a fearless reading practice is evident too in "Shame and Identity: The Case of the Coloured in South Africa," which I discussed at some length above. Here it is worth reiterating that Wicomb's speculations about the reasons for a majority of coloured voters in the Western Cape province having cast their ballots for the National Party, the party of the former (white, apartheid-era) regime, in April 1994, is centrally concerned with the overlapping politics of gender and race. The famous case of Sara (Saartjie) Baartman, the so-called Hottentot Venus exhibited across Europe in the early nineteenth century, serves as an example of the objectification of the body of the brown woman and its role in discourses of shame and propriety.[56] Baartman's status as a new heroine for posttransition South Africa, an autochthonous mother-of-the-nation, also (however) confirms a rush to fetishize the indigenous and a tendency to overlook the sufferings of slave women in eighteenth- and early nineteenth-century South Africa. The long shadow of the apartheid system's investment in discourses of purity and stigmatization of miscegenation can clearly be seen here. "What the problem of identity indicates," Wicomb argues, in particular in relation to the contested modifier coloured/Coloured, "is a position that undermines the new narrative of national unity: the newly democratized South Africa remains dependent on the old economic, social, and also epistemological structures of apartheid, and thus it is axiomatic that different groups created by the old system do not participate equally in the category of postcoloniality." We need to find other ways to talk about postcolonial experience, she suggests, than in biological metaphors and theoretical keywords (like "hybridity"). The essay, first published nearly twenty years ago, may continue to be generative as affect studies influences discussion of postcolonial literature more broadly.[57]

Finally in Part 1, "Remembering Nelson Mandela," a tribute that appeared in the *New Yorker* magazine on 16 December 2013, in the "Talk of the Town" section (as one of a suite of short essays: the other contributors were Philip Gourevitch, Nadine Gordimer, and Nuruddin Farah), operates as an obituary that defies description or classification. Wicomb characteristically refuses to perform in any received or expected mode, instead meditating on the meanings of Mandela's hair and imagining what might have taken place during his famous meeting with Betsie Verwoerd, widow of the late apartheid-era prime minister Hendrik, at Orania, an enclave of white separatists, in 1995 (they took tea together; no one has revealed the details of their conversation). Wicomb's speculations are both amusing and moving. They offer an affectionate portrait of Mandela, but also a clear-sighted sense that all we can really know about the man is the myth that has grown around him—his magnanimity, his sartorial fastidiousness. Consequently, Mandela's significance is best decoded by a semiotician or a novelist, and in Wicomb we have both. This short essay, offered here in a full-text version that was abridged in its *New Yorker* appearance, offers an adroit reading and remembering that is, like much of her work, both playful and profound.

RACE, TRANSLATION, CONVERSATION

As an author reading the work of other writers, Wicomb excels at explicating the mechanics of the "business of writing" for the general reader, and her work on other authors necessarily also involves reflection on the meaning of this "business" in her own practice. The essays grouped together in Part 2 of this collection show us Wicomb as careful reader of "literary narrative"—while also attentive to the overlap in questions about ethics and pragmatics with work on "natural narrative," the text of the everyday. In the first four of these essays, we see her attending to questions of race and of translation—as linguistic activity, metaphor, and injunction.

As noted earlier, Wicomb's extended family members were first-language Afrikaans speakers, giving the lie through their very existence to the fiction that Afrikaners constituted a purely white nation with Afrikaans as its (pure) language: it was always already a creole, spoken by a heterogeneous group. One of the earliest printed texts in recognizable Afrikaans is in fact an Islamic primer, printed in a modified Arabic script by the Ottoman state printer in Istanbul in 1877—an inconvenient fact for apartheid ideologues.[58] In "Five Afrikaner Texts and the Rehabilitation of Whiteness" (Chapter 9), Wicomb reassesses the claim of whiteness on Afrikaans and the work done by white Afrikaners in the early years of the transition to grapple with the legacy of their community's national-linguistic-racial project through the twentieth century. (The essay, incidentally, surely has one of the most arresting opening lines of any South African essay: ""One of the more refreshing qualities of apartheid was the abandon with which we all talked about and identified ourselves in terms of race.") Focusing on a range of work by a number of important Afrikaans-language writers—Antjie Krog, Etienne van Heerden, Marlene van Niekerk, and Chris Barnard—Wicomb considers their attempted revisions of the meaning of whiteness in relation to conceptions of the "other," to language, and to geography. In short, in all of these works, she finds a "revised Afrikaner self . . . staged before a back-cloth renovated from the old picturesque, horizontal surface of landscape to the land in cross section," one reimagined in such a way as to recognize the claims on the land of others. Self-definition in relation to the otherness of black South Africans, in particular, becomes a crucial feature of these works, one that shifts Afrikaner self-identification away from the land to interpersonal, relational processes of becoming that rely in complicated ways on processes of othering. "One of the less predictable phenomena to develop" in the postapartheid period, Wicomb notes in another very quotable formulation, "is the current scramble for alterity." Her analyses of a number of significant works of the transition period, not least Van Niekerk's novel *Triomf* (1994) and Krog's work of creative nonfiction *Country of My Skull* (1999), make this essay indispensable for understanding postapartheid writing in Afrikaans.

Wicomb's skill at reading between the lines and against the grain, at marrying close textual analysis with an interest in linguistic and critical theory, is perhaps nowhere more in evidence than in the repeated engagements with the work of her near contemporary, J. M. Coetzee, a writer whose engagements with his own Afrikaans-speaking family would become clearer in the years following the publication of Wicomb's essay on Afrikaners and whiteness. Wicomb's first published assessment of Coetzee's work was in an essay entitled "South African Short Fiction and Orality" (2001), first delivered as a conference address (in 1997), which in fact treats as short stories two fragments from what would turn out to be longer works.[59] Several years later, Wicomb returned to Coetzee in a bravura reading of *Disgrace*, included here as Chapter 10, "J. M. Coetzee's *Disgrace*: Translations in the Yard of Africa," indisputably one of the most original and important early readings of this seminal novel. At its heart is a consideration of tropes of translation and of transition, which Wicomb discerns not only in Coetzee's explorations of the politics of gender, race, and language in the immediate posttransition period but also at the level of the novel's form. *Disgrace*, she notes, is a "text that struggles with *translation* as concept-metaphor for the postapartheid condition" and which contains at its center deep anxieties about the relationship between original and "target." Here she revisits a number of theoretical engagements with the idea of intertextuality as translation—George Steiner on what Wicomb calls "intracultural translation"; Mikhail Bakhtin's dialogics; Julia Kristeva on intertextuality; Roland Barthes on the "vast stereophony" of textuality. Wicomb offers her own revision to these positions, suggesting that the "function of the author . . . is both junctive (tying together narrative and citational utterances) and translative (transferring utterances from one textual space into another)," and that it is because of its "translative possibilities that intertextuality as writing strategy has become such a staple of postcolonial discourse." I shall return to her thoughts about intertextuality shortly.

The assessment of the translation metaphor in *Disgrace* pays particular attention to Coetzee's treatment of temporality and of the perfective form of the verb in the text. The fact that David Lurie, *Disgrace*'s complicated protagonist, broods over the perfective (glossed in the novel as "signifying an action carried through to its conclusion"),[60] as if to draw attention to its structural complexities, suggests that the process of transition cannot so easily be completed, Wicomb argues. A key question in this essay is how appropriate the metaphor of translation is for postapartheid South Africa, in which "apartheid has to be translated into democracy." If translation is never transparent or absolute, if there is always a "residue" of the untranslatable, then what residue remains from the process of translation to a new political order? *Disgrace* demonstrates, Wicomb claims, that the postapartheid nation will inevitably be "hamstrung by the double bind of translatability and untranslatability," for "the modalities of the past—sex, race, violence—continue to prevail": they are the residues of the project of national translation.

Leon de Kock, himself a noted translator (including of Marlene van Niekerk's *Triomf*), turns Wicomb's conclusions back from the broadly national-psychological to the question of the literary; Wicomb means the conclusion cited above "to carry well beyond merely an interpretation of" Coetzee's novel, he argues: "practices of translation in South African writing, one may suggest, are more generally implicated in the kind of double bind Wicomb describes" (the imperative that there be translation between language communities, yet translation entails inevitable failures and residues).[61] De Kock understands this in terms drawn from his own important theoretical intervention in the study of postapartheid fiction, by observing that "the only way to bridge the gap from the first-person singular to the first-person plural, from 'I' to 'us' (and therefore from subject to nation in political terms), is via the transitive zone, where literary acts cross over, trying to suture the fissures of language, culture, class, race, ethnicity and gender. But in doing so, the mark of the suture remains: a representational seam, inscribing difference in the same moment that it seeks to smooth it out, conjoin it or resolve it. This transitive-translational seam, I would argue, in its various forms has come to mark, to scar, one might say, what we today talk about as 'South African' writing."[62]

The difficulties of communication across barriers of language (and barriers mediated by language—including of class, race, and gender) likewise concern Wicomb in the next essay in Part 2, "Rereading Gordimer's *July's People*," an unpublished piece based on papers delivered in 2005 and revised in 2014, the year of Nadine Gordimer's death. Here Wicomb returns to the late Nobel literature laureate's landmark 1981 novel, a speculative work that imagines the implications of a future civil war for a white, middle-class family from Johannesburg and their black servant, whom they know as July and who offers them refuge in his village in a "homeland" to the northeast of the city. Much has been written about the novel's enigmatic ending, in which Maureen Smales, July's former employer, runs either toward or from a helicopter, which bears either government (or allied) soldiers or fighters of the (black) opposition.[63] Responses that attempt to determine what precisely happens, Wicomb writes, "reveal a will to interpret, which is to say produce a meaning other than the literal event at the end: Maureen running to something unknown." But they also suggest that Gordimer implies that "the story of the dissolution of apartheid is coordinate with the story of . . . the white woman of liberal persuasion." By contrast, Wicomb argues, Gordimer's novel "accommodates yet another kind of reader, one whose interests do not coincide" with Maureen's destiny, and for whom the actions of Maureen are not to be understood from the Smaleses' perspective but instead considered "literally as her removal from the site of the story." The unclear ending, then, allows for a "return to central questions of the masters' construction of the black subject and the role of language in articulating such subjectivity." Wicomb consequently returns to the figure of July, significantly also as a reader in the world, "from the vantage point of a different time, the New South Africa struggling with the legacies of apartheid." Focusing on July,

Wicomb contends, takes seriously Gordimer's text's "concern with the articulation of language as a medium through which a culture in transition is explored."

Here, then, is a focus on the business of writing—and reading—that revisits many of the defining concerns of Wicomb's early essays, but in relation to the activity of rereading, and from a future those early essays could really only imagine, though whose discontents they could certainly foretell. Also in evidence is Wicomb's insistence that the remaking of the constitutional order, even large-scale investment in infrastructure, would be all very well, but the ethics of interpersonal relationships would be the ground on which real change might be possible—and very difficult. As Deborah Posel notes, "geographies of distance and proximity were fundamental to the apartheid project": "apartheid institutionalised the intimacy of strangers, and the uncertainty, ignorance, fear, threat and temptation" that inevitably arose because of the deformation of personal relationships—or the impossibility of these—in and across "racially distinct spaces of community, schooling, friendship and mutuality, along with sites of routinised interracial contact and dependency, be it in the factories, on the mines or in white homes employing domestic workers."[64] If Coetzee's *Disgrace* explores the residue of any translative project, Gordimer's *July's People* stages what Wicomb calls "the buckling of an interpretive horizon under unequal conditions, the failure of face-to-face engagement when one of those faces has for years been deferentially averted."

If there is a suggestion here of Emmanuel Levinas's influential metaphor of the otherness of the other, imagined as categorically "other," as an encounter with a (sometimes inscrutable) face, Wicomb draws on Levinas directly in the essay that follows, Chapter 12, "Natural Narrative and Tall Tales: Remembering District Six," in which we see an ongoing concern with translation, otherness, memory, and the analysis of speech. Here, though, the subjects are *"real"*: what we witness is the *practice* of ethical engagement with the narrative of another. In this essay, Wicomb considers "natural narratives" by two former residents of Cape Town's fabled District Six as they reminisce about their youths in the neighborhood, a mixed-race, inner-city area demolished by the apartheid government after 1966. Wicomb collected the accounts in the early 1990s, during a brief period spent working in Cape Town. As she explains, what interests her is "the discursive mechanisms by which subjectivity is achieved and self-worth is displayed" in these men's accounts: "I look at the ways in which the narrative of the past (1960s) is inflected by the demise of apartheid (at the time of storytelling in the 1990s); in other words, how the relocated subject as victim is represented in the postapartheid era through storytelling." Their code-switching shows both their communicative abilities, she observes, but is also "a meaning-ful device with particular narratological and ideological functions."

Wicomb also addresses what she calls "the popular equating of narrative with knowledge" that informs, for example, the ways in which oral accounts have been made to function in postapartheid museums (including the District Six Museum). She considers this "in relation to troubling aspects of the narratives: their apocryphal nature, and the denigration of women that structures the sto-ries." "What kind of knowledge claims can therefore be made for narrative?" she asks. This is a question that has in fact structured her own experimentation with narrative voice and occasion of narration in her short stories and novels. "Natural narrative, like its literary counterpart," she concludes, might "be consid-ered a mode of discourse that produces and reproduces cultural values, and in that sense is bound up with cultural knowledge in a productive way, so that cultural knowledge cannot be viewed as a ready-made repository from which information about a culture is simply extracted." Both Chapters 11 and 12 make use of theoretical turns that foreground the situatedness of the agent of inquiry, the problem of the authority of the one inquiring and her influence on the sys-tem being observed. Wicomb engages here, as elsewhere, in a sensitive testing of the insights of poststructuralism, always conscious that any supposed "West-ern 'crisis of legitimation' is of little relevance to the condition of dispossessed South Africans who, after the first democratic elections, expected to see their narratives of resistance and emancipation legitimized."

"CROSS-MIXING . . . REFERENCE AND PHENOMENALISM": MEMORY, SETTING, REALISM

Repositories of cultural knowledge—and memory—are at issue in Chapter 13, "'Good Reliable Fictions': Nostalgia, Narration, and the Literary Narrative," the first of two essays that engage with the work of Ivan Vladislavić (b. 1957), long well known in South Africa and gradually gaining international attention for a body of work that probes the absurdities of apartheid and the complexities of the postapartheid period with a surrealist's wit and an artist's (and proofreader's) eye.[65] Wicomb discusses Vladislavić's 2010 novel, *Double Negative*, written to accompany a selection of sixty years' worth of celebrated photographer David Goldblatt's images of Johannesburg.[66] There is also treatment of historian Jacob Dlamini's *Native Nostalgia* (2009), a nonfiction exploration of the nature of Dlamini's own memories of growing up in a township in the last two decades of apartheid rule. Each grapples with the nature and politics of nostalgia in chal-lenging ways: Vladislavić interrogates the costs and consequences of white liberal nostalgia, while Dlamini asks in forthright fashion what it means for black women of his mother's generation to remember aspects of their lives under apartheid with fondness. Wicomb uses both texts to ask whether nostalgia can be "mimetically represented without its sentimentality detracting from the aesthetics of a literary work." Casting a critical eye on Svetlana Boym's well-known distinction between reflective and restorative nostalgia as well as on the co-implication of the uncanny and the nostalgic, Wicomb argues that nostalgia, in the most significant evocations of its limits in South Africa, "hovers on the threshold of representation, . . . its intransitivity in representation . . . manifested in . . . simultaneous evocation and dismissal." Such complex attraction and repulsion structures the responses of characters in Wicomb's fiction, too. In *October,* for example, Mercia Murray bewails her "need to recollect a past that cannot be considered without irony" and wonders whether this is what constitutes nostalgia; she has turned recently to memoir (even as she is "skeptical of the genre") to provide respite from the intolerable "cant" she finds associated with "local versions of postcolonial memory," the subject of her academic work.[67]

Of all South African writers, Bessie Head has most often engaged Wicomb's attention and provided an example to which she has returned in her literary and cultural criticism. In the interview with me included in this volume, Wicomb notes that she "had not heard of Head until the early 70s," which is to say until she had arrived in Britain, but that she immediately "felt an affinity with her." Head's early novel *Maru* (1971), Wicomb claims, had given her "the courage or perhaps permission to write." Head's work is the focus for the next essay, "Identity, Writing, and Autobiography: The Case of Bessie Head's *The Cardinals*" (Chapter 14), in which Wicomb turns her attention squarely on Head for the first time, focusing on *Maru* and on the posthumously published *The Cardinals* (1993). These texts, Wicomb notes, are most often discussed in relation to Head's own biography and to "the tradition of black women's autobiography," approaches from which Wicomb departs. (It is worth noting the uncanny instance of the unauthorized use of a picture of Wicomb on the cover of the Heinemann edition of *Maru,* to which she alludes in her interview with me: the specter of the biographical reading in relation to Head's *and* Wicomb's work could not be represented more powerfully or troublingly.)[68] Rather than the biographical reading, Wicomb aims instead to examine how Head's work "explores racial and gendered subjectivity" via what she calls a "creative rewriting of the self." "The discursive modalities of both writing and not-writing about the self, or rather the relation between these modalities, manifested as traces in the texts," Wicomb suggests, "constitute a discourse of liberation" that must be read alongside the story of Head's victimization by apartheid legislation, of her exile to Botswana, and indeed of her struggles with mental illness. The essay suggests that Head uses both writing and the law as tropes in order to "rehearse self-reflexively the production of not-autobiography"—a term Wicomb uses to problematize the category of writing about the self that rewrites the self.

When Wicomb writes in this essay that "the argument for the authority of experience is . . . precisely what underpins the current reception of black women's writing," we sense that she is writing too about her own experience. *You Can't Get Lost in Cape Town* was read too easily by many of its first critics and reviewers as a work of autobiography. "While the genre has been rehabilitated, the tendency to treat black women's texts, whether written in the first or third person, as autobiography, persists," Wicomb observes, while "writing that cannot be mistaken for autobiography has, as bell hooks discovered with her own experimental, nonlinear narratives, little hope of finding a publisher, a situation that is not unconnected with what Gates has called 'the sociological fallacy.'" Not only is this essay suggestive for thinking about Wicomb's own work, or indeed Head's, it also makes an important intervention in the study of postcolonial autobiography, seeking to reposition the way in which only apparently straightforward life writing by black women is routinely read.

Wicomb reckons in the following essay, "Setting, Intertextuality, and the Resurrection of the Postcolonial Author" (Chapter 15), with this expectation that an author's work is necessarily autobiographical.[69] Her response, apart from drawing ironic attention to the ways in which authors are routinely invited to "'speak as a writer,'" is to consider the ways in which setting operates as intertext to mediate the experience of a writer's location for a reader, particularly in postcolonial texts, in a manner that engages debates about the "death of the author" in complex ways. Wicomb builds the essay on a reading of another Vladislavić text, the short story "'Kidnapped,'" particularly of its postmodern effects. She begins with the apparently simple claim that "setting" does more in postcolonial writing than supplement characterization, that the representation of surroundings "bound up with a culture and its dominant ideologies" might be seen instead to function *like* intertextuality. "Postcolonial theory"—she observes—"does address the question of place, of how the postcolonial writer revises the empty space of colonialism and through writing and naming turns it into place," and yet "displacement is invariably discussed in terms of ambivalence, in the separation and continual contact between colonizer and colonized." Instead, Wicomb prefers to highlight a "more mundane aspect of place: the mise-en-scène or setting of fictions that for any writer is rudimentary and that for the emigrant writer can be problematic."

Wicomb can be seen here to be searching for a way of addressing the ongoing importance of South Africa in her fiction, and to be returning to the question that has long vexed her—that of the relation of her own life story to the lives of her characters, something she claims elsewhere evidences the peculiarly reductive expectation of sociological or anthropological equivalence from black women writers in particular. "I am fortunate in having a personal ready-made topic that is happily legitimated by the postcolonial keyword 'transculturation,'" she writes (and it is not difficult to hear a wry chuckle). "The questions that this condition entails are as follows: Why when you have lived so long in Scotland do you write about South Africa? When will you set your fictions in Scotland? Can you go on writing about a place in which you do not live?" "Setting, Intertextuality, and the Resurrection of the Postcolonial Author" concludes with a characteristically deft if dizzying displacement in which space is rendered metaphorical (perhaps it is always thus, which is in part Wicomb's point). "The writer's envelope of space," she writes, "finds a ready metaphor in the house of fiction, a structure that occupies a circumscribed place, the setting of which is literally foundational, which is to say that it can be taken for granted. It is the homeliness of that constructed space that allows fictional characters to act and interact in the context of a shared history and a common identity." And yet here Bhabha's suggestion that the postcolonial writer finds creativity in "the unhomely world" (Wicomb is quoting from Bhabha's *The Location of Culture*) strikes Wicomb as a "brave view" that is worth considering: "How possible is it to build such a house of fiction in a foreign world? I fear that what comes cravenly to mind is a construction that promises to be none other than a folly."

Quite apart from its usefulness for reading works by migrant and diasporic writers, this essay includes one of the most interestingly self-reflexive comments in her nonfiction, one that might be taken as descriptive of her own staging of acts of writing as recuperation or curation. The "foregrounding of the authorial" in postcolonial writing, Wicomb argues, is certainly "a departure from the usual traffic with subjectivity," but "instead of staging representation, such resurrection of the author is also concerned with asserting an ethics of authorial responsibility in an ostentatious coupling of author and narrator." This observation casts very interesting light on the writer, artist, and amanuensis figures in all of her prose fiction: *You Can't Get Lost in Cape Town*, *David's Story*, *Playing in the Light*, *The One That Got Away*, and *October*. And yet . . . ever cautious to impute too direct a link between the setting of fiction and anywhere "real," Wicomb brings us back to the text itself, to the surface of the page, to the writer's activity in setting the world before us to read as we see fit.

This collection ends with one of Wicomb's most accomplished and sophisticated essays, a reading of the complex network of substitution and proxy at play in one of Coetzee's most puzzling fictions, *Slow Man* (2005), a novel that, with its self-conscious metafictional aspects, divided critical opinion. Wicomb tackles the problem of reading the novel head on, as a fellow novelist *and* as a scholar thoroughly versed in a range of methodologies—from linguistics and pragmatics to theories of postmodernism. Offering analysis that ranges from close reading of passages to thematic critique, she argues that what she calls the novel's "insistent cross-mixing of reference and phenomenalism" offers "a heuristic device for alerting the reader to the complex relations between author, narrator, and character." Coetzee's novel in fact offers its own "lesson in reading, which is to say rereading," and so "demands the reader's active tracking of the relationship between representation and the real, or rather levels of the real," she contends. It "offers insights into the business of writing" itself. Drawing on her familiarity with contemporary art and art historiography, Wicomb makes comparisons with Rachel Whiteread sculpture and, through a wonderful quotation of Hal Foster in her penultimate paragraph, reveals precisely what is at stake in this analysis, if not in her criticism more generally: "In contemporary art practice," she observes, "Foster identifies a bipolar postmodernism in which the real, repressed in poststructuralism, returns as traumatic. Both the textual model of culture and the conventional view of reality are dismissed by artists who wish to 'possess the obscene vitality of the wound and to occupy the radical nihility of the corpse.'"

This is perhaps only a more extreme, contemporary art-world version of Wicomb's insistence on hearing the beggars at our doors, on holding open the claims of a variety of voices that battle against any attempt to broadcast a single message about national identity or "official" culture. No settled version of any cultural formation should be allowed to stand, to ossify, to assume final authority. So, too, with an introduction, and so how better to end this one than with Wicomb's own final words in the final essay in this collection, in which she addresses "the irony of an arrest in interpretation: *Slow Man* offers itself as prothesis, lays out on the credence table its own hermeneutic. It waves its flags; there is ultimately nothing hidden; I can only describe what-has-been-read." And now, lucky reader, it is over to you.

Part One

HEARING THE VARIETY
OF DISCOURSES

1

TRACING THE PATH FROM NATIONAL
TO OFFICIAL CULTURE (1991)

Culture is a weapon of the struggle. That has for some time been a rallying cry of the African National Congress (A.N.C.), a slogan for the liberation movement, and indeed public political events during the period of resistance, whether at home or abroad, have since the 1980s routinely been accompanied by cultural expressions such as music, dance, or poetry.[1] Such practices were partly dictated by the apartheid laws against political gatherings that then could be called a cultural event, and partly by the movement's strategy of popularizing resistance so that it indeed became a "people's resistance." The development at political gatherings of the *toyi-toyi*, a vigorous, high-stepping march-dance accompanied by chanting, not only became an intimidating display of solidarity, but signaled the fact that celebration of *indigeneity* and *resistance* went hand in hand. (So welded has the culture-politics dyad become, even abroad, that the BBC seems never to offer a news broadcast of political events in South Africa *without* the accompaniment of song, a practice that continues well into the 1990s.) The practices, at public gatherings, had also, in the 1980s, been formalized through the formation of popular A.N.C. dance troupes, presented as the exemplars of cultural renewal in South Africa. These depart significantly, however, from their origins in the resistance movement: they are "nativist" in their assumption of traditional dress and movement. It is this phenomenon of cultural expression, the contradictions inherent in cultural renewal that at the same time appeals to tradition and that not only constitutes a self-definition of a people but has come to represent the New Nation, that I wish to investigate in this essay.

My point of departure is the Sechaba Festival of Culture, a mixture of political discussion—with city councilors and trade unionists—and diverse cultural events, held in Glasgow over five days in September 1990, the year of that Scottish city holding the title of European Capital of Culture.[2] Earlier in the year, Glasgow hosted Amapondo, a contemporary band of musicians who had become especially popular for dressing up in a miscellany of "tribal" wear. Sechaba, too, offered the hallowed spectacle of musicians with drums, and dancers scantily clad in animal skins. In Glasgow, where they were sedately applauded by white trade unionists and A.N.C. officials in four-piece suits, a Scottish clansman followed with kilt and bagpipes, suggesting an equivalence in the national appeal to tradition.

Discussions at the Sechaba festival demonstrated that culture had come a long way from the received view of the best that is known and thought, that it has severed itself from so-called civilization, but the Arnoldian notion seems to have been replaced by a commonsense view of culture as something that is simply the way people live, and a reflection of these ways of living in forms such as drama, fiction, and poetry, hence the popularization—especially—of people's poetry. However, a contradiction arises when we scrutinize the equivalence between African and Scottish practices. Not only does Hugh Trevor-Roper's work on the invention of tradition in Scotland suggest that the clansman's ethnic kilt was in fact invented in the eighteenth century;[3] rather, more pertinent to this discussion is the case that the kilt has since its invention been a visible presence on Scottish high streets and at popular gatherings (weddings, ceilidhs, and so on), whereas the presence of anyone clad like the Sechaba players on South African township streets would indeed be a spectacle. The commonsense view of culture conveniently refused to address the phenomenon of the dancers.

Traditional dress may not have been entirely abandoned in rural areas, but it does not reflect the way of life for urban black South Africans, forgers of the new national culture. The reflectionist model has in any case been demolished by Raymond Williams, who points out that culture "is never a form in which people happen to be living, at some isolated moment, but a selection and organization, of past and present."[4] To speak of cultural renewal, then, would be to discuss how, what, and on what basis selection and organization occurs. Instead, the phenomenon of the dancers highlights the problematic issues of *nation* and *tradition* that are already implicated in the notion of culture. It is these notions and their confluence in material practice that I wish to investigate.

Cultural renewal is deemed necessary in South Africa, where the corrupt and vulgar culture of apartheid has held sway. Centuries of colonialism had, in the name of Christianity and civilization, undermined indigenous cultural expressions. Decolonization held out the promise of reclaiming those very practices, and of imbuing them with value, a reversal of the colonial black consciousness of shame and inferiority. It is the very process we find represented in Frantz Fanon's pathbreaking essay "On National Culture," where Fanon comments on the early phase of the native intellectual that is marked by a high value set on "the customs, traditions and appearances of his people; but his inevitable, painful experience only seems to be a banal search for exoticism . . . each native who goes back over the line is a radical condemnation of the methods of the regime."[5]

That the Sechaba extravagances of "traditional" dance are offered in the name of a national culture is clear from the context in which they are found. Generally, whether at home or abroad, these displays accompany A.N.C. speeches, so that it is reasonable to assume that the visual information of the performance is intended to illustrate or support the linguistic information. In Glasgow, speakers expounded on the new democratic order of the A.N.C.'s legal, political, and cultural positions, but relations between the visual and textual information do, as I discuss elsewhere,[6] produce meanings that contradict the apparent political messages. Mendi Msimange persuasively explained how tribal killings are a construction by conservative elements in the apartheid government, and gave an account of a highly industrialized, urbanized society engaged in a culture of resistance. Govan Mbeki, newly released from Robben Island, recommended that alongside the local, South Africans should also develop a "universal" culture in the interests of both cultural diversity and internationalism. In both cases, however, the accompanying visual information of the Sechaba dancers clad in animal skins foregrounded tradition. It is inevitable that where the imagery is contradictory, viewers are pressed into rereading the political message at the intersection of visual information and text, and necessarily find that all is not well. The bonding of nationhood with black tradition and culture is found in the very logo used by Sechaba. Taken from the A.N.C. journal of the same name, which means nation, the image adopted for the festival is an adaptation of the journal's logo: a spear and shield held by a black male in loincloth more or less segue into a paintbrush alongside the outline of Africa, which metamorphoses into a palette. It is perhaps this fusion of cultural activity with the armed struggle that can, after all, brook no ambiguity, that has precluded the use of irony in the transitional culture of resistance. (That nationhood is so often represented as unambiguously male is an issue I address elsewhere, too.)[7]

If a culture has been arrested and tipped into alien trappings, then tradition becomes a hypothetical notion. We have to imagine how certain practices, given certain conditions, would have developed, or whether they would have been retained at all. To haul up traditions through the centuries is to do what

Johannes Fabian accuses European anthropologists of, a "denial of coevalness,"
or of believing that we do not experience time as the European does.[8] Europe
renders others the object of its investigation by assuming that such people exist
in an eternal present, an assumption that has allowed anthropologists to codify
and classify their customs and manners in a way that fixes them in time. Since
tradition is not a monolith dragged along through the ages, the idea of keeping
it alive or reviving it is surely problematic. Raymond Williams cites tradition as
"an instance of cultural reproduction in action . . . a selection and reselection
of elements of the past."[9] Only certain elements of the past are retained; others
are dropped gladly, and various groups would ideally select which ones, and
how, according to their own interests. The discussions at Sechaba offered neither an examination and questioning of the criteria for retaining, abandoning,
modifying, or reviving certain practices nor an interrogation of the conflated
concepts of culture and tradition. Again, we could do no better than turn to
Fanon, who pinpoints the relationship between the two: "Culture has never the
translucidity of custom; it abhors all simplification. In its essence it is opposed
to custom, for custom is always the deterioration of culture. The desire to attach
oneself to tradition or bring abandoned traditions to life again does not only
mean going against the current of history but also opposing one's own people.
When a people undertakes an armed struggle . . . the significance of tradition
changes . . . during the period of struggle traditions are fundamentally unstable
and are shot through by centrifugal tendencies."[10] Williams's notion of selection
is implicit in Fanon's description of opposing the people since the historical
phase of assimilating colonial culture, or of passive resistance, is excised in this
embrace of certain traditions.

Fanon's characterization of the unstable and centrifugal tendencies of tradition during the period of struggle is suggestive, for far from the obviousness of
its meanings and expressions, it is *interpretation* of tradition that is here at stake.
If the very meaning of tradition is destabilized by the armed struggle, then it
severs itself from custom and, in the ambiguous spin, collides with culture. In
literary terms, this is the very stuff of irony that both states and undermines its
own statement; which effect depends fundamentally on a process of interpretation, rather than on what it appears to say. However, the Sechaba-type spectacle
of dancers is sadly devoid of an irony that would accommodate its inherent contradictions. For even if, as Fanon so persuasively argues, the nostalgic desire for
the past is misguided, the very fact that it exists implies its representability, if
only with the deployment of irony. And this brings me to the question of why
irony has had such a bad press in the resistance movement.

It has been an unspoken edict in the case of writing that irony being inaccessible to the "ordinary reader" is not a suitably radical trope; it cannot be relevant to the political reality.[11] A reason given for this is the close relationship between cultural renewal and the armed struggle, which cannot brook any ambiguity. Moreover, irony is seen to exemplify the decadence and depoliticized nature of Western postmodern strategies. In terms of the history of European cultural criticism, *Kulturkritik*'s stance against democracy, as exemplified by Thomas Mann, may have much to do with the alignment of irony with reactionary politics. According to Mann, it was irony, "the self-betrayal of the intellect in favour of life," that would serve as a bulwark against the radical threat of modernity.[12]

An alternative theory of irony, one that does not implicate it in a spuriously romantic opposition between intellect and "life," suggests that it is anything but a detachment from the social and political reality. It may not be seen as relevant to political struggle, but Sperber and Wilson's relevance theory offers a cognitive account of how an ironic or oppositional meaning is arrived at in the process of interpretation.[13] Relevance theory starts from the premise that the use of language signals an intention to communicate, thus what is said or stated comes with a guarantee of relevance to a situation that a listener or reader will work out. If a first, obvious proposition is contradicted or ridiculed by a second meaning, it is because the first proposition is an interpretation of an attributed thought, one that is articulated elsewhere. Thus irony is seen as an echoic utterance, presented in order to be undermined. What needs to be ascertained is where the echo originates from, or whose thought is being ridiculed, and to what purpose.

Sperber and Wilson give the following example: "When all was over and the rival kings were celebrating their victory with Te Deums in the respective camps."[14] Voltaire is not implying the opposite: that neither side won the battle, nor that both sides lost and bewailed their defeat, which is the traditional explanation of irony. Instead, he is echoing claims made by the rival kings, and expects the reader to reason that one of the claims must be false. By leaving the echo implicit, the author opens up "a whole new line of interpretation" and "suggest[s] . . . that he shares with his reader a whole cynical vision."[15] Relevance theory does not develop the ideological implications of echoic utterances, but it is manifestly the case that irony appeals to shared or given knowledge. Through this appeal, the reader who may never have considered the absurdity of postwar claims is, in the cognitive activity of processing the statement, pushed into retrieving the source of the echo, and assessing the common belief of warmongers. Relevance theory, in foregrounding irony's effect of making us question the given or shared knowledge, denies its reliance on a particular poetic sensibility. Instead, it shows how ideology is crucially implicated in our understanding of irony.

I will briefly consider ideological implications and the ways in which received views are challenged in Twain's *The Adventures of Huckleberry Finn* (1884), a work that over the decades has suffered much cultural policing. When Huck protects Jim, the escaped slave, there is nothing in the text that contradicts or ridicules the obvious meaning—that Huck is struggling to tell the truth and abide by the law but fails to do so. ("I got aboard the raft, feeling bad and low, because I knowed very well I had done wrong.")[16] Twain's use of a common expression quoted in the following passage where Huck has misgivings about helping Jim to escape, is a reminder that he is echoing received views about slavery: "It most froze me to hear such talk. He wouldn't ever dared to talk such talk in his life before. Just see what a difference it made in him the minute he judges he was about free. It was according to the old saying, 'give a nigger an inch and he'll take an ell.' Here was this nigger which I had as good as helped to run away, coming right out flat-footed and saying he would steal his children—children that belonged to a man I didn't even know; a man that hadn't ever done me no harm. I was sorry to hear Jim say that, it was such a lowering of him."[17] The commonly held view that an "inferior human being" can be owned by another, and that Huck therefore has a moral obligation to give Jim up, is echoed here. But a second, contradictory meaning arises when we consider that Jim's humanity had been established over the course of their journey and thus that his children cannot belong to another. Huck's innocent acceptance of slavery is ironic. He thinks that he has failed morally by lying to the slave catchers, but the reader, who processes the echoic utterance as morally untenable, understands that by deciding to protect Jim he embraces a new moral code. Even if we believe that Huck simply responds to the moral claims of friendship, the ideology of slavery would deny such a claim because it decrees the impossibility of friendship with a black slave. The irony then has the specific function of undermining the ideology of slavery.

Sperber and Wilson's claim that "if you look at . . . affective effects through the microscope of relevance theory, you see a wide array of minute cognitive effects"[18] is borne out. The reader, who would already have encountered irony in relation to Huck's views on Christian civilization, is affectively caught up in the bond of friendship established between Huck and Jim in an unfamiliar situation. This in turn has the cognitive effect of dismissing the universality of a belief that can hold sway only in the familiar master-slave situation. Huck's self-condemnation for not betraying Jim is shown to be an echo from received beliefs, one that does not stand up to scrutiny. Part of the pleasure in identifying irony is bound up with the "recognition" of assumptions so naturalized by ideology that recognition comes as a revelation. Irony may not be a counterdiscourse, but alternative views, produced by the thinking/reading subject herself, and oppositional to received ideological beliefs, may well have radical effects. According to relevance, then, the branding of irony as an elitist discourse is a misconception.

Cultural renewal cannot be a switch from the old to the new, but rather is a continuous process of assessment and criticism that includes an assessment of the very forums in which such commentary occurs. If criticism takes place within the general relations of all cultural work, then the conference where the subject is debated is *itself* an instance of cultural reproduction. And if cultural activity expects genuflection rather than analysis, then the atmosphere of prohibition is itself constituent of the transitional culture. Edward Said's observation that "all intellectual or cultural work occurs . . . on some very precisely mapped-out and permissible terrain, which is ultimately contained by the State,"[19] is pertinent, for even in the case of an emergent order, a palimpsestic map already exists and institutions stand at the ready to install their sacred cows. Cultural renewal demands that we study the map, however faint it may be, explore the terrain, and check its relation to the democratic principle.

It is commonplace to speak of meaning being generated by context, and the very coexistence of the performance with the political speech points to its ritual function of illustrating or affirming the speech. It is this affiliation of certain forms that raises the specter of a path between national and official culture. Cultural practice is not simply derived from, or a reflection of, an otherwise constituted social order, but is itself a major element in the constitution of that order. If culture is, as Williams describes, "a *signifying system* through which necessarily (though among other means) a social order is communicated, reproduced, experienced and explored,"[20] this convergence means that we dismiss questionable practices repeatedly promoted as examples of a national culture precisely because such practices *constitute* the social and political order.

Postcolonial culture stands in opposition to Western postmodernism in its embrace of nationalism as a radical force that will mobilize resistance against colonialism, and in the case of South Africa, will counter apartheid's strategies of division. But it is worth noting that the meanings of the terms "nation" and "culture" are transformed when they are welded together to form the popular phrase "national culture." The pluralism implicit in the separate terms—where nation refers to a whole country and culture to the way we live as well as all our diverse forms of expression—is lost as hegemony creeps into the meaning of the combined form. From the rhetoric of the liberation movement we gather that a national culture never simply exists; it is always something that has to be forged, a process, something in the making. However, in the fixed syntagm of the combined form, both the process of forging a culture and the inherent cyclical nature of that process is suppressed. It is interesting to note that terms like women's culture and black culture never become bonded in this way, precisely because in a white patriarchal society such cultures can never be hegemonic. The adjectival function of *woman* or *black* is retained, but *national* becomes in a sense nominalized, to assert that the cultural form in question is naturally welded to the nation.

There is, of course, nothing natural about it. Those in power decide on cultural expressions that are deemed suitable for export; a national culture is indeed synonymous with export culture; it refers not so much to how we see ourselves but rather how we wish others to see us; that is, we promote a particular image of ourselves that we offer as representative. If we press the relation between cultural production and the market economy, we arrive at something like Outspan, the name for South African oranges not eaten at home (where children die of malnutriton and vitamin deficiency), but rather packaged for foreign consumption. However, we know that Outspan oranges are chosen for their size, color, uniformity, and wholesomeness. That qualifying criteria are not discussed seems to be inherent in the fixed syntagm of national culture. Which practices, for instance, are excluded and why?

Benedict Anderson's interpretation of nationalism as an imagined political community is persuasive: "*imagined* because the members of even the smallest nation will never know most of their fellow-members, meet them or even hear of them, yet in the mind of each lives the image of their communion."[21] But Anderson makes an important distinction between imaging or creating and inventing or fabricating. The notion of simultaneity, or temporal coincidence, is necessary for representing the kind of imagined community that is the nation. Members of the community then must be aware that the things they do are being replicated simultaneously by others whose existence they do not doubt. By way of analogy, Anderson refers to the structure of the realist novel, in which characters who do not know each other are interrelated through a narrative. Simultaneity, and community, is enacted as these various characters affect each other without realizing that their actions link them together. It follows that a national culture will embody that simultaneity: that we imagine everyone wanting to sing "Nkosi Sikelele i'Afrika" on particular occasions.[22]

But just as a nation is an imagined community, a national culture as communal expression is imagined. And here slippage so easily occurs: the narrative that demonstrates simultaneity becomes the master narrative; to regard a particular expressive form as the national cultural expression—always by the agencies and institutions of an authoritative order—is also about limiting the imagination, about becoming official. The institutions of church, universities, the A.N.C. cultural office, and so forth, will make pronouncements on culture that will also be about exclusion and differentiation, the most obvious and necessary being those expressions that support an old repressive order. As Edward Said explains, culture is a "system of exclusions legislated from above . . . by which such things as anarchy, disorder, irrationality, inferiority, bad taste, and immorality are identified, then deposited outside the culture and kept there by the power of the State and its institutions."[23] To instate a popular form like the vigorous traditional dance may be an attempt to draw in the culturally disenfranchised, but the term "popular" masks obvious exclusions: the dance can be performed only by physically able, strong, young people.

If we look at the tradition in whose name such a performance is defended, further problems arise. Under colonial rule, cultural practices were stifled so that the period is characterized by rupture. Since the fabric of society has changed under the pressures of urbanization and industrialization, it is inaccurate to haul up practices of the past in the name of an authentic tradition, when tradition itself is bound up with temporality and is reliant on a temporal continuum. Historians like Jeff Guy and Sandra Burman have commented on institutions like *lobola*, or bride wealth, which "no longer fulfils the same function as it did in pre-colonial societies; it is only at the most superficial level that it can be seen as the perpetuation of a traditional social feature."[24] In the precapitalist context, bride wealth based on productive female labor brought security and respect for women; in the postcolonial context, it necessarily becomes commodified as part of a wider system of accumulation based on wage labor and thus can be read as the demeaning sale of women. "Traditional" dances like *iqhawe*, marked by "traditional" dress, drums, singing, and sexually provocative movement, can be analyzed in the same way. In the past, when sexuality was celebrated within the parameters of agrarian codes, the dance would have evolved as a desirable form that allowed the young to pick their future partners. Such a dance as export culture, however, no longer serves that function, but, more important, *can* no longer serve that function in a society reared by television series like *Dallas* and *Dynasty,* in which sexuality is commodified and fetishized through multinational capital. In other words, the iqhawe is not and cannot be iqhawe: it occurs in a new context, a political event, where participants do not choose sexual partners; it is a representation of a form of the past and as such must forfeit its claim to authenticity.

If we take the meaning of a work to be determined by its context, not only of production but also of reception, then we have to attend to how meaning is produced for a *Dallas*-fed audience among which racist views of black hypersexuality still abound and where otherness is reinforced by the dance. Which is not the same as saying that our practices must be circumscribed by European perceptions of us, but rather that affirmative statements about our undervalued culture require thoughtful negotiation with negative stereotypes.

One criterion that is not disputed is, of course, that the national culture must be founded upon resistance to the old order. And a close look at the process of establishing the national culture goes some way toward explaining its criteria. It is inevitable that a subordinate culture should be in dialogue with the official culture of the regime, in other words, react against it in order to transform not only the official forms but also oppressed people's self-perception. So if the dominant culture undervalues our way of life, our customs, our mode of dress, and our language, with the result that we have distanced ourselves from these forms, a resistance culture reacts by boldly reclaiming these cultural expressions and, gloriously indifferent to dominant perceptions, inflects them with the politics of resistance. Or reacts, by rehabilitating forms like the miners' gumboot dance that previously had been given a degrading function by the repressive system. But this process surely must continue; attempts at arresting it at this stage turn the reactive (that which opposes an unjust system) into reactionary (that which opposes further change). Such a movement from reactive to reactionary parallels the shift from a national culture, an imaginary entity that fires our will to be free, into an official culture that is an ossification, an attempt to fix certain forms, to authorize and validate them as *the* desirable, correct forms. The process, of course, will continue regardless. The cycle will repeat itself: the official culture can only lead to a new culture of resistance as the unofficial voices struggle to be heard.

If resistance is endemic to culture, then the slide into official culture can only be avoided by acknowledging this fact and by gathering the notion of resistance into the concept of a national culture. For a society fighting for independence, there is clearly a need to imagine a community with common aspirations, but it is unrealistic for such a national culture to aspire to common expressive forms. It may find its material form in the highly symbolic national anthem, but there can only be one such anthem. To instate traditional performance as artistic expression of comradeship will always be what a dominant group imagines the legitimate expression for the subordinate to be. That is what our discourse about culture ought to confront; an emerging democratic order must acknowledge the fact that even within such an order there are power relations at play. And the reflectionist model of cultural expression, that it simply mirrors what we experience, conveniently conceals the relationship between culture and power.

It is the reflectionist model that allows the documentary to be privileged by the democratic movement as the desirable cultural form, and, according to this model, the traditional dance can be read as documenting the past. However, a look at photography—which in South Africa has become synonymous with documentation—offers an example of how the question of power is evaded. The documentary does, of course, play the important political function of providing information in a state of emergency, or of presenting information that conflicts with that put out by a repressive regime. In a recent issue of *Creative Camera*, Neville Dubow writes of photographic practice as if it could be nothing other than documenting the violence in South Africa. He refers to "standards of technical excellence" that presumably allow the photographer to record more accurately.[25] As a new direction, he recommends David Goldblatt's *The Transported of KwaNdebele*, a work that required the photographer to make a daily grinding bus journey with the people of the KwaNdebele homeland to their place of employment. Goldblatt took photographs during the journeys, and his collaborator took statements from the people.[26] The work, we are told, is an accurate documentation of their lives, a cultural form that reflects the real world of apartheid. The camera, jolted during the journey, testifies to the authenticity of the experience.

It does, however, seem foolish to imagine that contemporary practices in the wider world of photography are not relevant to South Africa. Manipulation of the medium in order to explore it as an ideological tool has long since superseded the focus on technical excellence. Radical feminists in the West use photography to expose the myth of the camera's objectivity and to question the belief in vision as the privileged means of access to truth. The work of American artist Martha Rosler, for instance, problematizes documentation of the dispossessed by the socially committed photographer who "inevitably functions as an agent of the system of power that silenced these people in the first place."[27] Rosler writes in relation to her image-text project *The Bowery in Two Inadequate Descriptive Systems* that "the photographs are powerless to deal with the reality that is yet totally comprehended-in-advance by ideology."[28]

The sociopolitical situation in the United States is, of course, different. Goldblatt's work about KwaNdebele does bring into the public domain that which is suppressed by the regime. The work is also undoubtedly valuable as an instance of the artist immersing himself empathetically in the world of exploited people; it tells us about his extraordinary experience. Dubow's reading of the work, however, conflates the artist's experience with that of the photographed people, and so suppresses the unequal power relations that the project cannot fail to exemplify.

Writing strategies too can be discussed in terms of power relations. In "What Is a Minor Literature?" Félix Guattari and Gilles Deleuze deride the dream of so many literary movements that assume the status of a major literature, "to offer themselves as a sort of state language, an official language."[29] In this study of Kafka they use the spatial metaphor of territorialization that characterizes literature produced by an oppressed or marginalized people, written in the language of the oppressors. For Kafka, as a member of a Jewish minority, the available choices were, first, to enrich Prague German artificially, in other words to infuse the language with Jewish mysticism (chiefly Kabbala and alchemy). Deleuze and Guattari call this an attempt at symbolic reterritorialization that "accentuates its break from the people and will find its political result only in Zionism and such things as 'the dream of Zion.'"[30] The second choice is reterritorialization through dialect or patois, a vernacular language filled with archaisms to which the writer will try to give a contemporary sense. Kafka, they say, chose deterritorialization by writing in Prague German, thus exploiting the very poverty of the deterritorialized language, and pushing it further in the direction of deterritorialization, "to tear out of Prague German all the qualities of underdevelement that it has tried to hide."[31] There are obviously problems with Deleuze and Guattari's reference to the poverty of Prague German. However, if we leave aside such linguistic misconceptions and read their description as a metaphor for the political inflection of language, then the notion of territorialization seems a useful one to apply, not only to literary but to all cultural practice in the emerging New South Africa.

If we look at apartheid's project in geographical terms, that is, at the establishment and underdevelopment of the homeland system in the name of maintaining indigenous cultures, then deterritorialization becomes more than a metaphor. A truly national state, the abolition of an unjust geography, would coincide with abolishing notions of a master narrative, of so-called truthful documentation, of turning minor vernacular forms into major official ones. In terms of the geographical metaphor, the privileging of traditional dance as an expression of national culture can be seen as an act of reterritorialization. Since the dance is itself a reworking of tradition that seeks to conceal that transformation, coming clean or coming to terms with such transformations seems essential. We can no longer ignore popular cultural fusions or the obvious hybridizations popularized, for instance, through the new media networks.

I return to the issue of irony in relation to the representation of tradition via a reading of Njabulo Ndebele's story "The Prophetess," one of the few examples in contemporary black fiction where the complexities of a hybridized urban culture are explored. Michael Vaughan, however, critiques the story in terms of tradition: "The problematic identity of the inner life, the sophisticated scepticism of the narrative voice . . . have no *organic* connection with oral culture and oral narrative."[32] He goes on to offer a truism: "The wider, non-reading population cannot engage . . . with the writer's practice."[33] The "sophisticated scepticism of the narrative voice," which he derides, is of course precisely Ndebele's deployment of irony, lamented for not reproducing traditional storytelling. Ironically, Vaughan overlooks the radical aspect of Ndebele's treatment of the very issues of cultural renewal and ossification.

Ndebele's narrative of a prophetess's supernatural powers is constituted of a set of contiguous events that question what is popularly seen to be "authentic" or "traditional" culture. Contiguity is of significance since it is the placement of different and apparently unrelated events alongside each other that impels the reader to make cross connections. Although one of the events is a memory, in other words a movement back in time, the story insists that it is not only temporality (as theorized in Anderson's description of the simultaneity of events that serves as a metaphor for nationhood), but rather the conjugation of time and spatiality, the next-to-ness, through which culture is articulated. Thus without considering the particularity of the events, their very arrangement places a question mark over the popular, diachronic view of cultural practice being rooted in tradition, and posits the validity of juxtaposing apparently unconnected phenomena. An analysis of the story precisely bears this out.

The unnamed central character, a boy, is sent by his mother, a nurse, on an errand to a prophetess to bless a bottle of water that the mother believes will cure her ailment. On approaching the prophetess's house, the boy is scared by the dark tunnel of vine, said by local people to be coated in an invisible glue that holds captive those who steal her grapes by night. The boy experiences the prophetess and her rituals as both mundane and awesome. She blesses him and his bottle of water, but on the way home he accidentally loses the water. He replaces it with unblessed water from a tap, which nevertheless appears to have the desired effect on his mother. The story ends with the boy feeling grateful: "He had healed his mother. He would heal her tomorrow, and always with all the water in the world."[34]

The two contiguous events presented on either side of his encounter with the prophetess are connected by sticky liquids that are invested with mythical power, and that operate as fetishes within the mini-narratives. The first event is a loud conversation held by passengers in a bus, recalled by the boy as he walks through the scary tunnel of vine. There a skeptical washerwoman asks whether anyone has proof of the prophetess's glue that catches thieves, and a debate ensues into which is drawn the gendered nature of skepticism. A young man described as applying "the final touches of saliva with his tongue" to a rolled up cigarette makes a lewd and senseless contribution: "'That's it good ladies, make your point; push very strongly. . . . Love is having women like you' . . . and his rolled up cigarette looked small between his thick fingers."[35] The cigarette as metaphor for penis becomes clear in the second event, when, on his way back from the prophetess, the boy encounters a gang crowding around a youth who boasts of just having had intercourse with a sought-after girl. He shows them the sticky liquid dripping from his penis, but the authenticity of the semen is comically disputed by the others:

> "Look! See? The liquid? See? When I touch it with my finger and then leave it, it follows like a spider's web."
>
> "Well, my man," said someone, "you can't deceive anybody with that. It's the usual trick. A fellow just blows his nose and then applies the mucous there, and then emerges out of the dark saying he has just had a girl."[36]

The boy watches the penis, described with echoes of the cigarette between the lewd man's fingers as "a thick little thing . . . it looked sad. It had first been squeezed in retreat against the fly like a concertina before it finally disappeared."[37]

Both events are cast as debates that remain unresolved. What is unmistakably linked in them is the aggressive sexuality of young men whose contemporary claims to traditional male behavior allows for the abuse of women. These "real" bodily fluids—mucus, saliva, semen—serve as metonymies for the authentic black bodies that claim precolonial practices such as domination of women as "authentic culture." The fluids are contrastively linked to the artful glue of the prophetess's vine; the boy's observation of worms crawling over the vine marked by prohibition ("'Don't touch that vine!,' was the warning almost everyone in Charterston township knew")[38] echoes the "thick little thing" of the transgressive penis. It is the hermeneutics of contiguous events that unmask an unspoken aspect of tradition, aggressive male sexuality. But the bodily fluids also contrast with the tap water of urban modernity for which the question of authenticity does not arise, but which remains in the realm of the ineffable. The magical powers of the prophetess may be questioned by the washerwoman and dismissed by the educated man in the bus as foolish superstition, but the fake holy water administered to the mother has the desired medicinal effect.

It is innovation and syncretism that are valorized in the text. In blessing the boy the prophetess sings a brand new hymn created by herself rather than found in "the dead leaves of hymn books"; her prayer is for the water to bring the "flower of newness" to those who drink it; her parting words are, "'My son, we are made of all that is in the world. Go and heal your mother.'"[39] Indeed, the blessing ceremony is a happy mixture of old and new, of Christian and pagan; the African mask and the laughter of the prophetess turned to unearthly shriek coexist with the images of the cross and the sacred heart of Jesus that adorn her home. Western customs, beliefs, and knowledges have not driven out the old, but at the same time their existence within a colonized culture is not denied; rather, the coexistence has produced something new, something that has developed within time and sitting alongside the old will not be dismissed and derided. It stands in opposition to the appeal to a precolonial, traditional and "authentic" display of the stereotyped virile black body.

In his essay "Redefining Relevance," Ndebele distinguishes between artist and propagandist in terms of irony: "If the writer has an ideological goal, and he always has, he has to reach that goal through a serious and inevitable confrontation with irony."[40] The ironies in "The Prophetess" operate in complex ways, and in terms of relevance theory rely on a number of echoic utterances. The story about thieves glued at night to the vine is elaborated in a description of the prophetess who in the morning "would come out of the house with the first rays of the sun, raise her arms into the sky, and say: 'Away, away, sinful man; go and sin no more!' Suddenly, the thief would be free, and would walk away feeling a great release that turned him into a new man."[41] Here the readily recovered biblical echo of a redemptive Christ offers an ironic equivalence between the opposing "superstitions" of the pagan, and the so-called rational beliefs of the Christian. The prophetess occupies a space in between that refuses to prioritize either.

For the sexualized man in the bus who subscribes to precolonial beliefs, phallocentricity is in ironic contradiction with the prophetess's creation of a "new man." The efficacy of the stand-in (unblessed) water constitutes a dramatic irony which is double-edged in its political implications, and which establishes the story as one that refuses to have its meanings fixed. On the one hand we could see from a modern, urban perspective the contradictory, placebo effect of the blessed water as one that is both responsible and not responsible for the healing. On the other hand, there is the irony of a "rational" explanation for the "supernatural": having also blessed the boy himself, the prophetess may have conferred on him the magical powers that necessarily transfer to the new water. If innovation, creativity, and therefore the boy's improvisation on his accidental loss are privileged in the text, then it is the case that traditional, pretheoretical knowledge is likewise valorized. Improvisation in the modern world of the nurse is precisely about being in dialogue with the past, so that in Ndebele's own words African readers are given the opportunity to experience themselves as "makers of culture in their own right."[42]

"The Prophetess" is a far cry from the Sechaba spectacle, in which colonial rupture is denied in an uncomplicated step into the past to recover an authentic culture. Significantly, it is Ndebele, the critic, who has launched the most searing attack against the stultifying nature of antiapartheid cultural practices offered in the name of relevance to political struggle. While his indictment of the hegemony of spectacle is primarily aimed at writing, the spectacular nature of South African culture described as follows, readily applies to the drum and dance routine: "The spectacular documents; it indicts implicitly; it is demonstrative, preferring exteriority to interiority; it keeps the larger issues of society in our minds, obliterating the details; it provokes identification through recognition and feeling rather than through observation and analytical thought."[43] The technological revolution has given all cultures an internationalist aspect, and conservative forces in South Africa have drawn on this to forge a popular culture as represented, for instance, on television or syndicated magazines from *True Love* to *Tribute*. Rather than pursue authenticity and tradition, a radical culture would engage with such representations, expose the poverty in their glossy images of the corporate black, intervene in their presentation, and represent them in ways that explore and challenge power relations. We may have to give up beloved notions of correct forms for expressing a national culture, but engaging with innovation will, as Ndebele urges, "help to break down the closed epistemological structures of South African oppression, structures that can severely compromise resistance by dominating thinking itself."[44] It may very well prevent the perilous slide into official culture.

2

NATION, RACE, AND ETHNICITY: BEYOND THE LEGACY OF VICTIMS (1991, 1992)

We have all been horribly bullied by Father Culture and Mother Nature, that binary pair who define the terms of our production in the old language of the West—race, ethnicity, nation. Not that these have not changed: race has for some time been dressed in quotation marks, and we must now ask the question, in what sense can the concept of nation be refurbished? How could these mediating terms inform writing? How are they constituted through language? These are the questions I will address, but I am wary of what sounds like an invitation to find new guidelines. What lies beyond the legacy of victims, Father Culture alone knows.

I am not sure that this should not be a study of place names: the New South Africa, like New South Wales, New York, New Orleans, with the preferred prefix of colonialism, which through naming keeps the new tied to the old and so points the way to repetition and mimicry. But my title points to the rupture that the New South Africa represents, a rupture that must necessarily influence the course of writing.

In another period of rupture, the Natives Land Act of 1913, which drove black South Africans off the land, Sol Plaatje was driven to write the first black novel, *Mhudi.*[1] Plaatje was also an executive member of the South African Native Congress, later to be known as the African National Congress. The significant replacements, African for South African and National for Native, are indicative of the kind of unity that was deemed suitable for a culture of resistance.

Mhudi reveals the textual construction of nationhood through a fictionalized Mzilikazi. Throughout the novel the Matabele king is represented as the villain, his tyranny, imperialism, and bloodthirstiness contrasted with other black chiefs'. When, at the end, Mzilikazi is defeated by the gunpowder of the

Boer-Baralong alliance, Plaatje undertakes the complex task of rehabilitating him. This process takes place through a shift in the mode of narration: from third-person report where his behavior is explicitly linked to the European imperialist project, to a first-person lament in which Mzilikazi's voice allows him to be deconstructed into a tragic hero. Land as well-known metaphor for nation is explored in his argument for waging war against his black neighbors and taking their land: "It was my desire to incorporate them with ourselves, so that together we could form one great nation."[2] Nationhood then is presented as an alternative to the unholy alliance between Boer and black, and Mzilika-zi's passionate denunciation of that alliance amounts to a prediction of the Natives Land Act of 1913, a prediction of apartheid. Significantly Mzilikazi uses as an analogy a traditional narrative, a truth which has been orally transmitted and which he repeats as a speech act of exhorting his people.

It is a folktale about Zungu who rears a lion's cub as a domestic animal, only to find one day that the grown lion has ungraciously eaten the Zungu family. In other words, an alliance between different genuses goes against nature. He carries on to predict: "They [the Boers] will despoil them of the very lands they have rendered unsafe for us; they will entice the Bechuana youths to war and the chase, only to use them as pack-oxen; yea, they will refuse to share with them the spoils of victory . . . they shall take Bechuana women to wife and, with them, breed a race of half man and half goblin and they will deny them their legitimate lobola."[3] Mzilikazi's appeal to a black nationhood thus relies on the notions of race and custom, delivered in a language in which difference is inscribed through the pronouns, a language that echoes the biblical Law of Father Culture.

Nationhood thus can be seen as a concept that comes into being at a particular historical juncture, a concept for survival. But built into it is also entropy, and in order to examine its inevitable collapse, it is necessary to look again at one of its linchpins, race.

Apartheid has claimed a monopoly on racism for so long that our perceptions of its operations have been distorted. For instance, we speak as if only whites practice racism; we do not note the racism among the different white groups. Robert Miles in his study on race discusses British immigration law, where an explicitly racist discourse is modified, "becomes silent but neverthe-less embodied in the continuation of exclusionary practices or in the use of a new discourse."[4] It is precisely such transformations, when discussion of race goes underground, against which we must be on guard. The civilized world agrees that there is no scientific justification for using the term: "The use of the word 'race' . . . is an aspect of the social construction of reality: 'races' are so-cially imagined rather than biological realities."[5]

But race does acquire meaning through signification or the process of representation, meanings that are tailored according to ideological needs. Bessie Head, in the novel *Maru*, explores this and locates it in language. Her subject is not the white-black opposition; instead her concern is with the inherent reproductive nature of race as a sign of difference: "And if the white man thought that Asians were a low filthy nation, Asians could still smile with relief—at least they were not Africans. And if the white man thought Africans were a low filthy nation, Africans could still smile—at least they were not Bushmen."[6] Head goes on to explain how studying the Masarwa is considered no different from examining the teeth of a zebra: "The zebra is not supposed to mind because it is an animal. Scientists do the same to Bushmen and they are not supposed to mind, because there is no one they can still turn round to and say, 'At least I am not a——.'"[7] The dash, the absence of another group from which to differentiate themselves, ensures that the Masarwa remain at the bottom of the scale. What is as important as the gap is the fact that the incomplete sentence "At least I am not a . . ." is formulated at all, suggesting the possibility of reproducing that sign of difference, the desire to find an other to occupy the gap. The sentence is formulated in direct speech, a quotation in the sense not only of an actual utterance, but also as an echo repeating that which is infinitely reproduced in the culture. As it happens, being at the bottom of the scale, the mouth of the Masarwa must remain hanging open: there is no group with which to replace the formula, and absence or silence marks their subjection and repression.

This section, early in the novel, ruptures the writing. Head abandons the narrative to speak directly to the reader. Stepping out of her role as narrator to address a topic beyond the fictive boundaries, she invites us to step outside our role as readers of fiction. We are confronted with the relationship between fiction and the world; we are addressed directly as "you." We are reminded: "You were a child yourself," forcing us to recognize ourselves as perpetrators of racial violence. But the sign "you" also takes another meaning—"you," the victim: "Children went a little further. They spat on you. They pinched you. They danced a wild jiggle, with the tin cans rattling: 'Bushman! Low Breed! Bastard!'"[8] Again the calling out, the articulation marked by the inverted commas of direct speech, a speech event recalled within this speech event where we are addressed by the author. Language as marker of difference is exploited: the pronoun "you" has meaning only in opposition to and differentiated from "they."

Head's narrative allows Margaret Cadmore, the central female character, to assert herself as subject by breaking the silence of the Masarwa, by uttering the unspeakable. Her reply to Dikeledi, who asks about her racial origins, is given without hesitation: "I am a Masarwa." The incident demonstrates how language or discourse provides the possibility of subjectivity for someone who is seen as object, a subordinate race despised by all. Language, the act of speaking and specifically of identifying herself as Masarwa, establishes the "I"—Margaret as subject, differentiated from the "you" of her interlocutor. She is able to sustain this position in spite of her friend's response, which is to urge her back into silence, the accepted condition of the Masarwa: "'Don't mention this to anyone else,' she said, shock making her utter strange words. 'If you keep silent about this matter people will simply assume you are a Coloured. I mistook you for a Coloured until you brought up the other matter.'"[9] Dikeledi is unable to utter the word "Masarwa": she calls it "the other matter" when it is in fact the matter under discussion.

Such construction of race through language can be seen as a precursor to the construction of nationhood. Race has the double-edged function of playing primary roles both in oppression and in the fostering of nationhood that aims to overthrow oppression. Subjectivity of the oppressed then is asserted through language, through the utterance: "We, the oppressed majority of South Africa, will no longer do as they say." And following Anderson's view of nation as imagined community, those who do not know each other can speak for each other, claim the right to speak for each other, and in the process of doing so, redefine and re-present their racial difference. The pronouns allow for reversal: "we" assert ourselves as subject: "they" become the morally flawed other. It is the moral content that allows for a racially defined nationhood to reshape itself, to articulate itself in a new linguistic construction: "We who oppose apartheid . . . ," the racial content etiolated.

As the New South Africa heaves itself into place, we find the inevitable happening—the notion of nation is under siege. Elsewhere I have outlined the process by which a national culture becomes the official culture that attempts to fix, authorize, and validate certain forms.[10] The vigorous ethnic performance culled from fond notions of tradition is an example, where the reactive (a necessary phase) becomes reactionary. The official culture will of course produce its own resistance, its own disclaimers, for the truth of the matter, the irony, is that there is little to differentiate between the visual excesses of Zulu nationalists in the Inkatha Freedom Party and the insignia of South African export culture—the so-called traditional performance, complete with animal skins and feathers.

But ethnicity will not go away. We may think of nation as imagined community, but community itself is of course not imagined; rather, it is the lived expression of people who interact with each other, as in a speech community that shares a common language. The question of a national language has always been at the heart of the notion of nation. Brought into being by language, the concept of nation then becomes subsumed by language.

Nation and ethnicity are always cast in hierarchical terms—nation as developed, and of the privileged category of unity, while ethnicity is seen as primitive, belonging to a different mentality, made up of opinion, custom, prejudice, forms of knowledge that are not valued. If both were recognized as pragmatic concepts that find legitimation in particular sets of practices, particular political needs, we might find their conflicting demands easier to negotiate. We have to recognize the dialectical relationship between the two. When the question arises, "In which language have we said, 'We who oppose apartheid . . .' and asserted our subjectivity?" we could do worse than reflect on the common root of the words "dialect" and "dialectic," which relates to discourse.

We envisage at present not only this nonracial "we," but also the imagined "we" of a united, all-embracing society. What language theory, however, does not take into account is the material reality of people's lives. For many who are able to speak and include themselves in the resisting "we," otherness remains a condition of their lives. The reality of exclusion manifested in hunger, homelessness, and illiteracy sits uncomfortably with the happy notion of nation.

As for writing, the question is not simply how to transform our racially inflected chants, the fixed syntagms of we-the-oppressed-majority or we-who-fight-apartheid, the victims of the title. The question is surely what to do about those real voices that intrude upon us as we sit down to write: how to continue the activity of writing that is disturbed by the beggars beating at our doors for food: how not to think of writing in this context as a shameful activity that does little or nothing about redistributing cultural and linguistic capital. It is difficult not to sound pious, but the horror of life on our streets raises crucial questions. I have no grand statements to make about the writer and her writing; all I have arrived at is a set of questions.

How do liberal humanist assumptions about the function of art, of writing, relate to those who cannot read? What place could the dispossessed decently occupy in our schemes of representation? Mindful of the popular and indecent practice of objectifying and othering the poor in documentary photography ("'victim' photography," as Martha Rosler so aptly puts it),[11] is there really a case for privileging representational art? Is there a case at all for giving writing a central position in our culture?

3

CULTURE BEYOND COLOR? A SOUTH AFRICAN DILEMMA (1993)

In Bessie Head's novel *A Question of Power* (1973), there is a rare moment of hilarity when a Danish development worker in Botswana proudly makes the following comments about Denmark: "In our country culture has become so complex, this complexity is reflected in our literature. It takes a certain level of education to understand our novelists. The ordinary man cannot understand them"; "There's a whole lot of novelists no one can understand."[1] South Africa, too, is extremely complex, but then we do not produce much by way of literature, and when we do our writing-from-the-roots movement recommends that everyone understand it, including the illiterate. The draft document of the newly constituted Federation of South African Cultural Organizations (FOSACO), dated March 1992, insists, after numerous references to common nationhood and national pride, that cultural workers, including oral storytellers, have a central role to play in the reconstruction of the country, and demands that the constitution guarantee cultural rights.[2] The protection of the arts in the New South Africa will not, then, protect works from being understood but aims for broad cultural development and conservation of our cultural heritage. Respect for our tradition, which the New South Africa, frightened by its own newness, invokes almost as often as it does the imagined community of the nation, will ensure that our oral and written literature stays alive.[3]

Given this central role in the New South Africa, writers, also known for their knowledge of the future, are often asked what its writing will be like. Indeed, in the plethora of conferences in Europe and the U.S.A., writers are routinely asked whether the removal of apartheid will not also remove our subject matter and therefore the impetus to write, a question that perversely casts apartheid as an enabling system. In a sense the answer is already inscribed in a description of writing from the old South Africa, to which the exciting new writing would be diametrically opposed: there will be no protest writing, no stereotypes of idle madams lounging at swimming pools and attended by flagging servants, no missionary English, no patronizing publishers or critics waxing lyrical about our least attempts, and much experimentation with new forms. But I fear that we will be disappointed. What my list does not make explicit is that it speaks of black writing. It cannot speak of an interracial culture; the New South Africa is too much like the old and is therefore necessarily a racial affair.

Our new society remains umbilically linked to the matrix of apartheid so that parturition is a slow affair. Since we are shaped by race-specific conditions, the protracted and bewildering weaning from the old is radically different for different racial groups. Moreover, we have all become rather perversely attached to apartheid. How will black people, long accustomed to dispossession and deprivation, adjust to a new condition of not being racial victims? Our chant of we-the-oppressed-black-majority with its moral upper hand has at times a curious ring of comfort, since it absolves us from taking responsibility for our own condition, precisely because our more assertive cries have never had any perlocutionary effect. How will we transform that chant, invent a new language for reconstructing ourselves to replace the fixed syntagms of the discourse of oppression? And will our writing be about these kinds of painful psychological adjustments? I have no idea, and there seems little point in speculating. What does seem clear is that an interracial culture is a long way off—that to think of an achromatic writing is simply premature, if not altogether a mistake.

My experience recently of attempting to judge the interracial Bessie Head/ Alex La Guma Fiction Award says something, I think, about the politics of culture.[4] These anonymous manuscripts were not only easily identified in terms of race, they were all about race, and our criteria in a context of reconstruction cannot ignore race. To imagine our society as achromatic, as an interracial competition would suggest, seems a serious anachronism that can do little more than perpetuate inequities. After years of underdevelopment by apartheid there can surely be no such thing, since white writers with their cultural and linguistic capital will necessarily walk off with the prizes, and to award them to less competent black writers for trying hard is no solution. The response that one should recognize and reward potential, that natural ability, genius, and talent will shine through, is of course misguided. Linguistic research has shown that there is no such thing as a literary language that certain gifted people somehow will access; there is only language that a writer will comfortably use and abuse to her own advantage. In our situation, where apartheid conditions have militated against the linguistic development of black people, both in the imposition of European languages and in the neglect of education, the function of the literary prize becomes obvious. Not only is it inappropriate or inadequate as a means of encouraging writing, it actively perpetuates inequity by rewarding those who have been privileged.

To speak of the politics of a culture is to speak of the ways in which the culture represents itself, the structures that privilege certain forms of representation and the means by which such forms are legitimated. The National Arts Policy Plenary (NAPP),[5] a cultural Convention for a Democratic South Africa (CODESA), is currently bringing together politically diverse groups to formulate recommendations for arts policies, structures, and funding mechanisms, and it will no doubt play a significant part in establishing the cultural politics of the New South Africa. The NAPP's draft document does not explicitly address our official resistance culture, with its conservative appeal to tradition and its privileging of the documentary; its broad endorsements of freedom of expression cannot, however, guarantee the covert replacement of A.N.C. resistance culture with another set of prescriptions or, at best, predilections of those in control. In many ways it does not matter that structures exercise pressure on individual production: culture, which can be tautologically defined as that which already is, ensures a growing gap between what is actually produced and what legislative bodies imagine it ought to produce.

What does matter and what literary arbiters so often forget is that writing is made of the common mundane material of language. Far more basic than Virginia Woolf's room of her own and so many pounds per year as a necessary condition for writing is the question of literacy and education, and the material conditions of production predict a dismal future for writing in South Africa. Where illiteracy is high and educational opportunities narrow, people simply will not, cannot write. The divided system of apartheid is still in place when schooling for black children, administered by the segregated Department of Education and Training, is a brutalizing experience of fighting for space in overcrowded buildings with impossible teacher-pupil ratios.[6] Attempts made by frustrated pupils, who are being taught outdoors or in a "platoon system" of shifts, to occupy empty school buildings in white areas have been met with police defense of the Department of Education and Training's properties. The government continues with its "rationalization" program, by which it means closing down schools and making teachers redundant. There are no jobs for black teachers who graduate at the end of this year.

It is no accident that the most vibrant cultural production among black people is in the visual arts, where poorly educated artists, in their mining of low culture, depart from the symbolism of traditional African art. I am thinking of

Fig. 3.1. Vusumuzi Derrick [Derek] Nxumalo, *Drakensberg Mountain*,
felt-tip pen on paper, 1987. Photograph © Gavin Younge, taken with
permission of the artist, and used with permission of the photographer.
Source: Gavin Younge, *Art of the South African
Townships* (London: Thames and Hudson, 1988), p. 53.

Derek Nxumalo or illiterate artists like Chickenman Mkhize and Tito Zungu,[7]
who engage directly with writing and with language as social semiotic. Their
images have in common an interest in issues of communication and their orthographic inscription in the geospatial terrain: Nxumalo's roads, railways, road
signs, and place names constitute the physical planes of a curious rural-urban
landscape, the world(s) inhabited by the black work force (see fig. 3.1). The role
of language in the culture is encoded in the sociosemantic exchange between
linguistic and visual information where, for example, toponymy and topography are linked in bold signs of mountain names that visually replace the referent. Mkhize roughly copies "found" language in both Zulu and English in a
typically illiterate hand and with no regard for word breaks onto wooden placards
balanced on a crude circular wire stand. These three-dimensional objects, con-
sisting of triangle with rudimentary image above a rectangle with text, resem-
ble road signs that not only explore writing as visual information but invite us to
make meaning at the intersection of image and text (see fig. 3.2).[8] Zungu started
making art by decorating letters that his migrant workmates would send home

Fig. 3.2. Chickenman Mkhize, *Full Cream,*
Creamline, mixed media, c. 1990, collection R.
Palmer / Z. Wicomb. Photograph by Roger Palmer,
reproduced with permission.

to the Bantustans. Where literacy is basic, letters, often dictated to a scribe and read to nonliterate wives, are valued as much for their symbolic meaning as for their contents. As an act of communication, the images covering these public/ private letters become tropes of desire that speak loudly of cultural difference, of access and exclusion. Zungu's images of airplanes, ocean liners, trains, and cityscapes communicate to rural recipients the language of the metropolis. In- cluded in the meticulous detail of Zungu's drawings are the linguistic signs of industrial enterprise, such as "SUB[S]IDIARY COMPANIES" (see fig. 3.3).

Concern with literacy and the symbolic power of language can be visually articulated in challenging works by artists in ways that cannot be explored in writing, which relies on linguistic competence. It is strange, then, to speculate

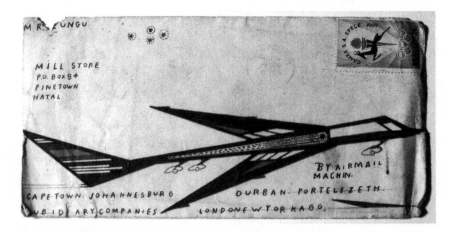

Fig. 3.3. Tito Zungu, Untitled, felt-tip pen on paper envelope, c. 1969.
Photograph by Roger Palmer, reproduced with permission.

on postapartheid literary production when learning to read and write involves jostling and struggling within an educational system that offers no alternative to the brutal conditions of the township. If we think more broadly of culture, the way in which people behave, then it may be more appropriate to talk about our ravaged culture of violence. Where other countries speak with hope about the dominant culture being regenerated from below, from the marginalized everyday culture of the people, we can only remain silent. Our corrupt and sterile official culture of apartheid has nothing to offer; our everyday culture has in turn been brutalized by it. Endemic violence characterizes both the operations of the old regime and the culture of resistance during the period of transition. If the resistance culture was successfully mobilized by a revolutionary call to make the country ungovernable, the new South African government will itself be hamstrung by the legacy of that call, by a citizenry that has grown into being through violence necessitated by apartheid's intransigence. Besides, the distortions of apartheid that admitted whites to privilege and gain on the irrational basis of being white have been vulgarly translated into apartheid's obverse of irrational entitlement by virtue of being black. And both violence and entitlement will continue to be fed by the gross economic inequities that postapartheid culture stands to inherit. Transitional culture, then, is necessarily a jagged affair, subject to repetitions and inversions, or dangerous translations that do not offer a desirable route to social transformation.

In order to discuss the polite subject of literature, we may first have to speak about the unspeakable, and I have in mind the Afrikaner cultural activity of the *braaivleis*, the bonhomie of the barbeque, translated into township necklacing, the burning of human beings who are alleged *impimpis* (informers) or traitors to the state. Rian Malan in *My Traitor's Heart* describes his investigation of a braaivleis, a "profound cultural ritual," where drunken jolly-japing by the side of the swimming pool includes the torture of a black man. Malan describes "that quintessentially South African tableau of braaivleis, rugby, sunny skies, and torture. It was all so fucking, heartbreakingly traditional. Dennis Moshweshwe died a completely traditional South African death. There is even a traditional word for it in the Afrikaans language: he died of a *kafferpak*, meaning a 'kaffir hiding,' a brutal beating of the sort whites have been administering to blacks since the day we first set foot on this continent."[9] Malan's narrative is partly framed as an act of translation. The story of Moshweshwe's death is told by his girlfriend to a black journalist, Eugene, who translated it into English. Malan's account of the actual torture is told in a stilted language in which is embedded its history of actual speech, translation, and the author's repetition/ translation into writing. This discursive rewording in its successive forms raises the issue of what George Steiner calls "topologies of culture," by which he means that cultural expression is characterized by metamorphic repetitions.[10] We do not have access to the necessary transformations through which Malan's story has passed, but the translation can be seen as a model for the "rewording" of braaivleis as necklacing, where a number of invariants underpin these cultural activities.

The most obvious recursive feature is the act of burning as a communal activity—necklacing, like the braaivleis, is never a private affair. Both activities are marked by the iconography of postindustrial culture: the swimming pool (itself a wry transformation from the veld) and the discarded tire (waste from another coveted marker of bourgeois culture, the motor car) that is placed around the victim's neck. Both originate in the need to survive: Boers trekking from British domination relied on shooting buck and eating the roasted meat in the open veld; necklacing eliminated those who endanger the community by spying for the government. Necklacing, then, is about displacing Boer culture both physically and symbolically. It is about positioning: placing the victim as other within an isolating circle of fire and outside the community; replacing the decorative necklace with the destructive tire, a symbolic reminder to victims of where they have placed themselves as they embraced the enemy with its lure of lucre; and positioning the necklacers above such treachery.

Amid hunger and homelessness, even the piffling amount that the South African Police offer to informers is hard to resist. The hungry, homeless, and outraged communities respond with acts that challenge our liberal humanist assumptions. Necklacing does not tell us about communities pitted against each other, it tells about cohesion within communities who take collective responsibility for such a death and who honor the dead with sympathetic ululations as if it were a natural one. The barbarism of such cultural activity becomes peaks of a topological process, a generative transformation in the barbarism of official white culture. Necklacing responds to the countless deaths in the townships recorded as unrest related and therefore not worthy of investigation, deaths caused by the agents of government who use impimpis to destablilize black communities. The "official" status of necklacing was confirmed in a recent news report of its use in Maputo, in Mozambique, where the community used burning tires as punishment for theft, yet another transmutation of our export culture.

The question of what kind of literature such a culture will produce cannot take priority. Legislation on the arts, the well-meaning documents produced by our cultural organizations, will only lead to shrewd investments by those who already have cultural capital, unless we address the question of literacy, the raw material for producing poetry. And how can a literary culture be interracial if it conducts its business in a minority language and its minority dialect of standard English that few have access to? Without a decent, compulsory, multilingual system of education for all, we cannot move toward the national interracial culture of which our policy documents or euphonic conference titles speak. We need a radical pedagogy, a level of literacy that will allow our children to read works of literature that will politicize them into an awareness not only of power, but also of the equivocal, the ambiguous, and the ironic that is always embedded in power. We need a radical pedagogy that will sensitize those whose privilege has blinded them to the ironies of power. Only then can we speak of an interracial culture of readers and writers who are not passive consumers of culture, but rather who interrogate received views, who interrogate the magisterial discourse of the New South Africa and its cultural institutions, and who above all interrogate the fixed positions that we have allowed ourselves to adopt and assign to others in our practice of necklacing. And with competent readers, who knows, we may even develop a way of reading, which is to say disambiguating, those complex and incomprehensible Danish works.

4

Reading, Writing, and Visual Production in the New South Africa (1995)

It is the popular privileging of speech and the phonological aspect of language that we find in the fond reference to reading and writing as the two Rs which prompts me to address an absence in my title, the question of orality. Thus the following observations have less to do with literary production and the reading of literary texts than with the relationship of these modalities with what has been cast as their opposite—orality. And while it is hardly necessary to rehearse the claims for literacy made in recent decades, I shall very briefly do just that in order to attempt a reading of the ways in which the orality-literacy dichotomy has been figured in South Africa where social change, if not yet an actuality, has symbolically taken root.

The dismissal of writing and claims for the primacy of speech, by Plato, Rousseau, Lévi-Strauss, and linguists like Bloomfield and Sapir, have been challenged by Ong, Havelock, Goody, McLuhan, and others, who claim that the technologizing of the word had far-reaching cognitive effects. Writing was responsible not only for new forms of discourse and for metalingual activity, but, most significantly, for the restructuring of consciousness itself, making us capable of abstract, context-free thought. The new forms of social organization brought about by writing and print, then, are associated with progress and individual liberty; collective political skepticism, according to Goody, comes only as a consequence of literacy.

Arguments for the inherent qualities of literacy have, however, been contested. Ruth Finnegan, in her study of the Limba people of Sierra Leone, analyzes the ways in which their oral literature indeed functions as a vehicle for objectivity and abstract thought, and remarks on its concern with the metalingual and reflexivity in storytelling.[1] There is no such thing, she says, as a primitive preliterate mentality; the extravagant claims of Ong and others can be dismissed as an ethnocentric, technology-based, Great Divide theory.[2] Similarly, Brian Street's ideological model, skeptical of the claims of literacy, shows how the teaching of literacy reinforces and extends inequalities, and how the purpose of teaching people to read and write, as in the case of UNESCO's "functional literacy" approach, is often to promote multinational interests, resulting in further exploitation of the poor.[3] What passes for the testing of literacy is none other than "the social conventions of a dominant class, rather than universal logic."[4] Following Jenny Cook-Gumperz, Street discusses the celebrated literate mentality as a social construct rather than as an inherent condition.

Literacy, then, has to be considered in relation to the social and cultural institutions that give meaning and value to particular practices of reading and writing. In South Africa, where historians have uncovered the manipulative methods by which orthographies for indigenous languages were established by missionaries, we have perhaps good reason to be skeptical of the gifts of reading and writing. Patrick Harries, in his study of Tsonga as a written language, argues that its delineation and codification "was a product of nineteenth[-]century European discourse rather than a reflection of local reality," resulting in the construction of a Tsonga "tribe" or "nation" because of their perceived linguistic affiliation.[5] Setswana, according to Sol Plaatje, was equally corrupted by missionary intervention. Plaatje, who had written extensively in his own language, as well as having worked with the London phonetician Daniel Jones, spoke scathingly of "Se-ruti," the name used to describe the version of Tswana used by the missionaries and codified in Brown's Tswana dictionary of 1925. Failure of the missionaries to agree on an orthography for Tswana had prevented publishing in that language. Plaatje found the London Missionary Society's choice of the Tlaping dialect for their own publications incomprehensible; however, it did not shake his belief in the importance of a written literature to maintain the culture.[6]

Cognitive claims for literacy have had the effect of downgrading oral cultures, so that, in our era of careful language use, the term "illiteracy" has been replaced by "nonliterate," one which is deemed to be less negative and which hopes somehow not to brand more than half the world's population as incapable of what we call rational thought. Concepts like "varieties of literacy" and "varieties of knowledge," or Walter Ong's subsequent claim that writing itself can paradoxically liberate us from our chirographic bias, are an attempt to bridge the divide.[7] Such amelioration, however, makes no impact on the fact that cultural production is routinely associated with literacy, that in our world of texts the illiterate are seen not as producers or contributors to dynamic cultures but rather as themselves "texts" to be read by others. Oral history projects and studies in oral "literature" undoubtedly play an important role in the preservation of cultures, but they have not succeeded in undoing the conflation of *culture* with *literacy*.

What is overlooked or undervalued by the conflicting positions on literacy is that writing has made the word visual, that it is as closely related to graphic art as it is to speech, and that a complex of relations between writing and visual representation has developed. Thus contemporary visual works in South Africa have outstripped the need for apologias on behalf of the nonliterate or poorly educated who produce art forms that in their use of writing curiously coincide with postmodernist practices in the overdeveloped West. Nevertheless, commentary on cultural production has largely been confined to the literary and has failed to examine other works that exemplify the literacy/orality dialectic as it operates in South Africa.

Before Albie Sachs, speaking from the sanctioned position of the African National Congress (A.N.C.), found it necessary to lift the injunction of culture as a weapon of the struggle, writer and cultural theorist Njabulo Ndebele lamented the stultifying effects of apartheid on writing, which, in the name of revolution, had settled into redundant messages about the suffering and oppression of the black majority.[8] Ndebele redefines politically "relevant" writing as the discovery—or rediscovery—"of the ordinary," and locates the greatest challenge of the revolution "in the search for ways of thinking, ways of perception, that will help to break down the closed epistemological structures of South African oppression."[9] But such a search presupposes and relies on the medium of literacy. Tracing in his essay entitled "Towards Progressive Cultural Planning" the conservative functions that literacy has served in black culture, he focuses on the transformation of the function of reading in a New South Africa: "Politically, reading will be seen and regarded as an important extension of the democratic process itself."[10]

Nadine Gordimer, while subscribing to the A.N.C.'s notion of a People's Literature, is aware of the contradictions inherent in the term. She points out that functional literacy can produce neither literature nor competent readers of literary texts; instead, education, libraries, space in which to write, and the valorization of indigenous languages are prerequisites to a democratic literary culture: "If there is to be a People's Literature it will come about only if there is state interference in a future South Africa, and if social conditions ensure that comic-book literacy, disseminated through the long-established colonial agencies which continue to monopolize distribution of publications in the entire African subcontinent, does not become the people's literary culture, as it has in so many parts of the world."[11] While I can only agree that we have politically and aesthetically been infected by the vulgarity of apartheid, or, as I have argued elsewhere, using the model of a topology of culture, that our most apparently divergent practices are metamorphic repetitions or recursive transformations of apartheid culture, I am concerned with the consistent association of culture with high literacy. No one would argue against an enabling education or the advancement that literacy could bring, but in the face of massive illiteracy and the new government's inability to provide compulsory education, it is salutary to look at how such sectors of our society have made an astounding contribution to the New South Africa. Disparaging references to comic books, itself problematic after Roy Lichtenstein's re-presentations, may have to be reconsidered in the light of new ways of reading that the intersection of image and text in comic books demands and the new works of art engendered by such image-text encounters. To view culture in terms of high literary culture alone is to ignore the ways in which culture from below constantly challenges official and canonized forms; to focus solely on lack is a pessimistic view that overlooks the ways in which the nonliterate people of South Africa during the optimistic years of revolution have translated and transfigured that lack into a vibrant visual culture. Not only are many such works overlaid with the trace of illiteracy, they have successfully managed to escape the vacuousness of struggle literature that Ndebele laments.

Ironically, it is precisely the lack of literacy that has allowed such works to escape the epistemological structures of apartheid, a condition that is not so surprising when we consider the political history of literacy and the central role played by British missionary presses like Lovedale.[12] If this missionary educated class laid the foundation of a black literary culture, the contemporary underclass, schooled in Bantu education, has no choice but to turn to the palliative of comic books. Nevertheless, the 1980s, a period of optimistic political defiance, is marked not only for its production of oral "struggle poetry," often delivered at funerals and mass gatherings, but also for the vigorous growth of visual work within the dispossessed, nonliterate class. For instance, in the rural areas of the north, the erstwhile apartheid-era homelands of Lebowa, Gazankulu, and Venda, sculptors using local wood and clay and home-produced technology have responded in new syncretic modes to their interacting worlds of the traditional and the urban industrial cultures that they service. And in the townships, tourist art flourished and developed into work that outgrew its origins.

Thus came into being the new label "transitional art," which refers in part to the political transition from apartheid to democracy, manifested in the celebration of hybrid forms and the creative recycling of urban waste. Colin Richards, in the Oxford Museum of Modern Art catalogue of the landmark 1990 *Art from South Africa* exhibition, refers to the transitional as "the place where migrations of the (semi) rural workers and the cosmopolitan tourist intersect. It lies somewhere between the global and the local village."[13] But for all this locatedness, Richards's point that the transitional also "signals development" is surely a covert reference to the fact that the term presupposes a destination, which begs the question of what that might be. If it is seen as a movement from periphery to center, from local to global, then in a sense it is also a movement toward literacy, since a central irony in transitional work is that many nonliterates who have turned to visual representation incorporate writing in their work. Street's emphasis on the mixed and interacting modes of literacy and orality might thus be explored not only in terms of situational use (as in different registers), but be recast in terms of cultural production that inscribes the speech/writing divide as visual information, at the same time thus deconstructing that divide. Many nonliterate or poorly educated artists, in other words, use the visual representation of language(s) that they may or may not be able to read.

Contemporary use of language in artworks can be distinguished from earlier works such as the famed woodcuts of John Muafangejo.[14] In the shaky hand of the functionally literate, he introduces linguistic information that carries propositional meaning insofar as the words record thoughts or events and appear to anchor certain meanings suggested by the polysemous image. However, the trace of orality remains, for example, in a work (see fig. 4.1.) that carries the following lines of text above three horizontal visual frames arranged successively in comic-book style:

> The Ancient People had a long beard. Why we dislike the
> beard People?
> The Middle ages People had short beard and She divids the
> beer
> In this days People wear the new Fashion.

The second and third horizontal strips are each divided into two. It is the influence of speech, the phonological slippage from "beard" into "beer," that produces a frame in the second strip with an image of two drinking vessels and a bare-breasted woman holding a ladle above a calabash. The next frame in the same strip represents two naked men with short beards holding ceremonial objects. In Muafangejo's usual succession of frames, the one of the woman with calabash disturbs the coherence of the discourse on beards; moreover, unlike the line of language, read from right to left the image asserts its own contradictory mode of viewing by reversing the order of the beer and the short-beard

Fig. 4.1. John Muafangejo, *The Ancient People had
a Long Beard*, © The Estate of John Muafangejo
(The John Muafangejo Trust). All rights reserved.
DACS 2017.

frames. ("She divids the beer" [*sic*] is above the image of the short-bearded men
in the next frame.)

Cohesion is nevertheless achieved when the final frame in the third strip, illustrating "the new Fashion," prominently repeats the visually salient circular
motif found on the beer calabash. Thus the presence of the old in the new is
asserted, but the viewer/reader is also alerted to signs of old and new other than
beards, such as race and clothing, that are not linguistically encoded. In the
first frame of the final strip, a white woman shakes hands with a black man;
both are dressed in formal Western clothing. They do so under the sign of a tree,

suggesting the postlapsarian, but replicated from the first strip of ancients with long beards. The final frame in this last strip includes a black priest towering over three heads of people either seated or kneeling. As Barthes would have it, it is the less common function of relay (rather than anchorage) that the linguistic information achieves: "Text and image stand in a complementary relationship; the words, in the same way as the images, are fragments of a more general syntagm and the unity of the message is realized at a higher level, that of the story, the anecdote, the diegesis."[15] Thus the slippage from "beard" to "beer" does not only carry the orality of storytelling; it also allows for a diegetic leap into colonial history.

Numerous contemporary South African artists who are poorly educated or might be called "nonliterates" depart from Muafangejo's narrative work and engage with language as social semiotic. Language, rather than carrying propositional meaning, is used instead by artists like Tito Zungu, Derrick Nxumalo, and Chickenman Mkhize for its visual properties.[16] Chickenman Mkhize, after being made redundant from his work on a dairy farm, began making art objects to sell on the streets. He roughly copies "found" language, in Zulu and English, in a typically illiterate hand, with no regard for word breaks or the meaning of words. His three-dimensional objects consist of a rectangle of plywood boards painted with words, above which is balanced a triangle with a painted red border and a rudimentary image (see fig. 3.2, in Chapter 3). These are held together with a supporting strip of wood, and the whole balanced on a circle of wire. The reference to road signs is clear. The works explore writing as purely visual information, inviting the literate viewer to make meaning at the intersection of image and text where disjuncture often occurs.

Chickenman was "discovered" by the then director of the Tatham municipal art gallery in Pietermaritzburg, Lorna Ferguson, who encouraged him in his work. Since then he has situated himself at the periphery of the establishment art world, a postcolonial positioning, as he spreads out his wares and gets on with his work on the paved area in front of the gallery. The entrance to the gallery displays a dull commissioned work, *No Stilettoes Please*, which presses him into the role of sign maker and fails to acknowledge the significance of his representation of writing as visual sign stripped of its ideational content. In an interview with South Africa's *Sunday Times* newspaper in April 1989, Ferguson had the following to say: "The first thing I admired about him was his entrepreneurial drive. He has a flair for attracting attention, but he is never pushy. He has never abused the interest and support shown, but waits modestly for orders and requests from collectors and galleries."[17] With such patronage, steeped in colonial values, it is not surprising that Mkhize's deferential waiting at the gates of the gallery is in the financial interests of collectors. Functional literacy or nonliteracy of artists renders them vulnerable to economic exploitation by the art establishment. While Mkhize occupies the position of "international" artist by exhibiting in the MOMA group show at Oxford, he has no idea of the inflated art market, and still sells his signs for R10, which at the time of writing is not quite the price of two bunches of flowers. Similarly, when we visited Noria Mabasa in the very period that she was exhibiting at the Venice Biennale, it transpired that she knew nothing of that event.[18] Her sculptures at home were still selling for R100.[19]

Finally, consider the case of Jackson Hlungwani, a nonliterate South African artist whose extraordinary reading practice is more pertinent to my investigation than his visual art. Hlungwani has been producing wood sculptures in his remote Gazankulu village for some thirty years (since he suffered an industrial accident as a migrant worker in Johannesburg).[20] His monumental works, huge totemic carvings of symbolic religious figures, represent his apocalyptic vision of an old world about to be replaced by the new (see fig. 4.2). Evil and hatred, he believes, will give way to truth and life, a vision that has sustained him, and one that is available to all, if only, he says, we knew how to read the world. His language is strewn with references to reading and interpretation. We encountered him in the veld where he was working on a huge tree trunk; he insisted that we go to his house where he would give us a lesson in reading.

Hlungwani laid out his books, homemade scrapbooks into which he had pasted news and magazine images, scraps of text, and also images from a book of Renaissance reproductions that a visitor had brought and that, instead of awed contemplation, he had cut up to contribute to his own book. Hlungwani launched into a reading of his books, roughly put together and incomprehensible to me, weaving around the images narratives that allegorize the coming of the New South Africa, a process that he says has been going on for a long while and that will never be complete, hence his continuous reading and rereading of the books. The reading itself, in his brilliant broken English, is a humorous narrativization of figures represented in the pictures. The dignity of an overdressed businessman comes to an ignominious fall with the turn of a page when Jackson exclaims, "Look Sharp!" and announces his tumble into a travel-brochure lake. Unlikely images of the British Queen Mother and princesses, fodder of the popular magazines, interact in narratives with Moses, a long-haired local popstar, who leads them out of slavery. Hlungwani has no knowledge or interest in the real-life identities of his characters, except for Nelson Mandela, who has special saintly status.

There is an element of Snakes and Ladders to the reading process. At times Hlungwani returns to an earlier page to reinterpret the action of a hero who has

Fig. 4.2. Jackson Hlungwani. Photograph by Roger
Palmer, 1993, reproduced with permission.

fallen from grace, or to assign to him new roles as he introduces new subplots
in these distinctly nonlinear narratives, allegories of social and political
change. In an autobiographical book that includes personal documents like
an old apartheid-era passbook, or documents relating to his previous life as a
worker, these humiliating texts are reread in terms of his new life as artist and
priest, marked by a passport recently acquired for his exhibitions in Zimbabwe.
When, with much laughter and exclamations of "look sharp," we reached the
end of the reading lesson, Hlungwani, to my dismay, returned to the beginning, ready to start with a new story.

South African newspapers and magazines are, in the face of a plethora of real-world events, remarkable for their paucity of stories and images: we have our interchangeable scenes of violence, our pious-faced politicians, and to cheer us up the vagaries of the British royal family or the vacuous ugliness of beauty queens crowned weekly in every dusty dorp. Jackson Hlungwani's recycling and re-production of this dreary fallout from the literate, industrial world is an extraordinary act of transformation of the limited supply of readymades. The frame of the master narrative of salvation hovers over the images, but the performance itself undermines that Christian narrative as the images from the world of mass media are regenerated into narratives of political liberation. Thus the pictures are not mnemonics for a predetermined story, but rather, through strategic selection and combination of pictorial elements, they produce a plenitude of texts. Reading and narration become one, complete with self-conscious shifts in focalization such that any narrative at the immanent level of the picture is subjected to constant refiguration, one in which the notions of change or altered states function as central tropes in the storytelling itself. It is also the event character of speech that is retained in Jackson Hlungwani's reading: word soon spreads that the books are out on display, and neighbors drift along to hear the new versions from the well-known books.

What then seems to be overlooked by the theorists of literacy and orality is the practice of a visual literacy that makes a considerable contribution to communal cognitive lives. While Walter Ong does refer to a secondary orality demanded by the new media, he does not acknowledge the importance of the visual skills that the reading of such media requires and also develops. Hlungwani's practice could be seen as evidence of Ivan Illich's term "lay literacy," glossed as "symbolic fallout from the use of the alphabet in literate cultures," a "distinct mode of perception in which the book has become the decisive metaphor through which we conceive of the self and its place."[21] But it is equally evidence of how nonliterate people defy the label of deficiency by engaging with representations of writing through a visual heuristic.

Jackson Hlungwani's Reading Lesson can be viewed in parallel with the Writing Lesson in Claude Lévi-Strauss's *Tristes tropiques* (1955), a correspondence that raises problems for my attempt to valorize the culture of nonliterates in South Africa. Lévi-Strauss discusses his work with the Nambikwara, characterized as a people who "have no written language, but . . . do not know how to draw either, apart from making a few dotted lines or zigzags on their gourds."[22] When Lévi-Strauss tries to teach them to write, the chief, although still unable to do so, produces some squiggles and, by so pretending to write, enhances his status among his people, who believe that his writing has accomplished a bartering transaction. Lévi-Strauss dismisses the decorative art on calabashes as nondrawing; similarly, he does not appreciate the chief 's understanding of writing to be of aesthetic rather than propositional value. Thus the anthropologist interprets the Chief's behavior as deceitful, which confirms for him that writing is corruptive and serves only to exercise power over others.

In his lengthy analysis of the incident in *Of Grammatology*, Jacques Derrida challenges the label of illiteracy for a people who are not allowed to use proper names. Such a taboo, Derrida explains, is evidence of speech as arche-writing, an originary writing that is captured in the definition of writing as absence of a signatory or a referent; writing, then, does not derive from speech. To use a proper name is to erase it precisely because the proper name is only possible through its function within a classification and therefore within a system of difference, and it is only within a writing, retaining the traces of difference, that the interdict is possible. "If writing is no longer understood in the narrow sense of linear and phonetic notation, it should be possible to say that all societies capable of producing, that is to say of obliterating, their proper names, and of bringing classificatory difference into play, practice writing in general. No reality or concept would therefore correspond to the expression 'society without writing.'"[23] While the hierarchical opposition of literacy and orality is in need of deconstruction, as I hope Jackson Hlungwani's reading lesson demonstrates, it is difficult to conceive of anything other than the ethnocentric and material notion of writing so elegantly dismissed by Derrida. And I wish to delay the vulgar question of what difference it makes to the dispossessed, nonliterate people of a contemporary culture to know that they practice "writing in general" in order to explore first the Derridean notion of writing-within-speech in relation to literary texts themselves.

In South African writing we often find representation of literacy and the desire to write, and recursively embedded in these the desire for speech, which, far from being natural and accessible (for black women writers especially), is something that has to be learned. Paradoxically, then, and in accordance with Derrida's dismissal of speech as originary (the contention that it always and already contains the trace of writing), it is often through writing that we learn to speak and come to trust that our speech will produce perlocutionary effects, that its propositional content will not evaporate. It is such narratives of breaking out of the restrictions of apartheid through speech and writing, such prefigurations of democracy, that still—for those of us who remain optimistic—inform our idea of a New South Africa.

One such text is Gcina Mhlope's story "The Toilet," in which writing is specifically linked to spatiality, to a place where language is allowed to assume material form. It is narrated in the first person by a young woman, a factory worker who lives clandestinely in the servant's room of her sister's employer, where she must be still and silent. Thus she spends many hours in an underused public lavatory, at first viewed as a place to shelter from the rain. As an alternative to the confined servant's room, the lavatory, where she reads and begins to write, offers sought-after privacy; it is a cozy space, described as "very small—the walls were wonderfully close to me—it felt like it was made to fit me alone."[24] Here writing becomes visceral, a form of incontinence, something she cannot control: "It was some kind of pain that pushed me to do everything at double speed and run to my toilet."[25] But her daydreams disclose that the writing bears the trace of its opposite, a desire to be in a "big hall doing a really popular play with other young actors."[26] Barred from such opportunity, she find in the restricted space of the toilet not only liberation from being locked up in her sister's room, but also the freedom to write. Space, however, remains a consideration when she starts her first story: "She hoped there were enough pages left in [her] notebook."[27]

Writing is figured as transgressive. The opening sentence—"Sometimes I wanted to give up and be a good girl who listened to her elders"[28]—declares the ease of conforming to expectations. The narrator's sister complains that she reads too much, that it is no training for being a good wife. The story she tries to write about, a real event, the theft of dresses that she fails to report to her supervisor in the factory, is not only a reference to the "unlawful" aspect of writing, but also to the expectation that she would be a "good girl" who defends her employers' possessions.

Writing—in her little notebook and in the confined privacy of a small public toilet—opens up her world, so that when she finds the toilet locked that day, her fear and disappointment are momentary; she confidently crosses the road to a public bench and starts writing her story anyway. Physical freedom within the desired/imagined framed space of a stage is already present in the restricted space of the toilet, imaginatively transformed in its representation as enabling space. In the movement from toilet to bench we have the metaphoric expansion of the boundaries of apartheid through the agency of writing.

It is perhaps not so surprising that in a number of postcolonial literary texts the questions of literacy and its political implications have been figured explicitly in terms of a lesson, a character learning to read or write as an event within a narrative. Implicit in such representations is the question of agency, the hierarchal nature of teacher-pupil relationship, and the implied function of literacy. Perhaps the most poignant of such representations is found in Bessie Head's first novel, *The Cardinals*, written in 1961, just after the Sharpeville massacre and during the optimistic period of independence elsewhere in Africa. The manuscript, for thirty-odd years in the custody of the poet Patrick Cullinan, was published just before the first democratic elections, in 1993, an extraordinary time for reading a work so skeptical of politics. Johnny, the voice of truth in the novel, indeed speaks of the importance of freedom and individual rights, but doubts "if any political party can ever really guarantee that."[29] And the comment that "Africa is the one thing I can't afford to be uncommitted about and yet I, and every writer, should be—especially at this time of change, of patriotism and nationalism,"[30] while reminiscent of the maverick Head's misguided admiration for D. H. Lawrence, cannot be too easily dismissed.

The story is of a child given to a working-class woman in a Coloured slum near Cape Town. When the adopted father molests the girl, she runs away and spends her childhood in various foster homes. On writing a letter of complaint to a new black newspaper, *African Beat*, modeled on *Drum* (for which Head had worked), she is offered a job as a journalist. It is here that she meets her mentor, Johnny, who falls in love with her and encourages her to write creatively. What is interesting in terms of the orality-literacy representation, and pertinent to Derridean deconstruction, is that there appears to be a taboo on the central character's name. In the course of the novel she has three names, none of which is ever used by the narrative voice. At the end of the opening section, the name of the baby is presented in inverted commas, reported to the reader in a curiously artificial dialogue:

> "What have you thought to name her?" Lena asked.
> "Miriam," she said.[31]

The only other time this name appears in the novel is in bold uppercase, as orthographic representation of the child's first attempt at writing. Again, the report of this event is preceded by dialogue in which the old man who teaches her to write asks her name. The narration, switching from direct speech, simply gives the information: "She told him."[32] This has no diegetic function, but serves purely to mark avoidance of uttering the name.

When the child, as she is referred to, runs away from her abusive adopted father, she is taken into care and refuses to speak or utter her name, a self-imposed taboo highlighted by the interrogatives that frame the sentence "To all these questions she kept silent."[33] A social worker gives her a new date of birth and, it is reported, the name of Charlotte Smith, one that next appears in the text in an italicized representation of a letter written by the white editor of *African Beat*. He addresses her once as "Miss Smith," but after her interview she is immediately dubbed "Mouse" by her colleagues, a name by which she is referred to throughout, while the narrator maintains a strategy of avoidance. The character's self-imposed taboo allows her to accept this humiliating name without demur, and the reader has no choice but also to refer to her as such.

The proper-name taboo, in which Derrida locates arche-writing, and which here is so consciously coupled with the marked orthography of uppercase or italics, also signals the reader's hermeneutic encounter with silence, prohibition, and literacy. The child first breaks her silence to approach an old man who serves as community scribe in the slum. Her name, not used in the text, is obliquely reported when we are told that the old man, who "with a shaky hand in bold print wrote MIRIAM," teaches her to trace over the letters. From an illustrated book found on the rubbish dump, he teaches her to read by identifying words with pictures. As an adult, her first attempt at creative writing is cast as a lesson. Reminiscent of the Nambikwara chief who insists on the relationship between writing and visual art, her teacher asks her to sketch the town before writing about it. The lesson is bound up with the taboo of incest: unbeknown to them both, Johnny, her teacher, who is about to become her lover, is also her biological father.

Finally, a reading of the real world, a look at that reluctant and unwieldy beast, the New South Africa, faltering over its alphabet. I must also confront the question of how nonliterate people will participate in a democracy equipped with the dubious attribute of an arche-writing immanent in proper-name taboos. Let me take as example the real taboo of *ukuhlonipha* in Xhosa and Zulu cultures, a practice that prevents a married woman from using the name of her husband, or, more pertinently, that of her father-in-law. Where such a name or part of such a name coincides with a common word, as it often does, the woman must use synonymic expressions in order not to utter the taboo word in everyday speech. Older female members of the family will instruct the new wife on accepted substitutions, terms that over generations of the same clan have been conventionalized, but the very nature of language use is such that convention will not suffice; the taboo demands linguistic creativity from the speaker.

In a sense the taboo also applies to female interlocutors, who, in deference to the woman, will not use the proscribed words either. Thus, where a number of women are in conversation, the avoidance of many words will demand an incredible degree of linguistic ingenuity in order to encode that which is unsayable. What necessarily develops in traditional women's speech, then, is a circumlocutory style, an expansion of the taboo word into synonymic clauses or a metaphorical mode. This devolves easily into the folkloric belief about women's language being long-winded and ineffectual.

The taboo and its consequences for women's speech are surely not unconnected with the current problem of new women parliamentarians after 1994, who, at the end of their twelve-minute limit on speaking, frequently find that they have not yet made their point. The fact that at funerals, where orations are the norm, women are given longer to speak than men perhaps suggests a tacit acceptance of their linguistic disadvantage, and points to the Eurocentricity and androcentricity that persisted after the transition, in the years of the Government of National Unity. Predictably, there have been no responses to the linguistic behavior of these parliamentarians other than the reinforcement of prejudice against black women. It is the women themselves, frustrated by the ineffectualness of their speech acts, who are now collectively taking measures to tackle the problem. And predictably, they see the solution as one of learning to read and write more effectively, a recognition of the essayist literacy that governs speech in the magisterial discourse of government.

In the face of such debilitating traditional practices, the acquisition of literacy for women is, of course, a necessity. But there is also something to be learnt from Jackson Hlungwani's reading lesson: that arche-writing, undoubtedly present in the creativity engendered by ukuhlonipha, is convertible and can rescue the so-called direct, lexically dense discourse of writing from its distanciating effect; that the speech/writing divide can be deconstructed in practices that do not conflate culture with literacy. And let us hope that, unlike with the Nambikwara chief whose writing was interpreted as deceit, the literacy of women parliamentarians will not result in them being denounced by the people on whose behalf they govern.

5

To Hear the Variety of Discourses (1990)

The second issue of the South African journal *Current Writing: Text and Reception in Southern Africa*, published in October 1990, is devoted to the condition of feminism in South Africa: it questions the appropriateness of Western theory in the African context and addresses the shift from apartheid to democracy from a feminist perspective. Such interrogation, fraught with anxiety about the correct ways in which to negotiate the modalities of race and gender, is necessarily circumspect in its assessment of liberation's official discourse. Concern about perceived commitment to the national liberation struggle finds perhaps its most famous example in Nadine Gordimer, whose vociferous stance against feminism is posited as a commitment to antiracism.[1]

The debate in *Current Writing* is initiated by Cecily Lockett, whose position paper, "Feminism(s) and Writing in English in South Africa," laments the transference of Anglo-American or French feminist theory to the South African context, especially since such imported models are unable to connect the theoretical with indigenous politics. By way of solution she advocates Alice Walker's term "womanism" and the Nigerian critic Chikwenye Ogunyemi's exposition of a womanism that appeals to the experience of oppression shared by black men and women.[2] Lockett also warns white feminists against the appropriation of black women's issues. Her main concern is that feminist theory in South Africa has overlooked the racial dimension in the oppression of women. Perhaps, she writes, "we will have to develop a more sympathetic womanist discourse for considering the work of black women in this country in place of the current feminist paradigms which only tend to condemn and silence black women writers."[3]

In this essay I examine Lockett's argument for womanism and its relevance in the transitional culture of South Africa in the late 1980s and early 1990s.

Through a reading of black women writers invoked by the proponents of womanism, I focus on the contradictions inherent in the attempts to negotiate between race and gender to argue that, in spite of Lockett's well-meaning exhortations, the endeavor to formulate a single approach fails to acknowledge the variety of discourses produced by black women.

I start with an event in May 1990. Albie Sachs, exiled revolutionary, on this his first visit back, is late. We have seen photographs of him in the newspapers and we wait in the Jameson Hall at the University of Cape Town, not only to hear about the new constitution on which he is working, but to see in the flesh the iconoclast who has pronounced from the heart of the African National Congress (A.N.C.) establishment that culture must no longer be considered a weapon of the struggle. We are both audience and spectators. While we wait we listen to a band of young black men making the township music so closely associated with the struggle. (Music, Albie says, has mercifully escaped the stultifying demands of relevance to the revolution.) It is during the second number that four young women leap onto the stage in a state of undress. They have no instruments to play; they grind their hips and shake their breasts. The choruses, which offer the female voices an opportunity to harmonize, are about freedom. For a half hour we are entertained by the spectacle of women in faux-jungle-print bikinis that speak the colonial discourse of nouveau ethnic fashion and assert black indigeneity. There is great applause followed by hoarse *Amandlas!* and *Vivas!* and *Longlives!* from the floor. Thus do we prepare for the speaker whose dangling sleeve is a potent visual reminder of the armed struggle against political domination and repression. Comrade Albie speaks on equality and the need to enshrine in the new constitution the right to be the same as well as to be different.[4]

The contradiction between the linguistic and the visual discourse of the event ought to be interrogated, but questions remain unasked or are drowned in authoritative toyi-toying of liberation politics. And heeding Cecily Lockett's advice to develop a more sympathetic discourse that takes as its object of study a wider cultural expression, I attempt to read the event in terms of womanism. This proves difficult. The orthodox position of deferring matters related to gender in the interest of racial liberation overlooks such contradiction, and womanism, dwindling into its mandalic core, reveals itself to be more desired state than theory. By its own definition it must meet the spectacle with silence.

Alice Walker's aesthetic account of womanism as the color purple—in relation to feminism's lavender—has proved less than helpful in translating her novel of the same name into film. There colonial discourse in the representation of Africa happily coexists with the womanist content of love between women and a female protagonist's arrival at a sense of self. In the film, aesthetic cuts allow for collocation across linguistic, aural, and visual information, so that a seamless world of continuity (as opposed to the discontinuous epistolary novel) is presented, a world in which Africa is artlessly othered.

What these examples suggest is that a necessary linking of race and gender is not adequately theorized in the concept of womanism. Ogunyemi's explanation of womanism as a practice is alarming: "The intelligent black woman writer, conscious of black impotence in the context of white patriarchal culture, empowers the black man. She believes in him."[5] If white patriarchal culture is about unequal power relations, how can we fail to infer that empowering black men will at the same time advocate the mimicking of white patriarchy? In the interest of more civilized gender relations, it is just as well that those of us of lesser intelligence look elsewhere for a model.

Ogunyemi's development of womanism rightly insists on a sociohistorically based analysis of race-gender relations. Her question—"How do we share equitably the world's wealth and concomitant power among the races and between the sexes?"—offers a welcome emphasis on the politics of domination.[6] Not only does it see oppression in the context of global capitalism and neocolonialism, it also addresses the problem of linking theory to political action. What does seem lacking in her account and why it cannot explain the Jameson Hall event is the failure to examine the categories of race and gender in terms of their dominant discourses. If we think of these categories not as biological realities but rather as social constructs created through language, then it is a puzzling omission. That a historical perspective shows how such discourses do not run in neat parallel but necessarily diverge and intersect, and within specific discursive formations are in open conflict, is presumably what Ogunyemi would agree to. However, what her account suppresses is that divergence and conflict, centered around the material reality of women's oppression, point to areas of commonality between womanism and feminism. To suppress commonality is as dishonest as Euro-feminism's denial of "difference."

The search for a literary or cultural theory to suit the South African situation must surely take as point of departure a conflictual model of society where a variety of discourses will always render problematic the demands of one in relation to others and where discursive formations admit of cracks and fissures that will not permit monolithic ideological constructs. Womanism, then, presents only one side of the story, and it does so precisely because "in the context of white patriarchal culture" it is not legitimate to speak of the contradictions. Discursive practice being characterized by what Foucault calls "delimitation of a

field of objects, a definition of a legitimate perspective for the agent of knowledge and the fixing of norms for the elaboration of concepts and theories," we
need to look at the prohibitions that govern a black woman's discourse.[7] Black
patriarchy, deciding on legitimate portrayals of black gender relations, does so
in the name of racial solidarity. Those who control discourse, whom a culture
authorizes to speak, will not tolerate exposure and, indeed, will construct it as
treacherous and politically unsound. The reinscription of patriarchy in the film
of *The Color Purple* is not only an example of the dominant culture's appropriation and domestication of a dissident voice, but also an example of patriarchal
pressure on a chastised Alice Walker. The transmogrification of the novel into
popular filmic discourse indeed represents a shift from feminism to womanism.
Its "dynamism of wholeness and self-healing" is injected into the narrative so
that the reinstituted Father, ambiguously represented as preacher and biological father to Shug Avery, gathers the dissident female into the fold of black
unity. Historicizing her narrative might have overcome the limitations of both
Euro-feminism and womanism, but the film, which has Walker's blessing and
collaboration, rather reveals discourse as an expression of desire—desire for a
homogenous black community that will stand united against racial oppression.

It could be argued that black solidarity would be more solid if men behaved
in such a way that there were nothing to expose. In South Africa the orthodox
position, while celebrating the political activism of women, is that the gender
issue ought to be subsumed by the national liberation struggle. In "'A Bit on the
Side?'" Jo Beall, Shireen Hassim, and Alison Todes argue convincingly against
this view. They look at the ways in which women participate in the struggle and
conclude that, like men, they fight issues not as natural subjects, but as gendered
beings. For instance, many are drawn into the conflict as mothers defending
their homes and their children. The politicization of women's domestic role is
indeed a departure from the Euro-feminist view of motherhood as a condition
of passivity and confinement but, while recognizing such difference, I can think
of no reason why black patriarchy should not be challenged alongside the fight
against apartheid. Beall et al. demand that the liberation movement ask the
important question of why issues like prices, housing, and General Sales Tax
are women's demands, and how these are related to oppression. They assert the
importance of socialist feminism as a political discourse and practice that will
allow women's struggles to transform the very nature of the national liberation
and class struggle.[8]

To develop a suitable feminist literary theory for the South African situation
is no simple matter, but Lockett's puzzling challenge to "find a method that goes
beyond the limits of the white middle-class text, something that American fem-

inism has so far failed to do," suggests that we might start at the level of nomen-clature.[9] Should we understand by "America" the U.S.A.? And do African Americans not enjoy a hyponymic relation to that federation? In which case can the substantial body of work by Barbara Johnson, Gayatri Spivak, Susan Willis, bell hooks, Deborah McDowell, Hazel Carby, and so on, which deals precisely with the complexities of race and class within gender studies, really be overlooked and American feminist theory be presented as if there were no black theorists? I would like to suggest that a literary theory for South Africa has much to learn from these black feminists who insist on the incorporation of class and race as interlocking factors, and who, like Carby, argue for a historically specific, anties-sentialist criticism, or, like McDowell in her contextual approach, seek to expose the conditions under which literature is produced, published, and reviewed. Spi-vak's work on the politics of interpretation and her application of postmodernist theory to third-world texts, which at the same time questions the cultural specific-ity of theory, would be an obvious reply to Lockett's belated challenge.

It is just as well to bear in mind that feminism itself is a hegemonic term. Pragmatically its meaning refers to heterosexual white women only, so that in order for a black or lesbian to define herself as feminist, she has to add the mod-ifier that will specify her different emphasis. Dabi Nkululeko, quoted by Lock-ett, refers to "feminist socialists" in quotation marks, presumably as a comment on this linguistic hierarchy, but also, more specifically, as a gloss on "Euro-settler women." Lockett does not question this labeling of white women; instead, she endorses Nkululeko's recommendation that "settler women must work among their own people to create conditions for the destruction of oppression, while their counterparts among the native women must do the same within our own ranks."[10] To locate white women's experience within a historical colonist-settler context is, of course, correct, but to refer to twentieth-century socialist feminists as "Euro-settler" women is no less offensive than the term "immigrants" for blacks born and bred in Britain. That different power positions are inscribed in these politically inflected terms does not sanction their use in discussions com-mitted to political transformation. Problems on the lexical level also alert us to the need for revision at the level of discourse. Hazel Carby, while deploring a sisterhood that overlooks class and racial "difference," suggests the following de-parture from the accepted discourse of race within gender studies: "We need more feminist work that interrogates sexual ideologies for their racial specificity and acknowledges whiteness, not just blackness, as a racial categorization. Work that uses race as a central category does not need to be about black women."[11]

Even that strand of "American" feminism that Lockett considers to be unsuit-able because of its "political and historical emphasis on experience" can I think be of value to the South African situation.[12] It is after all the case that white feminists, having identified the traditional site of female veneration—home, motherhood, family—as the very one of their oppression, sought their liberation outside the home. While they participate in the male world of power, achieve economic independence, and enjoy liberation from the drudgery of domestic-ity, South African white women can nevertheless ensure that their homes con-tinue to run smoothly by replacing their unpaid labor with that of poorly paid black women. Thus the situation of the black woman is unique: her "liberation," unlike that of her European counterpart, does not necessitate any change in gender relations. Her man, joyously secure in his continued domestic comfort, has not needed to rethink traditional sex roles; his behavior has not had to change. Neanderthal attitudes thus persist and, according to womanism, must necessarily filter down to inform black patriarchy.

The experience of white women's liberation therefore in material terms rep-resents the oppression of black women for whom, in the context of restrictive apartheid laws, the notions of home, motherhood, and the family have become characterized by desire. Analogies with slavery are clear, and in African Ameri-can writing these issues can be traced as tropes of desire that adapt and trans-form received ideas of womanhood, manhood, motherhood, dominant domestic ideologies, and gender relations. Toni Morrison's *Beloved* (1987) is an exciting example of such exploration where the history of slavery is re-presented and the use of the supernatural, itself an expression of desire, raises the question of pro-hibition in relation to the kind of knowledge that is considered legitimate or worthy of recording. As discursive practice, the novel elegantly articulates a black feminism that is a far cry from the crude womanism of empowering men or asserting an imaginary wholeness. Instead, discourse as desire is movingly acknowledged in the narrator's observation at the end of the novel: "He wants to put his story next to hers."[13]

Lockett's recommendation of a "sympathetic womanist discourse for consid-ering the work of black women in this country" sits uncomfortably with the in-junction that we listen to the voices of the worker-writers in the Congress of South African Writers' (COSAW) *Khulumani Makhosikazi*, who speak of the material conditions of their oppression.[14] While Boitumelo Mofokeng, Nise Malange, and Roseline Naapo offer insightful accounts of the socioeconomic reality that prevents women from writing, they do not protect patriarchy. Mofo-keng, lamenting the dissipation of female talent and energy, says with unmis-takable bitterness: "We shall not forget how our marriages contribute to our lack of participation."[15] Malange describes the "triple oppression, at the workplace, in organisations and in the domestic sphere," where women suffer at the hands of bosses, fellow male trade unionists, and husbands.[16] Similarly, interviews with women in *Vukani Makhosikazi* speak of male oppression that weakens the womanist case. While spokespersons in the trade unions may insist on the equality of women, the experience of women is one of conflict where their political activities are at odds with the expectations of husbands within the home. It is the testimonies of workers themselves that are often ignored by liberal theorists who, embarrassed by feminism's neglect of race, insist on hierarchizing the issues in the order of race, gender, and class.

In the face of *Vukani Makhosikazi* testimonies, Ogunyemi's fabulous question—"What after all, is the value of sexual equality in a ghetto?"—can be given the obvious answer: the possibility of putting your feet up for five minutes after a hard day's work and being given a cup of tea.[17] A "union wife" complains: "So you have to have a job, be in the union and run the home all at the same time. . . . If the man comes earlier he hasn't the ability to go and fetch the child. . . . He expects the woman to fetch the baby, put it behind her back, get to the stove and cook for him . . . and he's busy reading the paper."[18] A feminist criticism might be more usefully engaged in studying the discourse of the worker women rather than selectively culling contents to support our arguments. To suggest that illiteracy is no obstacle to textual production is presumably not as absurd as it sounds. However, while I do appreciate the point that Naapo, from the Domestic Workers Union, tries to make about cultural maintenance and recording workers' experience, Lockett's respectful quotation of "You can say whatever you can say without knowing how to write. The next person will write it for you and it can be compiled into a book" is surely misplaced and constitutes a misreading.[19] Far from offering a new paradigm for art and writing (who would recommend illiteracy for the writer?), it tells us something about the conditions of textual production, about naive attitudes toward the mediated text, and points to an area of inquiry where the voices in texts struggle for dominance. Our culture boasts of a number of such ambiguous collaborative auto/biographies of illiterate servants written by white women whose mediating voices cannot be effaced.[20] How can we attempt to read these opaque works without considering the question of how meaning is produced? A feminist linguistic theory—whether developed in Europe or elsewhere—could fruitfully be applied to investigate how power-related interests intersect in the sign, or how language as conductor of ideology comes to mean. It is surely in women's interests to insist, against purist arguments for its autonomy, that theory should be applied to a particular set of circumstances, hence we do not in every instance, and thus tautologically, arrive at the same conclusion. Application, if it is at all possible, is then always a question of adaptation.

Lockett's citation of negative reviews or normative criticism of Miriam Tlali's work is no indictment of poststructuralist theory, which rather focuses on how meaning is produced. Besides, the recommended womanist approach to Tlali proves impossible in the reading of her story "'Fud-u-u–a!'" which explicitly undermines a basic tenet of womanism in its account of sexual abuse of women on the crowded trains. A character says, "What is even more annoying is that no one wants to even *talk* about this whole 'nonsense,' as they regard it. It is *not* nonsense because who suffers? We suffer. They just don't care. They treat us exactly as animals."[21] Tlali's mode of narration is significant. There are no male characters, no actants who perpetrate the abuse. The shameful incident is narrated in a whisper by a woman to her companions, who have similar stories to relate. The abuse takes place in the horribly crowded trains for which the politics of segregation is squarely blamed, but the floating deixis in the passage above points to female reluctance to identify black men: the ambiguous "they" can refer both to men who control female discourse and to the authorities who create conditions in which abuse becomes possible—that is, "they" create extenuating circumstances for men. Concealment, then, becomes a trope for the woman writer who has to negotiate the conflicting loyalties of race and gender.

Through the use of speech marks, exclamation mark and expressive phonology, the title of Tlali's story asserts itself as utterance. An asterisk refers us to an explanation of the word as a chant by commuters who have to turn their backs to train doors and wriggle their bottoms in order to make space for themselves in the train. The chant has specific illocutionary force: those inside are forced to shift, to reoccupy the space in order to accommodate more people, and the contextual meaning of the title quietly transfers to the story and whispers its plea. It is in the body of the text that the lexical meaning is given as "stir the pot." Which is precisely what Tlali's story does: stir that which an official policy keeps still, in order that a new space can be created for the crushed and degraded female to articulate her plight. Significantly, in the story it is the custom of singing in the train, of communal expression in which women themselves introduce the singing, that provides a shield for sexual abuse. There is no chance of the victim's protest being heard; the abuser is concealed by the community so that the very definition of community is thrown into question and womanism is exposed as self-destructive. More importantly, a feminist reading that draws on a theory of discourse will alert women, through divergence between race-gender discourses and tropes of concealment, to the dangers of insisting on the wholeness of a community where apartheid ensures that there is no such wholeness. "'Fud-u-u–a!'" allows us to do so without losing sight of the racial politics that provides a hospitable environment for female abuse.

Equally interesting in the accounts of the worker writers in *Khulumani Mak-hosikazi* is the conflict that marks their discourse, the unease with which they speak of feminist strategies. Mofokeng's words offer a good example: "Since the ground is fertile within organizations we could establish not a separate forum but a special one, to give women a chance to be themselves, to work on their ideas, take initiatives and produce their own work."[22] Prohibition is encoded in the quasi-distinction between a separate forum and a special one, a prohibition that is grammatically expressed in the anxious fronting of the negative. A possible approach, then, to South African women's writing would be to examine discursive strategies by which the orthodox tendency of hierarchizing the evils of our society—racism, sexism, classism—is resisted, or the ways in which the conflicting demands of representing these are textually articulated.

Ignoring the language of such texts is implicit in Lockett's view of black women's writing as being "primarily socio-historical" and of its purpose being "to record the experiences of black people in South Africa under Apartheid."[23] That works by writers as diverse as Ellen Kuzwayo, Miriam Tlali, Gcina Mhlophe, Nise Malange, and worker women "become part of a coherent development" is equally puzzling. The reception of our work as autobiography, or artless record, as that genre is curiously considered, also prevails in the white cultures of Europe and the U.S.A.: whether written in first or third person, we produce social documents that speak of personal experiences and grievances, and that therefore are primarily of social and anthropological value. Henry Louis Gates's comment on the interest in the "functions of black texts in non-literary arenas rather than with their internal structures as acts of language or their formal status as works of art" is not a prim demand that writing be kept in literary purdah.[24] Rather, since writing is necessarily a political act, Gates would suggest that an exploration of *how* issues are inscribed in texts is of political significance. Black criticism, then, like any other, is in dialogue with the literary establishment that includes an aligned feminist criticism; it engages with the fact that "the structure of the black text has been repressed and treated as if it were transparent."[25]

Lockett's view of black writing as documentary has prescriptive implications and suggests expectations of the realist form. To decide on a collective purpose for a body of writing is surely a mistake: it effaces the differences that undoubtedly exist between individual writers. Besides being black and female, we may also have significant lives as, for example, mothers, lovers, or invalids. It is in any case unwise to presume intentions to which the reader cannot possibly have access: decentered as subjects, lost in Derridean difference, and caught in ideological cross fire, we cannot rely on the stability of such intentions. Also,

jouissance under apartheid may seem more than predictably *triste*, a depressing pursuit for oppressed women; nevertheless, a Miriam Tlali cannot be
denied engagement with the libidinal because of a prescribed concern with
oppression. Indeed, Tlali's story "Devil at a Dead End" could be read in terms
of jouissance in conflict with the phallic law, which is linguistically resolved by
a woman's ingenious claim that she is afflicted with venereal disease.[26] This
utterance that "saves" her incidentally questions Lockett's essentialist reference
to patriarchal language.

Bessie Head, in spite of her avowed antifeminism, can similarly be read in
terms of the fissures in her discourse through which "illegitimate" meanings are
percolated. Ogunyemi's womanist reading, for instance, in which "ostracism
and ethnicism rather than sexism cause the development of the strong woman"
in Bessie Head's *Maru* (1971), overlooks the furtive negotiation of race and gender in the novel.[27] The key to deconstructing the marginal-central casting of
race and gender in that novel can be found in Head's handling of representation itself: both the heroine's visual representation of her dreams and the sketch
of her dead mother are cast as problems in the text.

The heroine paints her dream which is in fact a projection of the desire of
her powerful suitor, Maru, and which later, when he sweeps her off into marriage, is translated into reality. But, by separating the scene of his desire into
discrete paintings, in other words, by denying the unity of his composition, Margaret disrupts the realization of his dreams, so that the opening chapter of the
novel in which their marriage is represented also shows how he fails to possess
her. The circular structure of the text may appear to collaborate with the closure of Maru's quest, but Head clandestinely represents the heroine's resistance to
total subjugation through creating a space in which she might insert inventions
of her own, representing her own desires that contradict a happy ending. The
Masarwas' racial liberation, which Margaret's marriage to the Batswana chief
promises, can thus not be secured without addressing her subjectivity as woman.
Resolution of the story does not constitute fulfillment; story and discourse diverge, and the complexity of negotiations between race and gender in visual
representation can be read as a figure of concealment in the text.

The text explains how, unlike other groups, the Masarwas' inability to fill in
the gap in the sentence, "At least I am not a——,"[28] marks their subjection. Where
language is explicitly posited as the site in which difference is reproduced, the
account of a sketch of the protagonist's dead mother opens up the issue of meaning and scripto-visual relations. An artist had written beneath her sketch of the
dead Masarwa woman "She looks like a goddess," curious words that cannot be
read as caption. A caption would simply say "Goddess," from which a viewer

would infer the comparison. But the proposition "She looks like a goddess," if it is true, is surely redundant, since the visual information ought to tell us about the goddess-like qualities. We infer then that the artist does not believe that visual representation of a Masarwa woman could communicate such qualities to a viewer in a society that believes in her subhuman status. In other words, a reading of the image will say the opposite of what the artist wishes to communicate. Thus it is left to language, in the discursive form of the utterance, to assert the goddess-like qualities of the woman. The represented image then can be altered through language: apparently contradictory relations between image and text demand that the image be reread, and reassessment of the visual information involves a change in the underlying presuppositions. The transparency of the image is questioned; the process of rereading brings home the fact that what we see is ideologically mediated and that alternative intervention in the process of seeing can produce a new meaning for the Masarwa woman. In the same way the proposition that starts off as false can, through cross-readings between image and text, become true.

To return to the meeting in Jameson Hall: the display-while-we-wait, the pretext, which speaks loudly of putting gender aside while mighty matters of national liberation are addressed, allows us through its contradictory relations to reread the linguistic information. Where the visual degradation of woman is presented as part of the discourse of liberation, we are necessarily drawn to the pragmatic meaning of such liberation. The "revolutionary" text reads as the opposite of its semantic meaning, as a pretext for domination, since coercion of women to participate in their own degradation, which is also what our silence on the issue amounts to, can surely not amount to a *national* liberation.

6

MOTHERHOOD AND THE SURROGATE READER: RACE, GENDER, AND INTERPRETATION (1994)

Africa is Woman. This cry of the early colonial poets galloping through the land echoes warmly in the chants of the New South African poets singing their praise songs to Mama Afrika. Woman as Mama remains a metonym for Africa; protean woman, who once also served the colonial project, has been refashioned to serve the national liberation movement. For the imagined community of the nation, with its reliance on "tradition," woman as mother, whose reproductive and nurturing powers are foregrounded, is a revered symbol of survival. It is her body that is written as a map: its rivers and plains and peaks, landmarks and boundaries of early colonial struggle, are also discursively drawn in the struggle over reproductive control.

It comes as no surprise that advertising, taking its cue from both high and popular culture, should promote the feminization of Africa and the role of black woman as mother. A full-page advertisement for maize (a traditional staple supplanted by Western processed foods), found in a number of newspapers and magazines in the early 1990s, has the following bold print:

I am woman.
I am the nation.
I am the maize generation.

Reference to motherhood, the reproduction of the "maize generation," and women's role in maintaining tradition are inferences promoted through the parallel structure of the sentences. The false equivalence can of course be seen in the absence of an article in the first sentence, where woman is a self-declared abstraction, a notion as imaginary as that of nation. The accompanying—updated—image of motherhood is that of a sleek young woman with processed hair, rather than the "traditional" turban-wearing Mama. For all its reference to tradition, the advertisement cannot succeed without reshaping the image of motherhood, itself a tradition in need of constant reinvention.

In the April 1989 issue of *True Love,* a popular black South African monthly magazine, eleven advertisements for food products address the reader directly as a mother who is responsible for the physical well-being of husband and children. With such reliance on the reproductive function of woman, the advertising of contraception or birth control would seem to pose a problem. The following study of a family planning advertisement from this issue of *True Love* focuses on the contradictions inherent in the magazine's construction of womanhood and on the ways in which the reader/viewer is directed toward drawing these contradictions into a particular ideological reading.

To argue that an advertisement for family planning genders the reader and directs her or him toward a specific position in the text might perhaps be a tautological claim, but my analysis aims to show how the text, produced and consumed in the specific context of South Africa during the period of its transition to democracy, strategically inscribes a gendered subject. The contradiction inherent in the concept of revered Mama/subordinate woman demands a flexible negotiation of her position in the text: while the advertisement positions woman as mother, it must at the same time discourage her from being a mother; while it addresses woman as subject of the text, she is simultaneously subjected to a hidden male addressee. The text does not construct a fixed subject position for the reader; instead, conflicting interests demand that a male reader be stealthily inscribed in a text ostensibly addressed to a female, thus reproducing male control over reproduction and maintaining the unequal gender relations that prevail in this society. In a culture in which references to sexual relations often invoke "traditional" differences, advertising must be careful not to offend patriarchy in its reinvention of womanhood.

Criticism of advertisements, typified by Judith Williamson's influential *Decoding Advertisements,* generally focuses on the ways in which they produce and reproduce the dominant values of capitalism and shape behavior in accordance with a consumer society. I do not depart from such criticism, but in order to uncover the complex negotiation between contradictory positions of real and surrogate readers, I rely on the following analytical approaches: firstly, a pragmatic analysis that explores the role of inferencing in the production of meaning; secondly, a foregrounding of the relationship between image and text, and an exploration of linguistic categories as a model for analyzing the image; and thirdly, an acknowledgment that the particular medium of the magazine provides a local context for the generation of meaning.

The advertisement in question addresses itself to a female reader who is apparently able to make decisions about her own reproduction. My analysis, however, hopes to show how the gendered reader constructed by the text is necessarily unstable. Such a reader is aware of another, reading over her shoulder: she sees herself and her understanding of the text in relation to and dependent upon another's understanding. This other is a male to whom the text is not addressed directly but whose role as surrogate reader is crucial to the female reader's production of meaning. These unstable positions intersect in a variety of discourses, most notably the common discourses of race, nation, and tradition. My analysis attempts to uncover the inscription of race in the text, and to show how—at the intersection of race and gender—a particular reading is generated.

White magazines of this period do not carry advertisements for family planning; studying the textual strategy of gendering alone would therefore be inadequate since the target group is not only women, but specifically black women. Where population development advertisements do occur in white newspapers, women are addressed as responsible members of a new democratic nation whose duty it is to educate the less fortunate about family planning. Significantly, such advertisements in daily newspapers dispense with imagery and rely for visual impact on uppercase typography alone. The slogan "Helping Women to Help Themselves," culled from feminist discourse, neatly outlines the difference between the racially coded categories of those who have too many children and those who can offer advice to their poor, ignorant, and fecund sisters.

Advertising, which has the unambiguous intention of selling a product and thus affecting the behavior of the reader, readily lends itself to a pragmatic reading that is concerned with language in use. Pragmatics then studies meaning from a functional perspective. The following exchange

A: It's the phone
B: I'm in the bath
A: O.K.

is a textbook example of how the meaningfulness of a text does not always rely on its grammatical structure. A reader, drawing from her knowledge of the world, must contextualize the situation in order to make sense of the exchange. Aspects of meaning which are not grammatically encoded, and for which semantics cannot account, are thus dealt with pragmatically through the process of inferencing.[1]

Speech-act theory, developed by Austin and Searle, a pragmatic area of inquiry that considers language as a form of action (since it constitutes performatives such as declaring, promising, asserting, and so on), offers a useful theoretical tool. It allows for a distinction between sentence meaning and utterance meaning, which may diverge precisely because an utterance takes place in a particular context that in turn influences its particular illocutionary force.[2] Thus the sentence *I am cold* could in a certain context have the perlocutionary effect of a window being shut by the addressee.[3]

A reading that relies on the relationship between meaning and context is concerned with the implicatures and presuppositions drawn from cultural knowledge: an utterance will be connected to its context by a bridging assumption.[4] But, as Norman Fairclough notes in his critique of mainstream pragmatics, the application of speech-act theory or Gricean implicature often results in a "Utopian image of verbal interaction which is in stark contrast with the image of critical language study of a sociolinguistic order moulded in social struggles and riven with inequalities of power."[5]

In this essay I try to extend the application of pragmatics from its usual single utterances or short exchanges to include extended discourse and its participation in ideology. Thus I hope to show how revised images of race and gender relations, promoted in popular magazines like *True Love*, remain bound to the old apartheid social order. Unequal social relations are produced through discursive formations that I investigate using Michel Pêcheux's theory of the grammatical inscription of ideology.[6] My analysis relies on Pêcheux's notion of "interdiscourse," by which a subject's multiplicity of relations can be understood as being determined by existing discourses. Through linguistic analysis, I uncover the interdiscourse by which flexible subject positions are inscribed for readers. A scripto-visual analysis ought to show how the contradiction in the notion of womanhood is also visually constructed, and how the relationship between image and text generates further meanings that reproduce the conflicting interests of male and female.

SCRIPTO-VISUAL ANALYSIS: MEANING AT THE INTERSECTION OF IMAGE AND TEXT

Although linguistic analysis of advertisements is a much-needed departure from semiotic or content analysis, such replacement of focus would amount to a denial of the material reality of advertisements, of the fact that they constitute both image and text. Saussure's suggestion that language could be used as a paradigm for the study of *all* sign systems has led to the widespread use of terms such as "photo-grammar," or "visual syntax." However, critics neglect to explain what precisely such terms might mean. Gillian Dyer's *Advertising as Communication*

(1982) simply lists twenty or more rhetorical figures with examples of advertisements explaining the difficult Greek names. How this taxonomy could help us
toward the meaning of an advertisement is left unexplained.

Image-text readings generally rely on Roland Barthes's influential "Rhetoric
of the Image," in which he gives a semiotic account of scripto-visual relations in
a Panzani advertisement. The analysis focuses on the distinction between denotation and connotation or literal and ideological meaning. The text, according to Barthes, performs the function of anchoring the image, which is
polysemous—that is, it fixes "the floating chain of signifiers in such a way as to
counter the terror of uncertain signs."[7] Barthes's account of the production of
meaning is thus a one-sided operation of text on image, with no cross-readings
that allow for an image to influence the reading of a text. Nor is the common
phenomenon of contradictory relations between the two discussed.

Judith Williamson draws on poststructuralist theory to explain ideological
meanings in advertisements, foregrounding the role of the reader in the production of meaning. For her, it is the "referent system" that ensures that things *already* mean to us, and that "we give this meaning to the product, on the basis of
an irrational mental leap invited by the form of the advertisement."[8] The reader
is positioned in such a way—in this understanding—that a cognitive leap is the
only means of making sense of an advertisement. The example used, the unidentified face of Catherine Deneuve behind bottles of perfume, demands that
we make the link between the two units: to be beautiful, we must use Chanel
perfume; in the process we are constituted as female subjects. But Williamson
does not reflect on the cognitive process by which women are constituted *as*
subjects, nor does she take into account the context in which such advertisements are *read*. No information is therefore given on where the advertisements
were found. That the process of inferencing is not considered crucial is evident
from the way she refers to the cognitive activity as *irrational*.

A pragmatic reading of advertisements is outlined by Trevor Pateman, who
uses an example of a fine-art image transposed to the context of advertising. His
discussion of Barthes's denotation/connotation distinction is a welcome departure from the semiotic approach that dominates analysis of advertisements.
While his argument against denotation is not convincing, Pateman's critique of
connotation—for relying on what he calls the "Dictionary fallacy"—is suggestive.[9] This dictionary assumes the preexistence of connotations such that all
meaning is seen to lie *in* the text or the image. Such a view, Pateman points out,
cannot accommodate new connotations, nor does it recognize the activity of
inferring meaning or the cognitive activity of working out the kind of connotation

appropriate in a particular context. Connotations may be valid in semantically conventionalized examples (such as in roses connoting romance), but even so the conventionalization "shortens the inferential circuit" without eliminating it, he contends.[10] Instead, Pateman argues that the theory of relevance, advanced by Dan Sperber and Deirdre Wilson, which assumes an intention to communicate and therefore guarantees relevance, will allow the viewer to work out the relevance of the topic to the comment.[11]

While relevance is useful, a single way of reading images is not feasible; images cannot always be read in terms of topic and comment. Many sophisticated advertisements make no reference to the topic, as in the famously enigmatic Silk Cut cigarette advertisements. Instead they refer self-reflexively to previous images used in the campaign, or rely for their effect on oblique associations. The topic is deliberately suppressed in order to insist on a negotiation of meaning between the visual and the linguistic information.

Victor Burgin uses the term "scripto-visual" in his discussion of a photograph that, he claims, is "invaded by language in the very moment it is looked at" so that it "prompts a complex of exchanges between the visual and verbal registers."[12] His analysis foregrounds ideological meanings that exploit the "popular preconscious" and the "pre-text" concepts not unrelated to presupposition.[13] But Burgin's reliance on semiology in his discussion of specific advertisements does not allow for the role of pragmatic inferencing in the construction of meaning. While the pre-text *does* refer to that which already exists as common cultural knowledge, such knowledge is simply a given entity onto which the manifest text is somehow attached in the preconscious. Burgin locates the production of meaning in this process, which takes place in the act of looking.

The nature of exchanges between the visual and the verbal information could, however, be examined more fully. Cross-readings or pragmatic negotiations between image and text—as is also required in the reading of image-text artworks—involve secondary inferential processes, which are unavoidable when making sense of contradictory meanings generated by the two media. Each provides a context for the other from which inferences can be made. The various accounts of the image as a visual *language* remain metaphorical and offer little help in understanding it. It is surely the case that many viewers, baffled by contemporary images, are not enlightened by the claim that they themselves construct meaning in the act of looking. What follows is an attempt to explore the metaphor and develop a pragmatic way of reading an image.

PRAGMATICS OF THE IMAGE

A semiotic reading of the image, based on the code model of communication, has limitations precisely because—as in the case of language—not all aspects of the image are in fact coded.[14] Since I hope to argue a case for the pragmatics of an image, it is useful first of all to determine which of its aspects are stable and coded in the manner of a grammar.

A distinction between meaning and syntax, as in Noam Chomsky's example "Colourless green ideas sleep furiously," could be applied to a photograph in which the following system of rules exist independently of its meaning: firstly, the imposition of a frame on spatial continuity provides its basic form, just as a syntagmatic arrangement of words forms the sentence; and secondly, three-dimensionality is encoded in the two-dimensional presentation of a photograph. The reproduced example by the Dutch photographer Jan Dibbets (see fig. 6.1) can on one level be seen as an analogue to Chomsky's sentence. In terms of the above elements, we read it as a well-formed image, but the structural qualities do not help us to make sense of it. Instead, the reader is spatially disorientated: there is no correspondence between the image and something in the world (no denotation). We see part of a room with a square on the wall that does not make sense. In order to understand the image, I will test the use of pragmatic categories like inferential procedures and speech-act theory.

The art photograph, just like the commercial image, exists within a context, and as such can be studied from a functional perspective. An image viewed as goal-orientated behavior will generate meaning that we can infer from a context in which the viewer interacts with the image. In advertising, the image sets out to persuade the reader to buy a product; in the context of an art gallery, the Dibbets image demands that the reader make sense of it by visualizing an original rhomboid shape, drawn on the wall by the artist, in such a way as to compensate for perspectival distortion that would produce a square in the photograph. The linguistic distinction between "sentence meaning" and "utterance meaning" could be applied here: the image on the wall is, without the viewer, one of spatial distortion (natural meaning), but interaction with it demands the application of certain maxims orientated toward behavior (Gricean nonnatural meaning).[15]

All photographs require the participation of a "reader" who must either scale the image up or scale it down according to her knowledge of the world. Similarly, tonality in black-and-white photographs must be translated into color; color photographs, too, are only *approximations* of color in the world. The composition of an image is also dependent on focus (total, middle-distance,

Fig. 6.1. Jan Dibbets, *Perspective Correction, My Studio I, 1: Square on Wall,* © 1969, black on white photograph on photographic canvas, 110 cm × 110 cm. Courtesy of the Gladstone Gallery, New York.

near, and so on), from which the reader infers relative importance of the elements. Thus pragmatic methods for deriving meaning from an image will be used where the viewer contextualizes the scene of the image.

In terms of Gricean implicatures, we can speak of Dibbets's flouting of the maxim of *quality* since the space is falsely represented. But the following bridging assumption restores the cooperative principle: in fulfilling its function *as art,* the image questions the basic tenet that a photograph represents from a *single* point of view, so that we are invited to work out how the distortion occurred.[16] More economically, Sperber and Wilson's relevance theory, which assumes an intention to communicate and therefore a guarantee of relevance, suggests that the art viewer will calculate how the image has been distorted and will infer the relevance of such spatial disorientation.

Similarly, Austin's speech-act theory can usefully be applied to determine how an image attempts to modify our behavior. Instead of accepting the point of view that Dibbets offers, we recognize its separation of two different sorts of illusion: three-dimensional space (of the room), and two-dimensional space (of the square). We are directed to imagine the shape that has been drawn on the wall, but since this proves impossible from the viewing position offered by the photograph, another cognitive response to the "illocutionary force" is mobilized. We attempt to step into the (illusory) three-dimensional space to assume a new point of view that will accommodate the shape as square.

Such pragmatic analysis of the art photograph could be applied to an advertising image, where the wider context of the total advertisement as persuasive device is clear. As I show in my reading of the family planning advertisement, the text constitutes an immediate context for the image, and vice versa. Our interpretation of an image will thus intersect with that of the text to allow for a proliferation of meaning beyond the potential of any one of the media.

MAGAZINE AS CONTEXT

Meaning is also produced by a reader participating in the wider context in which the advertisement is consumed, namely, the magazine in which it is found. In "Understanding Advertisers," Kathy Myers comments on the way in which magazines promote advertising messages: "A quantifiable benefit to advertisers is that magazines provide a hospitable environment for the digestion and assimilation of advertised information."[17] Such environments are created by articles and features that provide an inferential pool, from which readers draw presuppositions in order to make sense of an advertising text.

Collusion between magazine and advertiser occurs in a number of ways. In the issue of *True Love* magazine carrying the text with which I'm concerned, the following examples can be seen to support the message of the advertisement. Articles on successful businesswomen listed in the contents page as "People in Focus," or the feature in this edition "on the first black woman nursery owner" (listed under Gardening), activate the suppressed message in the family planning advertisement: that fewer children mean economic success, the first requirement of the New Bourgeois Black who is regularly promoted in the magazine. Another example is an article on a new morning-after pill, developed in France, which strongly condemns abortion, a view supported via a survey. Interviews with "responsible" women who are also public figures explain why such a pill is unsuitable for the black community. The hazards of any new drug are highlighted, and the survey reports that a majority favor state-controlled contraception. The pill, on the other hand, is said to be unreliable since irresponsible behavior on the part of individuals cannot be discounted. In terms of women as nation, the foregrounding of France as foreign country is significant: South African women, with their national culture of collective action, stand opposed to foreign practices and products that target the *individual*.

That the cover of this issue of *True Love* promises "16 pages of Mother Love" while at the same time advertising family planning is, of course, not a contradiction. What is of interest is the discursive formation that constitutes the entire magazine whereby its subtitle, *For the Woman Who Loves Life*, and the very notion of motherhood promoted in the advertisement (as well as in supporting articles), is defined in economic terms. What remains suppressed in this incubation of meanings is the role of the state in determining such meanings, or indeed their function in resisting social change.

Supportive readings also rely on other advertisements that demonstrate how marketing practices address certain target groups. Advertisements for food products in this issue of *True Love*, as well as in other popular magazines like *Pace* and *Tribute*, offer an instructive illustration. Food is routinely presented as the concern of mothers. African women, interpellated in the text as Mama, are urged to prepare or serve the product, most often for their husbands or male offspring. It is suggested that the product, with its emphasis on health and growth, ensures the maintenance and reproduction of the species. But far from contradicting the advertisement for family planning, such emphasis on female responsibility for nurturing and reproducing is crucial for the presuppositions on which population control is founded. My analysis of the family planning advertisement will consider in detail the contradiction offered by a lengthy feature in the same issue of *True Love* on forced contraception in the workplace.

A further context on which inferences rely is the wider one of power relations in South Africa. The very growth of black magazines, funded by white financiers at the time of the demise of apartheid, demands scrutiny. Other magazines of the same month—*Pace*, *Drum*, and especially the glossy *Tribute*— show only too clearly their function in the construction of a new South Africa: to foster and co-opt a black middle class whose interests do not always coincide with those of the mass democratic movement. Given a stake in the economy, the New Bourgeois Black becomes invaluable during the period of the transition in helping to determine the direction of the economy. And such direction is in turn determined by a revised construction of nation in which reproduction, controlled within the institution of the family, has a crucial role to play.

To ensure that the reader reads "correctly," that is (i) as a woman who is persuaded that having fewer children is desirable, (ii) as a man who is persuaded
that reproduction remains within his jurisdiction, and (iii) as a black person who
sees that a small family makes economic sense, the advertiser must accommodate a range of meanings. Several contexts of conflicting interests render untenable the unitary notion of a gendered reader. During the period of struggle
and transition to democracy, gender was seen as a distraction from national liberation, thus race and gender became contending spaces in which to locate the
self as a reader. Furthermore, the family planning advertisement in *True Love* is
also meaningful in the specific political context in which a structure of dominant white-minority norms, concerned with demographic survival, interacts
with black norms related to economic survival. Such interaction is conflictual,
just as gendered readings of a text advocating "responsible" reproduction will
conflict. How, then, are conflicting interests resolved within the image-text of
the advertisement?

Where we believe the discourse of advertising, which is clearly signaled, to
be separate from that of the magazine, we may fail to appreciate the power of
the latter in promoting consumerism. Not only do the contents of magazines
reveal overt collusion with advertisers, they also offer support by apparently contradictory advertisements. Black magazines can be read in Pêcheuxian terms as
discursive formations in which their entire contents constitute a discursive-
ideological process that sets up dependency relationships between articles and
advertisements; each becomes meaningful for the New Bourgeois Black in relation to the other. This relation may appear to be contradictory, but Pêcheux's
definition is helpful in making sense of the contradiction: "I shall call discursive formation that which in a given ideological formation, i.e. from a given
position in a given conjuncture determined by the state of the class struggle,
determines 'what can and should be said' . . . words, expressions, propositions
which are different literally can, in a given discursive formation, 'have the same
meaning,' which if you follow me, is in fact the condition for each element
(word, expression or proposition) having a meaning at all."[18]

Coherence, or inferable relationships of meaningfulness between different
parts of the discourse, can be found in the April 1989 issue of *True Love* magazine, where an article on forced contraception (on page 56) coexists comfortably with a family planning advertisement (on page 36; see fig. 6.2). The article
exposes factory employers' insistence on a three-month Depo Provera injection
as a condition of employment for all women to ensure maximum industrial production. A black doctor employed by the factory explains the Depo-related
complaints suffered by women, and points out that the expense of medical fees

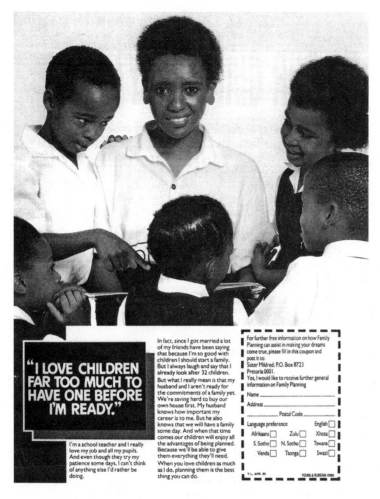

Fig. 6.2. Advertisement, *True Love* (April 1989), 36.

for the treatment of such complaints does not make economic sense. The report focuses on Madadeni, a town in the so-called KwaZulu homeland, where birth control in the workplace was introduced by the Department of Health. Factories have their own nursing teams who administer Depo Provera, and the report's humanist emphasis is on the scandalous reason for contraception: not administered because of a crisis baby boom, but rather to increase industrial production. With the help of Pêcheux's theory of the grammatical inscription of ideology, the contradiction generated by the widely known fact that Depo Provera is routinely used by government-sponsored family planning, also advertised in the same magazine, can be understood. Pêcheux claims that we call up a body of ideas, or interdiscourse, from the dominant ideology from which to make bridging inferences. What then appear to be

metonymic relations between propositions are in fact the addition of inferences.

Pêcheux cites the "impossible" sentence "He who saved the world by dying
on the cross never existed" as evidence for the functioning of language as ideological discourse.[19] The existence of conflicting domains of thought from the
discourses of atheism and Christianity within the same sentence becomes possible through what he calls preconstruction, by which an external or independent construction thought elsewhere or before (someone saved the world by
dying on the cross) opposes the global assertion of the sentence (that no
one saved the world by dying on the cross). Thus he shows that it is syntactic
embedding, or the relative clause, that accommodates the preconstructed in
discourse. For instance, the sentence "Black women, who love children, will
not have any of their own" contains the following propositions:

1. Black women love children (from the discourse of tradition).
3. Black women will not have children of their own (from the discourse of
   the New Bourgeois Black).

But we can insert the following sentence between 1 and 3, a preconstruction that
arises as a bridging assumption between them:

2. Love of children precludes having any of your own.

Sentence 2 intervenes as support of a thought contained in 1 to form a "sustaining effect," an implicature that allows for "articulation" between 1 and 3. Sentence 3 falsely assumes a causal relationship with 1:

3. (Therefore) black women will not have children of their own.

The explicative or nonrestrictive clause is thus shown to generate relations of
cause and effect (articulation) between the preconstructed and the main clause.

Pêcheux's division of discourse into intradiscourse, interdiscourse, and transverse discourse provides a framework for the investigation of discursive formations. By intradiscourse he means "the thread of the discourse," how what is said
now relates to what has been said before and what will be said afterward. Such
cohesion is a product of various relations of substitutability that are achieved
through markers such as coreference, lexical replacement, reiteration, synon-
ymy, hyponymy, paraphrase, and so on.

Interdiscourse refers to the preconstructions from which inferences are drawn
or connections between words, propositions, and expressions are made. It determines the range of possible substitutions or bridging assumptions available in

any society. Ideology operates within discursive formations precisely because interdiscourse remains disguised, or rather is absorbed/forgotten in intradiscourse. The process of this absorption, the crossing where interdiscourse simulates intradiscourse, is called transverse discourse. Thus what appear to be innocent markers of cohesion, or merely functions of grammar, are in fact a set of bridging inferences based on metonymy (relationships of part to whole, cause to effect, and symptom to what it designates).

Pêcheux uses the following example of substitution to illustrate the operation of transverse discourse: "We observe the passage of an electric current. The deflection of the galvanometer. . . ."[20] The replacement suggests that the two terms are synonymous, but it is, of course, not the case, since one is caused by the other. Thus substitution can be seen to yield a supplementary construction in which causality is embedded: "We observe a deflection of the galvanometer, which indicates the passage of an electric current."

ADVERTISEMENT AND ARTICLE AS DISCURSIVE FORMATION

Pêcheux's example above could be developed to encompass the two extended texts in *True Love* I have mentioned; both might be considered discursive formations within the magazine. More specifically, the key information outlined in the forced-contraception feature invokes a series of opposites to the family planning advertisement, which nevertheless makes for textual cohesion. For key factors in the article that are considered undesirable, the advertisement substitutes positive features as follows:

1. Factory workers are affected by forced contraception versus the professional woman as agent.
2. Callous production control versus considered reproduction as reason for contraception.
3. Local factory nursing teams versus national institution for administering contraception.
4. The KwaZulu homeland as exemplary site of political exclusion versus Pretoria, administrative capital, suggesting political inclusion.
5. Compulsory mass contraception versus thoughtful individual choice.
6. Ill-health and repression versus health and well-being.

However, our reading of the apparently contradictory texts—(a) that Depo Provera in the workplace is bad; and (b) that Depo Provera dispensed by governmental family planning is good—establishes an interconnection that becomes what Pêcheux calls the transverse discourse of the magazine. Through the six antonymies listed above, (a) and (b) become syntagmatized in a relationship of cause to effect, thus generating an accessory statement or "sustaining effect" along the lines of: "The exposure of forced contraception in the workplace indicates the necessity of individual choice as offered by the Department of Health's Family Planning."

The linear axis of (a) to (b) forms an intradiscourse by which textual cohesion—mainly through lexical reiteration, collocation, and substitution, since both texts deal with the relation of female reproduction to the socioeconomic system—can be established endophorically between the two magazine texts.[21] A logical distortion occurs: far from (a) producing an unfavorable reading of (b), by which readers would be put off by family planning, the interdiscourse or preconstructed elements provide an inferential base for a supportive reading of (b).

That Depo Provera is routinely used by the Family Planning Association is a contradiction suppressed in the transverse discourse of the magazine, by which we come to see it as desirable when properly and nationally dispensed to an upwardly mobile middle class that freely acknowledges its value.[22] Birth control is by no means the only contradictory element in *True Love*. Surrounded by advertisements for hair straighteners, facial creams, and other aids for black women aspiring to normative Western standards, the regular feature "Punchline" upbraids the same black middle class for abandoning its indigenous culture in favor of the alien West. As an afterword on the last page, the article offers final reassurance: all is well, and traditional values can comfortably be kept alive despite accommodations with reformist capitalism; the two are not incompatible. In the analysis below, we see how the contradictions that operate in South African society are held within the image-text of the family planning advertisement.

FAMILY PLANNING: ADVERTISEMENT

The visually prominent text "I love children far too much to have one before I'm ready" (see fig. 6.2) is marked in a number of ways to propose an equivalence between viewing and reading. Firstly, it is lifted out of the context of the speech situation that makes up the main part of the text. Secondly, it extends the context—in the sense that we can imagine the teacher at work through the visual synecdoche of the blackboard. The design allows this black rectangle with white print to lift out physically with the help of its visible shadow, in blue in the magazine. This typographic projection finds an analogue in the image above: the teacher who participates in a scene or event with the children is like the text board, lifted out of that scene in the manner of televisual address where interaction is interrupted so that the commentator can speak to camera, or participate in a different speech event with the audience.

A discussion of the relations between participants in the photograph reveals the image to contradict or undermine the authoritative text. In this intimate scene, the deictic center is unstable, and like the insertion of a male addressee shifts between the older boy and the teacher. The group forms a circle, reinforced by the way the teacher is touched by the senior boy and girl. Their hands are prominent, and respective curvature suggests a visual chiasmus with the body of the teacher as connecting space. Deixis (here graphically represented by the boy's index finger) points to the spatial context delimited by the circle, but the visual salience of the finger also puts the boy in a position of centrality. While the children are all engaged in something related to the papers held by the teacher, the sight lines between the children reveal the topic to be an exchange between the two boys; the older girl looks to the older boy for his response, and the younger girls focus on the younger boy. The teacher is almost redundant in this scene. Although the papers are held by her, her responsibility or agency in the production of knowledge is removed as she participates in quite another scene, that of direct engagement with the viewer. The male children are in control: the older boy rests his hand proprietorially on the shoulder of the teacher. Her youth questions her authority and suggests an equivalence with the older boy, her shirt being of the same cut as the school uniform. Her meek, pretty smile bridges the gap between professional and private, teacher and mother, thus allowing her to be lifted out of the teaching scene to utter the main text.

It is, nevertheless, her position as teacher through which we read the black/white rectangle: we view it as a blackboard upon which an authority figure has written the didactic words, converted into a slogan by the quotation marks. The blackboard text demands to be viewed and read: like children learning to read, we look-and-say, repeating her words. Teaching conventions thus permit the deixis to float. Every one of us can voice the slogan and, if we are responsible black people, can become the subject of the text, uttering the words as our very own. In other words, we are not interpellated by the image as text; instead, we produce our own subjectivity as responsible mothers-of-the-nation.

Careful design of the text area, reminiscent of a label that wraps around a can, insists on reader participation. A consideration of the relationship of rectangles and their potential for spatial transformation makes for persuasive graphics that might be considered in terms of an illocutionary act, or an attempt to accomplish some communicative purpose within a given context. The felicity conditions for the directive to send away for further details include both the authority of the teacher to direct the reader and the reader being a responsible person who responds to such a directive.

The blackboard rectangle on the left (white writing on black) lifts out pictorially, that is, asserts through its blue shadow a separate material reality that encourages the reader to consider the separate material reality of the analogous rectangle on the right (black on white). The blackboard shape lifted out of the "label," which is yellow in the magazine, carries illocutionary force, inciting the viewer to material action: act upon the conventionalized dotted line, cut out the coupon on the right, and send away for more information. The curious affirmative—"Yes I would like to receive . . . Family Planning"—on the coupon text underlines perlocutionary take-up as a response to the speech act.

FAMILY PLANNING: ARTICLE

Conflict, played out in the contest over access to public amenities in South Africa, shows how government reform has alerted the white population to a crucial fact that segregation had concealed: the extent to which they are outnumbered. Town councils now have to address the problem of public amenities being "swamped" by blacks as so many letters to the newspaper editors would have it, and advertising is one way of addressing the problem. I hope to uncover in this reading the conflicting interests of male and female, black and white, urban middle class and traditional rural blacks. This conflict is also expressed in the contradictory relations between image and text, although speech-act theory shows how the total visual presentation in fact offers forceful support for the advertising message.

Personal deixis establishes a speech situation in which a schoolteacher addresses the reader directly. The text is her testimony, spoken in the first person by a professional woman who is also surrogate mother. Thus the values of a traditional culture, where many children represent wealth and fertility, are cleverly transferred to a new context, a professional one, which accommodates many children as well as a maternal figure. The professional woman is simultaneously stripped of her negative connotations. This balancing act is maintained throughout: love of children *and* the undesirability of having children.

The opening sentence, "I'm a school teacher and I really love my job and all my pupils," ensures that we do not assume loving all the pupils to be an entailment of loving the job. The premodifier "all" makes possible a scaling down to loving her job and *some* of her pupils, something of which our teacher is not guilty. "Really" loving her job emphasizes her professional status, but the transference of love via the "and" allows the job to embrace the pupils, but as new information, specific to *her*. The speaker is therefore no ordinary, "unnatural" professional woman; her profession includes love of children, "all" ("her") children, just as a mother would not discriminate between her offspring. Sentence 2 reinforces the link between teacher and mother: "Even though they try my patience some days." Neither would wish away the children. Thus she negates any causal relationship between her pupils' behavior and her love for them: loving children is simply natural.

The next stage of the argument exploits traditional culture's attitude that caring for children extends beyond caring for one's biological offspring alone: "I already look after 32 children." To abandon thirty-two for one of her own would be nonsensical; it would amount to a betrayal of her pupils. The sentiment also draws from the discourse of nationhood: a mother-of-many is easily substituted by mother-of-the-nation while at the same time reconstructing the traditional mother in terms of a career.

Paragraph 2 reports the teacher's conversation with friends in which marriage as a prerequisite for reproduction crops up as a preconstruction in the relative clause, "since I got married." The conventional implicature is that she would not be expected to have children before marriage. And to have a child is expressed in the fixed syntagm "start a family," thereby anchoring reproduction in the institutions of marriage and the nuclear family. For all its reliance on tradition, the grammatically inscribed values clash with traditional social organization, where the birth of a child cannot be seen to *start* an extended family. Nor do these values coincide with the social reality of urban life where many women have children within a matrifocal household without male support.

"In fact, since I got married a lot of my friends have been saying that because I'm so good with children I should start a family" is the only complex sentence in which the hierarchical nature of the propositions is not reflected in the order of the clauses. Instead, the order is temporally determined: something cannot happen unless something else has already happened; the ideological world is shaped through the use of verbal aspect. The verb "got married" is followed by the progressive "have been saying" of the main sentence, which precedes the future "should start." And the time conjunction "since" reinforces the embedded notion that reproduction cannot take place before marriage. "In fact," which fronts the first subordinate clause, "since I got married," functions pragmatically as a cataphoric reference to caring for her pupils. Not only does it allow the reproduction-marriage relationship to slip in as a preconstruction, it also presents the text as a speech situation.

Between paragraphs 2 and 3, as in the cinematic process of suture, the presence of an addressee is pragmatically sewn into the text.[23] The privileged position of the reader as confidante can be inferred from the semantic distinction between "I always laugh and *say* . . ." and "But what I really *mean*," to which the addressee is given access. Where the first is a rhetorical response for friends, the second (a revelation for the reason underlying the first) is reserved for those more intimate than friends: a nameless category to which the reader by dint of the very speech act has been admitted.

The saying-meaning distinction also signals a decentering of the speaking subject to include the thoughts of a husband who concurs in the reasons for delaying reproduction. The addressee is destabilized: men too are addressed, if indirectly, and readers can choose to read either as female or male (there is in any case no difference in perspective, or so the text asserts). Deixis accordingly shifts from I/my to we/he/our.[24] Men, as surrogate addressees, are thus assured that women are not taking matters in their own hands, and the husband's response is presented as knowledge that implies discussion prior to this explanation: "My husband knows how important my career is to me. But he also knows that we will have a family some day." The near-parallel construction of these sentences appears to establish, through the husband's knowledge, an equivalence between career and family. But there is an important difference between his knowing *how* and knowing *that*: both are arguments of the verb, but the first presupposes the second. That her career is important is a presupposition needing no reassurances, so that the job in fact takes precedence over having a child, a necessary weighting for the ideological definition of a family that follows.

More than a mere biological unit, the family as ideological construct becomes the base from which the advertising message operates. The lexical item "family" in paragraph 3 is presented as part of a prepositional phrase, which as postmodifier is subordinate to "commitments," as in the noun phrase "commitments of a family." And these commitments are economic, so that buying a house *before* having a child is the key constituent, and by implication those who do not follow this order are irresponsible. The obvious result of a woman having a career is not mentioned; we are left to infer that more money will contribute to achieving a family. The promotion of middle-class values, material welfare in order that our children will enjoy all the advantages of being planned, reveals family planning as a euphemism for not having children. Homeownership in the townships is severely restricted; it follows from the advertisement that only the small number of blacks regarding themselves as middle class ought to reproduce themselves.

In the final paragraph, the reader is addressed directly. The speaker reminds us that she loves children, and offers herself as yardstick for the caring woman. Her position as teacher is doubly exploited; she has the authority not only to be the model, but also to utter the final homily: "When you love children as much as I do, planning them is the best thing you can do." This can be read as an implicit performative, urging the reader to follow the teacher's example. The advertisement achieves much of its persuasiveness from presenting itself as a speech situation. Typically, informal language, conversational contractions like *I'm, we'll, they'll,* avoidance of crude advertising imperatives, and simple sentence structure, contribute to its authenticity. But the force of the last sentence turns it into a speech event, "or culturally recognized social activity in which language plays a specific role . . . like teaching in a classroom."[25]

CONCLUSION

We can of course resist sending away for Sister Mildred's free information on how to reproduce ourselves, just as we do not have to accept the advertisement's construction of parenthood. But the question of succumbing or resisting is not the whole story. Kate Linker points out that "representation, hardly neutral, acts to regulate and define the subjects it addresses, positioning them by class or by sex, in active or passive relations to meaning. Over time these fixed positions acquire the status of identities and, in their broadest reach, of categories. Hence the forms of discourse are at once forms of definition, means of limitation, modes of power."[26] While a reader is unlikely to define herself in terms of a position offered by a single advertisement, it seems equally unlikely that she would remain immune to positions constantly mapped out in discursive formations of which such advertisements form part. However, the very existence of Linker's statement shows that ideological meanings can be resisted, and if meaning is negotiated between reader and text, then the variation in the effect of ideological messages could be located in both reading practices and a particular reader's interests.

Michel Pêcheux offers a useful method for examining the cultural assumptions that enable us to make sense of a text, but his ideological determinism does not allow for a level of political awareness that rejects the interdiscourse into which we are interpellated. Willed resistance is patently possible, but dependent first of all on prior understanding of the ideological message, and understanding in turn relies on close reading and a reader's linguistic and cultural knowledge. As Mills points out, an advertisement, unlike a poem, does not invite close reading. However, the oppositional close/slack reading may itself be in need of deconstruction, as may be the distinction between real and professional readers.[27] A continuum between casual and professional readers can surely be assumed where people read slackly if the product is of no interest to them, and carefully when it is.

In this essay, while uncovering the flexible gendering of the reader, I also raise the problem of tracing the reader's position in terms of gender alone. For all its simplicity, the family planning advertisement succeeds in holding together some of the contradictions that operate within society. Thus I use the context of South African politics as an inferential pool for a pragmatic analysis. The unstable positions offered to the reader are seen to be determined by a complex of existing discourses of national liberation and apartheid's reform. The discourse of nation and tradition, routinely used to boost the black liberation movement, is also used to maintain male domination. Caught between the discourse of apartheid's reform and that of its overthrow, feminist concerns have been branded as a distraction from the more urgent task of liberation. While reconstruction recognizes the need to enshrine women's rights in the constitution, women are no less vulnerable. Gangs of jackrollers, youths who rape young girls with the avowed purpose of impregnating them and disrupting their education, roam the townships with impunity.[28] In the overcrowded black university hostels, female students are routinely harassed and "disciplined" in the name of tradition.[29] Such invented tradition does not only serve to justify sexual abuse, it also intersects with the discourse of race, thus allowing perpetrators to argue that those who tackle the question are guilty of racism and cultural imperialism.

Given this context, black women are likely to read population-control advertisements with some care and anxiety. The reader is not positioned achromatically; she is gendered either as a black woman or as a white woman whose different interests, recognized by adverts that cannot afford racial conflation, are differently addressed. Thus the notion of a monolithic real reader, whose identity is determined in opposition to the literary analyst, seems less than useful in studying textual strategies and their ideological effects.

An important question raised by close reading is what the purpose of extracting an even lengthier text from the advertisement might be. Criticism, which nowadays borrows much of its terminology from the language of politics, often sees the exposure of ideological meanings as a political end in itself. It is unnecessary to dwell on the difference between writing on advertisements and being sexually assaulted in shanty townships, but perhaps one could explore connections. Close reading, put to pedagogical use, has an important interventionist function, and attempts at changing slack reading habits may well be useful. Knowledge of language and its ideological functions and an awareness of how advertising exploits existing discourses could lead to material changes in people's lives: the resisting reader could be moved to resist more actively.

I hope to have shown how language-in-use could be a paradigm for analysis, but my medium of language necessarily privileges the linguistic. Advertisements are traditionally analyzed as if they were literary texts, with a focus on identifying rhetorical strategies and lamenting ideological meanings. Learning how we are manipulated by advertisements is worthy, but this need not leave us with the pessimistic message that being vigilant is all we can do in a world artfully manipulated by advertising. The study of advertising could be turned into an empowering activity where techniques are uncovered and used in alternative practices. Image-text art by women like Barbara Kruger, Maude Sulter, Carrie Mae Weems, and Martha Rosler, which addresses issues of gender, race, and class, could be studied to show how the techniques of advertising can be used to question the dominant culture rather than conserve its values. These scripto-visual works intervene in the culture by compelling the reader/viewer to question not only representations of gender, race, and class, but the medium itself. Rather than producing passive recipients, charmed by the aesthetic impact of advertisements, such fascination could be harnessed to produce works that use the techniques of advertising to challenge cultural assumptions.

7

SHAME AND IDENTITY: THE CASE OF THE COLOURED IN SOUTH AFRICA (1995–98)

> Also: brown contains black—(?)—How would
> a person have to behave for us to say of him that
> he knows a *pure, primary* brown?
> We must always bear in mind the question: How do
> people learn the meaning of colour names?
> —*Wittgenstein*, Remarks on Colour

In the 1980s South Africans discovered the Khoi/coloured woman Saartjie Baartman, once known as the Hottentot Venus, who was exhibited in London and Paris from 1810 to her death in 1815. In nineteenth-century Europe, as Sander Gilman points out, the display of her spectacular steatopygia and its generation of medical discourse on the Khoikhoi genitalia established the iconographic link between the black woman and sexual lasciviousness.[1] Since the last decade has seen her well referenced in South African visual art and writing, popular outrage has resulted in the government's application to France for the return of Baartman, whose remains were held by the Musée de l'homme in Paris (though they were removed from public display in the 1980s). Having in the New South Africa become an icon of postcoloniality, Baartman's case can be seen as one of several initiatives toward reconstructing a national cultural past.

Although the project of recovery is propelled by the ignominy of sexualized display before the imperial eye, the discourse around the return of Baartman is cast in terms of injury rather than shame, and a question that has not as yet been resolved is what we will do with her remains.[2] The popular consensus is that the violated body must be covered with native soil, given a decent Christian burial in her own country, specifically in the Eastern Cape province, where she

114

originates. Perhaps the more pertinent question is whether her burial would also bury black woman as icon of concupiscence, which is to say bury the shame of having been the object of the European gaze, but also the shame invested in those (females) who have mated with the colonizer. Miscegenation, the origins of which lie within a discourse of "race," concupiscence, and degeneracy, continues to be bound up with shame, a pervasive shame exploited in apartheid's strategy of naming of a Coloured race, and recurring in the current attempts by coloureds to establish brownness as a pure category, which is to say a denial of shame. We do not speak about miscegenation; it is after all the very nature of shame to disguise itself and stifle its own discourse. What the case of Baartman shows is how shame, cross-eyed and shy, stalks the postcolonial world broken mirror in hand, reproducing itself in puzzling distortions.

"O shame, shame, poppy shame!"—Salman Rushdie, narrativizing shame in his novel about Pakistan and postcoloniality, maps its complexity as he tells the story "in fragments of broken mirrors."[3] Its English formulation, "tainted by wrong concepts and the accumulated detritus of its owners' unrepented past," in other words by the very shamefulness of colonialism, is replaced by the indigenous term: "*Sharam*, that's the word. For which this paltry 'shame' is a wholly inadequate translation. . . . A short word but one containing encyclopaedias of nuance."[4] Rushdie, investing shame with materiality, gives an ironic listing of political chicanery, its shamefulness reflected into that which Sufiya Zinobia Hyder, the character who embodies shame, blushes for. Such acts as "lies, loose living, disrespect for one's elders, failure to love one's national flag, incorrect voting at elections, over-eating, extramarital sex, autobiographical novels . . . throwing one's wicket away at the crucial point of a Test Match . . . are done *shamelessly*. Then what happens to all that unfelt shame?"[5] Throughout the novel, shame is connected to concupiscence, to a pathological female sexuality, so that the idiot Sufiya's release of absorbed shame is also finally brought about through the body, in the voracious sexuality and violence of the mass killer.

Following Rushdie's nuanced usage, my project is to find a way of discussing the textual construction, ethnographic self-fashioning, and political behavior of coloureds in South Africa, which is to say our condition of postcoloniality, through the concept of shame.[6] Stuart Hall's notion of transcoding ethnicity, of contesting its meaning within a new politics of representation—"It is only through the way in which we represent and imagine ourselves that we come to know how we are constituted and who we are"[7]—informs my reading of popular and literary texts. In order to shift the debate out of a local political discourse into culture in the wider sense, I trace the construction of colouredness through postmodernism's reconceptualization of geographical space and of the body. Not only can the body be thought of metaphorically as a text, as explored in recent Euro-feminist theory, I also wish to consider the actual materiality of black bodies that bear the marked pigmentation of miscegenation, and the way in which that relates to political culture.

Saartjie Baartman, whose very name indicates her cultural hybridity, exemplifies the body as site of shame, a body bound up with the politics of location. I adopt her as icon precisely because of the nasty unspoken question of concupiscence that haunts coloured identity, the issue of nation building implicit in the matter of her return, her contested ethnicity (black, Khoi, or coloured?), and the vexed question of representation. The Baartman case also neatly exemplifies some of the central concerns of postmodern thought—the inscription of power in scopic relations; the construction of woman as racialized and sexualized other; the colonization and violation of the body; the role of scientific discourse in bolstering both the modernist and the colonial projects—and is thus a convenient point around which to discuss the contested relationship between postcolonialism and postmodernism.

In etymologyzing terms, the death of apartheid and achievement of liberation from settler colonialism signals a condition of youthful postcoloniality. However, the shameful vote of Cape coloureds for the National Party in the first democratic elections in April 1994 throws such a label into question. Our electoral behavior, which ensures that the Western Cape is the only region without an African National Congress (A.N.C.) majority, coincides with the resurgence of the term "Coloured," once more capitalized, without its old prefix of "so-called" and without the disavowing scare quotes earned during the period of revolutionary struggle when it was replaced by the word "black" to indicate both a rejection of apartheid nomenclature and inclusion in the national liberation movement. Such adoption of different names at various historical junctures shows perhaps the difficulty that the term "coloured" has in taking on a fixed meaning, and accordingly exemplifies postmodernity in its shifting allegiances, its duplicitous play between the written capitalization and speech that denies or at least does not reveal the act of renaming—once again the silent inscription of shame. Yet, within the new, exclusively coloured political organizations that have sprung up in the Western and Northern Cape provinces, in particular, since the 1994 election, attempts at blurring differences of language, class, and religion in the interest of a homogeneous ethnic group at the same time seem to defy the decentering thrust of postmodernism. What the problem of identity indicates, however, is a position that undermines the new narrative of national unity: the newly democratized South Africa remains dependent on the old economic, social, and also epistemological structures of apartheid, and thus it is axiomatic that different groups created by the old system do not participate equally in the category of postcoloniality. Theoretically, the situation can be cast in terms of the diverging interests of postmodernism and postcoloniality, or it may indicate the need to revise popular definitions of the latter to include the coexistence of oppositional and complicit forms. However, in practice, such an absorption into a single category would gloss over the real threat to the task of establishing democracy, at least in the Cape.

The failure, in coloured terms, of the grand narrative of liberation (how else to describe the vote against nonracial democracy?) demands fresh inquiry into the questions of postcolonial "hybridity" and identity, as well as the territorialization or geography of belonging within which identity is produced. This I will attempt through a discussion of cultural practices as, for instance, in our complicit construction of District Six—an inner-city community marked by poverty and crime and destroyed by the Group Areas Act after 1965 (which forcibly removed people to the dreary, far-flung suburbs of the Cape Flats)—as ethnic homeland. Our postmodern suppression of history demands a strategy of relocating and rehistoricizing our own situation lest we come to believe the myth of our collective birth in Cape Town's District Six in the 1960s.[8] The making of the subject and the script of shame imbricated in such ethnographic self-fashioning as well as in the discursive construction by others needs to be examined in the light of the narrative of liberation and its dissemination in the world media that constructed oppression in particular ways.

The assumption of District Six as ethnic homeland illustrates not only the fictional nature of identity construction but also the postcolonial relationship with the politics of location. Since its earliest representation in fiction by writers like Alex La Guma and Richard Rive, it became a ready-made southern counterpart to the loaded signifier of Soweto. Site specific as media signifiers of oppression had become, District Six had the advantage of being urban, and having been demolished—therefore patently about loss, as well as being associated with forced removals, to which far fewer coloured than black communities were in fact subjected. The self-fashioning of a totalizing colouredness located in a mythologized District Six of the 1950s and 60s found its expression in the 1980s in the popular eponymous musical, devised by David Kramer and Taliep Petersen. Here ethnicity was constructed within a politics of nostalgia that sentimentalized the loss. The contradiction of forging an "authentic" culture— ironically also the overt theme of *District Six—The Musical* (1989)—through North American cultural conventions and musical forms seemed to escape its audience enraptured by the process of being constructed in the tepid, amniotic fluid of pastiche. In the heady months before the unbanning of the A.N.C., the show's self-conscious reliance on pastiche, a mode described by Jameson as "the imitation of a peculiar mask, speech in a dead language: but a neutral practice of such mimicry, without parody's ulterior motives,"[9] signaled its refusal to engage with collocations of colouredness, or with interacting identities in a larger framework of South African citizenship. What is significant is that the musical was in fact produced during the period of mass identification with the liberation movement, that the spatial overidentification with District Six was temporally linked to identification with the black nationalist struggle. In other words, while such modalities of belonging clearly existed historically, they did not find their way into a politics of representation. The popular attempt at inventing an authentic colouredness illustrates how representation does not simply express, but rather plays a formative role in, social and political life.

The title of Richard Rive's *"Buckingham Palace," District Six* (1986) refers to the parodic mode so conspicuously absent in the musical and its sequels. In this work of deliberate generic ambiguity, italicized texts written in the first-person autobiographical genre serve as foreword to each of the three sections of fictionalized vignettes of what we are assured are real-life remembered people: "And in the evenings we would stand in hushed doorways and tell stories about the legendary figures of District Six, Zoot, Pretty Boy and Mary."[10] Thus authenticity—or denial of the fictive—is inscribed in a text that apparently already exists in oral and communal representations of these very characters. While neither the place nor the affectionate portrayal of characters is sentimentalized, the autobiographical text is marked by the ethnographic. The past-tense modal form "we/they would," used throughout these sections, provides nothing less than a generalized customs-and-manners description of coloured life that takes us through the week ending with the Sunday dessert of jelly and custard and the boys' occasional trip to the museum to giggle at "the models of Bushmen with big bums."[11] Here Baartman's European viewer is replaced by the puerile gaze of coloured boys, and steatopygia itself is shifted to colonial *representation* of "primitives" in a museum, a shift that covertly and uneasily refers to shame.

As early as 1962, Bessie Head lamented in her first novel, *The Cardinals* (first published posthumously in 1993), the representation of the coloured and the mythologizing of District Six. Johnny, the voice of truth in the novel, advises his colleague to give up writing: "I don't even have to read this one to know it's about another prostitute walking down Hanover Street, shaking her behind. Where you see all these prostitutes is beyond me. I've never ever seen a prostitute walking down Hanover Street, shaking her behind. She wouldn't dare. . . . Every single story I've read of yours is about the happy little Coloured man and the colourful Malays. Why don't you leave that crap to those insane, patronising white women journalists who are forever at pains to tell the Coloureds how happy they are."[12] Thus the location of colouredness in the colorful District Six is firmly linked with coloured complicity in its construction, including the stereotype of female sexuality inscribed in the spectacular Baartmanesque behind.

It is instructive to look at how, in the 1960s, rejecting the label of coloured, Bessie Head, in exile in Botswana, responds to the question of ethnicity. In an essay called "Africa," she discusses her identity through addressing the country as a fickle, flesh-and-blood lover. Her discomfort is stylistically encoded in an archaic, inverted syntax, and using a trope of traveling without direction she describes her identity in terms of lack: "Not now, not ever, shall I be complete; and though the road to find you has been desolate with loneliness, still more desolate is the road that leads away from you. What do I do now that your face intrudes everywhere, and you are yet essentially *ashamed* of me as the thing of nothing from nowhere? Nothing I am, of no tribe or race, and because of it full of a childish arrogance to defend myself against all of you."[13] Through the rhetorical figure of chiasmus, shame is identified as the recognition of being the object of another's shame. Morphological forms of the word thus indicate changes in meaning that relate to a shifting subjectivity and to the interrelatedness of different subject positions. (Rushdie's Zinobia is also wife to Omar Khayyam, who is immune to the feeling of shame.) For Head this shame is supplanted only by an Africanist politics of liberation that allows her to say of the Pan Africanist Congress (P.A.C.) leader Robert Sobukwe, "He gave me a comfortable black skin in which to live and work."[14] Here the word "comfortable" stands in significant contrast to the word "proud," a black consciousness term that betrays its continued relationship with shame.

That black nationalist struggles gained an unstable popularity among coloureds is not simply a matter of postmodern skepticism of grand narratives of emancipation. There is the question of language or the ways in which political discourse relates to the figuration of colouredness in cultural texts. For instance, apartheid education ensured that coloureds do not speak the indigenous languages, and the Soweto uprising of 1976, characterized as a revolt against Afrikaans as the language of the oppressor, produced a movement among coloureds in the Cape to rescue their first language from its association with oppression. Thus arose in the eighties a flurry of poetry in nonstandard Afrikaans that had only the previous decade, along with its lone practitioner, Adam Small, been ridiculed as a shameful "gamtaal." Renamed and valorized as "Kaaps" (of the Cape), this local and racialized variety of Afrikaans as a literary language came to assert a discursive space for an oppositional colouredness that aligned itself to the black liberation struggle. But, as Hein Willemse points out, English-language writers like Richard Rive saw Kaaps as "propounding the acceptance of a brand of Colouredism in the face of strong anti-racism" and falsely claiming "the right to a special, ethnic literary existence."[15] This was indeed an unfounded and linguistically conservative assessment of Kaaps itself, but raising the specter of ethnicity at such an unlikely stage was curiously prophetic of coloured responses to black nationalist discourse in the nineties when the local variety of Afrikaans was once again appropriated by reactionary forces.

In literary representations, shifts in coloured-black relations are captured in short stories published in 1979 and 1991 by Mtutuzeli Matshoba and Don Mattera, respectively. The mood of racial conciliation in Matshoba's "A Son of the First Generation" is exemplified by an African woman giving birth to a mixed-race child who is forgivingly accepted by her black husband. The story ends with an epilogue in which, stepping outside the fictive, the narrator dedicates the following words to his "Coloured brothers and sisters": "To me a so-called 'Coloured' human being is a brother, conceived in the same black womb as I. Child of a sister robbed of the pride of motherhood by the man-made immorality laws."[16] Thus Matshoba's writing of black solidarity embraces the newborn coloured as male, constructed through a narrative of illicit sexuality, female concupiscence and shame. Don Mattera's "Die Bushie is Dood . . ." ("The Bushy is Dead . . .") tells a very different story of ethnic tension confirmed in the death of a coloured youth stabbed at a Soweto rally by black comrades who do not trust coloureds and who question his right to be there, just as the young man's family question his meddling with black politics. The tension in the story is marked by nomenclature: a tussle between the youth and his brother when the latter speaks of "bantu" and "darkies"; the use of the derogatory "Bushie" (from Bushman) by a black man to indicate the young man's lack of belonging as opposed to the term "comrade" used by his friends.[17] Thus the narrative of assimilation witnessed in the political activism of the 1970s and 1980s is replaced by Mattera's representation of an ambiguous coloured exclusion and self-exclusion from national liberation politics.

The majority vote for the National Party in the Western Cape in 1994 came as no surprise to the A.N.C. Max Ozinsky and Ibrahim Rasool, in their discussion of an A.N.C. election strategy for the coloured areas in the province, offer an account of the history of struggle in this area.[18] The paper, while correctly warning against the use of the term "coloured" to cover heterogeneous sets of communities differentiated by class, language, and religion, points out the demographic significance of the group, who compose 52 percent of the region's population in comparison with 25 percent Africans and 23 percent whites.

Ozinsky and Rasool comment on the vibrancy of the resistance movement in the eighties when the radical United Democratic Front (U.D.F.) captured the determination of diverse coloured constituencies not to be co-opted into the ruling bloc. The paper asks the following rhetorical questions: whether a legacy of organization and structures had been left in coloured communities; and whether the 1980s had indeed created nonracialism, acceptance of African leadership, and a sense of common nationhood. The failure of the movement since its unbanning is attributed to the fact that, after its legal relaunch, the A.N.C. was not seen to have a clear program for work in the communities. When politics became centralized there was no focus on mass work, and the racial tension that developed when the oppositional coloured Civic organizations, which had contributed significantly to the demise of apartheid and now became subject to the A.N.C., is quaintly characterized as an "ambiguity." This, the authors argue, led to the dissipation of much of the inherent strength of mass politics in coloured areas. What the document does not address is the question of regionalism and ethnicity, the way in which coloured activists considered themselves to be marginalized since the dismantling of the United Democractic Movement. Its rehearsal of the party line—"The main content of our national liberation struggles is the liberation of the African majority. The African majority is the most reliable force for the completion of the tasks of national liberation"—thus fails to take into account the reality of regionalism, that the majority in the Cape is in fact coloured. The working paper ends limply with recommendations for more A.N.C. branches focusing on community issues in the Cape, an example of the euphemistic use of the word "community." What the A.N.C. failed to predict was that the National Party, with its superior resources to mobilize working-class coloureds around issues like housing, and with propaganda about alien concepts like affirmative action, would lead them to believe that Africanization necessarily meant depriving them of their homes, schools, and jobs, and ultimately their culture.

Mahmood Mamdani, in his analysis of the differences between Afrikaner and coloured in apartheid South Africa, distinguishes between cultural identities, which illustrate differences along a continuum, and political identities, which were bipolar opposites: "Afrikaner was an identity of power, while 'coloured' was a subject identity."[19] But the volte-face of the National Party's false appeal to a shared culture centered in the Afrikaans language, the Dutch Reformed Church, and mutton *bredie* (stew), was overlooked by Cape coloureds as they cast their shameful vote. And the shame of it lies not only in what we have voted against—citizenship within a democratic constitution that ensures the protection of individual rights, the enshrinement of gay and lesbian rights, the abolition of censorship and blasphemy laws—but in the amnesia with regard to the National Party's atrocities in maintaining apartheid. Our postmodern effacement of history stretches back to the very memory of our origins. Robert Ross, in his study of the history of slavery at the Cape, remarks on the difficulty of research when virtually nothing by way of folktales, stories, or songs has been retained, and when the only sources are records of the Court of Justice covering the period of the Dutch East India Company rule. His account of the rebel slave Leander Bugis and his band of runaways at Hanglip, their insurrection including an attempt to burn Cape Town to the ground in 1736, is indeed of a figure ripe for legend and mythology, but such stories have not found their way into folk history. Ross explains the amnesia in terms of social history, but also in terms of denial: "The continued oppression of large numbers of ex-slaves by their ex-masters and . . . the concern of those who had escaped from this position to set themselves apart from the rural scene."[20]

This failure or inability to represent in popular forms, and consequently the total erasure of slavery from the folk memory, has its roots in shame: shame for our origins of slavery, shame for the miscegenation, and shame, as colonial racism became institutionalized, for being black, so that with the help of European names coloureds have lost all knowledge of Xhosa, Indonesian, East African, or Khoikhoi origins. Significantly, the reference to slavery in our self-naming as *Gam* originates not in memory but rather in apartheid's legitimizing reference to the Old Testament narrative of Noah's son Ham, who looked upon his father's nakedness and so earned the curse of slavery. It is no coincidence that the very word "shame" has acquired a peculiar semantic attenuation into an utterance of tenderness, sympathy, or empathy so that we would exclaim "Shame!" on seeing a baby or a beggar, while the meaning of disgrace has been excised in common usage.

The shame-bearing coloured finds her literary origins in Sarah Gertrude Millin's eugenicist novel *God's Stepchildren* (1924), where miscegenation, as J. M. Coetzee points out, is expressed in terms of "blood, flaw, taint, and degeneration."[21] Similarly, in what is arguably the first African Nationalist novel, *Mhudi* (1930), Sol Plaatje's rehabilitated Mzilikazi in his grand nation-making speech warns against the Bechuana's alliance with the Boers, who will "take Bechuana women to wife and, with them, breed a race of half man, half goblin"—although he wrongly predicts that "they . . . will waste away in helpless fury till the gnome offspring of such miscegenation rise up against their cruel sires."[22] Shame is still inscribed in the tragic mode routinely used to represent coloureds where assumed cultural loss is elevated to the realm of ontology as in Liz Gunner's enigmatic story "You, the Lioness." Here a black singer speaks of "women [who] heal with water and prayers—things I half understand because it's only half mine, and we of mixed blood, Coloured, that word! . . . I don't know where we belong."[23] (The answer, I fear, is in the Cape!) Such perception of culture as something divorced from the performative and curiously defined as that in which you do *not* participate is typical of this mode; more worrying is the metaphysics of race that allows difference to exclude an individual from what others in her own community intuitively know.

As Gunner suggests, the shame is located in the very word "coloured," a category established by the Nationalist government's Population Registration Act of 1950, where it was defined negatively as "not a White person or a Black." But it is worth remembering that as several groups found the term unsuitable, amendments to the Act for additional categories such as "Other Coloured" or "Griqua" were made. Subsequent shifts in nomenclature have further supported the idea of a fragmented coloured subject as a postmodern "ontological 'fact'" that can only 'find' itself in language."[24]

Postcolonial theorizing of the coloured also takes its cue from the notion of fragmentation, as witnessed in Homi Bhabha's analysis of the following passage from Nadine Gordimer's *My Son's Story* (1990). "Halfway between: the schoolteacher lived and taught and carried out his uplifting projects in the community with the municipal council seated under its coat-of-arms on the one side of the veld, and the real blacks—more, many more of them than the whites, 'coloureds' and Indians counted together—on the other. His community had a certain kind of community with the real blacks, as it did with the town through the Saturday dispensation; but rather different. Not defined—and it was this lack of definition in itself that was never to be questioned, but observed like a taboo, something which no-one, while following, ever could admit to."[25] Gordimer's representation of racial identity—in terms of the popular nationalist discourse of the authentic selves of "real blacks" and coloured indeterminacy—is taken up in orthodox postcolonial terms by Bhabha. He makes an ontological leap from the mytho-geographical, so that the "borderline existence" for the coloured marks a "deeper historical displacement" and represents a "hybridity, a difference 'within' a subject that inhabits the rim of an inbetween reality."[26] Here, surely, are echoes of the tragic mode where lived experience is displaced by an aesthetics of theory. How, one is tempted to ask, do people who live in communities inhabit, spookily and precariously, a rim of in-between reality? Symbolically, of course, and therefore, according to Gordimer, inexpressibly, in silence, the shame of it all encoded in the word "taboo." Surely relegation to such a space relies on an essentialist view that posits a "pure" reality that is experienced in the space inhabited by the racially pure.

Continuing the spatial metaphor of the home suggested by Gordimer's narrative, Bhabha speaks of the halfway house of "racial and cultural origins that bridges the 'inbetween' diasporic origins of the Coloured South African and turns it into the symbol of the disjunctive, displaced everyday life of the liberation struggle."[27] This link, assumed between colouredness and revolutionary struggle, seems to presuppose a theory of hybridity that relies, after all, on the biological, a notion denied in earlier accounts where Bhabha claims that colonial power with its inherent ambivalence itself produces hybridization: "Produced through the strategy of disavowal, the *reference* of discrimination is always to a process of splitting as the condition of subjection: a discrimination between the mother culture and its bastards, the self and its doubles, where the trace of what is disavowed is not repressed but repeated as something different—a mutation, a hybrid."[28] In this language of eugenics, Bhabha explains how ambivalence revealed within the discourse of authority enables a form of subversion; however, in the case of the coloured, racial hybridity,[29] as in the previous quotation, is somehow itself responsible for a necessary subversiveness— much like Plaatje's prediction of the hybrid race rising against its sire! But in the very narrative that Bhabha examines, coloured complicity rather than subversion is affirmed: Gordimer's schoolteacher, who becomes an A.N.C. activist, remains after all an anomaly in his extended family who continue uncommittedly to "picnic in the no-man's-land of veld"; there is no coloured community of activists. And the narrative charts the activist Sonny's decline in the movement because of his sexual relations with a white woman.

Bhabha's theory of hybridity cannot account for the postapartheid coloured politics where it is precisely the celebration of in-betweenness that serves conservatism, as in the use of the word "brown," introduced into the unwieldy title "Coloured Liberation Movement for the Advancement of Brown People," launched at the beginning of March 1995. Slipped in tentatively as a prepositional phrase, the word bears the trace of shame in its capitulation to the National Party's expedient use of "Brown Afrikaners," which successfully drew in the coloured vote, as well as in its evocation of country folk, an attempt at fabricating a traditional past to foster the notion of a coloured nation. The association of brown with mid-century Afrikaans-speaking farmworkers whose customs and manners had been ridiculed, and whose difference has been racially codified by Afrikaner writers like Mikro, shows both the amnesia and the contradictory nature of this construction: the apposite terms "liberation" and "advancement," "Coloured" and "Brown," thus have the task of amelioration that will efface history and reconcile contradiction. Amnesia is most crassly demonstrated in another new coloured political party, the Kleurling Weerstandsbeweging (K.W.B.; Coloured Resistance Movement), with its unseemly echo of the right-wing Afrikaner Weerstandsbeweging (A.W.B.).[30]

That coloured politics presents a problem for representation seems to be a central concern in *My Son's Story*. Gordimer, who is admirably free of the postmodern anxiety about representation and has never missed a chance to comment on the good, strong legs or large buttocks of black female characters, problematizes the representation of the coloured in her very title. The narrative is of Sonny, the coloured teacher turned political activist, who has an illicit affair with a white woman. It is his son, Will, consumed with disgust and anger on his mother's behalf, who writes the story of his father's infidelity and his mother's subsequent adoption of the struggle as a gunrunner. The final words of the novel, "I am a writer and this is my first book—that I can never publish," present a deictic complexity that points to the displacement of the "my" in the title, where the referent in the phrase, "my son's story" refers to Will's father, the man who cannot represent his own "shameful" story. (Rushdie's ironic reference to extramarital sex as a source of shame is pertinent; here it is, of course, a shame refracted through the comrades' ejection of Sonny.) In the very act of representing the coloured activist, the possibility of representing him is disavowed in Will's final words. What cannot be represented, one suspects, bearing in mind Gordimer's careful charting of the history of the struggle, is not the coloured but the coloured activist within the A.N.C. whose relations with the organization turn out to be problematic, not least because of his concupiscence. In contrast, Coetzee's virginal coloured vagrant, Michael K, whose life remains isolated from a community or a resistance movement of which he has no knowledge even as the revolution rages about him, is indeed representable.[31]

The narrative voice in Gordimer's text alternates between Will's first-person account and a third-person center of consciousness, itself focalized through either Will or his father. But we are told at the end of the novel that the events focalized through Sonny had all been Will's inventions; in other words, Sonny as source of the information about himself is denied; he cannot tell his own story. Will is able to write their story as a private act precisely because he has been excluded from liberation politics, a decision that is taken by his mother, Aila, much to his resentment. But he cannot publish it. The coloured story is destined to be suppressed; the narrative of Aila's surprising contribution to the struggle is marked by silence. In the space between writing and making public lies a shame steeped in its originary interracial sex.

Gordimer's account of the "spectator status" that coloureds adopt as they speak of black insurrection from a distance is communicated in an imperfect transcript of direct speech in the Afrikaans syntax that characterizes ordinary coloured language:

> There was fervent stoep and yard talk, *they going to moer the lanies   you'll see ou   they quite right make the Boers shit their pants there in Pretoria   what you think you talking about they going to get a rope round their necks   that what they putting up their hands for, bracelets man bullets up the backside you can't win against whitey.*[32]

This curious discourse, situated somewhere between the political and idle gossip, significantly takes place on the *stoep* or in the yard, the ambiguous space between inside and outside, between public and private, which makes it possible to present the dialogue among indistinguishable participants as if overheard. Thus it is marked by ellipsis, the most marked being the indicator of direct address, the *ou*, a modifier which is never used in face-to-face communication without being followed by the addressee's name. Instead of identifying the speaker, there is typographic space, a replication of the symbolic no-man's-land where the unpoliticized Sonny and his young family used to picnic. The dialogue, drawing attention to itself through the use of italics, presents the available positions of resigned acceptance of the power of apartheid as well as a vague empathy with black resistance, but not of active participation in the Movement. Thus Gordimer's unidentified speakers, represented through ellipsis, express through their own enunciation their political identity as lack.

Significantly, this family do not live in the Cape, home of the coloured, where we find instead of an articulation of lack of identity, a shameful excess, an exorbitance of identity expressed in the construction of coloured nationhood that has surfaced since the elections. This situation questions several of the metropolitan articulations of postcoloniality. For instance, Homi Bhabha's location of the condition in the "history of postcolonial migration, the narratives of cultural and political diaspora,"[33] would seem to prove inadequate for a group who in the suppression of their diasporic slave origins have adopted an excessively proprietorial attitude toward the Cape. Similarly, the indigenists' dismissal of the postmodern critique of nationalism as imagined community needs to be reconsidered in the light of the new fissures. The coloured valorization of rootedness at the Cape also brings to mind Aijaz Ahmad's sneer at the postcolonial myth of ontological unbelonging that is linked to diasporic cultures. In his critique of *Shame*, Ahmad complains about postmodern dislocation and the fact that "the idea of belonging is itself seen now as bad faith, a mere myth of origins, a truth effect produced by the Enlightenment's 'metaphysic of presence.'"[34] However, such bad faith may well serve as antidote for the equally mythical excess of belonging or exorbitance of coloured identity. Instead of denying history and fabricating a totalizing colouredness, "multiple belongings" could be seen as an alternative way of viewing a culture where participation in a number of co-loured micro-communities whose interests conflict and overlap could become a rehearsal of cultural life in the larger South African community, where we learn to perform the same kind of negotiations in terms of identity within a lived culture characterized by difference.

As I write this (in 1995), there is news of Winnie Madikizela-Mandela declaring the A.N.C. Women's League an Africanist organization, the meaning of which we euphemistically choose to construe as a riposte to the League being called a femi-nist organization. News also comes of the walkout at the A.N.C. Youth League's annual general meeting in the Western Cape by coloured comrades who claim that discrimination against them has become intolerable. The comrades' choice lies in either being shamefully aligned with the Browns or remaining silent on the margin of the movement, hugging to themselves their refracted shame. Other-wise there is the retreat into culturalism with a rallying mumble of diversity that hardly constitutes the excision of shame that we would like to think it is.

It is in the spirit of the new postcolonial internationalism that I choose to end with the African American artist Carrie Mae Weems's image-text work *Then What? Photographs and Folklore*, recorded in an artist's book of foldouts.[35] One of these constitutes a series of black-and-white informal photographs of six young black people with a continuous text running below:

DEEP BLACK, ASHY BLACK, PALE BLACK, JET BLACK, PITCH BLACK, DEAD BLACK, BLUE BLACK, PURPLE BLACK, CHOCOLATE-BROWN, COFFEE, SEALSKIN-BROWN, DEEP BROWN, HONEY BROWN, RED BROWN, DEEP YELLA BROWN, CHOCO-LATE, HIGH-BROWN, LOW-BROWN, VELVET BROWN, BRONZE, GINGERBREAD, LIGHT BROWN, TAN, OLIVE, COPPER, PINK, BANANA, CREAM, ORANGE, HIGH YALLA, LEMON, OH, AND YEAH CARAMEL.

In this self-consciously discursive text where a speaker rattles off gradations of color, ending affirmatively with the remembered "CARAMEL," difference is lin-guistically inscribed in the range of metaphoric colors. But in the disjuncture of accompanying images of black people who are of the same color, difference is also at the same time disavowed: at the intersection of image and text there is a space where people can resist received racial descriptions, where they make their own meanings, oh and yeah, new discursive spaces in which modalities of blackness can wipe out shame.

8

REMEMBERING NELSON MANDELA (2013)

In April 2013, as joyful chants of "Maggie, Maggie, Maggie, dead, dead, dead!" reverberated through the streets of Glasgow, where I live, I heard the echo, as all South Africans surely did, of the floppy-bow-tied Iron Lady, Margaret Thatcher, calling the African National Congress (A.N.C.) a terrorist group.[1] Nelson Mandela became a byword for virtue all the same. Every schoolchild knows of his contribution to democracy in South Africa, of the sacrifices he made, of his status as an icon of reconciliation. Mandela's image, banned in South Africa during the years of his incarceration, circulated throughout the world. But what did he *actually* look like? There were no photographs of him from prison. The A.N.C. released images of a pugnacious young lion. There is the famous one of a boxer foregrounding his gloved fists in 1957, another of the urbane lawyer at the Rivonia trial who embraced his incarceration with warrior words.

When I was a student in South Africa, these photographs were banned, but the rest of the world chanted to the outdated image of an ill-favored young man with the curious hairstyle of colonized Africa: a severe European side parting gouged into resistant black hair, and his oddly close to the center. How, then, could we have recognized the man who stepped out on the balcony of Cape Town's City Hall in 1990, blinking in the sunlight? Mandela looked nothing like the artists' renderings of an aging boxer, which had been circulating. That day, a tall, handsome stranger strode into the world. His face, instead of bearing the signs of the usual havoc that time wreaks, had been transfigured into sculpted planes that spoke of bygone Xhosa-Khoisan relations, and the ugly hair parting had gone. Mandela walked out in beauty. Supermodels and philosophers sighed alike.

Hendrik Verwoerd, the prime minister and "architect of apartheid" under whose government Mandela was imprisoned, benign-looking and sporting a standard hair parting on the left, had long since been assassinated. (He died in 1966.) He could not have imagined that Mandela's life sentence would be a gift to the A.N.C. Mandela, kept pristine in prison, was spared that inevitable slippage from idealism to corruption that war and military values bring; he came out *skoon*, an Afrikaans word meaning both squeaky clean and beautiful. The banality of apartheid, to adapt Hannah Arendt's phrase, threw back through Mandela its counterimage of the thoughtful, the beauty of a mind given to reflection and introspection. And the beautiful man did not have to follow the gray ways of parliamentarians in four-piece suits. He donned a colorful shirt, metonym for *ubuntu* and the Africanicity he would come to represent.[2]

We are sentimental about Nelson Mandela. We use words like "love" and "beauty." We did not only love him; we wanted him, after his years of deprivation, to be enveloped in love. We did not want him to die. We wanted to know about his private life: the unsuccessful first marriage to Evelyn; the public collapse of his marriage to Winnie. And we delighted in his marriage to the good widow Graça Machel. Now we also know of the widow Cachalia, who had turned down his marriage proposal, exhausted by a life devoted to the struggle against apartheid and who, mindful of Evelyn, did not see her way clear to marrying a nation.[3]

But what did Nelson Mandela say to the widow Verwoerd? In the scramble for alterity that followed the demise of apartheid, forty unreconciled Afrikaner families, led by Verwoerd's son-in-law, retreated to Orania, an exclusive enclave established in the Northern Cape. It is here that Mrs. Betsie Verwoerd retired. In Orania, people lead pure white lives, unsullied by blacks, which is to say free even of black workers and servants, a lesson they had surely learned both from the failure of apartheid and from the example of virtue that Mandela had garnered in isolation. Here Nelson Mandela visited the unprepossessing widow Verwoerd, in 1995. We know that tea, coffee, and the iconic Afrikaner *koeksisters*[4] were served, presumably by lily-white hands. Then Mandela was left alone with the widow. Almost certainly they spoke in Afrikaans, the language of the oppressor, as it was dubbed by blacks in the Struggle era. Mandela learned the language in prison, while children in Soweto protested against its imposition as medium of education in schools. What passed between them? Mandela reported nothing. Tight-lipped Betsie Verwoerd never spoke of it. (She died, aged ninety-eight, in 2000.) Were her lips sealed throughout the meeting? In the Karoo, there is no point in speaking about the weather, because it never varies. The meeting in Orania must remain the stuff for fiction.

Part Two

———————◆———————

INTERTEXTUALITY AND THE POSTCOLONIAL AUTHOR

FIVE AFRIKANER TEXTS AND THE REHABILITATION OF WHITENESS (1997–98)

One of the more refreshing qualities of apartheid was the abandon with which we all talked about and identified ourselves in terms of race, a situation that compares rather favorably with European cultures where official "antiracism" takes on a peculiar locutionary force that stifles its own discourse and produces in natives a nervous throat-clearing with the utterance of the words "white" and "black." And this notwithstanding avowed awareness of the constructedness of race and ethnicity. It is, I fear, in such advanced societies, where whiteness as a category is masked, that apartheid will be sorely missed as a ready-made Other whose aggressive naming of white and black has, in the popular imagination, come to mean racism. In South Africa, where the material effects of institutionalized racism linger, ethnicity as a contrastive system ensures that not everyone wishes to let go of racial naming: black people jealously guard their blackness, coloureds cling to the colouredness of a mythologized District Six, the moremorious-than-thou Afrikaner Weerstandsbeweging (A.W.B.) howls for a white homeland, and only "English" liberals are puzzled by the persistence of their perceived whiteness.[1]

Whiteness, the condition once assumed by diverse European settler communities, is no longer a condition to be cherished; "white" is no longer a nice word. Whiteness does not collocate with the key words of our narrative of freedom so there is no potential for discursive appropriation or refiguration of its general field of meaning. As a construct, whiteness cannot be fully addressed; indeed, it appears to be only from within and bound up with the meaning of a specific ethnic group that a revision can emerge. It is not surprising that Afrikaners, the group most in need of rehabilitation, are engaged in such a discursive struggle. In this essay I examine a number of contemporary texts concerned with Afrikaner identity, and focus on some textual strategies through which Afrikanerhood has been refigured in relation to whiteness.

An article on the Truth and Reconciliation Commission in the British newspaper the *Guardian* is a convenient point of departure precisely because investigation and disclosure appear to be common tropes in the literary discourses of a revised Afrikanerness.[2] An entire page of the broadsheet of 18 January 1997 is devoted to the issue, and more than a quarter of the page constitutes a closely cropped, larger-than-life photograph of the crumpled face of a black woman whose chin rests dejectedly on her right hand. Looking directly into the camera she cries with abandonment: her eyes are narrowed, a plump Tretchikoff teardrop trembles on her cheek, through parted lips we see her clenched teeth; from the tonality of her lower lip there is a suspicion of slavering. In the left-hand corner, below the injunctive headline "Cry, Beloved Country," with its evocation of Alan Paton's patronizing liberalism, is a passport-size photograph of the Afrikaner poet Antjie Krog, whose account as head of the team of radio reporters covering the Commission fills the rest of the page.[3] Besides the matter of size, there are other inversions in these photographs: Antjie's smiling face is tilted; her right hand appears to lift the chin, giving her a meditative air; the intelligent, penetrating look engages with that of the viewer where the black face is blanked with grief. The black woman's tears dissolve her subjectivity; there is no reciprocity as we are forced into an unequal, voyeuristic gaze.

The report, it turns out, is at odds with the images. There is no story of black tears. Instead, the scripto-visual text finds its cohesion in Krog's crying, her grief and breakdown as a result of the trauma of listening day after day to stories of atrocities and the horror of having to convert these into soundbites. It is of course perfectly appropriate that Antjie Krog (whose dissident credentials are well established in the British media) should cry, but the article raises the question of why the *Guardian* should want to translate her tears into that of a black woman, or why her text should be slid under the signification of blackness. Krog states her task as follows: "It was crucial for me to have the voices of the victims on the news bulletin. To have the sound of ordinary people dominate the news. No South African should escape the process." And so too in the *Guardian's* report of the report, where the nature of the *process* remains unexplained, but where we are given four extracts from the voices of victims. These are not racially identified, except one knows that the tea lady in the police station, who sees her grandchild falling down from the upper floor, is black, by virtue of her being a tea lady. We learn that her edited story was broadcast: "The voice of an ordinary cleaning woman is the headline. We lift our fists triumphantly. We've done it!"[4]

The other two texts are more difficult to identify in terms of the race of their speakers, but the voices are not stereotypical of dispossessed blacks. The final, most detailed account, is that of two families wiped out by an African National Congress (A.N.C.) bomb on the northern South African border—in other words, victims of liberation warfare. This gory story, told by an identified Mr. van Eck in "formal old-fashioned Afrikaans" and ending with "I sat for days . . . I simply sat . . . I lost my business. I am reduced to a poor white," has, it turns out, been previously represented. Reporting the request for a further soundbite, Krog tells of her instruction to a colleague to "send the one about where he was just sit-ting and remember to add that the newspapers of that day said that pieces of his son's hair and eyes were found in a tree near the bakkie [pickup]."[5] Such re-presentation of texts, as I will later show, is precisely what seems to be required to produce a revision of ethnic identity. Significantly, these accounts of atroci-ties, originally reported on different occasions, are dispersed in Antjie Krog's moving book on the Commission, *Country of My Skull* (1998). But it is the particular meanings produced by the specific recycling for the *Guardian* read-ers that I wish to discuss.

Class has come to replace race: the text suggests an equivalence between the ordinary black cleaning woman and the once prosperous white man, and Van Eck's identification of himself as a poor white amounts to an effacement of whiteness with its dominant meaning of privilege. Indeed, the word takes us back to a deeper historical memory of British oppression of the Afrikaners in the nineteenth century that drove them into the laager, the circular defensive position of a collection of ox wagons that has become a metaphor for closed-mindedness. British oppression is historically responsible for Van Eck's very geo-graphical location on the northern border. Atrocity, memory, and grief are in the liberal-humanist idiom shown to be categories that cannot admit of racial differentiation since that would hamper the process of reconciliation. If the assertion of a white right to grief is overt, what is covert in the text where white-ness is disavowed is the conjugation of Afrikaner ethnicity with blackness. Hence the peculiar anchoring of the linguistic message of Afrikaner tears with the visual information of a crying black woman. At the intersection of image and text, a new meaning of self-other relations is produced.

RELATIONS OF ALTERITY

One of the less predictable phenomena to develop out of the scramble for Af-rica is the current scramble for alterity. There is still the native other, the object of ethnography, whose difference and inferiority has been established in colonial discourse, but there is also the psychoanalytic other, closely related to the postmodern crisis of reason. The fashionable anthropological turn in critical theory, as well as in contemporary artistic production or struggle in the name of the cultural or ethnic other, might be seen in this vein as an attempt to engage the first in defense against the nihilistic tendency of the second.[6] Otherness, then, comes to acquire a peculiar valency within metropolitan culture, peculiar, that is, from the point of view of the native, who can only be baffled by her new symbolic status. Hal Foster, outlining the pitfalls in the American artist-as-ethnographer paradigm, where alterity is seen as the "outside, . . . the Archimedean point from which the dominant culture will be transformed or at least subverted," discusses such assumption of otherness as problematic and offers a solution of self-reflexivity for the artist to protect herself against overidentification.[7] The notion of textual strategies for the management of identification is suggestive and informs my investigation of the ways in which, with the decline of apartheid, Afrikaner writing appeals to alterity in the process of redefining Afrikanerhood.

Nowhere is the scramble for alterity more prevalent than in postmodern theory itself, which, in its negation of Truth and Reason, continues to idealize the other. For instance, theorists like Deleuze and Guattari may reject the term, but their aestheticized discussion of the minoritarian, located within a metaphor of territory and linked with a process of becoming, deftly blends the colonial and the psychoanalytic other. Alterity is conceived as a process of growth that is not bound to territory, indeed is deterritorialized: "One reterritorializes, or allows oneself to be reterritorialized, on a minority as a state; but in a becoming, one is deterritorialized. Even Blacks, as the Black Panthers said, must become-black . . . if Jews themselves must become-Jewish, if women must become-woman, if children must become-child . . . it is because only a minority is capable of serving as the active medium of becoming."[8] The overarching metaphoric system of A *Thousand Plateaus* is that of the land and its mapping, a system that is continued underground where the dominant representative model of the tree and its vertical root is replaced by the horizontal rhizome with its multiple entryways. Since otherness is clearly not a desirable condition for actual minorities, nor for the politically colonized who actively struggle for territory itself, it would seem that such an idealized view is essentially an albocentric, metropolitan one. However, it is the case that South African literary representations of identity during the period of apartheid broadly correspond to the Deleuzian-Guattarian model of territorialization. Afrikaner writing rooted its identity in an aesthetics of the land, whereas black writing, characterized largely by a "becoming of blackness," was not concerned with the translation of geography into landscape—indeed, as Sipho Sepamla's poem states, "I have never had to say / this land is mine."[9] Since the demise of apartheid, however, Afrikaners, who have constituted themselves as minoritarian, have been representing in literary texts their "becoming," a process in which black-as-other is necessarily implicated.

The textual construction of Africa as other to Europe has been well charted, and the description of black-as-other enthusiastically embraced by black and white alike. For instance, much of black resistance to the term "postcolonial" centers around exclusive claim to alterity: there is no basis, it is popularly felt, for a term that posits equivalence between the black condition and that of white colonials. This view claims race as the only site of alterity, or where the other axes along which identity is constructed, such as class, gender, or ideological positioning in terms of center and periphery, are acknowledged, there would be insistence on the foregrounding of race. But without having to resort to Homi Bhabha's theories of hybridity and mimicry, the homology of white/black and self/other is clearly inadequate and simplistic. At the level of common sense, it disregards the fact that even when racism succeeds in undermining or estranging the black self, there remains a residue in which people cannot possibly think of themselves as other. Thus Othello's negative descriptions of himself attributed to his blackness—as in the following examples "for I am black / And have not those soft parts of conversation / That chamberers have" (III.3.261) or "Her name that was as fresh / As Dian's visage is now begrimed and black / As mine own face" (III.3.383)—are, for black readers, even as expressions of irrationality, not possible utterances, and especially not by someone of Othello's social status. Such perception of his otherness is an albocentric view of the black entirely refracted through white eyes, one that fails to appreciate the double-exposure effect of a subjectivity that is acutely aware of being the object of white focalization.

I want to dwell for a moment on the word "utterance" as distinct from "writing." Textuality has come to mean the written word, and thus we have focused on the ways in which blacks have been represented in ethnographic and literary texts. We tend to overlook the popular spoken texts of the disenfranchised that demonstrate the inalienable—if residual—existence of a self in their construction of whites as other, in popular discourse, in jokes, derogatory naming, and contemptuous informal accounts of their cultural practices. In South Africa, such oppositional identity was not shaped purely along the racial axis of black-white, but in ethnic terms, so that it was barbaric Afrikaner behavior that was mocked and against which blacks defined themselves. The common homology of white/black, self/other is then clearly inappropriate, since textual othering of the white oppressor is routinely practiced, allowing for slippage between the sets. Such practice may not in itself overturn the undeniable power of the oppressor; rather, it serves as necessary rehearsal toward insurrection. Thus the oppressed cannot fully embrace a postmodern theory of decenteredness and loss of subjectivity as they cling, if periodically so, to the humanist notion of a core self that is essential to the very possibility of resistance. Such a sense of self readjusts and redefines itself in relation to different self-other dyads when a goal like the overthrow of apartheid is achieved. Identity, being something always in process, constitutes a constant realignment of intra-affiliations among ethnicity, class, and gender, as well as perspectival shunting between self and other. While there is a level on which blacks cannot see whites as having given up any power in South Africa, there being no material evidence of the latter having done so, there is nevertheless a sense in which white/black, self/other relations are manifestly in flux.

When black South Africans in the 1980s reinflected the word "Boer" (farmer) to signify something distasteful, they succeeded in making Afrikaners accept the revised meaning to the extent that the majority now disowns the name. In spite of the fact that "Boer," in accordance with Afrikaner power, was a name proudly chosen by themselves to signal their connection with the land, the word had become infected with black distaste, which culminated in the Pan Africanist Congress's chant of "Kill the farmer, kill the Boer," so that Afrikaners have abandoned what they now feel to be a racist term.[10] Since the balance of power in the New South Africa is shifting, it is perhaps not surprising that Afrikaners should assume the condition of otherness. I examine this assumption of otherness in relation to textual representations of the land, precisely because of the geographical origins of their name, and the traditional self-definition of the Boers as white in relation to the land.

AFRIKANER GEOGRAPHY AND THE LAND

Literary representations of the land have typically relied on the ideologies of nature and space, given categories with which humans interact or which somehow reflect society. Contemporary critical geography dismisses this model as one that separates social and physical space; however, as Neil Smith suggests in *Uneven Development* (1984), both nature and space are in fact produced by humans, enabling geography to demonstrate rather than simply assert the unity of space and society.[11] Those of us who would otherwise have been lost in high theory's cultural critique of spatiality—Jameson's spatial model of culture, Soja's postmodern geographies, or Foucault's cartography of power—found ready understanding in apartheid's crude commodification of space, the geographical division driven by economic exploitation. The "homeland" was a construct of ethnic groups that belonged "naturally" in particular undeveloped, arid, and scattered fragments of land, an improbable mapping of alterity that both included and excluded it from the South African republic according to the use value of its people. Its deployment of the ideologies of nature and space to boost unequal economic development is a clear example of how geographical space was produced and hierarchized during the apartheid era.

In accordance with the project of domination, the South African land was idealized and considered by settlers to underpin history. One of the educational staples of the apartheid years, Gie's 1942 *Geskiedenis van Suid Afrika* (History of South Africa) has a geographical appendix of some twenty pages, "The Geographical Foundations of Our History," by Dr. P. Serton, its title asserting the determining role of immutable nature in historical developments. In preparation for the National Party's establishment of apartheid in 1948, Serton offers the following bizarre physical description: "South Africa clearly forms an independent geographical unit, isolated by nature from other connected territory. Not only is the land surrounded by oceans on three sides, but in the fourth direction, to the north, it borders on tropical regions which are unhealthy for the white man and which in the past constituted a more effective line of separation than the broadest water expanse."[12] Thus the South African (is)land is produced, textually severed from the African continent by the white subject who identifies the borders of his territory from within the imagined space. The albocentric logic that constructs the southern part of the continent as a separate landmass on the basis that it accommodates the white constitution is also an appeal to nature to legitimize an occupation of South Africa. But anxiety about such legitimacy finds expression in fears of desertification. Serton refers to popular contemporary theories of diminishing rainfall that would show that "the white man would have settled in a land sentenced to death," before summarily dismissing such fears. He quotes the Drought Investigation Commission of 1922: "No proof of significant changes in the average annual rainfall of the Union in recent historical times has been delivered, and such change is considered to be unlikely."[13] Serton nevertheless comments on the problems of diminishing water supply as follows: "Rivers become more irregular in their flow and the veld becomes drier in many regions, whilst a great number of fountains have disappeared. These phenomena can however be fully explained by human influences. There is no need here to think of climactic change."[14]

The language of these extracts is remarkable for its expression of anxiety. Given the fact of diminishing water, the Commission not surprisingly adopts the passive voice to diminish responsibility for its assurances against desertification. In the legal metaphor of a death sentence, Serton betrays his awareness of transgression, although the settlers are metonymically displaced by the land itself, the land on which the sentence is pronounced. We are invited to infer that God, arbiter of divine justice, will not turn against the settler; indeed, the occupation of the land is sanctioned so that actual instances of water scarcity are irrationally attributed to unexplained human activity. What is, of course, suppressed in this geographical text is the Natives Land Act of 1913, by which black people, deprived of their ownership, were pauperized and forced into the cities in search of labor.

The geographer's anxiety about the land's refusal to support white settlers is also to be found in Afrikaans-language literature, especially from the 1920s to the 40s, in the genre of the *plaasroman* (farm novel) and other narratives about the farm, in which drought produces crises that are not only geographical but also moral. Here we find that land and nature are socialized into the farm; there is no romantic celebration of nature that is not embedded in the ontological concerns of a "boer" (farmer) who tills the land that yields or withholds according to the blessing or curse of God. In the conversion of land into farm, nature into culture, the homologous relationship with other and self is developed so that, apart from the land's commodification, the natural claim of the savage native is effectively countered. Awareness of such claim was, however, repressed as the early colonizers, both Boer and English, apparently encountered vast tracts of empty land that invited occupation, a construction of space that failed to include the presence of indigenous people. Such human absence allowed nature to represent freedom: expansion into the interior was after all a product of the Afrikaners' love of liberty, as they trekked away from the disciplinary social space of the Dutch colonial authority, and later from the liberal ideology of British imperialism (most especially after the emancipation of slaves throughout the empire).[15] Since they could not claim autochthony, the settlers adopted the myth of the Israelites, who, after trials and tribulations abroad, reached the homeland assigned to them by God. This they tilled and developed as farm, thus establishing an ethnic identity that relied on a slippage between nature and culture.

For C. J. Langenhoven (1873–1932), author of the old national anthem, "Die Stem van Suid-Afrika" (The Voice—or Call—of South Africa), such slippage is deployed in the description of a land voicing its geography—out of the heavens, the depths of the sea, the eternal mountains, the far-flung empty plains—that merges with human echoes and the groan of Boer ox wagons. The voice of the anthropomorphized land rises through a series of parallel prepositional phrases to articulate the relationship between demanding nature and Afrikaner culture in terms of a fulsome patriotism. The poem ends in a plea to God that "the farms of our fathers remain the farms of our children," in order that they may be free against the whole world.[16] The word "erwe," which I have loosely translated as farms, is in fact ambiguous, meaning both legacy and land. Edward Said's characterization of the shift from premodern biological filiation to modernity's affiliative mode (the passage from nature to culture) here finds an example as genealogy is set in the service of timeless land or farm. Thus the filiative comes to be represented in the larger social structure of the nation.[17]

Langenhoven's most anthologized poem is a diptych called "Die Onteiening" (The Disownment—by nature, according to his footnote), which deals with drought and destruction of a farm that is mirrored—formally, stylistically, and in terms of the narrative—by an account of rainfall and regeneration, except that the voice of the farmer in the second poem turns out, only in the last line (and in italics), to be a replacement of the first owner.[18] While it is not within the scope of this essay to consider the intimations of a split Boer subjectivity, the implied self/other slippage performed by the mirror figures of retribution and blessing is suggestive. The speaker's belated acknowledgment of the replaced farmer in the line "it's other voices that I hear," hints at a repression of the (disowned) other within the self, a voice that, to the excluded black South African, has always rendered into falsetto the loudly sung land.

LANGUAGE AND AFRIKANERHOOD

It is precisely this racialized geographical space that must be invoked and reinscribed in order to produce a revised non-Boer identity. In "Cry, Beloved Country," the *Guardian* text to which I referred earlier (later included in her *Country of My Skull*), Antjie Krog, after her account of Van Eck's horrific loss, reports her own anguished escape from the studio to look out on to the veld: "My eyes claw at the trees, the *kloofs* . . . see, smell . . . a landscape of paradise and a language from paradise: *mispel, maroela, tarentaal*, I whisper. The air is drowsy with jasmine and kamferolie. I sit down on the steps and everything tears out of me."[19] The response is a personal one, but it is also, in its references to landscape and to the communality of language, as Afrikaner, with a particular time-honored relationship with the land as paradise, that Krog reacts to the horror stories. The naming of flora and fauna invokes an Adamic correspondence between things in the world and language that is unmediated by ideology. Thus her breakdown is signaled by a breakdown of language, placing the Afrikaner's humanist response in the realm of nature. The italicized difference encodes the struggle within South Africa's binary definition of whiteness as English versus Afrikaans; it asserts Afrikaner identity, the untranslatability of the land into English, to turn "kamferolie" into oil of camphor. The sensuousness of Krog's Africa departs from Afrikaner Calvinism, and "tarentaal," or guinea fowl, carries a particular significance for such revision. In the iconography of an informal and popular antiapartheid movement of dissident, urban, mainly English-speaking whites in the 1980s, this bird assumed a central place. Its ubiquitous image dominated design from expensive craft shops to open-air clothing markets; as design icon it signified liberation, and the very speckled black-and-white pattern of the bird's plumage came to represent an alternative to whiteness, a new multiracialism that chose to embrace indigenous blackness. In other words, it became an image of desire. In this text, the iconicity is appropriated from that alternative whiteness to forge a link through suffering and victim status between black and Afrikaner. Overloaded as the icon has become, it must also carry the mechanism by which the well-known "language of the oppressor" can be translated into a "language from paradise."

Thus the troubled history of the Afrikaans language comes full circle. Early white rejection of it as "kitchen language" ("kombuistaal"), followed by denial of its evolution as a creole of Dutch (developed initially by Indonesian, Mozambican, and Malagasy slaves), and the subsequent nurturing of a white variety of long-voweled "beskaafde" (civilized) Afrikaans, enters yet another phase of rehabilitation. During the liberation struggle, the spoken variety of diglossic, nonstandard Afrikaans, known as Kaaps, with its typical code-switching into English, was valorized as a literary language.[20] Postapartheid white translation of Afrikaans from its oppressor status has taken a similar course. The nonstandard, urban, spoken variety previously associated with coloured or poor-white speakers is used in much recent writing, especially by women, which deflects the language from the old, discredited Boer identity.[21] Narratives from the late 1980s onward, whether in standard or nonstandard dialects, are crucially concerned with a laundered Afrikaner ethnicity, its whiteness effaced through an association with blackness.

Krog's naming of fauna and flora alludes to Genesis, to a desire for the prelapsarian, with an Adamic language that proposes a simple correspondence between things in the world and language, a desire that at the same time invokes the old "homegrown Calvinist myth in which the Afrikaner has his type in the Israelite, tender of flocks, seeker after a promised national homeland, member of an elect race (*volk*) set apart from the tribes of the idolatrous, living by simple and not-to-be-questioned commandments, afflicted by an inscrutable Godhead with trials whose purpose is to test his faith and his fitness for election."[22] Not only must the subject formation of a New Afrikaner necessarily scavenge from previous liberal discourses, it must also invoke such old myths and translate them into a new discourse of conciliation.

EFFACING WHITENESS

Let me return to my initial question: why is a report about Afrikaner response to the horrors of apartheid and the inscription of (male) Afrikaner as victim accompanied by a large photograph of a crying black woman? Contemporary theorizing about whiteness would seem to have an answer: that white is an empty signifier, both everything and nothing, that being invisible to itself it cannot acknowledge its existence, that it can only articulate itself in terms of the markedness of black, the contrast that supplies the meaning of white as the norm.[23] Its avowed transparency, its refusal to acknowledge itself as an examinable category, at the same time asserts the unthinkability of itself as object, or as other. As my earlier metaphor of focalization would suggest, black-as-other is a white narration of the marked category of blackness; whiteness, as a given, masks its existence, and therefore also cannot be seen as the subject of a narrative, not least because focalization through an other has been unthinkable.

Richard Dyer gives the following revealing account of a British experimental video that sets out to investigate whiteness as an ethnic category: "In an attempt to get some white people to explore what being white means, the video assembles a group to talk about it and it is here that the problem of white people's inability to see whiteness appears intractable. Subcategories of whiteness (Irishness, Jewishness, Britishness) take over, so that the particularity of whiteness itself begins to disappear."[24] Such denial was, of course, not the case in South Africa. The white minority in South Africa instead unashamedly celebrated and claimed privileges on the basis of their whiteness—with its varied history of self-representation, related to particular historical stages of the political program. In the establishment of apartheid in the 1940s, far from presenting itself as invisible, codification of whiteness as cultural and political dominance became necessary in the face of being outnumbered by blacks. Application to be classified as white, for instance, demanded an explicit set of criteria, including the infamous pencil-in-the-hair test. At this stage, too, the colonial terms "European" and "native," inappropriate for the new project, came to be replaced by "white" and "nonwhite," as whiteness assumed native status in the promised homeland. Thus came the invention of a privileged white "race," which ensured political and demographic domination by constructing various black "ethnic" groups that could be forcibly moved into far-from-paradisiac homelands. That a subgroup identified itself as "English," regardless of the fact that it was constituted primarily of Scottish and Irish settlers, as well as various Western European nationals and Eastern European Jews, was a response, based on preferred language, to the aggressive assertion of whiteness by Afrikaners who insisted on a separate ethnic and linguistic identity bound up with a special association with the land.

In his introduction to *White Writing: On the Culture of Letters in South Africa*, J. M. Coetzee offers a definition of the category "white." He explains his title, which refers to the post-1948 neocolonial period, in the following historical terms: "The phrase white writing [does not] imply the existence of a body of writing different in nature from black writing. White writing is white only insofar as it is generated by the concerns of people no longer European, not yet African."[25] In other words, Coetzee overturns the European paradigm by giving whiteness a marked meaning, the name for something incomplete, not fully adapted to its environment, something in transition, a meaning of in-betweenness caught in a process of acculturation, the presupposition being that whiteness must inevitably be absorbed into Africa. Coetzee's whiteness, far from being the transparent, irreducible category of Europe, is subjected to history and thus anticipates Krog's translation. Her news article, at the intersection of image and text, engenders a new meaning of Afrikaner that is slipped under the signification of capacious black woman.

ETHNICITY TRANSLATED THROUGH THE PLAASROMAN

In *White Writing*, Coetzee points out how the master of the plaasroman genre, C. M. van den Heever, "broadly came to integrate nature into the farm, that is to relate certain romantic commonplaces about the recovery of man's truth in nature to the thesis that the Afrikaner will lose his independence and (eventually) his identity if he loses his base in landownership."[26] It is this relationship between truth and the land that is being unraveled in postapartheid writing. Until recently, it was dissident writers in English who rewrote the genre: Coetzee's own *In the Heart of the Country* (1977) is a revision that explores elements repressed in the plaasroman, and Gordimer in *The Conservationist* (1974) offers a farm on which the corpse of a black man, buried in a shallow grave, resurfaces to challenge Afrikaner construction and appropriation of the land. Now, however, a trend in contemporary Afrikaans writing itself, concerned with re-presenting the land, is discernible. In this section I consider the ways in which influential texts by Etienne van Heerden, Marlene van Niekerk, Antjie Krog, and Chris Barnard investigate and rehabilitate Afrikaner identity through renegotiation of the traditional affiliation with the land and particularly through the redeployment of the plaasroman's old tropes of drought and water. Read within the political context of the Truth Commission and the postapartheid program of land redistribution and restitution, these texts would appear to clarify the meaning of a new non-Boer identity in terms of revised relations of alterity between white and black.

Textual construction of ethnicity is traditionally bound up with a narrative of genealogy, and the plaasroman's generic treatment of the family, those responsible for improving and developing the farm and so legitimizing its occupation, is characteristically concerned with filiative Afrikaner identity that is established through successive generations. Etienne van Heerden's acclaimed novel *Toorberg* (1986), translated as *Ancestral Voices* (1989, 1993), stages its events under the sign of Babel and around the proper name of the Afrikaner family. The novel starts with a diagram of the Moolman family tree that crosses over traditional racial lines to reveal the branch of their coloured relatives, known as the "skaamfamilie" (family of shame, the illegitimate relations). The Moolmans occupy a farm called Toorberg, and their coloured relations live on an adjacent arid territory called, according to the family paradigm, the Step-veld, a spatial division that allegorizes apartheid's geography. The original Afrikaans title (literally translated as Bewitched Mountain) is also the name of the mountain that towers over the farm, from which flows the coveted commodity of water fountains, which for the current generation has dried up, the drought serving as central symbol for the demise of a corrupt culture. The word "toor" derives from the Afrikaans verb "tower," which means to bewitch or enchant; "tower" is homonymously related to the English noun "tower," which in turn is symbolically related to "mountain." It is on the Toor Mountain that the Malay magician, a slave descendant, is consulted by generations of Abel Moolmans, and babbles his prophesies.

The prosperous farm is also a Babel in the sense that the Afrikaner family sets out to make a name for itself, a totalizing project that cannot, according to the narrative, be completed. Derrida's commentary on the story of Babel as a central figure of deconstruction is suggestive for this story of apartheid: Babel as trope for the built-in entropy of apartheid with its attempts at a totalizing construction, at giving both whiteness and blackness proper-noun status, and at replete translation of the indigenous culture. Babel, the name of the tower that means both confusion and God the Father, as Derrida points out, is not translated and occupies a status of both common and proper noun: "Translation then becomes necessary and impossible, like the effect of a struggle for the appropriation of the name, necessary and forbidden in the interval between two absolutely proper names."[27] *Ancestral Voices* tells of the Moolmans' vain attempts to re-place the natural mountain source of water with boreholes drilled into the earth. Thus Van Heerden replaces horizontal penetration into the interior (by which the Boer freely acquired land in the past) with verticality. The punctur-ing of the land recasts the plaasroman's conversion of nature into culture as delegitimation, a process that triggers a deconstruction of the entire series of culture/nature, self/other, and white/black homologies. Thus the narrative traces the demise of the Afrikaner, whose only form of survival is through melaniza-tion, in other words through assuming the condition of otherness.

The novel's intertextuality includes references to Sarah Gertrude Millin's *God's Stepchildren* (1924), a key text in the culture's myths about miscegenation and racial purity. The skaamfamilie is descended not only from Afrikaners, but also a Millinesque British missionary. The coloured Andries Moolman has in disgust spent his hard-earned savings to have his name changed to Riet, a ges-ture of disaffiliation that anticipates his son's commitment to the black revolu-tionary movement. It is a complex translation—from the Afrikaner name Moolman to Read, the name of his white missionary ancestor, and then indi-genized to Riet, an Afrikanerization of the English name, significantly inscrib-ing its hybridity in the coloured mother tongue of nonstandard Afrikaans. The new name Riet is at the same time an assumption of agency that undermines self-other relations as oppositional, and constitutes the first chiasmic move in a refiguration of the racial homology: the coloured subject can no longer be viewed as purely other as he attempts to throw off an identity of shame that is focalized through the Moolmans. Indeed, the act shows the naming of the skaamfamilie to be white displacement of shame. Coloured subjectivity is also inscribed in terms of location: the Riets move between the contemporary shack in the Step-veld and the mountain cave with its historical Bushman paintings and the skeleton of their Bushman ancestor. Horizontal space, in other words, is crossed with the verticality of time. Their implied identity as Cain, adversary of the patriarchal *Abel* Moolman, replicates stereotypical portrayal of the co-loured condition as marked, but it also constitutes a revision of the old Afrikaner-Israelite myth of exclusivity, for an actual physical mark of sterility is borne by both white and black members of the family. Thus Van Heerden seeks to in-state new affiliations that are not a re-presentation of the old filiative order.

Ancestral Voices offers an allegorical account of the hubristic story of apart-heid: the arrogant occupation of the land by generations of Abel Moolmans and the subsequent disappearance of the water without which the farm cannot any longer be paradise. Afrikaners have, through overweening pride, megalomania, and greed, forfeited the inheritance of the land, while their coloured shame family has turned against them to support black revolutionaries. The Moolmans' majoritarian intolerance of gentleness and dreaminess, their prejudice against blacks, Catholics, and English, result in an inbreeding that produces madness. Thus at the geographical margins of their estate are those they have cast out: the coloured, the poor-white, and the mad relations, all of whom are excluded from the dominant definition of Afrikaner. The family is avenged when the last of the patriarchs uses water diviners and a grand machine to drill a waterhole that drives his ancestors out of their graves. Van Heerden also deploys an idiot figure, a generic character in the plaasroman, where he "represent(s) a way of living wholly at one with the natural world."[28] In this case, however, Abel's subnormal grandchild, named both Noah (denoting flood) and Trickle (denoting drought), serves as deconstructive agent. Noah/Trickle falls into one of the boreholes and is, with the consent of the entire family, both coloured and white, shot by Abel, who himself dies during the investigation of the child's death. The gift of water divining borne by Noah (yet another figuration of the vertical or subterranean as site of transformation) was the last hope of breaking the drought. Modernism's romantic idiot-other deployed by the plaasroman to access Truth is here replaced by a racialized postcolonial alterity: the remaining son, Cross-Abel, is sterile, and the inheritance of the land as well as the perpetuation of the family lies in the prospective union of one of the poor-white Moolmans with his coloured second cousin, Kitty Riet, a melanization of the Afrikaner through indigenous black blood.

Significantly, the stories of the family, told in the voices of both the living and the dead, coloured and white, are in response to a judicial inquiry into the death of Noah/Trickle. But the magistrate can come to no conclusion: the investigation is belated, a full year after the dream-child's death; the stories refuse to translate into a coherent, transparent picture of the events of the past. As the ghost of OldAbel predicts: "You haven't got the guts to pronounce sentence on the sons of Abel," and it seems as if the one-armed magistrate, Abraham van der Ligt (of the Light), is himself an incarnation of one of the dead Moolmans.[29] He does not, in the end, produce a judgment; instead, things sort themselves out, or rather nature does, in the death of the current Abel. It is thus through an inclusive narrative, the Babelesque allegory that deconstructs an exclusive Afrikanerhood into its suppressed meanings (the poor-white relations, the coloured shame family, the self-extermination—or, in Derrida's terms, the "multiplicity of idioms"), that the old link between land and Afrikaner lineage is severed. But with it goes historicity: the story of the past cannot be reconstructed; the postmodern otherness that is being embraced denounces the old grand narratives of truth and justice.

The narrative of *Ancestral Voices*, framed as a judicial inquiry, prefigures the Truth and Reconciliation Commission, although its judgment asserts the need to draw a veil over the past. Not only is the truth irrecoverable, not only are the coloureds both wronged blood relations and accomplices in the crime, not only can there be no outcome, but an insistence on Truth and Justice would amount to something vulgar, a failure to appreciate the equivocal. In "Cry, Beloved Country," Antjie Krog also speaks of the crassness of Truth, the need for its deconstruction: "I hesitate at the word . . . I am not used to using the word . . . I prefer the word lie. . . . Because it is there that the truth lies closest."[30] The focus in *Ancestral Voices* is not surprisingly then on reconciliation: "I am quite sure . . . that your laws will have nothing at all to say about mercy," says the sensible Amy, last of the grand Moolmans, and the magistrate concludes that "perhaps it is forgiveness, and not the chill, focused jet of judgement and sentence, that is the clearest water of all."[31] Thus the refiguration of the Afrikaner as one who investigates his crimes, who acknowledges his coloured offspring, and sheds his arrogant whiteness is staged in the historical context of the inevitable demise of apartheid, and the future democratic elections in which the Afrikaner's hope of political survival would be the coloured vote.

While Van Heerden's narrative of genealogy traces the decline of whiteness through madness and melanization, genealogy is deployed in radically different ways by Marlene van Niekerk, whose representation of Afrikaners self-consciously refuses identification or any trading with black-as-other. *Triomf* (1994; literally, Triumph), the title of her award-winning novel (translated into English under the same title in 1999), is the actual name of a white suburb, previously the site of Sophiatown, from which black people had been forcibly removed. In this unflinching account, written in a scatological nonstandard urban variety of Afrikaans, the hallowed rural family and the romantic idiot figure of the plaasroman are replaced by the suburban horror of working-class Mol, her brothers (who sexually abuse her), and Lambert, their crazy incestuous offspring, who continues the abuse. Focalized through Mol, it is a sympathetic representation of the dystopic "family," two generations removed from farming the land. Simultaneously, the novel parodies the writing of ethnic identity through genealogy. The neighbors, a lesbian couple (who have not reproduced themselves), of whom the family is surprisingly tolerant, support the negative genealogy. Without the ameliorative presence of black characters, Van Niekerk's representation of Afrikaners disrupts the white/black, self/other homology; instead, alterity is explored from within the dominant meaning of Afrikaner, the Calvinistic self from which debased, landless "poor whites" have been excluded.

The "natural" white location of the farm is accordingly replaced with the social space produced by apartheid, the poor-white prefabricated houses, and again, as in the case of *Ancestral Voices*, verticality becomes a significant modality of space as Lambert obsessively excavates the yard to collect relics from the bull-dozed black homes that Mol contemptuously refers to as "kaffergemors" ("kaffir rubbish").[32]

In her 1992 collection of stories, *Die vrou wat haar verkyker vergeet het* (literally, The Woman Who Forgot Her Binoculars), Van Niekerk parodies reconstructed Afrikaners, the new dissident generation, who are shown to be marked by tension, neurosis, and ambivalence, in their assumption of otherness. "Kanonbaai" rewrites the traditional Afrikaans treatment of drought in the story of a water catastrophe. The eponymous Afrikaner holiday resort is flooded on New Year's Day, and even the knowledgeable coloured plumbers who are persuaded to help are unable to stem the flow. In Kaaps dialect they describe the catastrophe as the underground raging of a mad ostrich who should be left to wreak its full havoc so that the entire system might be repaired from scratch; once again, the underground serves as imagined site of transformation. Gustav, the artist, whom we first see in the act of piecing together an ancient Khoi ostrich shell once used for storing water, mediates between the coloureds and the unreconstructed older Afrikaners, who misread the presence of the plumbers as an act of submission and so expect them to take orders with humility. The ideological gap between old and young is described in terms of the child reproaching the father. Instead of immersing himself in political struggle for the sake of a better world, the child adopts, on the one hand, a position of "vrugtelose lots-verbonde opstand teen die vader en aan die ander kant in drome van 'n ontmoontlike paradys" (fruitless fate-bound rebellion against the father and, on the other hand, dreams of an impossible paradise).[33] Thus the genealogical shift from filiation to affiliation is also cast as ambivalence; it would seem that transformation cannot occur within the context of reproduction and the family.

Van Niekerk's trope of water offers an allegory that departs significantly from Van Heerden's: the flood, unlike the drought, offers no opportunity for racial solidarity; indeed, it excludes the plumbers, who wash their hands of the problem. This paradise gone wrong is something Afrikaners have to deal with themselves; it is invoked as an expression of their neurosis and ambivalence, and attempts at identification with the other are shown to be so much posturing. The ostrich shell that Gustav hands over to the coloured plumbers is an act of self-mockery as he invents a history of enslaved Khoikhoi forced to produce water from a treadmill for the settlers, thus showing the gesture to be one of post-modern nostalgia. The paradise that Van Niekerk so scornfully invokes is indeed a revision of the popular Afrikaner naming of the South African countryside, its history of violence ironically encoded in the name of Kanonbaai (Canon Bay) for a holiday resort. Paradise Mountain was what Van Heerden's FounderAbel at first thought of calling the farm he staked out for himself with the help of a "tame Bushman" and a coloured bondsman, that is, before the drying up of the fountain. The extraordinary naming of a largely arid land as paradise suggests an acknowledgment of the imaginary, mythologized view of the land as idealized space, an appeal to the prelapsarian and the nostalgia for precolonial innocence.[34]

THE LAND AND DESIRE

In "Cry, Beloved Country," Antjie Krog's language and landscape of paradise encode Afrikaner ambivalence, the desire for rebirth set against horrific accounts of apartheid atrocities. Krog is driven out of the recording studio to respond physically to the veld ("I whisper," "I sit down," "see, smell," "my eyes claw"). The image of evisceration—"everything tears out of me"—leaves the speaker as empty signifier, an Afrikaner without connotation and thus open to invasion by the dominant visual image of the black woman. This is surely what Krog's puzzling reference to a "process" of listening to witnesses relates to: a process of ethnic translation. This also goes some way toward explaining the extraordinary final paragraph in "Cry, Beloved Country," where her spirits are restored in a gesture of indulgence and ingestion: "When in despair, bake a cake . . . a bowl full of glistening colourful jewels soaking in brandy. I relish the velvet of 12 eggs, butter and sugar."[35] Marinating, mixing, and baking, as images of syncretic transformation, could be read as allegorical for writing the melanization of whiteness, but the luxurious excess of its ingredients also points to the unwieldiness of the trope in an unequal society. In this discursive struggle superordinate whiteness, with its connotations of gluttony and opulence, takes over so that Krog's attempt at then superimposing paucity on an image of excess—"I . . . eat small fragrant slices in the blinding blue Cape summer heat"—is doubly poignant in its symbolic attempt at recuperating, through ingestion, an Afrikanerhood revised through blackness-in-apposition, a translation of the white body into the marked category of blackness.

One of Krog's earlier poems, called "land," similarly invokes the white body in a relation of unbelonging to the land that in itself others the Afrikaner. Cast in the romantic tradition of a speaker's unrequited love, the land as indifferent lover is directly addressed. The poem starts with an acknowledgment of a history of inequity since the speaker's ancestors simply colonized or ordered its occupation, so that land at this stage also appears to be a metonymic displacement of native, a meaning we are forced to revise toward the end of the poem. However, in spite of her love and implied disaffiliation with her ancestors, the land (or native?) rejects her:

> but me you never wanted
> no matter how I stretched to lie down
> in rustling blue gums
>
> · · ·
>
> me you could never endure
> time and again you shook me off
> you rolled me out[.][36]

It is a syncretic vision gone sour. The rejection by this cruel lover robs the speaker of language and identity: "had I language I could write for you were land my land," which perhaps accounts for the peculiar syntax, and later she claims "I became nameless in my mouth," placing herself in the realm of the very nature that is indifferent to her desire. Desire, usually suppressed in self-other representations, is foregrounded by Krog in the dramatization of a lover who is other to the land. The land as subject-who-rejects here produces its object, an abject Afrikaner, othered by the land that she is now forced to relinquish.

However, the grammatical fronting of the object in "me you never wanted / me you could never endure" suggests an ambivalence in subject/object relations that replicates an ambivalence in the representation of time. The past is invoked in references to the named waters of "Diepvlei" that sustain cattle and to imported blue gum trees, in other words to land as cultivated farm. The present, in a final dystopic stanza, is described as commercially infected denaturalization where the land is "negotiated divided paddocked sold stolen mortgaged"—an undignified situation marked by typographic gaps of disbelief. It is "now . . . fought over," as opposed to its earlier (more genteel?) occupation. This is presumably a representation of the postapartheid program of redistribution and restitution of the land in which the wide natural space of Afrikaner mythology is about to be replaced by social space, sullied by financial transactions, while colonial occupation remains romantically inflected, without the vulgarity of struggle. The speaker is appalled by the land's current "unnatural" treatment, and the poem ends with the following:

> I want to go underground with you land
> land that would not have me
> land that never belonged to me
> land that I love more fruitlessly than before[.]

As in the case of the other texts, verticality is invoked here. The distinction between surface and underground heralds the end of a historical era, of the land's accommodating horizontality, as it retreats into its own depths. An obvious inference is that such a retreat is a protest both against Afrikaner occupation *and* against the new dispensation that goes against nature. One might well ask how going underground *with* the land could be accomplished, unless the connotation of revolution radically redefines land so that it simply can no longer be identified by its surface. The passive construction "now you are fought over" not only elides an agent (black?) but keeps land in the subject position; nature and space remain given; they most certainly are not, as critical geography would have it, produced.

All contemporary writing in South Africa is to some extent dystopic, even necessarily so, since the promises of a new order remain unfulfilled. Popular recoil from the epithet of the rainbow nation is not simply a response to the notion of nation, or an inability to attach such colorful syncretism to the chaotic aftermath of apartheid, but also evidences ambivalence toward relations of alterity. Krog's poem disrupts the old homological relations insofar as the unmentioned black struggle for ownership of the land allows the farm of the past to slip back into nature. Thus mutable land, or nature, prevents the native from usurping its subjectivity, and so it retains dominance over humans, an authority that the new mute and humbled Afrikaner abjectly acknowledges.

MELANIZATION AND SUBJECTIVITY IN CHRIS BARNARD'S *MOERLAND*

On the face of it, Barnard's project in his 1992 novel *Moerland* ("Motherland," or in the demotic sense, "Fucked-up Land") appears to offer, via the emotive question of language, a direct revision of Afrikaner identity as white. In that narrative an Afrikaner patriarch who had trekked to Angola to escape British imperialism gives his daughter to a native in exchange for land. He returns to South Africa, while the deserted daughter remains to raise her impoverished black child and grandchild as Afrikaners. Barnard then introduces a new ethnic category: Lukas van Niekerk, the grandchild, is a Black Afrikaner, suckled by his Afrikaner grandmother and raised on Afrikaans literature. When he escapes to South Africa during the Angolan war of independence, he is surprised to find himself unacceptable to Afrikaners, and so, spitting out "Africa's white nipple," translates himself into a black revolutionary with the new name of Sipho Mbokani.[37] Here disaffiliation from the land does not revise the tropes of the plaasroman; instead, the black stereotype of large-breasted Mama Afrika is invoked to include and at the same time reject whiteness. The investigating journalist, the narrator whose research on the role of standard Afrikaans in the postapartheid era frames the narrative, recognizes Lukas's speech as a white variety, "a flawless Afrikaans without any accent."[38] Barnard's exploration of Afrikaner identity based on inaccurate folk beliefs about language such as speech without accent, lack of variation according to class (as if there were no such difference among Afrikaners), and lack of influence from other languages where Afrikaans is spoken outside its speech community, finds its motivation in the desire to redefine Afrikaner to include blacks acculturated via the language and the improbable Afrikaner canonical texts that Lukas inherits from his poorly educated grandmother. Crude racism prevents this anachronistic story of Lukas's albescence from developing; instead, inclusiveness is achieved through melanization of the Afrikaner.

Afrikaners, the novel declares, can no longer be considered in opposition to black—indeed, as the frontispiece map of Africa with its inset of Angola suggests, it is a process of Africanization that defines them. Barnard's journalist-protagonist responds angrily to an Englishman who calls him Dutch: "If you have to call us anything call us half-castes [*sic*], but we're no more Dutch than you are . . . we're of mixed descent. We have Dutch forefathers, yes, but we also have French blood, German blood, Malay, Khoi, Portuguese, even English blood. . . . After ten generations in Africa we can hardly call ourselves a bunch of Europeans. . . . The name Afrikaner refers to a language rather than a continent."[39] Fear of relinquishing whiteness is expressed through the far Right, to whom the journalist's son is affiliated. The boy argues with his father for an Afrikaner homeland:

> "It's we Afrikaners who have tamed and broken in this land. Now, everything, you want us to just . . ."
> "And the English, and the Jews, and the Portuguese, and Greeks and Germans and Dutch and . . ."
> "Yes O.K. They too. But they all have countries to return to. All except us. If we can't get a little piece of the land for ourselves, Pa. . . . We are three million. What will happen to us amongst thirty million black people under a Marxist government?"[40]

Within the apparent dissolution of whiteness we find, however, that subject/object relations remain the same. Black can become Afrikaner through white agency, through the speech act of a white grandmother, or the journalist's acceptance of Lukas as Afrikaner via his competence in the standard variety of the language. Not surprisingly, then, the journalist's voice of reconciliation acknowledges only white contribution to South Africa, to the development of the land from nature to culture—hardly an invitation to partnership. And not surprisingly, his syncretic vision of Afrikaner as mixed race, of negating his whiteness, has its origins in the terrifying demography expressed here by the far Right. In this narrative there is no figuration of verticality; the underground is the conventional "revolutionary" space into which the son, as member of the right-wing movement, disappears, and disaffiliates from the liberal father in order to engage in the struggle for (horizontal) land. Strangely, the category of other is not applied to the far Right; it is instead the liberal who assumes otherness through association with the black.

CONCLUSION

Like any other diverse ethnic group, Afrikaners, while crucially concerned with a process of detoxification, rewrite themselves in a variety of ways, but what is noteworthy is the common redeployment of geographical tropes in the works discussed above. While these texts do characterize deterritorialization, they depart significantly from Deleuze and Guattari's celebration of the horizontal in the figure of the rhizome, their emblem of becoming. The revised Afrikaner self is staged before a backcloth renovated from the old picturesque, horizontal surface of landscape to the land in cross section, thus revealing an underground significant for its association with revised self/other, white/black, culture/nature homologies.

The practice of conjugating a New Afrikaner ethnicity with the ready-made category of black-as-other is, of course, not a felicitous one from a black point of view that would question the validity of the very category. Neither does the scramble for alterity guarantee rehabilitation of Afrikaner identity. Van Niekerk's *Triomf* would seem to be successful precisely for releasing a suppressed alterity from within the old Calvinistic image of buttoned-up Boer respectability. More importantly, it avoids overidentification with blackness by keeping black characters on the very margins of the narrative as a category over which the poor white can crow. If *Triomf*, through its brutalized poor whites or the madness of Lambert, rewrites Afrikaner as other, such alterity hardly represents that which has the capacity to transform the dominant culture, however. Filiation as the foundation of identity has imploded in the perverse incestuous family, and the possibility of transformation would seem to lie instead in the novel's figuration of the excavated hole, or verticality, as an affiliative appeal to memory and history. Mol's reference to the remains of black homes constitutes a humorous Boer version of history, but Lambert's excavations do uncover the material past of Sophiatown that makes for transformed social and neighborly relations—even if such a past gets covered over all too quickly under the new dispensation.

The peculiar coincidence of verticality can, of course, not be explained in terms of a single meaning. It seems to appeal to the humanistic depth model linked to modernity's faith in knowledge, truth, and transformation with which to revise the horizontality of colonial occupation and its apartheid connotations of surface, lies, and aridity. It invokes Edward Said's shift from filiation or biological continuity (horizontal) to social affiliation (vertical) and its implied revision of nature/culture relations. The subterranean then does present itself as site of "becoming," which, according to the texts examined above, is also bound up with the destabilization of the old homologies. In addition, the rewriting of Afrikanerhood seems to support Homi Bhabha's argument against orthodox representations of the horizontal spatiality of the modern nation (and for that matter against Jameson's postmodern cognitive mapping that focuses exclusively on space). Nationness, Bhabha argues, as a form of social and textual affiliation, requires also a temporality of representation: "The secular language of interpretation needs to go beyond the horizontal critical gaze if we are to give 'the nonconsequential energy of lived historical memory and subjectivity' its appropriate narrative authority. We need another time of *writing* that will be able to inscribe the ambivalent and chiasmatic intersections of time and place that constitute the problematic 'modern' experience of the Western nation."[41]

Afrikaner texts that are overtly concerned with memory and history indeed seem to replace the old dynastic filiation with geographical verticality that, as a new figuration of the land, crosses over between the spatial and the temporal. Thus we have—although with varying degrees of commitment—a reconceptualization of Afrikaner relations with the land as secular and nondynastic. That this is done in the interest of survival and is marked by ambivalence is not so remarkable. What is remarkable is that whiteness itself is being narrated, that not only do these narratives question the validity of the category and imply the liminality of white nationhood, but that narration itself is focalized through other marked categories such as the black-white Lukas, the disaffiliated "shame family," or the abused poor-white woman.

To return to my opening remarks about South Africans clinging to old racial identifications: what contemporary writing engages with is a new meaningfulness of racial tags, a probing of identifications that it would be dishonest to disown in a society riddled with inequities, ones that can be divested of received meanings and can be negotiated afresh. Ethnicity, as every schoolgirl knows, is agonistically produced; we use it in our struggles of self-assertion; we abandon it only when it becomes in our interests to do so. Commitment to the demise of apartheid does not mean an abandonment of ethnic tags, but it does—according to the texts discussed here—require a disaffiliation from whiteness. For the majority of black people whose material conditions have not changed significantly in the New South Africa, racial identity, although renegotiated, remains the platform from which the fight for equality will be staged. While, as Krog so poignantly points out in *Country of my Skull*, Afrikaner has become a disgraced category, and the struggle for rehabilitation crucially implicates the other, older binary opposition, relations with Englishness. And while English, in fact, assumes de facto national language status, that space of cultural and linguistic capital is one where whiteness is likely to skulk in silence and anonymity. But then textuality is, of course, not the whole story. In the world beyond texts where whiteness remains bound up with privilege and economic power, it cannot simply be written off, not least because those who ought to benefit most from its demise are unable to read of such well-meaning resolutions to the narrative of apartheid.

10

J. M. COETZEE'S *DISGRACE*: TRANSLATIONS IN THE YARD OF AFRICA (2002)

In his account of the style in which Pauline Smith represents Afrikaners, her "faux-naïf translation" or transfer from Afrikaans to English, J. M. Coetzee identifies the grammatical error of aspect as evidence that there is no actual Afrikaans original behind the archaic-sounding, ethnicized English: "No one speaking his own language makes errors of aspect: the time-system of the verb is too fundamental to language, and therefore to conceptualization, for that to happen."[1] Two issues in this position relate to my argument about Coetzee's celebrated 1999 novel, *Disgrace*, as a text that struggles with translation as concept-metaphor for the postapartheid condition. Firstly, there is the question of an original language Coetzee expects to find behind the English "translation" that claims to retain its trace. Secondly, I will address the grammatical aspect of the perfective not only in how it preoccupies David Lurie, the novel's central character, but also, in terms of cultural translation, for its marking of arrival at the target language/culture. In the following examination of the ways in which cultural translation is figured in the text, I also consider the relationship between translation and what has been called the period of transition in South Africa.

Translation is widely used as metaphor for the postcolonial condition, another example of theory's turn to the linguistic in order to engage with subjectivity; however, before testing the correspondences between vehicle and tenor, I want to start by looking at some of the postulates of interlingual translation. Taking their cue from poststructuralist theory, translationists question the old common-sense notions of fluency, fidelity to the source text, equivalence between languages, and the illusion of transparency; they also consider the power relations at play between languages. Walter Benjamin's idea of a residue of the source text retained in translation or Derrida's double bind of a text being both translatable and untranslatable—these have readily lent themselves to theorizing postcolonial identity, in particular that of the migrant. But contemporary practice also foregrounds the notion of an original text as questionable. Andrew Benjamin, in his investigation of Freud's definition of repression as "a failure of translation," concludes that there is no such thing as an "original event": the event of translation is always already at work within translation.[2] Venuti, in describing his own practice as both reproducing and supplementing the text, claims that his "interpretive translation exceeds the foreign-language text, supplementing it with research that indicates its contradictory origins and thereby puts into question its status as the original, the perfect and self-consistent expression of authorial meaning of which the translation is always the copy." [3] An "abusive fidelity" aims at freeing reader and translator from "the cultural constraints that ordinarily govern their reading and writing and threaten to overpower and domesticate the foreign text, annihilating its foreignness."[4] And from the retention of a foreignness in English-language translation, Venuti makes an inferential leap to describing his practice as a dissident cultural politics.

Homi Bhabha employs the translation metaphor specifically in terms of migration: "The liminality of migrant experience is no less a transitional phenomenon than a translational one; there is no resolution to it because the two conditions are ambivalently enjoined in the 'survival' of migrant life."[5] It is the ambiguity of "survival"—the migrant must be transformed into a new culture, yet at the same time something of the original must survive—that renders Venuti's denial of origins difficult to accommodate, and his dissident politics impossible to map on to the condition of migrancy. What is omitted in Bhabha's description is the question of agency. Translation would always seem to be a self-translation, although the very appeal to survival surely raises the question of volition. In his discussion of blasphemy in Rushdie's *The Satanic Verses*, Bhabha addresses the concept of limits within cultural translation: "Blasphemy is not merely a misrepresentation of the sacred by the secular, it is a moment when the subject matter or the content of a cultural tradition is being overwhelmed, or alienated, in the act of translation."[6] While agency again is effaced through the use of the passive voice, inequity and loss are hinted at. And here Venuti's notion of supplementing the text would seem to be anything but politically radical; instead, it could be seen to contribute to the process of exceeding and thus overwhelming a cultural tradition.

As for the period of colonization itself, where violence, both physical and ontological, marks the erasure of indigenous cultures, the benign translation metaphor seems more than inappropriate. George Steiner refers to loss as a necessary aspect of translation, and the following description raises obvious problems for its use in theorizing the colonized: "The enactment of reciprocity in order to restore balance is the crux of the *métier* and morals of translation. . . . The appropriative 'rapture' of the translator . . . leaves the original with a dialectically enigmatic residue. Unquestionably there is a dimension of loss, of breakage. . . . But the residue is also, and decisively, positive. The work translated is enhanced. . . . To class a source-text as worth translating is to dignify it immediately and to involve it in a dynamic of magnification."[7] This ethical dimension is of course missing from the colonial project, characterized by the asymmetry of domination, which by definition deletes the possibility of dignity, magnification, or enhancement. The act of reproduction that constitutes translation readily lends itself to a sexual metaphor. If Spivak, in the role of textual translator, asserts that one can only translate out of a language in which one can speak intimacies, and that the "surrender" to the text is "more erotic than ethical,"[8] Steiner emphasizes the ethical. His description echoes that of a sexual encounter between equals: the "appropriative rapture" of the act of translation can be seen as "a hermeneutic of trust, of penetration, of embodiment, and of restitution."[9] The ethical lies in Steiner's chronology: the framing of the acts of penetration and embodiment within a reciprocity of trust and restitution offers an ethical intersubjectivity that does not correspond with the asymmetrical relationship between colonizer and colonized.

In the period of transition the liberatory people, according to Fanon, "construct their culture from the national text translated into modern Western forms of information technology, language, dress";[10] in other words, they assume agency in the process of translation. Here translation is a necessary, self-imposed adaptation, a condition for liberation, so that the literal act of sartorial transformation does not compromise the native's cultural integrity. Removing a traditional costume and donning a Western suit that retains the trace of the former is in any case not the punctual act that it appears to be; instead, the native has over a period of time been acculturated into a transformed world. The question of agency interposes itself in the time lag between the initial violence of colonial contact and the transformed native, the acculturated agent who necessarily undergoes a self-translation. And the process of racial subject formation is crucially implicated in such a temporality.

Before discussing the appropriateness of the translation metaphor in a post-apartheid context, I wish to start with the arrival of Europeans at the Cape, a historical moment where the denial of origins in translation theory constitutes an obvious problem. The story of the indigenous Khoikhoi woman Krotoa and her exertions in the matter of dress is an exemplary case in which translation can be examined as a figure within the narrative of racial subject formation and in terms of its relationship with transition. In 1652, within months of Van Riebeeck's arrival at the Cape,[11] Krotoa, then aged ten, lived in the Dutch fort, where, on her conversion to Christianity, her name was "translated" into Eva. With her aptitude for languages, which soon gained her fluency in Dutch and Portuguese, her role became that of translator and unofficial diplomat; she is repeatedly referred to in Van Riebeeck's journals as "Eva, the interpreter." Related to the Cochoqua chief, Oedasoa, Eva's influence among the Khoikhoi made her an adviser and mediator between the Dutch and the indigenous people. Her much vaunted assimilation in the European fort must, however, be questioned not only because she went off frequently in search of the sociability of the tribe, but because of the manner in which she left: "Outside the fort [she] dressed herself in hides and sent her clothes home."[12]

This cumbersome procedure marks out the strict boundaries of cultural difference and the circumscribed nature of her translation. Elphick writes of her transculturation, of her moving "back and forth between the fort and the Cochoqua, exchanging her Batavian dress for Khoikhoi hides each time she went."[13] Significantly, a prior history of colonial rupture is already present in the Batavian dress that replaces the Dutch costume; in other words, the Khoi is translated into an already hybridized Dutch/Batavian culture. And all that restless coming and going, dressing and undressing between ethnic wardrobes, marks the process of fashioning a new fidgety self.

Studies of early settler society as racially inclusive and encouraging of mixed marriages do not take into account the psychic violence that characterizes the history of Krotoa's translation.[14] That such a translation was incomplete is suggested in the Van Riebeeck journals in which she is accused of duplicity in her role as interpreter and is "caught out telling untruths occasionally."[15] Steiner's description of translation as reciprocal and imbued with trust is absent in the case of Krotoa. In 1664, her marriage to Pieter van Meerhoff, a surgeon who became superintendent of the convicts on Robben Island, was the first between native and settler. The early death of Van Meerhoff, and Krotoa's subsequent degeneration into drunkenness and prostitution on the mainland, led to their offspring being orphaned and absorbed into Dutch colonial society while she was properly banished to Robben Island.

In the 1990s, however, Krotoa was symbolically rescued from the island and rehabilitated as originary Mother of the Afrikaner. Carli Coetzee, tracing the ways in which Krotoa had been represented in twentieth-century South African writing to serve various ideological projects, focuses on Antoinette Pienaar's 1990s musical, *Krotoä S*, in which she is reclaimed as founding mother of the

Afrikaner. ("In amateur genealogical circles, white people compete to discover that they are descended from Krotoa.") Coetzee's concluding injunction to Afrikaners, "better to remember that her silence is not a forgiveness,"[16] overlooks the significant speech act that earns Krotoa her banishment to the island. Her story climaxes in an exquisite moment on 8 February 1669, at a grand colonial gathering, where, in a classic Calibanesque gesture, she hurls drunken abuse "within the hearing of the Commander."[17] At whom her abuse is directed, or the actual words she uses, is not recorded; indeed, what is of significance is the breach of etiquette, the inopportune language used in an inappropriate space, that earns her admonishment and subsequent banishment to Robben Island. Eva-Krotoa offends and transgresses precisely through speech that proclaims her difference, and so asserts her resistance to translation.

The scandalous speech act falls in the space between her two names, pushing them asunder: the assimilated Eva, who is admitted to the governor's presence, and Krotoa, the indigene who asserts her otherness by disturbing the grand event. The disturbance already present in the proto-colony of the Cape is also an exemplary instance of colonial ambivalence, or the basic contradiction that constitutes colonialism's translation of natives: "the making of 'savages' into 'citizens' and at the same time fabricating ethnic, racialised subjects."[18] In the case of Krotoa, the contradiction that lurks within the colonizer's project is mirrored back at him, magnified through the translated Eva's rude speech, which proclaims loudly the fissure already there in the respectability of the gathering: the fact that colonial occupation constitutes a fundamental breach of civility. In terms of the translation metaphor, Krotoa the "savage" asserts her untranslatability, refusing to be the source text for Eva, the "citizen."

The contemporary Afrikaner claim to Krotoa as founding mother would, in accordance with the translation metaphor, seem to be a belated act of restitution. The gesture may well be the disavowal of a stigmatized whiteness, but its appeal is to the symbolic nature of her translated name, Eva, originary woman, a name that may be suitable for a revised identity but one that also embodies the violence of colonial translation. In other words the white refiguration of itself as coloured is to return Krotoa to the status of translatable source text, to drown her verbal abuse in a counterassertion of her translatability.

In Bhabha's discussion of migrant subjectivity and the interrelatedness of transition and translation, it is the residual in the source text that is of value, and it is paradoxically through that which is retained in translation that "newness comes into the world." Thus translation produces the productive Third Space of culture's hybridity, the site where self-other polarities can be eluded although the "'present' of translation may not be a smooth transition, a consensual continuity, but the configuration of the disjunctive rewriting of the transcultural, migrant experience."[19] This interrelation of transition, which operates on a progressive continuum toward a goal, and translation, with its punctual nature, does, however, disrupt temporality itself, a destabilization that can be seen in the narrative of Eva-Krotoa. The space between Krotoa and Eva, between self and other, is manifestly not a liberatory space, and this raises a number of questions: How appropriate is the translation model for the South African situation where apartheid has to be translated into democracy? If an element of untranslatability is axiomatic, then are we necessarily doomed to the residue of apartheid? How helpful is the conflation of transition and translation?

For Andrew Benjamin, who eschews the notion of origins, there need be no temporal disruption or distinction between transition and the event of translation. He introduces the idea of a "pragma," by which he both allows for the specificity of the event and refuses a homological relation between source text and translation, or a specific interpretation and the object of interpretation.[20] The copresence of both pragma and the event means that it is possible to think *being* within *becoming*. Not only is such a healthy-sounding condition difficult to read into Eva-Krotoa's history, the underplaying of transition, and in particular its goal-directedness, is politically dubious. Conflating transition and translation would seem to diminish the aspect of transformation, the need for something radically and recognizably different. Here it reduces Krotoa's condition to costume changes, confers on it a literality, such that Bhabha's "newness" turns out to be limited to a matter of style, a modality that Andrew Benjamin sees as crucial to the operation of translation: "the displacement that, in part, is style is the enactment of the process of translation."[21] What I go on to investigate are the ways in which *Disgrace* might be argued to explore the relationship between the original and the translated, between transition and translation, and how this is underpinned by temporality and the role of the perfective in the text.

Rather than deny origins, *Disgrace* invites the reader to consider the source text and intertexts, and through the perfective asserts the role of history in the articulation of the new order—or rather disorder—in South Africa. You do not make errors of aspect when you translate: in translation, the perfective is the site where the original is effaced and the time system of a new language takes over. Thus it is through the perfective, an act carried through to its conclusion, that translation is asserted and the relationship between source text and translation, or apartheid and postapartheid, is articulated. Temporality in *Disgrace* is described through key verbs—"burnt up"; "driven"; "usurp"; "drink up"—that connect the pedagogical explanations of the perfective to events in the narrative. The first example of the perfective comes from David Lurie's Wordsworth class, "usurp completes the act of usurping upon,"[22] a verb connected with the colonizer's illegal assumption of power. Lurie goes on to explain to the bored youth of the country the distinction between drink and drink up, burned and burnt.

Lurie, the sophisticated, liberal, "English" academic, is typically immersed in European high culture, his moral and aesthetic anchors being Byron and, among others, Wordsworth, Hardy, Yeats, and Flaubert, traceable sources for the canonical citations made in his name. But he finds himself in "Darkest Africa" where English, for instance, is an unfit medium for communication with Petrus, the black farmworker. His students are postliterate and immune to the language of poetry. For them he has to translate, both geoculturally and in terms of register, Wordsworth's response to Mont Blanc: "Wordsworth is writing about the Alps. . . . We don't have Alps in this country, but we have the Drakensberg, or on a smaller scale Table Mountain, which we climb in the wake of the poets, hoping for one of those revelatory, Wordsworthian moments we have all heard about."[23] The point is that we have not all heard about it, that we do not climb the mountain in the wake of English poets, that revelatory moments are perfectly possible without having heard of Wordsworth, which is to say that our feelings and experience of nature need not be structured by poetic discourses from the metropolis. That, after all, is what necessitates Lurie's translation of the European landscape into the native one.

Lurie is absorbed by the Byron story; he revels in the parallels with his own loss of love. But the Byron story, in spite of Lurie's affiliation with European culture, translates into the absurd, finding its expression in the accompaniment of the crude banjo. Finally, he understands his project to be ludicrous, and specifically so in the African context: "Plink-plunk squawks the banjo in the desolate yard in Africa,"[24] to which the doomed dog of his closing affections smacks its lips and prepares to howl, a dog with whose demise, "burned, burnt," the novel ends. David Lurie represents the white colonial condition that looks to Europe as the center of reference, and for whom the need to match up, the reminder of an inevitable cultural hybridity, is always a humiliation, a reduction, and in terms of translation, a failure.

As for the central action carried through to its conclusion, it is Lurie who articulates the condition of the perfective through interracial sex. Of Lucy's rapists he says: "It was not the pleasure principle that ran the show but the testicles, sacs bulging with seed aching to perfect itself."[25] This analysis is preceded by a scene in the theater with Melanie's boyfriend, who tells Lurie to stay with his own kind: "Who is this boy to tell him who his kind are? What does he know of the force that drives the utmost strangers into each other's arms, making them kin, kind, beyond all prudence? . . . The seed of generation, driven to perfect itself, driving deep into the woman's body, driving to bring the future into being. Drive, driven."[26] But Melanie was never driven into the arms of this unreliable focalizer. The reciprocity with which this passage starts is spurious and is soon glossed as a one-sided male drive to procreate. The parallel descriptions link Lurie with the rapists, and in his desire to penetrate the black female body, he is shown simply to reenact the old colonial appropriation. Thus Lurie represents a culture that remains in a crucial sense untranslated, marked by the old values of apartheid. If he represents the untranslated, the narrative events nevertheless trade in translations. Internally topological, they offer crucial repetitions and rewritings that figure a culture of pathologies. The father's disgrace for seducing one of his students is repeated in the daughter's "disgrace" (Lurie's word) in being raped. On one of his sexual encounters with Melanie, "she does not resist . . . not rape, not quite that, but undesired nevertheless, undesired to the core."[27] The committee of inquiry's Dr. Rassool speaks of the incident as "the long history of exploitation of which this is part"; we are told that "in a case with overtones like this, the wider community is entitled . . . to know."[28]

The colouredness of the student, Melanie, is never named, neither in the account of events focalized through Lurie nor in the reports of the committee of inquiry; Rassool uses the deictic "this" to imply a given, shared knowledge. Similarly, the blackness of the rapists is not named. But conspicuously unnamed as race may be, the mixing of races functions as hermeneutic key to the translation of culture. The colouredness of Melanie will be morphologically repeated in the mixed-race child to whom Lucy will give birth, and so the transition from apartheid, an ideology based on race, to melanization will be achieved biologically through the violated female body. The topologies spiral into the given intertext and the self-reflexivity of the novel: Lurie tries to write an opera about Byron, while Melanie, the drama student, acts in a postapartheid play; like Byron's abandoned mistress, Lurie is concerned about aging and sexuality. These repetitions are foregrounded as rewordings bound up with a colonial history that shapes the present.

In reply to his question about the extent to which culture is the translation and rewording of previous meaning, Steiner expounds a theory of intracultural translation in which the novel, too, for all its contingency and freedom from stylization, is subject to metamorphic repetition and critical revision. (Thus echoes of *Middlemarch*'s Dorothea Brooke in *Portrait of a Lady*'s Isabel Archer exemplify topological translation.) Steiner contends that "these metamorphic relations have as their underlying deep structure a process of translation," a topological view of culture that can be seen to be superseded by Bakhtinian dia-

logics and Kristevan intertextuality.[29] Steiner's examples are all drawn from the
texts of high culture, but translation can also be seen to be exemplified in popular cultural practices of the resistance period, although such acts of violation of
the human body—necklacing and rape—cannot with any measure of decency
be cast as texts.[30]

While Steiner distinguishes between direct variants and mere collateral links
between related texts, intertextuality is, according to Barthes, a condition of all
writing: "The text [is] . . . woven entirely with citations, references, echoes, cultural languages, antecedent or contemporary, which cut across it through and
through in a vast stereophony . . . the citations which go to make up a text are
anonymous, untraceable, and yet already read: they are quotations without inverted commas."[31] Not only is a text made up of discourses from a variety of
fields, the boundary between literary and nonliterary is dissolved, and its citations being untraceable, it dispenses with notions of origin. The author is dead.
Here intertextuality does not so much contribute to the reading process; it is
rather a theory of writing, but as such it stops short of accounting for the postcolonial writer for whom the involuntary references and already-there citations are
often oppressive, and for whom value-laden origins are not dispensable. Bakhtin,
on the other hand, in addressing the question of reading and the problem of
meaning, has a number of illuminating questions to ask of citations: "How does
this infiltration occur, how does the receiving context relate to it, in what
sorts of intonational quotation marks is it enclosed?"[32] Similarly, Kristeva comments on novelistic utterances: "The functions defined according to the extra-
novelistic textual set (Te) take on value within the novelistic textual set (Tn).
The ideologeme of the novel is precisely this intertextual function defined
according to Te and having value within Tn."[33] The function of the author then is
both junctive (tying together narrative and citational utterances) and translative
(transferring utterances from one textual space into another), which changes
its ideologemes. It is precisely because of its translative possibilities that intertextuality as writing strategy has become such a staple of postcolonial discourse,
and in *Disgrace* it serves as an internal device to undermine the authority of the
narrative voice focalized through Lurie. For instance, if we are tempted to ad-
mire Lurie's concern with the disposal of unwanted dogs, the citation of Little
Father Time's *"because we are too menny"* must surely question our belief in him.[34]
The narrative voice describes the site of the incinerator in terms of the same
injustice toward humans—social and economic exclusion as well as exclusion
from education—that culminates in the death of the children in *Jude the
Obscure:* "By the time the orderlies arrive in the morning with the first bags of
hospital waste, there are already numbers of women and children waiting to pick

through it for syringes, pins, washable bandages, anything for which there is a market, but particularly for pills, which they sell to *muti* shops or trade in the streets. There are vagrants too, who hang about the hospital grounds by day and sleep by night against the wall of the incinerator, or perhaps even in the tunnel, for the warmth."[35] Here the short answer to Bakhtin's question is non-naming. The citation establishes Lurie's unreliability; it allows him to avoid identifying such people within the specific political context; he need not consider them in terms of inequities produced within a society that has remained unchanged. Instead, and it is nothing short of an outrage, he refers disgracefully to "the social rehabilitation thing." If his self-marginalization and professed humility in the company of dogs is not simply a matter of hyperbolic posturing, it certainly escapes ethical engagement with the human condition.

The novel's most enigmatic intertext, one that invokes South Africa's Truth and Reconciliation Commission (whose declared aims were of *remembering* and *healing*), is Cicero's story of the Art of Memory. Significant non-naming is embedded in the story of memory, where history and repetition are most dramatically figured in the role of Pollux, the rapist. In the Greek story, the poet Simonides, famous for his odes to victory, is asked by a rich patron, Scopas, to perform at his banquet. Instead of a praise song to his host, Simonides spends much time praising Castor and Pollux, twin sons of Leda. The slighted Scopas refuses to pay the full fee, and at that moment Simonides is told that two unnamed young men wish to see him outside. No sooner does he leave than the roof of the banqueting hall collapses and all the guests die, their bodies horribly disfigured and unrecognizable. It is Simonides who, through reimagining the space of the banquet and positioning each person at the table, is able to identify the dead. Thus mnemotechnics, the art of memory, is born.[36]

Embedded in the story are not only a concern with verbal art, visual imagination, and spatiality, but also the themes of revenge and reversal. Simonides may not get his money, but Scopas pays a heavy price for diddling him out of his fee. Like the unnamed race in Coetzee's text, the enigmatic young men whom we assume to be Castor and Pollux are unnamed in Cicero's story. They are neither characters nor actants in the narrative, but nevertheless perform the Proppian function of helper. They introduce into the story the concern with a hybrid identity: as the twin sons of Leda but born of two fathers, one mortal, the other immortal, they are marked by indeterminacy and burdened with the politics of location. Pollux spent half his days in Hades and half with the gods in Olympus; his father, Zeus, had raped Leda in the guise of a swan, thus the name in *Disgrace* represents a metamorphic repetition of historical violence, doubling not only the theme of revenge but characterizing the culture as one of translative recursions. The history of the twins, Castor and Pollux, can be seen as an allegorical condition of postcoloniality: their twoness within an inseparable unity figuring the condition of hybridity is one that is also achieved by the rapists in *Disgrace*—crucially through rape and miscegenation. Thus what the novel also proclaims through the intertext of Pollux and the story of memory is the failure of the project of public memorializing, the naivety and inadequacy of that Christian discourse of remembering, forgiving, and healing.

The question of reversal, narrativized in the overturning of power relations between poet and patron, is then to be read with caution. Victory is indeed achieved not only for the disinterested Simonides, but for poetry itself, for the integrity of art that refuses the sycophancy demanded by a patron. (Lurie, the would-be artist, assumes the same disinterestedness in his dealings with the committee of inquiry; Lucy's disinteredness in seeking justice for her violation is bound up with reversal.) But such victory for the independence of art would seem also to partake of paradox: in the Simonides story of power and revenge, the poet comes up trumps, but the physically obliterated enemy, in being identified, is resurrected through the art of memory. The non-naming of race, for instance, may seem to constitute an achromatism which reverses apartheid, but which would be a politically naive definition of apartheid as purely prohibition of interracial sex. Such reversal manifestly does not constitute democratic transformation; it is a vulgar reading of translation.

As significant as the foregrounded translations and intertexts are the metamorphic repetitions bound up with history. Lurie sees his daughter as a throwback who has returned to the land, a sturdy young settler or "*boervrou*."[37] He is able to use the word in its benign colonial sense, and fails to see her attempts at translation from settler into something new, even if it does retain a residue of the old. Lucy sees herself not as boervrou exercising power over her farmworker, but rather as one who is prepared to cofarm the land with Petrus. To answer Bakhtin's question: here the receiving context confirms a resistance to the citation, where boervrou as already read is the liberal intellectual's ameliorative translation. Lurie's language that articulates the topological is reinforced by the syntactic repetitions of parallelism:

> A frontier farmer of the new breed. In the old days, cattle and maize. Today, dogs and daffodils. The more things change the more they remain the same. History repeating itself, though in a more modest vein.[38]

But the narrative events are not repeated in a more modest vein; instead the metamorphosis is that of intensification. Lucy's rape is a magnification of her father's seduction of a student, gang rape an intensification of the violation, the blackness of the rapists an intensification of Melanie's colouredness, illustrating Steiner's "magnification" of the original text. Walter Benjamin's simile is pertinent: "While content and language form a certain unity in the original, like a fruit and its skin, the language of the translation envelops its content like a royal robe with ample folds. For it signifies a more exalted language than its own and thus remains unsuited to its content, overpowering and alien."[39] Such amplitude or excess is figured in the improbable extravagant gestures on the part of the central characters, such as Lurie's visit to the home of the coloured girl's petit bourgeois parents in the town of George, where he expounds inappropriately to the father about the fire his daughter kindled in him, about his own lack of the lyrical, before stumbling into the bedroom of the mother and prostrating himself before her. These hyperbolic gestures, aimed at overturning the past, in Lurie's case a personal, unhistoricized past, border on the bizarre.

Cultural translation in Coetzee's text is thus figured as departing from the merely topological in its excess and magnification. Lucy's acceptance of the child in her womb is an excessive expression of white guilt, of remembering and making restitution. Petrus's bizarre offer of marriage translates the previous taboos of apartheid legislation, whether the Immorality Act or the Natives Land Act, into an appropriative entitlement. These extravagant gestures are patently pathological; they also demonstrate the failure of postapartheid culture, translations that hardly constitute an emancipatory politics, that certainly do not bring newness into the world. The pathologies can be read as elements of the untranslatable, the residue of apartheid—an overarching intertext—that continues its vulgar influence on its subjects. Lucy will not acknowledge the rape, will not speak about it, and will not report it to the police: behavior that could be read in terms of Freud's statement: "A failure of translation, that is what is known as repression." She is also a victim of what Andrew Benjamin calls the overdetermination of the term "translation." Translation, he says, involves a process of disambiguation that means giving a single determination, and "literality, or literal meaning emerges therefore as a secondary effect."[40] Lucy's literal interpretation of making amends, of accepting violence and humiliation, constitutes a kind of public memorializing, since for all her silence on the rape itself she decides to bear the mixed-race offspring. Thus the lesbian Lucy too is translated into progenitor through violation of the nondiscursive female body. One of Lurie's key verbs for explaining the perfective is here demonstrated: his daughter is driven to drink up, to drain the cup of white guilt.

Disgrace declares South African culture to be at the end of its appeal to transition with its progressive aspect, as a movement from old to new. The new—product of violence, racially mixed, ethically skewed—that is about to be born, turns out to be not so new. With the invariants of the old regime horribly present in the new translations, progressive transition has come to a stuttering halt, and in this moral stasis Bhabha's conflation of translation and an emancipatory transition is unthinkable. Lurie's brooding over the perfective—"signifying an action carried through to its conclusion"[41]—declares the failure of transition as a crossing over to democracy. It is not only the vulgar reading of translation as reversal that triumphs (Lurie replacing Petrus as dog-man; Petrus offering Lucy paternalistic protection), but where translation does appear to operate, as in Lucy's lifestyle or Petrus's attempts at farming his own land, it inevitably carries the residue of apartheid. We are, then, according to *Disgrace,* hamstrung by the double bind of translatability and untranslatability, and the modalities of the past—sex, race, violence—continue to prevail, carrying with them the echo of Eva-Krotoa's curses.

REREADING GORDIMER'S *JULY'S PEOPLE* (2005, 2007)

Not only was *July's People* (1981) one of the first of a number of novels to deal with an anticipated revolution in South Africa, its epigraph from Gramsci's *Prison Notebooks*, "the old is dying and the new cannot be born; in this inter-regnum there arises a great diversity of morbid symptoms," explicitly articulated the novel's concern with a culture in transition. The epigraph, describing the transitional as a process bound up with time, displacement, and ambiguities produced by the in-between condition of delay, readily translates into narrative indeterminacy. It is the reception of *July's People* in the 1980s and the manner in which its open-endedness has exercised critics that has prompted my rereading of the novel and its enigmatic ending.

July's People explores master-servant relations in the story of an imaginary revolution in South Africa. The white, liberal Smales family escape from Johannesburg with July, their servant of fifteen years' standing, to his village in an unnamed homeland, where he protects them and attends to their every need in the ambiguous role of host/servant. The novel ends indeterminately as Maureen Smales, hearing a helicopter about to land in the bush, leaves her family behind and runs toward it. A number of critical responses betray a desire for a known destination for Maureen and valorize such a destination in terms of embracing or rejecting revolution in South Africa. I name but a few in what follows. For Stephen Clingman, "the circumstances in which [the running] occurs are ambiguous, but their significance surely is not. . . . She is running from old structures and relationships, which have led her to this cul-de-sac; but she is also running towards her revolutionary destiny."[1] Nancy Bailey believes that "what Maureen runs to is a return to the illusion of identity created by a world of privilege and possession" and finds "the unqualified triumph" of the novel to belong to the black "matriarchs," July's wife and mother.[2] Nick Visser, while acknowledging a multiplicity of possible meanings and eschewing a physical destination for Maureen, nevertheless privileges a positive outcome. He reads convincingly from the parallels and verbal echoes in the ending the intertextuality of Yeats's "Leda and the Swan": "The imminent convergence of Maureen and the helicopter, like the convergence of Leda and the god-swan, heralds a new civilization, a new epoch for South Africa that cannot, particularly from within a moment of interregnum, be described but can only be symbolically prefigured in a prophetic gesture of revolutionary optimism . . . a moment of insemination from which new possibilities will emerge."[3] Elleke Boehmer dismisses Maureen's running as an "apparently open yet arrested ending" that refuses to anticipate "any ultimate end and therefore any possibility of a new beginning, a diffidence about 'registering' any final 'collapse.'" In common with other South African late-apartheid novels, the ending, according to Boehmer, "could not . . . be taken as other than a closing down or narrowing of possibility." [4] I do not understand this distinction between the indeterminacy of Gordimer's "ample . . . predictable" ending and real open-endedness that would make "room for new and various ways of thinking about the future,"[5] but it appears to be connected to the lack of a positive outcome for the Smaleses. For July and his family, Maureen's running is surely neither a closing down nor an opening up of possibilities; it is of no consequence in the face of a new order.

These responses to *July's People* reveal a will to interpret, which is to say produce a meaning other than the literal event at the end: Maureen running to something unknown. What they also suggest is that the story of the dissolution of apartheid is coordinate with the story of Maureen Smales, the white woman of liberal persuasion whose consciousness is explored and through whom so much of the narration is focalized. Gordimer's own comment on the state of interregnum as a state of Hegel's disintegrated consciousness would seem to support such a reading: "The interregnum is not only between two social orders but also between two identities, one known and discarded, the other unknown and undetermined."[6]

But to focus on Maureen is surely to disregard the title, an ambiguous possessive that cannot be resolved in the novel as its referent shifts between the white family and the extended black family's claims to belong to July. It is, of course, the possessive itself that is interrogated by the text: Who are his people? What does belonging to entail? How is power situated within the humanitarian possessive? How does it operate between affectionate familial (and quasi-familial) ties and the exercise of power over people? One of the concerns of the text, then, is bound up with the problem of the possessive—before Maureen runs she refers unambiguously to the villagers as July's people—an examination of master-servant relations in terms of a poetics of displacement.

In this essay I argue that the text accommodates yet another kind of reader, one whose interests do not coincide with those tied to the destiny of Maureen, for whom her running is not interpreted from the Smaleses' point of view but rather read literally as her removal from the site of the story, and for whom the indeterminacy of the ending allows for a return to central questions of the masters' construction of the black subject and the role of language in articulating such subjectivity. It is difficult not to read July primarily as the medium through which Maureen explores her self and her situation; that is, the calculated result of a narration sympathetically focalized through her, allowing for direct access to her thoughts and feelings. One of the effects, then, of an undecidable ending is to displace Maureen, allowing the reader to rake over forensically, as anyone would on the disappearance of a subject, that which precipitates her disappearance, the dialogues with July.

Thus I propose a return to July from the vantage point of a different time, the New South Africa struggling with the legacies of apartheid. To turn a spotlight on July is also to take seriously the text's declared concern with the articulation of language as a medium through which a culture in transition is explored. The narrative of *July's People* is demonstratively constructed around three germinal dialogues between July and Maureen, the final one of which is, as I will later argue, clearly connected with Maureen's running into the bush. As *dialogues*, then, they are as much concerned with Maureen's condition as with July's, and while the narration comments explicitly on hers, the dialogues themselves are available for scrutiny of July's. Indeed, I will argue that July's language, foregrounded for this very purpose, constitutes a rhetorical figuration of the transitional.

To call *July's People* dialogic is of course in Bakhtinian terms tautologous, since dialogization is a distinguishing feature of the stylistics of any novel: "Dialogue itself, as a compositional form, is in novels inextricably bound up with a dialogue of languages, a dialogue that can be heard in its hybrids and the dialogizing background of the novel."[7] Knowledge of the political background of an unjust homelands policy, so brutally articulated by a minister of justice who failed to imagine himself in dialogue with the subjects of his utterance—"The black labour force must not be burdened by superfluous appendages such as wives, children or dependents who could not provide services"[8]—is still necessary to make sense of Maureen's trump card in each of the encounters, the reference to July's town woman, Ellen.

But a reading at the beginning of a new century, when Gordimer's vision of political transformation has come to pass, should be instructive, since texts also acquire meaning in dialogue with our current concerns. One such current concern, for instance, is the issue of employing servants in a culture of mass unemployment. In the heyday of apartheid, characterized and caricatured in terms of the large white house with swimming pool and a liberal, idle madam attended to by servants, radicals found dignity in *not* having servants, in doing their own work. One of the painful lessons that Maureen has to learn is that the liberal-humanist belief that some kind of egalitarianism can operate within civilized or humane master-servant relations is false, that having a servant like July constitutes complicity in the migratory labor system. A decade and a half after *July's People* was published, the far Right in the New South Africa views apartheid's failure in terms of an incomplete project of separation, flawed for relying on black servants. In bourgeois households of the late-capitalist era, where cultural and educational capital ensures employment, the ethical position vis-à-vis servants has necessarily shifted as we have to choose between dispensing charity to the hungry people who knock on our doors for bread or guiltily offering them the domestic work they wish to do in exchange for money. Interaction with the dispossessed has become unavoidable—unless, as a result of the endemic violence that goes with dispossession, we have barricaded our homes so that dialogue constitutes the disembodied voices over an intercom. In the light of this protracted interregnum, the copresence of Gordimer's madam and servant, the uncomfortable and revealing dialogues, seem quaintly humanistic. Domestic worker relations have since been represented in a popular comic strip *Madam and Eve*, which first appeared in the *Weekly Mail* a decade after *July's People* appeared.[9] Significantly, it is through speech that the relationship between the madam and her servant is parodied.

According to Bakhtin, the novel is the form that incorporates heteroglossia, or the multiplicity of interacting languages in the very fabric of the text, where dialogue between characters creates a polyphony of voices. My textual analysis sets out to demonstrate that the polyphonic struggle is indeed the textual dominant to which the plot and the mode of narration in *July's People* are subordinated. Heteroglossia is always implicitly present when any one language is used, so that any utterance acquires meaning through a number of other languages with which it is necessarily in dialogue. Gordimer's novel draws attention not only to the contending languages within a multilingual South Africa—there are references to Afrikaans, Fanagalo (a pidgin developed and used as means of communication on the mines), and the language spoken in July's home village—but also to the agonistic element of voices in a multiaccentual English, the language of cultural dominance in South Africa. It is these contending voices, implicitly present in Maureen's standard English, her "translation" of her thoughts into simple English, and the representation of July's speech, that I propose to examine in detail. The broken English in which July communicates with Maureen is in turn in dialogue with the various other languages associated with him: the simple English used to speak with his wife; the narrative report of his mother tongue usage; and his actual translation of his native language into nonstandard English. All these are in dialogical relationship not only with one another but also with the standard dialect of the external narrative voice against which they resonate. (In particular, the narrational ambiguity produced by almost imperceptible shifts between internal and external focalization itself constitutes what we might consider a transitional stylistics.)

The linguistic interactions between Maureen and July are furthermore in dialogue with an established master-servant discourse, one that, following Foucault, is treated as sets of discursive events recalled and echoed by both participants in the new situation. The dialogues in the village are themselves represented as *events*; they have specific diegetic functions within the development of the narrative, and as such are constitutive of the power struggle between Maureen and July. The discursive event, according to Foucault, takes effect at the level of materiality: "It has its locus and it consists in the relation, the coexistence, the dispersion, the overlapping, the accumulation, and the selection of material elements . . . it is a question of caesurae that break up the instant and disperse the subject into a plurality of possible positions and functions."[10] While Maureen recalls with horror the order of master-servant discourse in her suburban home in order to cast it off, July's ploy is to recast it within the new locus of the village, the new material context of having taken control of the whites' *bakkie* (pickup) and of demanding a monthly wage for services provided. Foucault warns against "the reduction of discursive practices to textual traces; the elision of the events produced therein and the retention only of the marks for a reading,"[11] but a close reading of these dialogues will not elide the event, precisely because Gordimer represents the dialogues *as* events; it is through speech that the materiality of their condition is articulated.

In the novel's opening paragraph, July's utterance appears to announce the servant's usual role of waking his employers with a cup of tea:

> You like to have some cup of tea?—
>   July bent at the doorway and began that day for them as his kind has always done for their kind.

The knock on the door. Seven o'clock. In governors' residences, commercial hotel rooms, shift bosses' company bungalows, master bedrooms
en suite—the tea-tray in black hands smelling of Lifebuoy soap.
   The knock on the door
   no door. . . .[12]

July's broken English is meaningful not only in its conventional use for marking racial and cultural difference; its salient syntax also wrenches the act of
bringing tea out of the continuum of master-servant relations, so that the discursive event is marked as caesura and is located in uncertainty. The omission
of the modal "would" in July's utterance allows for the "you," the addressee and
recipient of the tea, to be fronted, thus undercutting the deference (according
to South African usage) expected from a black servant in this period. The omitted modal, which normally distinguishes between possibility and actuality, af-
fects the mood of the utterance: the punctuation indicates an interrogative, but
the syntax is declarative. The fact, however, that July has already brought the
tea, as we discover in the next paragraph, implies an imperative mood. As a
speech act its illocutionary force insists on the Smaleses' acceptance of the
tea. In the past the servant could have been sent away, or the tea left, but the
grammatical deviation also indicates the ambiguity of July's new role as ser-
vant/*host*. Politeness precludes refusal on the part of the guests, and the act of
bringing tea as he has always done indicates that for July, in spite of the new
circumstances, it is business as usual.
   July's utterance deviates in other ways from the standard form, "Would you
like some tea?" The use of two mutually exclusive idiomatic expressions, *some
tea* and *cup of tea*, foregrounds the materiality of the pink glass cups and the
condensed milk, registered by Maureen as markers of economic and cultural
difference. The redundancy of "to have" draws attention to the needs of the
Smaleses and establishes July as their benefactor. Later, in the struggle for possession of the keys of the bakkie, it is precisely this role as provider for their needs
to which July resorts. The representation of his variety of English is thus a stylistic choice that performs the conventional function of encoding his otherness,
but it also establishes from the outset the ambiguous nature of master/servant
relations under the new, yet undisclosed, conditions.
   The opening scene represents Maureen, surfacing confusedly out of a sleep
interrupted by July's voice. This voice conjures up the habitual knock on the
door, a remembered knock that in fact has not happened, since they are in a
hut without a door, and activates the old master-servant discourse common to
an entire culture, the shared cultural knowledge indicated by direct reference,

"*the* knock on *the* door." But the ambiguity inherent in the power relations between master and servant is raised through the question of agency: "July bent at the doorway and began that day for them"; their dependency, which becomes overt in the new situation, already inhered in the old, in the habitual act of serving tea. Repetition of "The knock on the door," now occupying a line on its own, also indicates slippage from external narration to focalization through Maureen as she wakes and registers "no door" (in the next line). She remembers that they are in July's mud hut, and her actual utterance, "*Bam, I'm stifling; her voice raising him from the dead, he staggering up from his exhausted sleep,*" italicized and presented as memory, recalls her unease in the night. The aspect of the verbs, indicating incompletion as the progressive does, links the past with the present, if unconsciously, and so demonstrates the transitional hitch. Maureen not only finds it difficult to enter into a new relationship with July; from the start, his kind ministrations bring unease.

The three dialogues between July and Maureen are explicitly about the struggle for dominance, and they center on the traditional Western fetishes of car and gun. In the first, Maureen returns the keys of the bakkie to July but cannot do so without a resentment that, in spite of her protests, is registered by him. He refuses to give up the madam-servant discourse of the past, but in doing so, in recalling it in terms of an event, presents it in a new light: "—You worry about your keys. When you go away I'm leave look after your dog, your cat, your car you leave in the garage. I mustn't forget water your plants. Always you are telling me even last minute when I'm carry your suitcase, isn't it? Look after everything, July. And you bringing nice present when you come back. You looking everywhere, see if everything it's still all right. Myself, I'm not say you're not a good madam—but you don't say you trust for me.—It was a command.—You walk behind. You looking. You asking me I must take all your books out and clean while you are away. You frightened I'm not working enough for you?—"[13] The trust that Maureen believed to have been there had simply been the cant of liberal discourse, now ironically echoed by July ("You tell everybody you trust your good boy"). The subjects of July's sentences, "you" and "I," are pitted against each other, with the majority of verbs predicating "you" in the present progressive, a further insistence by him on the continuation of the madam role for her. Although his inflections are not rule governed, there is remarkable regularity in his use of the verb-to-be, which assumes an auxiliary function—as in "I'm carry your suitcase." But the absence of -ing (as in "I'm carrying") would seem to shift the copula from being a tense marker to representing an existential form. Thus the ungrammaticality of the "I'm" sentences could be construed as a representation of the difficulty July has in constituting himself as a subject: *to-be* is here conflated with the actions of a self defined in terms of performing the servant's task as demanded by the madam. Disturbingly, he means to carry on in this manner, just as the progressive aspect of the verbs suggests that he expects Maureen to continue in the role of madam.

His triumph over Maureen consists precisely in the act of presenting his current discourse alongside the old discourse represented as a past *event,* with all its implications of discontinuity and transformation—a recognition that such things could never have been said in the past. Here, in discourse, we see the transitional represented as the old and the new in combat, the former refusing to be displaced by the latter, rather taking on a necessary complementarity. It is in this sense that the well-formed construction "Look after everything, July," surrounded as it is by broken English, is an echoic utterance, a repetition of her words, which, for Maureen, now carries a distortion. Similarly, the omission of the infinitive in "I mustn't forget water your plants" carries an echo of her command ("water the plants") that intrudes in July's reported speech. The mimicry is, as Homi Bhabha points out, a necessary aspect of the colonial project, but at the same time an act of subversion. The echoic utterance, which resonates within the spatiotemporal gap between there and here, between then and now, also produces difference in interpreting the past, functioning as an ironic comment on the perception Maureen has of relations between her and July. What is clear from this extended speech of his is that his is not a rule-governed dialect of English. Rather, it is Gordimer's stylistic choice, aimed at showing the complex nature of relations between madam and servant, of viewing through the new the old that refuses to be instantly displaced in order to suit Maureen's new requirements.

The second dialogue (on pages 94–101) is significant for the lacunae within the speech event itself, a splitting into three sections brought about firstly by the removal of July's sidekick, Daniel (July "spoke as if opening a conversation out of silence, as if they had not already been talking"), and secondly by Maureen walking away in fear of the anger she has aroused in him. When she returns, he again introduces a new topic, their need to report to the chief. In the first section, when she finds him trying to fix the bakkie, his reference to the past is by way of lamenting the tools left behind, thus to her horror betraying his political naïveté, his antirevolutionary sentiments:

What can we do. Is terrible, everybody coming very bad, killing . . . burning . . . Only God can help us. We can only hope everything will come back all right.—[14]

This is the pious statement of one unable to throw off the yoke of subservience but who at the same time wishes to assume power (prevent the madam from working in the fields with native women; insist they all go the following day to the chief) and retain the material benefits that the situation has brought (claim the bakkie as well as his monthly wages).

Another significant feature of the representation of the second dialogue is its self-referentiality, its numerous descriptions of July's language as a restricted code, as listed below:

(i)   When July says "I'm getting worried," the reader is told: "She knew his use of tenses. He meant 'am worried,'"[15] which draws attention to *her* knowledge of the coded aspect of *his* language, and her role as translator.

(ii) An aporetic moment, however, arises as July tries to prevent Maureen from picking spinach with the black women: "You don't need work for them in their place.—"[16] Maureen knows "He might mean 'place' in the sense of role, or might be implying she must remember she had no claim to the earth—'place' as territory."[17] Thus the coded aspect is shown to be inadequate, and we are alerted to the pragmatic problems of translating July's speech. Indeed, the ambiguity about role and territory can be seen as emblematic of the "problem of July" played out in the context of the homelands policy.

(iii) Toward the end of the dialogue, Maureen corrects herself: "—Why didn't you tell us before, if the polite thing—if it's nice to go and see the chief?—"[18] This condescension in the name of considerateness is countered by July's "—Now I'm tell you.—" which follows shortly after his "—Yes, I'm say that."[19] The latter is the first repetition of the "I'm" as used in the previous dialogue. But here its implication of subjectivity is no longer predicated on subservience; rather it asserts a knowing self whose assumption of agency lies precisely in speech, in dialogue with July's combatant. The unnecessary self-translation by Maureen of "polite" into "nice" is a reminder of the very first dialogue, in which we learn that "she didn't know, either, if he understood the words; she dropped fifteen years of the habit of translation into very simple, concrete vocabulary. If she had never before used the word 'dignity' to him it was not because she didn't think he understood the concept, didn't have any—it was only the term itself that might be beyond his grasp of the language."[20] While this could be read sympathetically, another reading would focus on what is overlooked in this statement, which is that July has learned his English from Maureen, that her talking down maintains his restricted code,

that avoiding abstractions constitutes linguistic deprivation. Her explanation of the frozen register of their conversations over the course
of fifteen years, presented as a given, sits uncomfortably with the implied understanding of their relationship, the moral development
bound up with discovering an other within her self. Fifteen years of
speech that never requires the use of abstract terms must be based on
an assumption that July's proficiency in English cannot improve, implying what Johannes Fabian calls a "denial of coevalness."[21] July is
incapable of acquiring the official language in the time that Maureen herself would have become fluent in several languages, in the
time that her own children, under July's very care, are becoming multilingual. (Even Es'kia Mphahlele's liberal madam of the 1960s, the
eponymous Mrs. Plum, is concerned for the education of Karabo and
encourages the servant to go to the social club, where her political
education develops apace under cover of Lilian Ngoyi's sewing classes.
The story is remarkable for being narrated entirely by the servant in
simple English.)[22] Although Maureen does not register the similarity
between the two modes, her condescending English of fifteen years'
standing is essentially no different from Fanagalo, "the bastard black
lingua franca of the mines, whose vocabulary was limited to orders
given by whites and responses made by blacks."[23]

(iv) The comment on Maureen's explanation of why she chooses to work
      with the women in the field describes July's English precisely in Fa-
      nagalo terms: "—I've got nothing to do. To pass the time.—But they
      could assume comprehension between them only if she kept away
      from even the most commonplace of abstractions; his was the English
      learned in kitchens, factories and mines. It was based on orders and re-
      sponses, not the exchange of ideas and feelings.—I've got no work.—"[24]

One of the difficulties in assessing Maureen's development as an ethical subject is the variable focalization that characterizes this novel. While thoughts and
events are in the main focalized unambiguously through Maureen and thus are
strongly aligned with her consciousness, there are instances where internal and
external narration seems indistinguishable. External narration, for instance, intrudes in the passage about July's use of "place" when we are told, "She spoke
with the sudden changed tone of one who has made a discovery of her own and
is about to act on it."[25] In the extract above, it is possible to read the focalizer of
the thought to be both external and internal. Read, however, as purely her
thought, inserted as it is between her two utterances, the collocation of "kitchens,

factories and mines" suggests a new understanding of her own complicity in the system, with the implication that the distancing "kitchens" includes her own. On the other hand, if Fanagalo once was regarded with shame by Maureen, July's broken English is not, which may suggest that the quotation above is not a representation of her thoughts but is rather that of an external narrator who undermines the pious empathy by connecting the two linguistic descriptions through repetition. Then the echoic element would allow us to read the thought as ironizing Maureen's understanding of the linguistic space between them. More plausibly, the variable focalization is specifically employed to produce ambiguity in the representation of relations between the Smales family and their host. In other words, Maureen's ethical development is subject to slippage, and the reader is situated in a position of ambivalence toward her.

Undecidability is thus not simply a feature of the final event but rather is integral to a mode of narration in service of ambiguity, or a transitional point of view. For instance, the story of a newborn litter of cats for which the children find a plastic orange sack as a nest focuses on their indignation at being accused by one of the villagers of stealing his sack (pages 85–86). The man comes to complain; the dialogue between mother and children about the accusation is represented; there is no reference to the presence of the man; indeed, the reader assumes that he is not there while the Smaleses discuss the validity of his claim, albeit in English of which he has limited understanding. It turns out that he is present while they talk about him as if he is not there, or so we infer from the following: "But all the parents did was give the man a two-rand note" (which happens to be far in excess of the value of the sack).[26] This sentence, following the child's "He mustn't say I stole," is ambiguous in its representation of an attitude toward their actions; it could simply mean that the parents do not reprimand the man as the child would have it, or put into question the ethics of their actions, including the speech acts. The external narrator had introduced the man as one who "had been appearing for generations at the back door, asking for but not expecting to get justice, only the redress of a handout."[27] In other words, nothing has changed.

It is, of course, not surprising that Maureen's position is indeterminate; she has, after all, years of apartheid conditioning to unlearn, and the fact that she is not aware of her own ambivalence precisely describes liberal ideology. In "Living in the Interregnum," Gordimer discusses the "distorted vision" that apartheid produces in whites, as if it does not produce distortion in blacks.[28] Distortion is not represented in the novel as race specific, however. Those of us who, along with Maureen, are disappointed or even shocked by July's counterrevolutionary stance are guilty of a popular assumption that oppression necessarily produces

ethical awareness, that it has a prerogative on human rights, and that powerless-
ness is somehow an index of worth. Oppression, unfortunately, has no such re-
deeming effects; the oppressor can claim only responsibility for the brutalization
of all his subjects and of the self. July's subjection and deprivation of cultural
and linguistic capital, as Maureen by her own admission and by her ongoing
linguistic condescension demonstrates, also necessarily distort his ethical awareness. Apartheid's oppression had the further unintended effect of persuading
the oppressed that all of the deficit would be made good by economic capital,
the visible benefits of privilege. This is nowhere better demonstrated than in *The
Spilling of Blood* (1999), Thabo Luthuli's popular novel about the armed struggle, in which, except in the case of a few traitors, political and ethical awareness
on the part of the oppressed is premised on a necessary historicity. In the process of justifying the morality of killing for a just society—partly through its endorsement by a British aristocrat, a Swedish magnate's wife, and a wealthy
Afrikaner entrepreneur (their female gender is significant)—a dubious ethics is
established in the text, that of economic integrity. The black protagonist and
his comrades find their self-respect in sharp dressing, driving expensive cars, being deferred to in luxury hotels, all by way of conspicuous consumption that is
presented (astonishingly) not for critique but rather in service of demonstrating
their equality with whites. The vision of a new South Africa presented in that
text is thus a depressing one of sharp-nosed/nose-tapping/overdressed bankers
with "good" social connections.

   Richard Rorty's liberal take on the question of the human rights culture that
characterizes the contemporary "civilized" world is worth considering here.
Rorty describes the conditions of Europe and North America as "sufficiently
risk-free as to make one's difference from others inessential to one's self-respect,
one's sense of worth."[29] Thus social intolerance, prejudice, and ignorance—or
indifference—to a culture of human rights are not to be dismissed as irrational
but rather to be explained by the fact that such views are held by people who
are deprived of security, sympathy, and education. I will return to the question
of rationality; however, it is surely the case that material welfare may reduce the
fear and fetishization of alterity but has nothing whatsoever to do with alleviat-
ing the conditions of the other, let alone contributing to his emancipation. The
enlightenment of the Smales family, their perceived freedom from apartheid's
vulgar othering, does not alert them to apartheid's and thus their own responsibility for producing July's politics.

   In *July's People*, the compromised position of the homeland dwellers is further explored in the visit to the chief, whose questionable ethics and speech can
be seen to prefigure Maureen's final encounter with July. Not only in terms of

the gun as topic—the chief wants access to Bam Smales's gun in order to kill the revolutionaries—but more significantly in terms of translation. The narration reports the use by the chief of his indigenous language so that July translates into and out of English. When the chief unexpectedly says in English, "And they want to kill you,"[30] translation is shown to be a farce; he has all along been perfectly capable of speaking and understanding English, a language again used strategically when he inquires about guns. The dialogical event is suffused with Bakhtinian parody (just as the chief's position represents a parody of power within the homelands policy). The eruption of farce within interlingual translation and within the Smaleses' solemn respect for cultural difference is reminiscent of the redundancy of Maureen's intralingual translation. And the chief, who calls July by his real name, Mwawate, draws attention to the untranslatability of the proper name. "One should never"—says Derrida—"pass over in silence the question of the tongue in which the question of the tongue is raised and into which a discourse on translation is translated."[31] It is precisely the linguistic imperialism of English, the language in which the question of translation is raised through the violent eruption of an utterance on violence, that is both foregrounded and threatened by the use of the native language. July as medium is rendered redundant; the lesson in translation surely warns us against seeing him as medium through which to read the story of Maureen's liberation, or indeed against reading the novel as the story of Maureen's liberation. Thus it is the very role of protagonist that is shown to be in a state of indeterminacy. Maureen's earlier well-meaning comments on translating July's language are rendered suspect; it is translation itself, as a figure of transition, that points to a system—both narrative and political—in deconstruction.

After discovering the theft of Bam's gun, Maureen goes in search of July, who, she realizes, knows nothing of it. July, outraged by her demand, abandons his servant's discourse: "Where I'm going to find it? . . . *You* know? Then if you know why you yourself, your husband, you don't fetch it?—"[32] In this third dialogue Maureen reminds him of the trifles he had filched from her suburban home so that, angry and humiliated, he erupts into his own language. Somehow, instinctively, she has access to this language: "She understood although she knew no word. Understood everything: what he had had to be, how she had covered up to herself for him, in order for him to be her idea of him. But for himself—to be intelligent, honest, dignified for *her* was nothing; his measure as a man was taken elsewhere and by others. She was not his mother, his wife, his sister, his friend, his people."[33] In this reported event, July's voice is doubly mediated. Our access is through the intuitive comprehension Maureen has, filtered through her consciousness. Rather than a rational translation, it is the dialogic reception of July's words, rendered as Maureen's own thought, which is represented. Bakhtin's comment that "there takes place within the novel an ideological translation of another's language, and an overcoming of its otherness,"[34] is borne out in Maureen's intuitive understanding. Its authenticity is proposed through a shift in focalization from Maureen to July, so that his voice remains audible in the free indirect discourse of "what he had had to be . . . his people," if overlaid with her translation.[35] Her instinctive knowledge precipitates the ending of the novel, where her running through the ford and into the bush is of the same irrational order. That dissolution of her self, the slippage into an instinctive other, relates to her intuitive absorption of July's words, which she is able to translate. Understanding, however, includes the realization that she is not of "July's people," that July is and has been her construction: it does not bring rapport with the other.

The question of translation is also pertinent to the conversations between July and Martha, his wife, which again is necessarily in dialogical relation with the broken English spoken to Maureen. The reader has to assume that the simple, grammatically sound English in which July communicates with Martha is a translation of the native language. This narration (on pages 130–37) is focalized chiefly through Martha and thus retains the trace of her simple language: "Now her man was in her hut, she was giving him his food, he was there to look at her when she said something."[36] The writer's choice in rendering another language in the dominant dialect becomes significant in terms of whether it reproduces or challenges the valorization of languages according to race. One of the questions that the simple English raises is whether the privileged and the simple varieties can coexist without inviting value judgment, or transferring the low prestige of the simple variety to the speakers.

The narrative conventions for dealing with the speech of nonnative speakers is described by J. M. Coetzee in his study of Pauline Smith's usage as follows: "Sometimes they are given 'broken English,' a dialect rarely particularized to the extent that identifiable native speech-patterns emerge, though the odd native word may be dropped in a moment of stress. . . . More often the practice is to give them a simple, functional, but on the whole fluent, even idiomatic English, which is understood to be a smoothed out rendering of some hypothetical original. . . . The rendering of the thought—as opposed to the speech— of such characters is not typed by language: the question of whether thought occurs within the patterns of the native language is by convention dismissed as academic."[37] Gordimer draws on both these conventions but radically reinscribes them. July's English is differentiated according to interlocutor, and as I hope to have shown above, the broken English is meaningful in pragmatic terms. Martha is given free indirect thought, but the simplicity of her language proclaims her deprivation, her ignorance of the lives people lead in the cities from which she and her children are prohibited. In her attempts to communicate with Maureen in broken Afrikaans, however, it is Maureen's limitations that are displayed: Maureen has no idea that the Smaleses' occupation of the hut is resented for having displaced July's mother; she does not understand that grass has to be cut for the thatching of the roof. The Smaleses, it turns out, are a source of tension between July and his family.

With Maureen, July takes an antirevolutionary stance, but it is in relation to the homelands policy that kept families apart and produced the phenomenon of extramarital liaisons in the backyards of employers that he, in conversation with his wife, reveals his understanding of and longing for political change: "He looked at her, painfully, pityingly, as if by so doing to block out seeing something or someone else. He spoke with the rush of an enthusiasm there was not time to examine.—When the fighting's over I'll take you with me, I'll take you back and show you, you'll stay there with me. And the children too.—"[38] The poignancy of July's words hover beneath the incivility of Maureen's references to Ellen, his town woman, who lived in the backyard with him. In each of their conversations, Maureen utters the unspeakable: she accuses July of fearing that she would tell his wife, and harangues him for not caring about what happened to Ellen. The pious concern for Ellen sits uncomfortably with the Smaleses' complicity with an unjust system, complicity by dint of accepting and prospering under the status quo.

The theme of how the migratory labor system impacts familial and sexual relations is one that Gordimer returns to in the story "Blinder," published two years after *July's People* (in 1983). In the light of (un)critical empathy with Maureen Smales, the ubiquitous overidentification with her, it is tempting to think of this story as an exasperated attempt on Gordimer's part to return Maureen to suburbia, to show her relations with a servant, her liberal humanism, in action at home. In "Blinder," the servant, Rose, lives in the backyard with Ephraim, who has a wife and children in a homeland. Her employer, the unnamed and generic "lady of the house," resembles Maureen in her tolerance, benevolence, her overlooking of the trifles that Rose helps herself to in the house, and her humane response to Ephraim's death, but the pitfalls of liberalism are more boldly drawn in the unambiguous representation of the employer. It is her colonial discourse, the fetishization of cultural difference, the different criteria for and the generalizations about blacks, on which the story focuses. The following comment is not only typical; the self-correction betrays an ambivalence, the latent sense of the unacceptability of racial prejudice: "She appears to get over

Ephraim's death very quickly, as these people do, after the first burst of emotion—perhaps it would be better to assume she has to take it philosophically."[39] And so the passage carries on shifting between crass stereotype, a primitive suspicion toward the other, and the unqualified sympathy of a shared feeling. The movements of the lady of the house, back and forth across this threshold, coincide with another exploration of liminality, the physical boundaries of house and servants' quarters, as well as the transitional space between the two, that of kitchen and backyard, a space that is denied in the political articulation of the homelands policy for which it serves as concept-metaphor within the story. Rose's transgression, with Ephraim's wife and children, into the family's dining space (where they are engaged in the cultural ritual of lunch), conjugates geopolitical space with sexual-familial relations. Thus cultural difference is re-presented in terms of Rose's embrace of Ephraim's family, an emotional flexibility alien to suburbia and the serial monogamy of the west.

In *July's People*, the liminal is cast in terms of language; Maureen transgresses across the boundaries of the permissible utterance—an indecency in the name of an imagined bond with Martha. Maureen's instinctive running into the bush and toward a helicopter of unknown identity would seem to endorse Richard Rorty's location of emancipation in sentiment, rather than in a rationality traditionally seen as the shared human attribute in which morality is supposedly grounded. Rorty describes this view through a critique of Kant's "unconditional moral obligation" as a transitional stage between spurning prejudice as irrational and belief in a more tolerant society. Kant, Rorty notes,

> wanted to make knowledge of a core self do what can be done only by the continual refreshment and recreation of the self, through interaction with selves as unlike itself as possible. Kant performed the sort of awkward balancing act that is required in transitional periods. His project mediated between a dying rationalist tradition and a vision of a new democratic world. . . . Kant's balancing act has become outmoded and irrelevant. We are now in a good position to put aside the last vestiges of the idea that human beings are distinguished by the capacity to know rather than the capacity for friendship and intermarriage, distinguished by rigorous rationality rather than by flexible sentimentality.[40]

This may well theorize the condition of Maureen, whose abandonment of rationality would seem to be accompanied by an intuitive, sympathetic understanding of July, but the reader for whom her removal from the site of the story signals a turn to July must at the same time engage with postmodernity's turn against the rational. Rorty's self-declared ethnocentrism is illustrated in the utopian notion of "interaction with selves as unlike itself as possible." In the real world this does not come on equal terms; power relations inherent in such encounters make it a one-sided affair. Detranscendentalizing reason may be desirable for a new paradigm of mutual understanding, but the reader must surely at this stage consider its implications for July. What can it possibly mean in practice? Is the "capacity to know" so negligible a thing for July? Can rationality be outmoded and irrelevant for one who has never had access to knowledge? To replace reason as Rorty does with an intersubjectivity based on an agreement in a shared language is shown in the novel to be an impossibility under the asymmetrical conditions imposed by an overarching system of apartheid.[41] Gordimer clearly shows that it is precisely Rorty's flexible sentimentality that makes it possible for an employer to say that her servant is her friend. July's systematic underdevelopment, his restricted language and restricted knowledge, makes intersubjectivity an impossibility; rather, it has itself produced the distorted vision of political conservatism.

It is helpful here to consider the difference between the two often conflated terms "reason" and "rationality," a difference that becomes clear in the use of the infinitives: "to reason" and "to rationalize." For July, it is precisely sentimentality and irrational affiliation with that which he knows, dependence on the Smales family, that keeps him apparently shackled to an unjust politics and a dubious ethics. The various metropolitan articulations, whether Habermas's communicative reason or Rorty's contextualism (and the notion of an expanding interpretive horizon constantly negotiated between the privileged subject and the other), are rendered useless with lack of subjectivity and lack of knowledge. No doubt for the native in edenic nature, philosophy (as Habermas explains) "needs a procedure of rationally reconstructing the intuitive pre-theoretical knowledge of competently speaking, acting, and judging subjects."[42] The valorization of pretheoretical knowledge can be nothing other than sickening for the postcolonial subject flung helter-skelter into modernity, and into the service of those who spend years boning up on theoretical knowledge. Reasoning requires a knowledge base: education.

Thus for the other reader I proposed at the beginning of this essay, the ending of *July's People* does not propose an emancipatory politics for either of the chief characters; instead it asserts the impossibility of emancipation at the beginning of revolution. But it lays bare the conditions for its possibility through language and narration. From Maureen's perspective, we may be persuaded of July's political naïveté, but Gordimer's variable focalization destabilizes identification with Maureen and so trips readers up in their liberal bourgeois assumptions. July, so lacking in political glamour, cannot be dismissed as a traitor; it is his economic dependence that binds him to the Smaleses and dictates utterances that he thinks they would like to hear from him.

What Gordimer proposes is the limits of dialogue between unequal subjects, the buckling of an interpretive horizon under unequal conditions, the failure of face-to-face engagement when one of those faces has for years been deferentially averted. Indeed, with the reconfiguration of the dialogical event itself in July's final speech, where his voice is both given and not given, ambiguity points to an absence—the intersubjectivity that is suppressed by apartheid and that cannot now be recovered. No wonder that Maureen runs "like a solitary animal at the season when animals neither seek a mate nor take care of young."[43] July too remains saddled with the legacy of apartheid. Thus the temporality of transition is foregrounded: liberation cannot be achieved overnight and simply through political change; rather, it is a slow affair of "morbid symptoms" before actual transformation occurs, which is to say the erasure of inequities that prohibit intersubjectivity and dialogue. The fact that July's friend Daniel has left to join the fighting suggests that the revolution is gathering momentum and that the remote village no longer offers a place to hide. The old order is fast breaking down. What *July's People* introduces into the inevitability of a new political order is the ethical and therefore the personal: face-to-face interaction on a new footing that will take its measure from new languages and new registers yet to be learned by interlocutors.

12

NATURAL NARRATIVE AND TALL TALES:
REMEMBERING DISTRICT SIX (2006, 2012)

One of the most newsworthy cases of apartheid discrimination in South Africa was the demolition of District Six, a vibrant inner-city district of Cape Town often described as a melting pot of class, race, and religions. Under the Group Areas Act, in 1966, the largely coloured community was destroyed and rehoused (until 1981) in various dreary far-flung suburbs of the Cape Flats in order to make way for white occupation. District Six has since achieved iconic status in popular culture's liberation discourse, as well as in literary texts: authors like Alex La Guma and Richard Rive set many of their most memorable fictions there. In this essay I examine natural narratives by two men, called Boeta (or Brother) Dickie and Boeta Alie, reminiscing about their youthful escapades in District Six. (An extract from Boeta Dickie's narrative is included in the appendices.)

Firstly, how did I find these stories? I was looking for a short diglossic speech with typical code-switching between nonstandard varieties of English and Afrikaans to use as a teaching text in a language course, and the content didn't matter much. One of my mature students told me about his evenings spent playing cards with neighbors, a group of older men in the Cape Flats township of Hanover Park, who often reminisced about their youth in District Six. So he asked their permission to record the evening's stories for academic purposes.[1] The fact that I did not set out to acquire oral accounts of life in District Six thus avoided the problems inherent in an interview. The three rambling stories do become less coherent or intelligible as the evening of drinking and smoking *dagga* (marijuana) progresses, but they lent themselves successfully to the project of teaching about features of speech, clause structure, and the pragmatic functions of code-switching.[2] The narratives *themselves*, however, also captured my interest. It was a recent visit to the District Six Museum, established in Cape

Town only a few months after the recordings were made, that returned me to the material, and one of the aims of this essay is to discuss the stories in relation to that official monument to District Six.

The speakers are ex-gangsters, Boeta Alie and Boeta Dickie, who tell their neighbor Boeta Roli of their adventures in the early 1960s. My aim is not to valorize the speech of the disadvantaged by uncovering its ingeniousness or pathos, or by offering it as evidence of the subjects' oppression.[3] These stories give no reliable information on life conditions before or after forced removal from District Six. Besides, any well-meaning intention of giving the underclass a "voice" would find its rebuff in narratives that themselves demonstrate and assert the volubility of the speakers and the fact that their voices are irrepressible. Instead, I am interested in the act of storytelling itself. For all their lack of linguistic and cultural capital, it is precisely in telling their stories that these disadvantaged speakers find a measure of self-worth. They do not perceive themselves as being silenced; on the contrary, it is—according to their tales—through their own language use that they assert themselves against authority. Self-report is, of course, notoriously unreliable, but what is at stake in these narratives is the telling that evidently transforms experience. Thus, what I examine is the discursive mechanisms by which subjectivity is achieved and self-worth is displayed. I look at the ways in which the narrative of the past (1960s) is inflected by the demise of apartheid (at the time of storytelling in the 1990s); in other words, how the relocated subject as victim is re-presented in the postapartheid era through storytelling. Finally, I address the popular equating of narrative with knowledge, instances of which we see in the postapartheid valorization of the people's oral accounts (as witnessed in the District Six Museum). This I consider in relation to troubling aspects of the narratives: their apocryphal nature and the denigration of women that structures the stories. What kind of knowledge claims can therefore be made for narrative?

The speakers' code-switching between nonstandard varieties of English and Afrikaans not only shows their competence at communicating but is in itself a meaningful device with particular narratological and ideological functions that I investigate in my reading of the stories. There is no space to consider fully the communicative effects of code-switching, but the following gives an idea of the kind of analysis pertinent to the study. Code-switching, as an aid to both the semantic and the performative aspects of storytelling, has a significant role to play in the production of the world of happening, of process and of becoming. Boeta Dickie's frequent switches from past tense to conversational historical present tense, often marked by a switch between English and Afrikaans, is not only a stylistic device related to the performative but is itself also a function of rheomodality that recreates a past mapped on to the recent politics of resistance and liberation. Boeta Dickie's story about female behavior can be shown to demonstrate the variety of discourse functions marked by the switch from one language to another. The common distinction between direct and reported speech or quotation is produced through code-switching, but as Suzanne Romaine points out, "it is the switch itself which must be significant, rather than the accuracy of the representation of the reported speech with respect to its linguistic form."[4]

In the following, the narration in English switches to Afrikaans: "Before I leave she ask me again and then it struck me. *hei daai buddie het gesê jy moet jou vrou* in total trust [hey, that buddy said you must trust your wife in total]." The switch occurs when Boeta Dickie introduces the representation of thought, but the significance of "total trust" is here foregrounded through an English borrowing within an Afrikaans construction. The narration continues in English until he returns to base time and introduces himself as speaker: *"ek sê vir haar* [I say to her] listen it's in the fig tree," differentiating between narration and direct speech through a switch. The English narration is next disrupted by the act of blabbing: "my sister ask her something about it. er. *vroumense geselskap en daar sê sy is innie vyeboom* [er women's talk and there she says it's in the fig tree]." When he narrates the female friend's treachery, Boeta Dickie adopts a parodic whining tone, and the illogicality of her dislike for him when she does not know him is foregrounded both through mimicking her voice and through code-switching: "the woman tell her *ja Diekie willie hoor nie ne hy's alweer innie moeilikheid ne* [yes Dickie won't listen hey he's in trouble again hey]." The subsequent turns between the sister, her friend, and finally the police are neatly differentiated through successive switches.[5]

In the 1980s, the culture of resistance in South Africa fostered the production of autobiographical genres in which the stories of ordinary people were seen to provide information about marginalized cultures that had been suppressed by apartheid policies. Oral history and oral literature projects proliferated, not only in response to a wider critical concern with language as discourse in a multilingual society but also as part of a restitutionary movement to include alterity. Since memory has a crucial role to play in oral narrative, storytelling by the dispossessed is also valued for the political act of remembering. Oral history projects set out to produce "history from below," an attempt to counter the official history of apartheid, and as such was distinguished from oral literature. Bill Nasson, commenting on the received images of District Six presented by dominant groups, claims that it is through oral history, "the personal testimony and life history of actual individuals, rather than through statistical abstractions, that we might begin to understand work, leisure, custom and the great repertoire of other activities which the inhabitants of District Six imbued with their own meanings."[6]

While the above hints at the subjective nature of such testimonies, Anne McClintock is explicit about oral history involving the "technological reproduction of people's memories; the unstable life of the unconscious; the deformations, evasions and repressions of memory, desire, projection, trauma, envy, anger, pleasure";[7] in other words, that there is little to distinguish it from oral literature. Thus doubt has been cast over the empirical value of oral accounts, and the analysis of oral material has only recently come to be informed by the methodologies of both history and literature.[8] For all the skepticism toward facticity, however, the study of marginalized cultures finds its very raison d'être in the referentiality of the tales, and oral narratives continue to be valued for "information" about a culture precisely because of the stifling or distortion of information during the apartheid era. Nor is the reliance on narrative as a valid mode of thinking merely a local trend. Martin Kreiswirth refers to the contemporary "narrativist turn," in other words the way in which a range of disciplines—economic theory, jurisprudence, psychology, visual arts, and so on—are being formulated in terms of a turn to narrative.[9]

The District Six Museum, established in Cape Town in 1994, is such an instance of oral history being given form. This space relies heavily on testimonies of ex-residents who make their marks in the museum, record their stories, and reflect on the past; it has no permanent collection as such apart from the remains of people's possessions excavated from demolished sites. The museum promotes the popular account of the rich diversity of community where people of different religions and race lived together, but an important corrective is the inclusion of African residents in the story of coloured dispossession. To this purpose a work called "Nomvuyo's Room," a domestic Xhosa interior produced by Nomvuyo Ngcelwane, occupies an actual room in the museum. Peggy Delport, the chief curator of the first exhibition, explains that "the focus included the notion of accessibility, the creation of a generative area for historical retrieval and interpretation and the interrelationship of historical method and aesthetics. These concerns were exemplified in the way in which the oral history was given form through the active engagement of narrators in assembling and interpreting their own materials within the museum space."[10] What this attempt at "historical retrieval" fails to acknowledge is that the act of narration, as in the case of writing, is itself generative and, as I later show, lends itself to fictionalization.

The narrative I discuss in this essay would not have found a place in the District Six Museum, undermining as it does the popular notions of harmonious community and solidarity against apartheid law. The bolt of cloth in the museum, which invites signatures and comments, includes nothing like Boeta Dickie's story—which tells of gang warfare and a particular instance of a rival gang informing on him to the police. His narrative concerns the police's search for the gun, and how Boeta Dickie manages to escape a prison sentence through his linguistic skills. His story shows that personal narratives cannot be taken as evidence of past events, that rather his is a creative, self-reflexive act of reveling in linguistic performance. As such, it is self-consciously concerned with story-telling and with the performance and presentation of a remembered self in a desirable light. There are several ways in which the notion of community is called into question, not only gangs at each other's throats, but also racist reference to "darkies," as well as gender conflict. It would seem that that the strictly male environment of drinking and smoking has a gendering effect on stories that encode and reproduce masculinity through its relational difference from women, and through masculinist belief that men are responsible for women.

What I argue is that the context of the 1960s intersects with the context in which the events are recounted, the 1990s culture of political resistance that retrospectively inflects the stories. My reading examines the ways in which natural narrative, including the strategy of code-switching, functions within the context of the 1990s New South Africa as a means of recasting the past. By this I mean how subjects constitute themselves through narrative, how informal storytelling becomes a speech act of resistance in which the speaker transforms himself, and, since the stories involve women, how folk-linguistic beliefs about women's speech—that is, speaking out of turn, speaking too much, and speaking with no regard for logic—are reproduced in the natural narratives.[11]

It is not surprising that the context of habitual performance, where men tell stories to one another and to younger members of the new community in which they reminisce about their youth, should shape their stories in particular ways, and that the hallowed space of a museum cannot accommodate such reprobate stories. While it is the case that the speakers are urban and literate (Boeta Dickie speaks of his "collar-and-tie job"), Isabel Hofmeyr's research on where and how people acquired storytelling skills in a Ndebele-Sotho chiefdom is pertinent. She found that "such acquisition had occurred in households strictly divided by gender and that such different 'gender' spaces served to differentiate what were, in effect, cognate narrative skills."[12]

The first notion of community I unpack is the linguistic idea of a speech community. Although I started out with the orthodox notion of speech communities, in this case Cape Flats Coloured English, the narratives themselves point to the limitation of such a notion. In her argument against distinct and homogenous speech communities, Mary Louise Pratt discusses language as a site of social reproduction and struggle that cannot be unified in the imagined utopian manner. She asks her reader to imagine the following alternative: "a linguistics that decentred community, that places at its centre the operation of language across lines of social differentiation, a linguistics that focused on modes and zones of contact between dominant and dominated groups, between persons of different and multiple identities, speakers of different languages, that focused on how speakers constitute each other relationally and in difference, how they enact differences in language."[13] Pratt's linguistics of contact/conflict offers a critical framework for discussing the stories in question, where men tell of conflict with agents of the law and rival gangs within the community, refer to diglossia, and represent their own speech in conflicting relation to female speech, a feature through which masculinity is constructed in the narrative. Moreover, the hierarchy of the languages between which they alternate is pragmatically exploited in the narration where the cultural dominance of English is reproduced. And yet the notion of a linguistic community cannot be completely discarded. Oral performance in this dialect occurs within a particular community on which it relies not only for its intelligibility but also for its empathy and indulgence toward the more extravagant aspects of the stories, even if such a community is crisscrossed with divisions and alliances. In her study of District Six speech and the necessary conditions in which code-switching is practiced, Kay McCormick alludes to the notion of community. The perception of Afrikaans as "unrefined," while a high status is accorded to English, does not deter speakers from using both languages: "If . . . social conditions between speakers of different languages are quite relaxed, there is less anxiety about linguistic borrowing."[14] In the stories I discuss, the context of telling allows for uninhibited code-switching, but what is striking is the speakers' belief in their linguistic competence in the standard dialects of English and Afrikaans and in the value of their bilingualism.

All three stories are about the speakers' skirmishes with the law and the ways in which they gain the upper hand. Contact with whites, which is to say with authority, plays an important role, and such contact ranges from inconsequential slights to outright conflict with the law. Where the field is explicitly that of criminality, the law assumes a structural role in the narrative: laws of masculinity, of solidarity against white authority even among rival gangs, and linguistic laws against women; these are produced in the act of storytelling and consolidated in the stories.

It is orality itself that is shown to be crucial in the process of transforming experience: the narratives are also always metanarrational in that they draw attention to the specific speech acts within them, and by implication to themselves, in other words to storytelling per se as speech acts. The presentation of events organized within the narratives is, in fact, a creative re-presentation that overtly depends on the protagonists' verbal skills. Boeta Dickie's story tells of the police coming to his house in search of a gun with which he had allegedly shot at a rival gang. He claims that he successfully talks himself out of trouble: "*die twee vat my storie* [these two (police officers) accept my story]," and that they leave, since "they saw they not gonna get anywhere by me." When later that day the police find that they had been duped, "*toe's die boere kwaad want die boere wat die oggend daar gewees het. ek het hulle mos geswitch* [then the boers were furious because the boers who were there in the morning—I managed to fool them]." Thus Boeta Dickie posits himself as agent, although subsequent stories show that it is not the case.

Boeta Dickie claims responsibility for preventing his sister, who is caught in possession of the gun, from being charged: "*en ek kry dit reg* [and I managed it] you see once they got me to the books. out is my sister." Later, when he is shouted at by members of the rival gang, he takes them on single-handedly: "[this plan you've got against me it's got a dick in its arse . . . because why if you're a man then don't wait until there are many of you. speak up like a man don't wait until I turn my back. now your flag is torn . . .] because in the district the code was . ja . thou shalt not squeal."[15] He claims that these words have a perlocutionary effect: by simply stating their "unmanliness"—the reference is to sodomy—and by reminding them of the code of solidarity against whites "thou shalt not squeal [tell tales] to the boere," the rival flag, we are told, is indeed torn. When Boeta Dickie ends up in court, it is the ejection of his crying baby daughter from the court room, in other words foregrounding his responsibility as a father, that galvanizes him against the enemy, imbues him with power, and guarantees his success: "fuck yous man now its on with me and yous [and there he made his mistake because when I chucked out the lawyer, then I just handled them man . then I handled them my way. let them speak. I just keep myself mister you know in perfect Afrikaans and so on]." From this account the implication is that he was found not guilty because of his verbal skills, which he knows to be superior to those of his lawyer. That these self-redeeming speech acts are vaguely reported, or their effects simply asserted, tell us not only about the apocryphal nature of the stories but also about storytelling itself as a socially symbolic act in which gendered subjectivity is constructed.

The metafunction of speech within the narratives is thus foregrounded, with causality embedded in specific speech acts. In another story about the advantages of bilingualism, Boeta Alie bamboozles a customs officer at the docks by claiming that he understood the English command, "Open the boot," to be the similar sounding Afrikaans words "OK *Boet* [brother]," which allowed him to do an improbable U-turn and successfully drive off to get rid of illegal goods. Boeta Dickie comments on the widespread practice of manipulating bilingual court proceedings by demanding interpreters for witness given in Afrikaans. The translation allows him more time to think and so to construct a persuasive argument: "we using it but the darkies [*sic*] using it even more to his advantage. *hy kan Ingels en Afrikaans praat dan seg hy nog altyd hy wil 'n tolk hê* [he can speak English and Afrikaans yet he will still ask for an interpreter] which gives him more time to figure out how to phrase and how to put down something."[16]

The second story, Boeta Alie's account of a group of young men verbally abusing a white woman, ironically comments on the referential aspect of the evening's stories and their convoluted relationship with the truth. He explains how he rightly confesses to the crime of molesting the woman, who, in an identity parade, wrongly identifies his friend as the culprit, upon which he, Boeta Alie, is charged: "They say I'm not the crook. I say I'm the crook an I AM the crook an they say what you wanna come tell lies here. Er. Then the magistrate say hey *vir jou sluit ons op jong* because why *jy praat nou er* [hey you, boy, we'll lock you up because why you're now talking er] . . . He chase me away to jail for *sommer* [just] nine months or six months for perjury." However, that story inexplicably ends with the lawyer congratulating Boeta Alie on his excellent lying, and by skirting around the issue of his actual imprisonment we are free to assume his subsequent acquittal. Such self-redeeming speech acts form the resolution and the basis of the coda in all the narratives.

Clearly the apocryphal nature of these stories raises questions for the fixed syntagm of narrative-is-knowledge, and suggests that the "bivalency of narrative,"[17] the fact that it encompasses both discursive performance and truth claims, cannot be ignored. The story Boeta Dickie tells about the gun shows that knowledge is indeed implicated in his deployment of narrative structure itself, in other words the organization and patterning of information, as well as the embedding of causality and temporality. The influential work by William Labov on natural narrative in his study of Black English vernacular in New York established that spoken and written narratives have common features. His analysis shows not only that what Basil Bernstein called the restricted code of working-class language was inaccurate but also that all Labov's interviewees structured their stories in an order which is formally similar to written narratives. Pratt concludes from this that since people do not organize their anecdotes around patterns they learn from reading, literary and natural narratives are utterances of the same type. We can attribute the formal and functional similarities, Pratt argues, to "the nature of the speech situation in which the utterance occurs, in which the speaker and his audience are engaged."[18]

This attention to context, and thus to the pragmatics of the performative-propositional double structure of utterances, also turns the spotlight on the speaking subject, who constructs reality through narrative form. Such construction is, however, not simply fictitious. Habermas, for instance, claims that "in adopting the narrative form we are choosing a perspective that 'grammatically' forces us to base our descriptions on an everyday concept of the lifeworld as cognitive referencing system."[19] To locate storytelling within cultural knowledge, however, and make claims for the operations of narrative as an instrument of cognition, should surely also take into account the truth claims of the story.

It is the fictional aspect of the story Boeta Dicke tells that prompts me to reconsider the ways in which knowledge is implicated or deployed in his narrative. His story about the gun is not only explicitly about knowledge, it also activates our knowledge of the Fall, a script that is mobilized in order to establish patriarchal law. The evening's storytelling is preceded by a discussion of the codes of friendship and loyalty necessary within groups to protect themselves against the injustices of apartheid law. Boeta Dickie's framing device is itself the formulation of a law: whether or not a wife should be trusted with information. Boeta Dickie starts his story by recalling a previous conversation with a friend who believes that a wife should be trusted "in total," and in spite of his own belief that he should "have a reserve," he decides to test his friend's view. Subsequent events show that telling one's wife a secret (for example, where one keeps one's illegal gun) unleashes a spiral of blabbing and treachery that rages through the family and the community, thus undermining the subject's successful handling of the police—who are subsequently led by women to the incriminating gun. At first, Boeta Dickie manages to placate the police with his representation of the situation, a muddled argument about how the people who started the trouble should know where the gun is by virtue of the fact that they had tried to shoot him. This argument is about to be legitimated, or turned into an official statement that evening, bringing closure to the case, but such legitimation is prevented by women who talk out of turn.

His wife, who wants to know where the gun is kept, does not manage to wheedle information out of Boeta Dickie; instead, he consciously experiments with woman's trustworthiness, and against his own good sense tests his friend's belief that a wife can be trusted with a secret. Woman's untrustworthiness is a presupposition drawn from common cultural knowledge, thus his act of telling her the location of the gun is presented as the legitimate testing of a dubious theory. The experiment fails; Boeta Dickie proves that women cannot be trusted, and he is thus able to establish a patriarchal law that excludes women from knowledge.

In Boeta Dickie's narrative, the deferral of blame between Eve and the serpent is attenuated into a chain of female betrayal that ranges from an innocence of sorts through to intentional treachery. Fatima, Boeta Dickie's wife, reveals the truth to her husband's sister in an unguarded moment of innocent babbling, a slip while engaged in "women's talk," which is to say idle discourse or thoughtless wittering. The meddlesome sister, who imagines that she is helping Boeta Dickie, actively intervenes by taking the gun out of the fig tree and carrying it to her friend; the friend, an older woman, deliberately betrays Boeta Dickie to the police.

Knowledge of the gun in the fig tree comically enacts the drama of good and evil in Eden, and woman's transferral of the phallic gun from the fig tree to the handbag suggests manipulative sexuality that leads to man's downfall; indeed, the behavior of Boeta Dickie's sister shows the illogical gap between her speech and her actions: she wishes to help him, but her weakness for talking out of turn leads to evidence landing in the hands of the police, enemy of all people of color. The final betrayal has many of the improbable elements of a fairy tale: as agent we have the older woman or witch, associated with jealousy, malice, and manipulation, who irrationally colludes with the enemy in spite of not knowing Boeta Dickie. His sister, in search of a solution, has brought the gun in her handbag to the house of the older woman who calls the police after sending the sister off on an errand ("leave your bag here," "post a letter") the transparency of which would have given any schoolboy pause.

In *The Post-Modern Condition: A Report on Knowledge,* Jean-François Lyotard posits storytelling as a central activity of the human mind; he calls it a mode of thinking as legitimate as that of abstract logic, and claims that as such it constitutes knowledge that does not take on an object but is rather an instance of ordering and uttering. Such knowledge, in opposition to technology's commodification or "exteriorization of knowledge with respect to the 'knower,' is what constitutes the culture of a people," Lyotard proposes.[20] In tandem with the knowledge equation is the widely held view of narrative's central concern with cultural legitimacy and with struggle. For Lyotard, knowledge, instantiated in oral discourse, also shows that "to speak is to fight, in the sense of playing, and speech acts fall within the domain of a general agonistics."[21] Walter Ong similarly defines natural narrative as knowledge embedded in the world of human life, so that orality "situates knowledge in the context of struggle."[22] This agonistic aspect is borne out in Boeta Alie and Boeta Dickie's stories, in their focus on conflict with authority and their representation of a community criss-crossed with difference.

Boeta Dickie's story on the very topic of knowledge—the strategic withhold-ing of knowledge from women and the police—is formulated in terms of codes of survival: don't trust your wife with sensitive information; don't "squeal" to the police (the boere). It is these precepts that provide a structure for what appears to be a loose, incoherent narrative in two parts: the storyteller giving informa-tion to a woman, and the rival gang transgressing the code of the district by giv-ing information to the police, significantly formulated in terms of a mosaic commandment: "Thou shalt not squeal." This would seem to support Lyotard's claim that knowledge is embedded in the deontic or ethical function of story-telling. The hero's successes, Lyotard claims, "bestow legitimacy upon social institutions" and allow the society in which the story is told "to define its crite-ria of competence . . . and to evaluate . . . what can be performed within it."[23] While the formulation of narrative as knowledge, often cited in terms of the ety-mological connection between the words themselves, is not concerned with what it is that the storyteller knows, it is crucially bound up with how narrative operates as an instance of mind in the construction of reality. The hermeneutic property that marks narrative raises questions, however, from a gendered per-spective about the benign orthodox formulation of narrative-is-knowledge. Boeta Dickie's story may urge us to conclude that women cannot be trusted with knowledge, but such nonsense also shows that to dismiss the question of *know-ing what* is done at the cost of severing knowledge from the ethical.

It is Lyotard himself who subsequently, in *The Postmodern Explained to Children* (1992), repudiates his earlier views on the importance of narrative, claiming that he had gone too far in identifying knowledge with narrative:

> There is an uncriticised metaphysical element in general narratology that ac-cords hegemony to one genre—the narrative—over all the others, a sort of sovereignty of minor narratives which allows them to escape the crisis of dele-gitimation. It's true that they escape, but only because they never had any le-gitimating value. The people's prose—the real prose I mean—says one thing and its opposite: "Like father, like son" and "To the miserly father, a prodigal son." Only romanticism imagined this prose to be consistent, to be guided by the task of expressivity, emancipation, or the revelation of wisdom. Postmo-dernity is also the end of the people as sovereign of the stories.[24]

While it is difficult to disagree that the concept of knowledge has been banalized in relation to narrative, I would also suggest that Lyotard's disidentification seems to be misplaced. Lyotard's characterization of the people's prose as inconsistent rejects by sleight of hand its claims to wisdom, expressivity, and emancipation, as if the latter are predicated on the former. One could argue equally that the cited aphorisms (they are *not* narratives, and they *are* expressive), produced as they must be in different contexts, demonstrate the existence of contradiction, ambiguity, and pluralism that necessarily operate in any culture, and also in narratives. The Western "crisis of delegitimation" is in any case of little relevance to the condition of dispossessed South Africans who, after the first democratic elections, indeed expected to see their narratives of resistance and emancipation legitimized. Such narratives of enfranchisement can surely claim legitimacy without recourse to the concept of knowledge, on the basis of an ethical imperative. Lyotard's characterization of knowledge in terms of consistency does, however, suggest a reinstatement of *knowing that,* which allows knowledge to take an object.

It is the introduction of the ethical into the equation that affords a way out of the problem. An understanding of knowledge in terms of *knowing that* and *knowing how* has shifted with Foucault's archaeology that renders all knowledge contentious, so that the problem of knowing now crucially embraces the question of *how* we know *what* we know. This is to include within the sphere of knowledge ethical and ideological as well as textual dimensions, and to acknowledge that Habermas's "lifeworld as cognitive referencing system," far from being a neutral given in the production of knowledge, is shot through with ideological assumptions that may have slender claims either to knowledge or to legitimacy. The ethical has of course been argued convincingly by Adam Newton, Martha Nussbaum, and others in terms of narrative structure.[25] The more mundane point I want to make here is that to dismiss narrative content (*knowing that*) is patently unwise.

Boeta Dickie's narrative not only reveals knowledge in terms of narrative structure but also confers legitimacy on the undemocratic beliefs Boeta Dickie has about women's linguistic behavior. His undermining of white authority by the same token establishes his own masculine authority, by which he is defined in relation to women. His speech produces power, whereas women's speech brings trouble, and thus folk-linguistic beliefs about women's speech are ratified and existing gender relations legitimized. The parallel narrative of the gangsters who betray Boeta Dickie to the police strategically negotiates the modalities of race and gender in order to confer on women both treachery and naïveté. It is around speech that the homologous elements in the narrative are centered: the male/female antithesis is embodied in women's thoughtless, misguided, or malicious talk that leads to trouble, while men's sparse, strategic, and directed talk gets them out of trouble and establishes self-esteem. Such female stupidity is reiterated in the white woman's wrong identification of her molester, while the act of molestation, presented cursorily as an instance of jolly assertion of manhood—and, by implication, of resisting the Immorality Act—is ameliorated through its link with apartheid legislation.

While there is no reference to the forced removals and the destruction of District Six, the events in these narratives are firmly located in particular geographical spaces, the importance of which is established in description of routes and reiteration of names of streets. For instance, in Boeta Dickie's narrative, the naming of Van der Leur, Constitution, and Hanover streets is largely irrelevant for the purposes of the story, but these emotive names, redolent of demolition, embed the story in a geography that surveys the participants' communal territory, marks the history of displacement from District Six, and confers a truth-value on the narratives. Boeta Alie's story about molesting a woman similarly traces the participants' movements through the streets, the names of which not only lend authenticity but also function as an aide-memoire.

Not surprisingly, "Streets," the first exhibition at the District Six Museum, comprised a vertical display of the original street signs, as well as large map of the area on the floor, on which ex-residents marked the site of their demolished houses.[26] Given memory's close mnemonic relationship with place and location, Isabel Hofmeyr asks the important question of what happens when people lose access to the topography that helps to uphold memory, and finds a process of corruption and transformation in their historical narratives.[27] Thus the apocryphal inevitably slips into narratives set in a space of demolition, and associations that are necessarily lost with the loss of memory are replaced by contemporary associations, in this case, of armed resistance and liberation from apartheid.

While knowledge surely entails the truth of what is known, it is also the case that a true description of the past is not possible, "not because there are and always will be lacunae in our evidence, but because earlier events will continue to receive differing descriptions through the relations in which they stand to events later in time than themselves."[28] Or, as Levinas puts it in terms of the speaking subject, narrative synthesis "recollects its temporal dispersal into past, present, future, narrates its existence as a finite and contemporaneous story [*histoire*], a totalizing copresence of past, present and future."[29] The crucial aspect of temporality can be seen in Boeta Dickie's tale of multiple betrayals, set in territory occupied by rival gangs, where black solidarity—albeit male solidarity in which differences are settled without recourse to white authority—is foregrounded. It is the appeal against white authority as well as the recent past of political resistance that allows for the gun to undergo metonymic displacement from its kudos as gangster accessory ("is *mos* few and far between that guys had guns that time man") to implied association with the guerrilla's AK-47. Apartheid legislation against black ownership of guns thus is assumed to decriminalize the story of gangster warfare. In other words, through narrative, reality is retrospectively constructed so that in the process of inscribing the self as subject, the boundaries between criminal behavior and political armed resistance are blurred.

According to M. A. K. Halliday it is not only through narrative but also through the hidden grammar of speech itself that reality is constructed: "Ordinary languages in their everyday, commonsense contexts embody highly sophisticated interpretations of the natural order, rich in complementarities and thoroughly rheomodal . . . with the further property that it is 'metafunctional': it is committed to meaning more than one thing at once, so that every instance is at once both reflection and action—both interpreting the world and also changing it."[30] Halliday translates sentences from their formal written language to typical informal speech, and discusses their different grammatical structures to show that these modes constitute different ways of knowing: the formal or synoptic mode with its characteristic nominalizations and lexical density represents a world of things, of product and of being, whereas the informal or dynamic mode of speech, which is clausal, represents a world of happening, of process and of becoming. Thus he concludes that natural language, specifically through clausal structures, "represents reality as what happens, not as what exists; things are defined as contingencies of the flow."[31]

Halliday's characterization of writing and speech as different grammars that constitute different ways of interpreting experience is suggestive, and the claim that ordinary language interprets and also changes the world is not as extravagant as it might seem. It is borne out in Boeta Alie and Boeta Dickie's stories where the world of process and becoming allows for the act of oral narration to construct power and self-worth for the narrators. The world related by them is shown to be one in which power relations are not what they appear to be. No reference is made to the forced removal from District Six or the impotence of protest movements against the razing of the district; instead, the stories show how the very edifice of the law can be penetrated by sharp talk. Thus the draconian world is transformed into a manageable space in which it is the speakers' own language use that produces control. The same events narrated at the time of their occurrence in the late sixties would surely not have been constructed in such a way as to inflect criminality with political subversion; in other words, the hermeneutic property that marks narrative would have encoded and processed "knowledge" in different ways.

It is the overthrow of apartheid through armed resistance that determines and inflects Boeta Dickie and Boeta Alie's stories about clashes with the law. Armed resistance provides a revised context and thus revised meanings for the ex-gangsters' tales of life in District Six, so that criminal violence, through oral narration, is ameliorated into triumphalist tales of resistance. Not only, then, is speech demonstrated in the narratives themselves to be central in undermining authority, the act of speaking, of telling a story filtered through a biblical script, allows the speaker to reinterpret the world and re-present it as one in which he establishes power over women, outmaneuvers authority, and legitimates his actions.

Annie Coombes cites the Truth and Reconciliation Commission as an important influence in the conception of the District Six Museum, and in the structuring of individuals' interactive responses within the space, which is to say their refiguring of the past. In the context of public remembering of loss, separation, and violation, she claims, "it is easier to understand the way that District Six has come to serve what we might appreciate as a 'necessary' paradigm of prelapsarian wholeness—a concept of 'community' that not only denied apartheid, but also presumed, at times, an (impossibly) harmonious and unified population prior to apartheid and possibly colonialism. The museum proposes nothing less than a utopian moment and, by implication, future."[32] In this sense Boeta Alie and Boeta Dickie's narratives depart from the reverential representations in the museum, offer a corrective to the imagined community, and as such indeed contribute to knowledge about District Six, but crucially this knowledge does not reside in what they tell but resides rather in how they tell and how we interpret their stories.

Natural narrative, like its literary counterpart, can thus be considered a mode of discourse that produces and reproduces cultural values, and in that sense is bound up with cultural knowledge in a productive way, so that cultural knowledge cannot be viewed as a ready-made repository from which information about a culture is simply extracted. Undoubtedly narrative performance is of value in that it allows the storyteller to construct himself as subject, but what the stories of Boeta Alie and Boeta Dickie also alert us to is the pitfalls in an unreflective adoption of the narrative-is-knowledge mantra that ignores the ethical aspect and truth-value of such knowledge. Foucault's view is instructive: "What is essential is that thought, both for itself and in the density of its workings, should be both knowledge and a modification of what it knows, reflection and a transformation of the mode of being of that on which it reflects."[33]

13

"Good Reliable Fictions": Nostalgia, Narration, and the Literary Narrative (2011)

After having read extensively about the critical rehabilitation of nostalgia, I no longer know what the word means. Yearning, which is an intense, overpowering longing, seems to be elided in contemporary accounts of nostalgia, so that the term attenuates into plain old fond remembrance. I will not here rehearse the arguments for nostalgia's critical, subversive, or empowering potential, or for its value as a conceptual or critical tool, but since this literature refers primarily to popular media, personal narratives, public memorializing, and historical discourse, I want to test the validity of these claims in relation to literary discourse— not least because literary narratives are distinctive in deploying a common feature, the concept of the uncanny, the immanence of the strange within the familiar, in the evocation of nostalgia. It is also my unease about Svetlana Boym's much-quoted *The Future of Nostalgia* (2001), which does deal with literary texts, that sets me off on this contrary course.

If nostalgia has, in the past, frequently been associated with facile sentimentality and thus with middlebrow writing, to what extent and how could its valorization impinge on a literary text? Indeed, how representable is nostalgia? I am not able to discuss here a body of work, so instead examine closely the ways in which nostalgia is represented in South African author Ivan Vladislavić's *Double Negative* (2010), a novel that accompanies a book of photographs, *TJ*, which reproduces a selection from six decades of photographer David Goldblatt's representations of his native city, Johannesburg. My questions include the following: Can nostalgia be mimetically represented without its sentimentality detracting from the aesthetics of a literary work? Are there narrative strategies or rhetorical devices specific to the narration of nostalgia?

But first, a detour via a nonfiction account of growing up in a Johannesburg township by one of South Africa's leading young historians and journalists,

Jacob Dlamini's *Native Nostalgia* (2009), not least because it offers a refreshingly nuanced account of remembering the bad old days of apartheid and also allows me to consider the troubling notion of sentimentality. That the thoughtful narration of Dlamini's own childhood experience is mercifully free of sentimentality suggests a need to distinguish between fond personal memories and a yearning for that past. But sentimentality has had a makeover, it turns out, embraced as it has been by postmodernism for opposing the rationalist ideals of the Enlightenment. Richard Rorty claims, for instance, that it is sentiment and the casting out of rationality that will save human rights. "Human beings," Rorty says, "are distinguished . . . by the capacities for friendship and intermarriage," by "flexible sentimentality" rather than by "rigorous rationality" and "the capacity to know."[1] If Boym's claim that "longing can make us more empathetic toward fellow humans" is unsubstantiated, Rorty's account of tolerance of the other, as an outcome for those who are economically and socially secure, is more convincing.[2]

I start with Jacob Dlamini's Mrs. Nkabinde, an older woman the author encounters in a township whose recollections of life under apartheid depart from the usual expressions of pain and suffering. "If the pass laws were such a hated symbol of apartheid, as many of us think they were," Dlamini writes, "why would Mrs Nkabinde remember them so fondly?"[3] The answer has in fact been given on the previous page, where he tells us that influx control is "remembered benignly" by his informant because "in her view the problems of today started 'with the influx of people and shacks. . . . There are too many outsiders.'"[4] Now it would seem here that benign memory *does* constitute nostalgia, since Mrs. Nkabinde would rather return to the halcyon days of influx control, even though she may have hated it at the time. Or would she? She has, understandably, not been asked that particular question, and there is no evidence that disillusionment with the current postapartheid government necessarily translates into desire for an actual return to the Pass Laws. In this case, I cannot see how Boym's celebrated distinction between restorative and reflective nostalgia holds.[5] Mrs. Nkabinde neither wants the past restored nor reflects on her views. Her intolerance of the outsider, an unspoken outcome perhaps of the struggle culture's fostering of support for the idea of nationhood in all its problematic senses of authenticity and exclusive belonging, and an outcome too of economic insecurity, surely fuels her fond remembrances of the past. What stays with this reader is the ethical implication of the insider/outsider opposition, of Mrs. Nkabinde's distaste for the strangers. The search for "authentic" tradition, so typical in the discourse of nationhood, is, of course, the mainstay of cultural nostalgia, and the imagined community of nationhood relies on its adversary, the foreigner.

Nostalgia, previously cast as false sentimentality, now in its rehabilitation asserts its authenticity. It is the indisputable fact of the individual's memory, whether accurate or not, as evoked by the bodily experience of the senses, that is valorized. But if Boym claims that nostalgia, "unlike melancholia which confines itself to the planes of individual consciousness," concerns "the relationship between individual biography and the biography of groups or nations, between personal and collective memory,"[6] she neither unpacks the notion of collective memory nor explains how this relationship is achieved. "Authentic" nostalgia, surely intransitive in its raw form, cannot transfer these bodily effects to an other and so serve ethical intersubjectivity. Except through the telling of stories, where rationality must once again step in, since it is through affective *and* cognitive processes that we encounter the narratives of others and make analogical links with the self, where the act of telling, the narration itself, engages us and produces empathy. What a pity that Mrs. Nkabinde has not had the chance to listen to the memories of displaced people, the stories of foreigners from the north. Or indeed to read *Double Negative*, where Vladislavić's central character perspicaciously states that he "would hate to be accused of authenticity."[7]

In her study on strangers, Julia Kristeva speaks of nationalism's tendency to isolate and hunt down the foreigner whose own "hard-hearted indifference" in turn is "no more than the respectable aspect of nostalgia."[8] She traces the slippage from universal man to nation in the French Declaration of the Rights of Man and Citizen, where "the lofty, abstract, fully symbolic notion of humanity" was replaced with "a local, national, or ideological membership,"[9] the legacy of which can be found in Germany's National Socialism. Kristeva's plea is, in the absence of a utopian society without nations, for "human rights"—which is to say for "an ethics . . . that espouses a concept of human dignity which includes strangeness."[10] It is Kristeva's appeal to the Freudian concept of the *heimlich/unheimlich* that returns me to the hermeneutics of literary narration. "In the very word *heimlich*," she writes, "the familiar and intimate are reversed into their opposites, brought together with the contrary meaning of 'uncanny strangeness' harbored in *unheimlich*."[11] Interestingly, Fredric Jameson, in his hysterical condemnation of what he sees as nostalgia's effacement of history, refers to its "occultation of the present" and its "casting of a spell."[12] The uncanny, a typical element in the *narration* of nostalgia, is surely what distinguishes nostalgia from fond remembering. So, in relation to *Double Negative*, a novel that stages the relationship between memory and nostalgia, I will also be looking at the inscription of the uncanny in Vladislavić's complex representation of nostalgia.

Vladislavić's title, *Double Negative*, references the genesis of the work as a collaboration with David Goldblatt's book of photographs, *TJ*. As a narrative about the experience of a young man called Neville—or Nev—Lister during the apartheid years and after its demise as well, it is also a meditation on history. Early in the text, there is a reference to Walter Benjamin's Angel of History, the commentary by Benjamin on modernity's loss of a sense of the past and of an inability to find ourselves in history. It occurs at the point where Nev first meets Saul Auerbach, the fictional photographer who is based on the real figure of David Goldblatt and whose works appear to coincide with Goldblatt's existing photographs (thus foregrounding the relationship between the real and the fictional). Nev reminds us that his narration is retrospective, that he is himself engaged in writing a personal history: "Had you seen me there, with the cold shell of the car against my bum and the morning sun on my face, you would have thought I was an overly earnest young man. You could not see Benjamin's Angel . . . leaning beside me with his wings folded across the bonnet. . . . If you had a sense of historical destiny, if you were sufficiently drunk with it, you might expect to ride out any storm. But I did not imagine I would be carried in one piece to a classless shore. History would break over me like a wave that had already swept through the manor house and bear me off in a jumble of picture frames and paper plates."[13]

If Benjamin's angel flies into the future looking backward, Nev's is stationary; history has stalled for him and will remain so until the demise of apartheid. I am troubled by Boym's claim that Benjamin's angel exemplifies "a reflective and awe-inspiring modern longing that traverses twentieth century art."[14] Not only is this a curious branding of twentieth-century art, but Benjamin's angel resonates with an image from antiquity (Barthes reminds us): "The Greeks entered into Death backward: what they had before them was their past."[15] The modern difference is what the past looks like. It is a refiguration of history, no longer tenable as a continuum, a teleological chain of events, linked through reason, which we have come to think of as progress; it is "a single catastrophe which keeps piling wreckage upon wreckage." It is this that, despite the storm of progress, must hold the angel's attention; hence "his face is turned towards the past."[16] There is nothing nostalgic in the angel's expression as he looks at this past: "His eyes are staring, his mouth is open, his wings are spread" (Benjamin tells us).[17] In other words, he is frozen with horror, unable to understand the past as the debris before him grows skyward. To identify this complex condition as nostalgia is surely to render the term meaninglessly elastic.

It is not for nothing that the photographer based on Goldblatt is called Auerbach in *Double Negative*. The name is a bold citation of the famous Jewish critic Erich Auerbach, whose work *Mimesis: The Representation of Reality in Western Literature* ends with a chapter on modernity and its stylistic concern with the representation of time. It is Edward Said who reminds us of the poignancy of Auerbach's project, the urgency to take stock as Europe hurtled toward ruin, the fact that Auerbach was writing this work in Istanbul, straddling the cultures of East and West, during the Second World War—in other words as a foreigner, a Jew escaped from Nazi Germany. It is such strangeness that is also attributed to the photographer in the novel and that finds expression in his art, which is not considered by the leftier-than-thou as exemplary antiapartheid work. The novel's referencing of *Mimesis* is pertinent to the fact that it engages, through documentary photography, with the making of fiction and explores the relationship between the artifact and the person or event in the real world.

Double Negative tells the story of a young man, Nev, who is disenchanted with life under apartheid, but who neither joins the resistance movement nor is able to continue as a student pretending to lead a normal life in a normal country. Dodging the draft, he lives in London for ten years. But before he leaves South Africa, his father insists that he spend a day with Auerbach, in the hope that he might become interested in photography. Later, he returns to postapartheid South Africa, where he works as a commercial photographer, a career into which he has fallen accidentally. The novel is, among other things, an elegy to the father, and as such it is associated with the typical themes of loss and continuity; it is a site that lends itself to a study of the inscription of nostalgia. What marks the writing is a gestural submission to nostalgia, followed by resistance to it, generally manifested in an acknowledgment of the nostalgic impulse and then an undercutting of it with irony. Sentiment is deliberately stifled, first in relating the death of the father, an event brimming with potential affect, especially since it occurs while Nev is in London. Here the fact is narrated on Nev's return, analeptically, in a subordinate clause, actually as a prepositional phrase in relation to the father's car: "I rediscovered my hometown in . . . the Mercedes he'd driven to work until a month before he died."[18] We have no access to Nev's feelings at the time of the death.

In this first-person narrative of witnessing we see Nev, the returnee, struck by nostalgia in his father's car, through that well-known catalyst, smell. The narration also evokes nostalgia's typical trafficking with the uncanny: "I felt him sitting next to me, a reluctant passenger, telling me to watch out and slow down and keep my eye on the road. He was so vividly present I could smell him. Later I realized it was no illusion: his aftershave was still in the leather steering wheel cover and the warmth of my own hands had drawn the scent out on the air."[19] If there is unavoidable evocation of nostalgia, a poignant yearning that conjures up the presence of the absent father performing the paternal role, the uncanny olfactory sensation is demystified through a rational explanation. The effect is an ironic distancing that undermines nostalgia. Stripped of sentimentality, the narration disavows the reproduction of nostalgia, while at the same time acknowledging its force.

Nev's exploration of the city takes him to the site of his old family home. Surveying new postmodern matchbox houses from the car, he notes that, uncannily, and "right on cue, the melancholy sounds of 'Stranger on the Shore' rose like fragrant smoke from the grills in the dash."[20] The sensory elicits a nostalgia that is simultaneously undercut by its association with the kitsch of the architecture. Again, the irony comes from an assertion of nostalgia uncannily revealed within the heimlich, which is then contradicted by a rational explanation. One is reminded of Derrida's injunction: "Beyond internalising memory, it is then necessary to *think*, which is another way of remembering. Beyond *Erinnerung*, it is then a question of *Gedächtnis*."[21] *Double Negative* demands cognitive activity on the part of the reader—the rational explanation of the old tape deck given much earlier in the text as "the soundtrack of my father's life" here has to be inferred, and the response elicited is laughter rather than sentimental indulgence of loss. Nev's homecoming is thus bound up with the unheimlich *within* the heimlich, a sentiment suppressed in the discourse of nationhood that surrounds him. The structuring of nostalgia as an absence in the text is evident again when we are told, incidentally and out of chronology, that Nev has sold the old Mercedes. No doubt it was painful to lose the car, but this pain is conspicuously elided. What these instances show is the problematic nature of representing nostalgia, particularly in the South African context.

While Dennis Walder argues convincingly for the value of self-reflexivity involved in nostalgia's negotiation between the present and the past, his investigation of nostalgia in postcolonial fictions points to the problems involved in representation. On Chimamanda Ngozi Adichie, for instance, he quotes biographical information from an interview in which Adichie declares that homesickness and nostalgia for Nigeria prompted her to start writing. "The nostalgic tone is unmistakable," says Walder of Adichie's biographical comments. But this cannot stand in for a reading of the novel itself. While it may be true that "Adichie's achievement is to have turned the nostalgia for her childhood into an indictment of independent, postcolonial Nigeria," the originary nostalgia has who knows when been transformed, for it is not represented in the novels and thus the reader has no access to it, and the critic cannot cite instances in the text.[22] No evidence beyond the biographical is given for what Walder calls the "consciously nostalgic recall of the post-independence past of the nation." Adichie's *Half a Yellow Sun*, for instance, he claims, demonstrates that "memory grasps history on the individual, microlevel, by means of a reworked nostalgia *refiguring* a family past,"[23] but the use of the word *"refiguring"* is disingenuous in this context. The fictional family's past has not been figured *before*; *this* text *is* its figuration. Boym performs the same sleight of hand in her discussion of Nabokov.

Vladislavić's novel differs in that it does attempt to represent nostalgia but in the process figures its very intransmissibility, or presents it as a structured absence in the text. Now irony, used in *Double Negative* to temper sentiment, is discussed by Linda Hutcheon as a close companion to nostalgia: both, she claims, are "doubled"; both share the "twin evocation of affect and agency."[24] I suggest a more adversarial relationship between nostalgia and irony, however, and would quibble with her understanding of irony as affective, as well as the notion of its transideological nature. A more persuasive theory of irony as an echoic utterance is presented by the linguists Dan Sperber and Deirdre Wilson. The speaker echoes a thought attributed to someone else, a type of person, popular wisdom, or general ideological belief or cultural aspiration, while dissociating herself from it with scorn or ridicule. Thus through an inferencing process irony appeals to shared knowledge, and the reader who may never have considered the absurdity of certain beliefs is, in the cognitive processing of the statement and in retrieving the source of the echo, pressed into reconsidering such a belief. In the case, say, of *Huckleberry Finn*, irony is clearly not transideological. Indeed, it would go undetected where those who believe in slavery are unable to retrieve in themselves the source of the statement: it is morally wrong to behave humanely.[25]

In evoking and ironizing nostalgia, *Double Negative* does not so much *reflect* on it as foreground the problem of its transmissibility. As raw material, nostalgia demands radical transformation. Yes, it happens, but the reader cannot savor it; the novel will not produce a copy of nostalgia. It fails to meet what Elaine Scarry in her meditation on aesthetics calls the "requirement beauty places on us to replicate."[26] Beauty prompts a copy of itself, Scarry insists, and cites Simone Weil's claim that beauty asks us "to give up our imaginary position as the centre. . . . A transformation then takes place at the very roots of our sensibility, in our immediate reception of sense impressions and psychological impressions."[27] The aesthetic, then, forces us to undergo a radical decentering, a process of "unselfing" that dissolves the self/other binary. In *Double Negative,* the dismissal of nostalgia as the self's "authentic" experience makes way for the ethical and produces the transferrable knowledge that narrative claims. Scarry puts it in narratological terms: "It is as though one has ceased to be the hero or heroine in one's own story and has become what in a folktale is called the 'lateral figure' or 'donor figure.'"[28]

What I now hope to show are the strategies used in Vladislavić's aesthetic project of unselfing the protagonist, and I start with the theme of photography. On the day that Nev's father insists Nev visit Auerbach, the photographer takes him and a British journalist on a trip to a hilltop, Langermann Kop, where, looking down to the streets below and guided arbitrarily by roof colors, they each pick a house in the suburb, Bez Valley, below. These they visit in the hope that Auerbach will be able to photograph the occupants, and indeed Nev witnesses Auerbach's way of engaging with his subjects as two photographs are made. But they run out of time, and the orange roof that Nev chooses has to be left unvisited.

Photography is explored not only as a medium that, in the popular imagination, is a catalyst for nostalgia but also for its relationship to mimesis, and here Vladislavić is clearly influenced by Roland Barthes's *Camera Lucida.* At the beginning of his study, Barthes, who appears to be sick of the dominance of theory *(Does the rise of nostalgia studies come from the same impulse?* one wonders), sets out his dilemma in terms of "the uneasiness of being a subject torn between two languages, one expressive, the other critical."[29] Wishing to turn to the affective and the visceral, to the nonstandard language of the heart, he asks: "What does my body know of Photography?"[30] He wants to explore photography for "'sentimental' reasons," a phrase from which he distances himself with scare quotes and acknowledges the problem of retaining "a view of the object which was immediately steeped in desire, repulsion, nostalgia, euphoria."[31] In Barthes's rigorous attempt to attend to both the intellect and the heart, he arrives at the concept of a punctum, a detail in a photograph that allows the viewer to be touched, that arouses sympathy and tenderness and so constitutes a "wound."[32] Despite his language dripping with the affective, however, Barthes's study leads to the conclusion that a photograph is "never, in essence, a memory . . . but it actually blocks memory, quickly becomes a counter-memory."[33] Thus for Barthes, "in front of a photograph, our consciousness does not necessarily take the nostalgic path of memory"; rather the photograph offers the certainty of the object it represents, authenticating the existence of the person in question. Given these unequivocal statements it is strange that Svetlana Boym should cite Barthes's punctum in support of her argument for reflective—rather than restorative—nostalgia.[34]

Vladislavić's title, *Double Negative*, referring as it does to the photographic negative and the making of two fictitious photographs, also literally means positive, and as such, containing within it its opposite meaning, serves as an analogical figure for the heimlich/unheimlich dichotomy. Photography's role in what Alison Landsberg calls "prosthetic memory"[35] is also ironized in Nev's memory of a photograph of apartheid-era cabinet minister Adriaan Vlok kneeling to wash the feet of the Reverend Frank Chikane, a struggle-era leader, since later Nev remembers that there was no photograph, that the story had simply been reported in the press.[36] Nev's verbal rendition of Auerbach's photographs and their making constitutes a double mimesis, a translation that speaks of transmissibility and that Benjamin calls the "afterlife" of the work of art.[37] It is reproduced with tenderness, but Nev will not allow it to be a hackneyed aide-memoire to the people photographed in Bez Valley: "Sometimes photographs annihilate memory; they swallow the available light and cast everything around them into shadow. Two of Saul Auerbach's images were like shutters on my mind: Veronica in her yard in Emerald Street, Mrs Ditton in her lounge in Fourth Avenue. Dense with my own experience, but held there in suspension, in chemically altered form. If I could seize them for myself, my time and place would spurt like juice between my fingers. But how to reach through the frame?"[38]

The second part of the novel, "Dead Letters," is crucially concerned with history and memory in the making of fiction, and is distinguished by its humorous flirtation with nostalgia. It starts with Nev in London, where he avoids South Africans, distancing himself from home. But the first democratic election brings a change. He explains that "it's not often that history steps down from its pedestal and comes to meet you in the street. Yes, we were making history too, I could see it that way if I squinted."[39]

At Trafalgar Square, where he has just voted, Nev is embraced, he recalls, by "strangers, fiercely, as if they meant to squeeze the breath of the past caught between us, and I held on as if my life depended on it."[40] He resists the euphoria that contains a ahistorical impulse to erase the past. The television images from home too show how "every face was turned to the future."[41] On his return to Johannesburg, however, he discovers that "now that it was safe to do so, every second person was joining the struggle, and backdating the membership form. In retrospect, everyone had done their bit. . . . Perhaps the freight of the past had to be lightened if the flimsy walls of the new SA were not to buckle. How much past can the present bear? . . . Good, reliable fictions, that's what the doctor ordered."[42] Instead of nostalgia, fictional reconstruction of that past is the healthier option for coping with the burden of history, certainly for those who had not participated in the making of the New South Africa. And that is precisely what "Dead Letters" dramatizes; it is an elaborate gloss on such "reliable fictions."

Now back in South Africa, Nev visits the orange-roofed house in Bez Valley that they failed to reach that day back in 1982 (in the first part of the novel). The house represents unfinished business, a historical lacuna, but also an incomplete aesthetic project: "It had crumbled away in the folds of my brain, leaving a residue as evocative as the smell of my father's aftershave. It had the appeal of an incomplete gesture, always on the tip of my memory."[43] The house had not actually been visited in the past, but this also underscores the liminal aspect of nostalgia—its occupation of thresholds, temporal and spatial; its own yearning for an unattainable aesthetic reproduction. "Thresholds," incidentally, is what Nev calls his own photographic work about walls in Johannesburg, the high guarded facades that have sprung up, and that inspire his "longing for the vanished city."[44] The "thresholders" are the people he photographs standing at the gates of their high walls, next to their weird letterboxes.

With his camera, Nev worms his way into the orange-roofed house, where he finds a Mrs. Pinheiro. To do so, he lies about writing a history about the boxer Rosco Dunn, in fact a fictitious character from a movie who, he claims, may have lived in the house. We see the generative nature of narration as further fictions are spawned in this encounter, marked by classic situational irony. Mrs. Pinheiro knows that Nev is lying, although neither the reader nor Nev knows that she knows; she, in turn, lies about her husband, Dr. Pinheiro, being ill, weaving her own fictions about him. Nev imagines the boxer as a child in the sealed room where Dr. Pinheiro supposedly lies ill, and we are told that, as Nev speaks, "the scrawny, ash-grey child matured into a portly, middle-aged man with an identikit face that took its black-rimmed glasses from Joe Slovo."[45]

Fiction and irony are the agents that open up the world of the Stranger and allow for empathy and the ethical. It turns out that Dr. Pinheiro is long dead; he had been a refugee, a foreigner with poor English, who lost his social identity as a doctor and who worked for the postal service during the apartheid era. His legacy is a bundle of secreted letters saved from the incinerator, so poorly addressed that they could not be deciphered and therefore delivered. It is here that strangeness is ameliorated, that the heimlich is secured through fantasy and fiction. Pinheiro's "dead letters" also refer to Herman Melville's strange character Bartleby the scrivener, whose standard response to his employer's requests is

"I would prefer not to." Bartleby's strangeness is attributed to the rumor that he had previously worked in the Dead Letter Office; in prison, where he ends his days, he is mistakenly thought to be a "gentleman forger."[46]

The dead letters, literally relics of semiliterate, displaced people and their underdevelopment, are a metonym for apartheid that refuses displacement through nostalgia. Mrs. Pinheiro shows them to Nev; together they decipher the sad contents. The mode of narration is interesting on two levels. First, concerning the temporality of narration: the full story of the letters and their contents is not narrated in base time. Rather, it is recounted to Nev's mother at a later stage, when there is an analeptic shift to the garden where Mrs. Pinheiro undid the bundle. It is Nev's mother, in the present flow of time, who mediates that past, and the analepsis, the narrational leap into the past, is significant in its mimetic enactment. It is also later that Nev finds a pamphlet about the postal system that gives the history of apartheid's denial of access to the poor, as well as instructions on how to write and address letters, and accordingly is a tribute also to the era of reconstruction.

As for the narration of the contents of the letters, rather than mimetic reproduction the mode shifts to magic realism as the letter writers are brought to life then abruptly closed down and slipped back into the envelopes. The estrangement of magical realism reminds one of the *Bilderverbot*, of the Second Commandment, which critics evoke in relation to the Holocaust: horror must not be represented and thus reproduced. In the weird setting of the Pinheiro garden, amid the doctor's collection of bizarre letterboxes, Nev and Mrs. Pinheiro read "until the air was so thick with stories it couldn't be breathed."[47] But these *are* and are *not* fictions; rescued by the Stranger, Pinheiro, they are the actual stories of migrant workers of the past, the people turned into strangers in their own country, heartbreakingly brought to life. From a padded envelope, "a paper chain of men and women, hundreds of them joined hand and foot clattered out like galleys from a printing press. . . . Free at last stretching their limbs and cracking their joints, they began to tell their stories . . . delighted to suck air into their lungs and born to speak."[48] Mrs. Pinheiro "unfolded a small girl into a shady corner," and "despite having resolved to stay out of it," Nev remembers, "I licked my finger and cleaned the corners of the child's eyes."[49] The style is self-reflexively alluded to in his observation that the scene was "unhealthy in a Latin American way"[50]—a significant departure from Melville's letters, in which are found "pardon for those who died despairing; hope for those who died unhoping; good tidings for those who died stifled by unrelieved calamities."[51] For all Nev's being "astray between real and imaginary," the undelivered letters have been opened; they *do* communicate; the writers have been brought to life. They are not only literally a repository of history but through narration also become a figure of history. And if nostalgia had originally driven Nev to the negative space of Auerbach's incomplete project, it has respectfully retreated in this literary representation of apartheid's disgusting past.

Let us now return to the theme of the father, or progenitor, in the novel, a theme that suggests continuity, and one that is linked to the generation of fiction. We see in Nev's choice of career as a commercial photographer (though Nev is now considered an artist) that Auerbach, named for the author of *Mimesis,* for all his absence in the young man's life, serves as father figure, and that the *ethical* instilled by the biological father finds its counterpart in Auerbach's *aesthetic* practice. Taking up photography is also metonymy for Nev coming to terms with his country: the older photographer's initials are S.A. Nev visits the orange-roofed house, pursuing Auerbach's incomplete project based on color and chance, driving the deceased father's car. There he learns about Dr. Pinheiro, whose incomplete project of collecting letterboxes Nev takes on in his own photographing of letterboxes and thresholds; in other words, the progenitive baton is passed on. Nev has inherited Dr. Pinheiro's dead letters, first read surrounded by Pinheiro's collection of letterboxes, out of which the man himself had fabricated fictions. Nostalgia for the authentic, biological father has not only been undermined by irony but also through the theme of fatherhood been transformed into filiation, a sociality that celebrates historical continuity and appeals to a wider ethics.

When Nev revisits Auerbach, another event wrenched out of chronology (a device used repeatedly to undercut nostalgia), this continuity is underlined by the photographer wearing the same clothes in a house with the same décor as years previously. Auerbach shows Nev the photograph of an adult Joel Setshedi, the son of the domestic worker, Veronica, whom they had found (and Auerbach had photographed) years ago, with her surviving babies, in the blue-roofed house in Bez Valley. Veronica, then, not mere subject of a photograph, has independent subjectivity; Goldblatt/Auerbach's works literally have an afterlife; the works, translated back into the world, give him access to people whose lives intersect with his own. Thus we are shown the artist as not only committed to his work but also as an example of empathy that, according to Simone Weil, produces "unselfing." We read that Nev "envied" Auerbach "his continuity. He had soldiered on, one photograph at a time, leaving behind an account of himself and his place in which one thing followed another, print after print." Nev's "story," by contrast, "was full of holes."[52] Or, as Nev says earlier of the scraps of news cuttings or found pieces on his pinboard, "the awkward truths of my life take shape in their negative spaces." Unlike official histories, they are "the last signs I can bring myself to consult."[53]

Double Negative ends with a traditional narrative coda, a flashback to Nev's childhood when his father played a game in the car. The child would lie down in the back seat while his father took strange routes, so that when they stopped the boy would have to guess where they were. More than an exercise in orientation, it was for the child an experience of "making rather than following a map and matching it not to the world but to an internal landscape, a journey in memory." Nev gets better at the game and recounts the journey where he knows exactly where they are going: "I had X ray vision, I could see through the leather seats . . . through the metal rib of doors," so that when his father asks the question "Where are we now, my boy?" we are given this final sentence: "I lay in the dark with the bitter knowledge that I had unlearned the art of getting lost."[54] Now this flirts dangerously with nostalgia. The edenic condition is cast in terms of the spatial, the geography of the city, which throughout the novel had been explored by car—hence *TJ*, the old car registration of a Johannesburg for which Nev longs—with an understanding that the struggle to orientate himself was itself the home of innocence, the heimlich. But that is not the whole story. Cognitive mapping denies sentimentality. The cryptic final sentence, stripped of emotive language save for the phrase "bitter knowledge," alerts us to the very mode of representation that establishes the new postlapsarian self. Cast as allegory, that most old-fashioned of tropes, the narration sidesteps nostalgia to assert indirectly that in the inescapable knowledge of where home is, the unheimlich itself is revealed.

Thus for all the narrative's dwelling on place, it is time, memory, the originary constitutive character of allegory, that signifies. Allegory went out of fashion precisely because it appears as a product of the Enlightenment and is considered to be excessively rational. Paul de Man says of allegory that it "designates a distance in relation to its own origin, and, renouncing the nostalgia and the desire to coincide, it establishes its language in the void of this temporal distance. In so doing, it prevents the self from an illusory identification with the non-self, which is now fully, though painfully, recognized as a non-self."[55] De Man also points out the enigmatic link throughout the history of rhetoric between allegory and irony, one based on their double temporality. Nostalgia's trading with double temporality is here evoked by Vladislavić as a trace at the end of the novel, where once again, failing to reproduce itself, it necessarily retreats in this project of unselfing, of turning the self into a stranger who paradoxically no longer gets lost. It is allegory and irony linked in their "common demystification of an organic world postulated in a mimetic mode of representation in which fiction and reality could coincide" that serve transmission.[56]

What I hope to have shown is that nostalgia's role in *Double Negative* is liminal and that, anterior to literary narration, nostalgia hovers on the threshold of representation, often structured as an absence. As authentic individual experience, its intransitivity in representation is manifested in the text's simultaneous evocation and dismissal. The famed distinction, then, between reflective and restorative nostalgia is unhelpful in the reading of the literary text that instead grapples not with content but with nostalgia's transmissibility. And in demanding a reader's cognitive activity in processing narrative strategies and tropes, that is to say the aesthetic transmission of unselfing, the ethical is invoked.

14

IDENTITY, WRITING, AND AUTOBIOGRAPHY: THE CASE OF BESSIE HEAD'S *THE CARDINALS* (1994)

Bessie Head's early novels, *Maru* (1971) and *The Cardinals* (1993), are routinely discussed in terms of the author's biography and the tradition of black women's autobiography. I wish to depart from such readings by examining the ways in which Head explores racial and gendered subjectivity through creative rewriting of the self. Such writing raises the question of "authority" that can be discussed within the context of the repressive apartheid laws of the 1960s. Thus I argue that the discursive modalities of writing and not-writing about the self, or rather the relation between these modalities manifested as traces in the texts, constitute a discourse of liberation. My essay investigates the ways in which Head uses both writing and the law as tropes in works that rehearse self-reflexively the production of not-autobiography.

Like Elvis, Bessie Head lives. Barthes may have declared the author dead, but Head's persistent inscription of her own life, her origins, and her experience in her fiction, and her insistence in interviews on the documentary aspect of all her work, has driven pretheoreticals and poststructuralists alike to her biography.[1] In South Africa, academics squabble anachronistically about uncovering the true story of Head's life: whether she has fictionalized her life or not; whether she has lied to her interviewers; how to match given information with fictional events in her novels; whether the truth lies in her speech or in her writing. And since Truth—as we postmodernists know—comes in many guises and has the habit of contradicting itself, squabbles continue and the writing itself is too often neglected or read in terms of her tragic life.

Head's life story is indeed sensational, and constitutes a paradigmatic instance of the effects of apartheid on real lived experiences. In her own words, she was "born on the sixth of July, 1937, in the Pietermaritzburg Mental hospital. . . .

The reason for my peculiar birthplace was that my mother was white, and my father black. No details were ever available about my father beyond the fact that he worked in the family stables and took care of their racehorses."[2] When Head was thirteen, she was told by her missionary head teacher: "If you're not careful you'll get insane just like your mother. Your mother was a white woman. They had to lock her up as she was having a child by the stable boy who was a native."[3] Head was brought up in an orphanage and a variety of foster homes. Her mother committed suicide before she was one year old, and literary gossip has repeated the claim made by her mother's family that she had been raped by their employee. And so stories about Head's life proliferate and are reproduced by those of us who would otherwise scorn the punter's prurient interest in the affairs of Tory MPs.

Autobiography, a previously marginalized genre, has through feminist and postcolonial theory and a growth in postcolonial writing been rehabilitated. It is now commonplace to focus on the narrativity, the textuality, the fictionality of autobiography, and theories of subjectivity have alerted us to the complexities of writing the self and the construction of identity in writing. Postmodernist theory is clear at least on the question of referentiality: that there is no such thing as an autobiographical self that exists independently of the text in which it is constructed. On the other hand, the dissolution of the genre of autobiography into fiction has been contested in South Africa by critics, like M. J. Daymond, who argue that it has a specific social and political function in encouraging an underclass to testify to its suffering under apartheid. The testimonies of readers "who take energy from an exemplary protagonist's claims of selfhood that is vital to her . . . validating what she recognises as her own experiences" are at odds with theoretical positions.[4] Daymond thus problematizes the negation of referentiality since it minimizes the atrocious experiences of real subjects in the world.

The argument for the authority of experience is, however, precisely what underpins the current reception of black women's writing. While the genre has been rehabilitated, the tendency to treat black women's texts, whether written in the first or third person, as autobiography, persists. And writing that cannot be mistaken for autobiography has, as bell hooks discovered with her own experimental, nonlinear narratives, little hope of finding a publisher, a situation that is not unconnected with what Gates has called "the sociological fallacy" that valorizes the social and polemical functions of black literature.[5] My use of the word "autobiography" in relation to Head's writing is thus fraught with problems, but I want to approach her work, perhaps old-fashionedly, from the writer's position. J. M. Coetzee puts it as follows: "In a larger sense all writing is autobiography: everything that you write, including criticism and fiction, writes you as you write. The real question is: This massive autobiographical writing-enterprise that fills a life, this enterprise of self-construction (shades of *Tristram Shandy!*)—does it yield only fictions? Or rather, among the fictions of the self, the versions of the self that it yields, are there any that are truer than others? How do I know when I have the truth about myself?"[6] Here the hierarchical opposition between fiction and autobiography is deconstructed, and Coetzee's formulation also implies the futility of searching for the author in the text. This is a view of writing that sits comfortably with theories of subjectivity, and it is one that seems to lie at the heart of Bessie Head's work. Many black critics, however, have difficulties with the critique of essentialism, the notion of identity as a linguistic construct, and with what is seen as postmodernism's incompatibility with a liberatory discourse. bell hooks, for instance, in her essay "Postmodern Blackness," while defending postmodern readings, expresses the following reservations: "It never surprises me when black folks respond to the critique of essentialism, especially when it denies the validity of identity politics, by saying, 'Yeah, it's easy to give up identity, when you've got one.' Should we not be suspicious of postmodern critiques of the subject when they surface at a historical moment when many subjugated people feel themselves coming to voice for the first time? Though an apt and oftentimes appropriate comeback, it does not really intervene in the discourse in a way that alters and transforms."[7] It seems possible to negotiate the thorny path between critical orthodoxies and to read Bessie Head in postmodern fashion, that is, as one more than willing to concede the constructedness of identity, but at the same time locating that position in Head's own experience, her own biohistory. I am going to argue that deconstructing identity politics is precisely what Head presents as transformational in her fiction.

Eight years after her death, with the publication of *The Cardinals*, her first novel and the only one set in South Africa, Head returned with yet another version of her life. Written in 1961 and 1962, just after the massacre of protesters at Sharpeville, a period during which state repression was stepped up, and while Head was working as a journalist for the *Golden City Post*, she failed to find a publisher for the work at home or in Britain. In a letter to Randolph Vigne she refers to various pieces she had given to the poet Patrick Cullinan, "even the novel." After thirty years, Cullinan submitted the novel along with seven short pieces to Cape Town publisher David Philip.[8]

The plot of *The Cardinals*, like Head's other novels, has obvious correspondences between her own life and that of her protagonist. A beautiful young woman hands a newborn child and five shillings to her washerwoman, who lives in a slum on the outskirts of Cape Town. At the age of ten, when her foster father attempts to abuse her, the child runs away and lands in hospital, where she refuses to answer any questions so that she is given a new name and birth date. By the age of sixteen, she has been placed in a variety of foster homes. She starts work as a tea girl and spends her time reading and writing. After a letter of complaint to *African Beat—The Paper of the People,* she is offered a job by the editor. In the offices of the newspaper, where she works with the white editor and two coloured men, she is given the name of Mouse because of her silence and her unattractive, unfeminine appearance, but one of the men, Johnny, falls in love with her.

Chapter 5, however, flashes back to Johnny's youth as a fisherman, and the reader realizes from the account of his passionate affair with a middle-class woman, who secretly gives birth to his child, that Mouse, unbeknownst both to her and to Johnny, is his daughter. The mother, Ruby, immediately after delivering the child to the shanty, had committed suicide. We thus read the events in the novel in the terrifying knowledge that the developing relationship is incestuous. But the situation of not knowing nullifies their biological identities, and this in turn nullifies the illegitimacy conferred by the social law, so that their innocence is *also* a dramatization of the relationship between being and knowledge.

Having started with the autobiographical, having inscribed it in my title, I wish now to erase it and to discuss Head's novel as *not*-autobiography, as a negation of autobiography. And I hope to show how the discursive modality of both writing and not-writing about the self can constitute a transformative strategy. I borrow the notion of trace from Derrida, who discusses in his essay "How to Avoid Speaking" what he calls apophatic discourse, or a denial of what we say or do of that which we especially say or do. But such denial is not to be confused with avoidance; in other words, Head's strategy is not one of avoiding her life story; rather it is one of engaging with it creatively, and by the same token interrogating the notion of identity.

Derrida comments as follows on the example of Heidegger's negative theology, in which Heidegger proposes—in his investigation of the notion of God—to avoid the word "being":

> The word being is not avoided; it remains readable. But this readability announces that the word may be solely read, deciphered; it cannot or must not be pronounced, used normally, one might say, as a speech-act of ordinary language. It is necessary to decipher it under a spatialized typography, spaced or

spacing, printing over. . . . This erasure does not then have avoidance as its essential function. No doubt, Being is not a being, and it reduces to its turns, turnings, historical tropes; one must therefore avoid representing it as something, an object that stands opposite man and then comes towards him. To avoid the objectifying representation one will thus write the word being under erasure. It is henceforth not heard, but is read in a certain manner.[9]

What Head so assiduously refuses to represent as something that exists is her origins, a biological and racial identity constituted by apartheid, one that can be recorded once and for all as autobiography. Instead, identity is something that has to be written, but repeatedly and under erasure, as Derrida's "spatialized typography," which can be read in a certain manner. The already written racial identity conferred by apartheid is a fixed one based on miscegenation, an identity marked by illegitimacy in terms of the country's notorious Immorality Act.[10] To avoid the objectifying representation of miscegenation, Head thus boldly rewrites herself across the laws of genre and across the racial laws of South Africa, asserting a fluid identity that can only be deciphered, repeatedly, in and through writing.

Writing and the Law constitute major tropes in the text. At the very beginning of the novel the child, at this stage called Miriam, overcomes her silence and approaches the man who serves as community scribe in the slum. She questions the fact that he copies out stock letters from a book entitled *The Art of Letter Writing.*

My dear Jonathan,
   It is with great sorrow that I learnt the news of the death of your beloved father. He was a great and worthy man. I and the family send condolence to you in your hour of loss and grief.
   Your devoted friend,
   Elijah[11]

That the first text read to the child Miriam, daughter of Sarah, is about the death of Jonathan's father, grieved by his devoted friend Elijah, is of course no accident. Not only do the biblical references conjure up the Judaic Law of the Old Testament (Elijah prefigures Christ), but the theme of the absent/deceased Father is here specifically inscribed into the Law. The letter, as introduction to literacy, suggests metonymic displacement of Head's bio-identity conferred by the Immorality Act.

The child's question about the same letter serving everyone's needs is a question about reading, about the replacement of proper nouns, names, that allows the text to be meaningful to anyone, and the fluidity of identity in the deictic "I" that can be substituted by any speaker and become coreferential with any name. But it is also a comment on the limitations of the scribe, the degree of literacy that allows him to perform only certain types of writing, an issue that arises later in the novel when Mouse the journalist has to be transformed into Mouse the creative writer.

Head gives a graphic and moving account of the child learning to read and write. She is taught to write by the community scribe who "with a shaky hand in bold print, wrote MIRIAM. He showed her how to hold the pencil and guided her hand to trace over the letters. After a few tracings she became excited and clutched the paper to her chest. He gave her the writing pad and she ran behind the tree. She traced the letters over several times then tried to write her version. . . . Soon she was able to copy out a letter from the book of letter writing."[12] Tracing, or the mechanical aspect of writing, simply repeating what is already there and reproducing the given, becomes a metaphor for autobiography and subjection to the Law. Gayatri Spivak's assertion—in her essay "Acting Bits/Identity Talk"—that the postcolonial subject "learn[s] identity letter by letter" is demonstrated literally in this scene.[13] It is only much later, when the protagonist learns to write creatively (which is also a return to linking writing to the visual), that she is able to overcome the Law. It is under Johnny's instructions that she first of all sketches a scene, avoiding the mundaneness of detail, and then writes about that scene in the same way, "without picking at bits and pieces of life," in other words *not* mimetically. Her success with the exercise unleashes in her a warmth and animation that according to Johnny renders her ready for sexual relations, that is to say ready to break the incest taboo. What the trace of the discursive modality of writing and not-writing the self thus enacts is the crisis of legitimation where the Law is rewritten through a rewriting of the self, and where illegitimacy or the taboos on miscegenation and incest are disarmed so that going to bed with the father, which coincides with transforming a debilitating biohistory into fiction, become acts of liberation. Writing then is a trope that functions as decolonizing strategy.

Head's account of the child learning to read is equally laden with meaning. Miriam is fascinated by the materiality of text, by the print that she touches, the object found on the refuse dump, which can be voiced into a narrative that is far removed from the location, one that transcends its squalor. She takes the illustrated book *The Adventures of Fuzzy Wuzzy Bear* to the old man who teaches her to read through associating words with pictures: "They read the whole book this way and she identified words he read out with objects in the picture."[14] This rudimentary reading thus occurs within an ideological framework that posits a simple one-to-one relation between signifier and signified, a crude correspondence between language and things in the world. Again she goes "behind a tree" to master the art of reading, a symbolic act of obliterating the self, an act that collocates with the proper-name taboo in which the acquisition of literacy is implicated.

It is when Miriam is confronted with the more overtly discursive text, the book of letters in which substitutable addressors and addressees are explicitly signaled, that she finds the inadequacy of associating words with pictures, of mimetic representation. The letter book "did not have pictures. Most of the words were meaningless strings of letters to her, and the old man, having a limited vocabulary, was unable to explain them."[15] The old man is the repository of knowledge, but the child in the process of reading comes up against the limitations of that knowledge. Culture, then, is transmitted through patriarchy, firstly through the old man who teaches her the rudiments of literacy, and later through her Father/Lover who teaches her to write creatively. When the old man dies she is described as the "silent, stubborn little figure possessed of an insatiable desire to learn to read and write, but not knowing at which point to start or where to go for knowledge. Strangely, it was her foster father who thrust her out into a new way of life."[16]

What is interesting here is the apparent lack of cohesion between the two sentences; "knowledge" and "new way of life" are not synonymous, but the textual grammar presents them as such. We learn in the next paragraph that the foster father's attempt at sexual abuse leads to her running away from home, an act that does not in fact lead directly to acquiring literacy. Her years in foster homes, "with the weekends of drunkenness, and violence and the crude, animal, purposeless, crushing world of poverty,"[17] had left her at the age of sixteen with only three years of schooling. Why, then, the textual link between knowledge and a new way of life? I think the answer lies in Head's conflation of sexuality or carnal knowledge with knowledge that comes from reading and writing that forges, through the narrative, a link between representation and a prohibitionary Law, a link that at the same time constitutes an absent—or rather deferred—narrative between the two sentences. The foster father may not be the repository of knowledge, but he nevertheless, like the old man, represents the patriarchal Law through which her acquisition of knowledge is mediated.

These nodal points within the narrative, the Law, identity, and representation interconnect in such a manner as to generate new meanings for the subject's relation to the law. But to talk about subjectivity is to follow, as Kristeva says, "the various configurations revealed by the different relations between subjects and their discourse. The subject *is* not; he makes and unmakes himself in a complex topology where the other and his discourse are included. One cannot possibly talk about the meaning of a discourse without taking this topology into account. . . . The production of meaning is . . . an actual production that traverses the surface of the *uttered* discourse, and that engenders in the *enunciation* a particular meaning with a particular subject."[18] The topological is a suggestive notion that allows for the shaping and reshaping or rewording of the subject in spite of the invariants of biology and the social law. In the case of Head's biohistory, repeated and reworded in various novels, the autobiographical self can be transformed and debilitating constructs like race can be denied and allowed to be subsumed by the Law. The discourse of others may deny her protagonist the corporeal act of speaking, her silence and impassivity may strip her of meaning for others, but through writing she reconstitutes or rewords her self.

Charlotte, as the child who has run away from home and who refuses to speak her name is called, moves from home to home learning "the lessons every unwanted stray has to learn: *Work hard. Do not answer back no matter what we do to you. Be satisfied with the scraps we give you, you cannot have what our children have. Remember we are unpredictable; when the mood gets us we can throw you out.*"[19] In this passage, orthographically marked by italics and so demanding a different way of reading, Head employs the language of the Law in its characteristic imperative mood. It is also the language of the earlier letter where the pronouns are substitutable deictics. The language is deliberately discursive, presented as the utterance or actual speech of an unidentified, universalized "we," who is the agent in all the sentences, with "you" as the affected, the recipient who has no choice but to obey. The Law is thus presented as an abstract that finds its instantiation in a variety of forms such as the incest taboo, the Immorality Act, and the linguistic registers of the newspaper and patriarchy.

At the offices of the *New African*, the protagonist is renamed Mouse—the silent, expressionless, impassive and unfeminine journalist who has difficulty in molding her writing into the sensationalist, politically conservative register of the newspaper. The variety of names she inhabits represents the erasure of the single racial identity conferred by the law. Instead, she learns to assume multiple identities in relation to the discourse of others and in relation to the various laws and taboos to which she is subjugated. Her silence and refusal to register emotion serve as a shield against the fixing impulse of the world around her; they are constituents of identity, whether racial or gendered, which operates as strategy rather than essence.

Mouse's reading habits confound her colleagues. Johnny comments on the unfemininity of reading about electricity. Her last foster father, a kind man who sends her to school and exposes her to Communism and protest literature, inadvertently gives her Darwin's theory of evolution, which she reads avidly "in spite of the man's protests."[20] Not only does her reading demonstrate the protagonist in conflict with patriarchal guidance, it also forges a secret connection between patriarchy and the inscription of race.

The relationship posited between identity and writing is one that is explored by Spivak in "Acting Bits/Identity Talk," where she discusses the postcolonial translation of culture within the politics of identity as a crossing over, a shuttling between cultures so that it is simultaneously about self-recognition and a stripping of identity.[21] Spivak foregrounds the performative aspect of postcolonial art in which identity, far from being essentialist or racial, is rather something staged. Bessie Head's constant rewriting or translation of her own life in the biography of her protagonists seems to constitute such a staging of identity. In relation to Head's own origins, the sensational racial element in transgressive sex is spectacularly absent in the biographies of her characters. Although the absent Immorality Act is lured into presence by the incest taboo, metonymically represented in the Law, the text denies the central position of race in constituting identity. In *The Cardinals*, the problematic of racial origins is replaced by class. Miriam's mother, a middle-class coloured woman, does not have the moral courage to pursue her intense sexual relationship with a working-class man and to confront the restrictive social taboos imposed by discrimination within the coloured community.

In the case of *Maru*, race is a function of language and representation, and Head focuses on the inherent reproductive nature of race as a sign of difference: "And if the white man thought that Asians were a low and filthy nation, Asians could still smile with relief—at least they were not Africans. And if the white man thought Africans were a low, filthy nation, Africans in Southern Africa could still smile, at least they were not Bushmen."[22] The parallel structure of these sentences reveals language as the site where difference is reproduced. Head goes on to explain how Bushmen cannot turn round to say, "At least I am not a—-." The dash, the absence of another group from which to differentiate themselves, ensures that the Masarwa remain at the bottom of the scale, but by implication there is always the possibility that an other could fill the place; the possibility of reproducing that sign of difference, of filling in the gap, remains. The sentence is in direct speech, a quotation in the sense not only of an utterance, but also of an echoic utterance, as repetition of an idea that can be infinitely reproduced. As it happens, there is no group to replace the formula and absence, which in spoken terms is silence, marks the Masarwa's subjection and oppression.

In *The Cardinals,* race is a figure reserved for white women; no other group is designated by race. Rather, the constructedness of racial identity in representation is suggested when Johnny condemns his colleague's writing about "the happy little Coloured man and the colourful Malays." Johnny asks: "Why don't you leave that crap to those insane, patronising White women journalists who are forever at pains to tell the Coloureds how happy they are."[23] When the Immorality Act explicitly surfaces in the narrative it is also presented as a problem of representation. Mouse, the journalist, because of the demands of the sensationalist newspaper, does not know how to write about a Norwegian sailor who is convicted under the Immorality Act. Johnny gives her the following lead: "A cop peeped through a keyhole and a young man and woman found themselves in the Magistrate's Court charged with contravening the Immorality Act."[24] In other words, it is the policeman as subject or agent who has acted and caused an offence, while the lovers are simply the affected and so are rendered innocent through the very grammar of the sentence. The event is staged for the reader through the representation of the court case where Head's account in the third person retains a trace of what Spivak calls the "withholding of translation," or the trace of the untranslatability of the sailor's experience is retained through his performance.[25] Stripped of identity as he refuses to cross over into the culture of apartheid, the sailor as character remains mute; we are given the translator's words in which the refusal of the sailor to accept that he has fallen foul of the law persists in his repeated fainting. He has refused to eat since his arrest, and the interpreter translates as follows, with the staccato of parataxis deliberately effacing the sailor's voice: "'The accused says that he has not been in a prison before. It has upset him immensely. He cannot understand why he was arrested. He was only looking for a bit of fun. . . . The accused says he cannot eat.'"[26] In the Derridean sense, "a trace has taken place. Even if the idiomatic quality must necessarily lose itself or allow itself to be contaminated by the repetition which confers on it a code and an intelligibility, even if it occurs only to efface itself, if it arises only in effacing itself, the effacement will have taken place."[27] And so, in the process of *not* speaking, the trace of the sailor's speech remains, his refusal to eat forging a link between sexuality and speech.

Wolfgang Iser talks about the decline of the mimetic component of representation in favor of the performative aspect of the author-text-reader relationship, "whereby the pregiven is no longer viewed as an object of representation but rather as material from which something new is fashioned." The play of the text is staged as a means of crossing boundaries; it stages transformation and at the same time reveals "how the transformation is done. Staged transformation makes that which is inaccessible both present and absent."[28] Head's staging in

The Cardinals includes an enactment of the process of writing the novel, a rehearsal of producing not-autobiography. Johnny gives Mouse an outline, some ideas, and she, "stiffly and uncertainly like a child learning to walk,"[29] produces a short story in which the protagonist is killed for refusing to join a local gang. The writing is about transforming the real-life story of Johnny into fiction. Pleased with her performance, he acknowledges it as his: "Omit one or two details and it's a pretty accurate picture of what I was like about twenty years ago."[30] But it is a narrative that resists closure in the sense that the death of the protagonist (in terms of the novel, Johnny-alias-Sammy, the father of Mouse the writer) is left uncertain. The final sentence, which literally ends with ellipsis ("He lifted his hand and pressed it into the wound but it continued to trickle through his fingers in hot sticky rivulets . . ."), allows for the possibility of a resurrection, and a new identity.[31]

This staging within the text of transformation from biography to fiction, or the rewriting of the self within topological boundaries, reveals the process of identity play as Mouse's narrative makes and unmakes the subject. But it also lures into presence the absent theme of incest: the act of killing/not-killing the father symbolically allows her to sleep with him/not sleep with him at the end of the novel. At the same time, it dramatizes the complex relationship of the gendered subject with the Law. While Johnny enables her to become a writer and animates her into accepting love, she is simultaneously subjugated by him. He fashions her into a "woman" by instructing her on taking up the hem of her skirts, learning to cook, speaking her mind, and expressing feeling, so that learning to write comes to collocate with all the other lessons she has to learn from him. The open ending thus does not only leave open the question of sexual relations with the father but also puts a question mark over the identity of the gendered writer who appears willingly to subject herself to the law of the father.

Finally, a postmodernist reading of Head's novel needs to be reconciled with the overt political project that straddles the narrative. Here I am reminded of Toni Morrison's words, in an interview, where she states that slavery propelled the black subject into postmodernity well before the West theorized postmodernism, an observation one could equally apply to the barbarism of the Immorality Act. I am reminded, too, of Lyotard's definition of postmodernity as a crisis not only in representation but also in legitimation, as the master narratives of the West lose their authority and come to be questioned. This is precisely what is staged in Head's text, where the narrative moves inexorably toward an undermining of the symbolic Law. Perhaps the paradigmatic postmodern moment occurs when Johnny confesses to his cynical editor that he is in love with Mouse. PK replies: "But Johnny. People don't fall in love these days. The

movies have made that kind of thing stale. They have robbed us of our capacity to feel through feeding us with cheap sensation. Ask any man and he will
tell you that he can't kiss his wife because she wants him to kiss her the way
Richard Widmark kisses."[32] This is not so far from Umberto Eco's characterization of postmodernism as a situation in which it is no longer possible to say "I
love you." (The subject instead has to present the words in quotation marks as
follows: "As Barbara Cartland would say, I love you desperately.")[33]

But the nihilism that adheres to postmodern thought is undermined in the
political agenda that inheres in the theme of writing. Head's novel is prefaced
with an explanation of the title: "*The Cardinals*, in the astrological sense, are
those who serve as the base or foundation for change." In Head's narrative,
where resolution on one level is found in Mouse learning to write, learning to
love, and learning to become a communicative being, Johnny, the father/lover/
tutor, explains why this is necessary: "A new way of life is emerging in Africa
and you and I, and many others, fit in somewhere. Africa may not need us but
we need a country like Africa. . . . A human life is limited so it has to identify
itself with a small corner of this earth. Only then is it able to shape its destiny
and present its contribution. . . . You cannot feel like the underdog and at the
same time feel you belong to a country. It is the duty of the conqueror to abuse
you, and treat you like an outcast and alien, and to impose false standards on
you. Maybe we can help throw some of those imposed standards overboard. It
is a great responsibility to be a writer at this time."[34] What is notable here is
the voice of Head, the Africanist, who admired Robert Sobukwe, leader of the
P.A.C. (she said he gave her a comfortable black skin in which to live).[35] The
sentence "Africa may not need us but we need a country like Africa" is a comfortable recognition of ethnic difference that does not interfere with a nationalist program and so promotes pluralism and social heterogeneity. This view of
writing may sound like the eighties slogan of culture as a weapon of the struggle, but the novel is explicit in its condemnation of party politics: "The crudest
expression of the power drive is in the gangster; the most subtle and disastrous
in the politician," says the all-knowing Johnny. In a discussion about freedom
and the rights of the individual, he says that these are "above the petty manipu-
lations of politicians. I doubt if any political party can ever really guarantee
that."[36]

15

SETTING, INTERTEXTUALITY, AND THE RESURRECTION OF THE POSTCOLONIAL AUTHOR (2004, 2005)

There is, I believe, a new spirit abroad. And all the writers I have questioned agree that a trend is manifesting itself at academic conferences and symposiums where they are invited to offer reflections on their own work. "Speak as a writer," the invitations invariably say. This, of course, constitutes a shift from the canonical position of not allowing a writer's biography to divert one from the text or not to be influenced by what a writer has to say about her work and practice. The departure is most probably bound up with the academicization of writing or the advent of higher degrees in creative writing where part of a submission is expected to be self-reflexive. There is also the phenomenon (which I will discuss later) of a number of prominent postcolonial fictions that revisit the orthodox distinction between writer and narrator. But those of us who have for so long meekly observed the silence of literary decorum will inevitably stutter through the task of speaking "as a writer." Do we follow funding council guidelines and groaningly produce research questions that underpin our works of fiction? With so new a phenomenon, should we presume carte blanche, or are there still areas of prohibition that have not yet been mapped? Should we fear that the vagueness of the request points to a gray area in literary etiquette where the vulgar at heart must needs betray themselves? In short, what are we supposed to talk about?

For the South African writer there has been the ready-made general question of whether there is anything to write about after the demise of apartheid, but that foolish inquiry has necessarily petered out. I am fortunate in having a personal ready-made topic that is happily legitimated by the postcolonial keyword "transculturation." The questions that this condition entails are as follows: Why when you have lived so long in Scotland do you write about South Africa? When will you set your fictions in Scotland? Can you go on writing about a place in which you do not live? These are the questions I will try to address in this essay, and thus my subject is the safe and seemly one of the setting of fiction.

Writing from the outside has always been celebrated for its special, insightful perspective. Joyce, we are told, would not have been able to write *Ulysses* in Ireland, and Auerbach, says Edward Said, was able to write *Mimesis* in Istanbul precisely because of the "agonizing distance from Europe." It was "the active impingement of his European selfhood" that made possible the monumental work on European culture.[1] I could say that the impingement of my otherness in Scotland necessitates my homely South African fictions, but it is rather with Ezekiel Mphahlele, for whom there was no executive value in exile, that I identify. He saw the compulsion to write about South Africa as a "tyranny of place" and wondered how long he could go on mining memory, a question that I imagine must be asked by many postcolonial writers, including, for example, Bernard MacLaverty, who lives in Scotland but continues to write about his native Ireland. In J. M. Coetzee's deliberate blend of fiction and autobiography, the ironized poet-protagonist of *Youth* expresses the problem in youthful histrionic mode: "South Africa is a wound within him. How much longer before the wound stops bleeding? How much longer will he have to grit his teeth and endure before he is able to say, 'Once upon a time I used to live in South Africa but now I live in England'?"[2] While I wince squeamishly at the word "wound" and cannot identify with the narrator, the formulation of the problem as a bodily act of uttering an unspeakable sentence is a suggestive one to which I will return.

The relationship between the mise-en-scène of fiction and the writer's physical location has been of little interest precisely because of the orthodox critical position of disregarding a writer's biography. Postcolonial theory does address the question of place, of how the postcolonial writer revises the empty space of colonialism and through writing and naming turns it into place; its concern is with the related concept of identity formation and the link with language. But displacement is invariably discussed in terms of ambivalence, in the separation and continual contact between colonizer and colonized, whereas I would like to focus on a more mundane aspect of place: the mise-en-scène or setting of fictions that for any writer is rudimentary and that for the emigrant writer can be problematic.

Turning to narratology, I find little more than references to stage-setting, to the ways in which setting provides facts, setting as evidence of a narrator, or its role in promoting verisimilitude. For Shlomith Rimmon-Kenan, physical surroundings in narrative or human environments are trait-connoting metonymies, in other words, setting becomes absorbed into character. Human characters are shaped by the places they occupy: "As with external appearance, the relation of contiguity is frequently supplemented by that of causality." Her example is from Faulkner's "A Rose for Miss Emily," where Emily's dilapidated house, with its clouds of dust and its dank smell, is a "metonymy of her decadence, but its decay is also a result of her poverty and her morbid temperament."[3] What is surely overlooked here is that that decadence is more than a personal characteristic, the dilapidation more than a local setting: this is also a story about the American South and Southern "aristocratic" values; it cannot be transported to the North through a mere change of setting. Thus, more than supplementing character description, setting is the representation of physical surroundings that is crucially bound up with a culture and its dominant ideologies, providing readymade, recognizable meanings. In other words, setting functions much like intertextuality.

Which returns me to the writer and her relationship to the culture in which her fictions are set. To recap Roland Barthes: intertextuality, a condition of all writing, strikes a death blow to the author and so liberates the reader from author-centered, theological meanings.[4] Thus the domain of reading and interpretation includes knowledge-based inferencing and an understanding of intertexts and their function in the new context. But for the postcolonial writer it is the transformative effect of intertextuality that is of significance. Frequently our settings in disjunction with citations from colonial texts produce postcolonial irony, and if we are doomed to echolalia it is also the case that repetition represents, reverses, or revises, or simply asks the reader to reflect on indeterminate meanings produced by citations, meanings that destabilize received views. In South African writing, for instance, settings like the servant's room in the backyard and the master bedroom in the suburbs operate as intertexts with readymade conventionalized meanings that interact with the narrative discourse and presentation of character to offer revised meanings. What the writer does, then, is to introduce dialogue between texts, whether they be written or spoken, and so brings into being the interconnectedness of the human world in a divided society. For instance, in Gordimer's story "Blinder," the intertextual function of setting is crucial to the meaning of the story. Apartheid geography, the impoverished homeland in relation to white South Africa, is replicated in the suburban house with its dining room—as site of culture or space of refinement—and servant's room, where Rose, an object of pity, mourns the death of her lover, a migrant worker, in uncontrolled fashion.[5] When Rose intrudes with the dead man's widow, the woman from the homeland, into the family's dining room, it is the values of the servant's room that cast a question mark over white culture's bourgeois morality. The civility that the dining room supposedly represents is called into question.

My project is to link the location of the author to her settings and to take on board the new requirement of reflecting on my own practice, but before I do so I would like to discuss a short story by fellow South African writer, Ivan Vladislavić, in which issues related to authorship, setting, and intertextuality are self-consciously staged. Indeed, Vladislavić's narrator, whose entire text is a comment on his writing, could be seen as a parodic instance of speaking as a writer. In "'Kidnapped,'" a third-person narrator finds an advertisement for a short-story competition entitled "Kidnapped," in celebration of the centenary of the Scottish writer Robert Louis Stevenson. The notice in the Johannesburg newspaper is placed in the "People in Crisis" column, between the "Parent and Child Counselling Centre" and "Lifeline," thus signaling Vladislavić's concern with an aspect of place that relates to mapping. It foreshadows his dramatization of the colonial's filial relationship with Stevenson, the abject relationship with the center, as well as the difficulties the protagonist will encounter in trying to write a story from the margins. We are told about the number of ways in which the task could be tackled, the contemplation of which in fact prevents the narrator from writing, so that the narrative of deferral also becomes a metaphor for the paralysis that the postcolonial writer experiences in relation to the metropolis.

The events of the story constitute a series of ideas, often introduced by the word "idea" in italics, that marks its failure to materialize. And each idea is abandoned as the protagonist confesses to his inability to produce a story, although he reports that the final idea is so elaborated that it exceeds the prescribed length of the story. A problem he identifies at the start is that of setting, whether to set the story in the Scottish Highlands or the South African Highveld, but the very homonymity introduces the problem of postcolonial translation. Highlands and Highveld, both terms for physical terrain, remind us of Derrida's meditation on Babel and the untranslatability of the proper noun. Derrida explains that when God descends toward the tower he proclaims his unpronounceable name, YWHW, imposes the confusion of tongues, and "with this violent imposition he opens the deconstruction of the tower, as of the universal language; he scatters the genealogical filiation. He breaks the lineage. He at the same time imposes and forbids translation. . . . Translation then becomes necessary and impossible like the effect of a struggle for the appropriation of the name, necessary and forbidden in the interval between two absolutely proper names."[6] It is under these precepts that "Kidnapped" must engage with translation, and in the very process of paying homage to Stevenson, must free itself of genealogical filiation.

Stevenson, the original author, occupies a prominent place in the narrative, not only appearing as a character from time to time in the story or in the ideas and plans for embedded stories, but as the subject of a biographical intertext. For instance, the narrator informs us that Stevenson abandoned an adventure story called "The Great North Road" to start working on his novel *Kidnapped*, and for that reason our narrator is drawn to a temporalized setting for his story, "in the interval between 'The Great North Road' and *Kidnapped*," that is to say between Dorset in England, where the author lived at the time, and the High-lands, where he set his story. Here setting fuses the author's real-life location and the mise-en-scène of his fiction, and the phenomenon of Stevenson as displaced author writing from the metropolis about his native Scotland is embedded in our South African writer's tussle with literature from the center. But in evoking England versus Scotland, the proposed setting also deconstructs the very no-tion of a monolithic center, itself subject to internal, hierarchical difference, which in turn could be seen to account for the paradox of writing a story, the one we read, where Vladislavić, the author, is distinct from his narrator.

The narrator-as-reader takes Stevenson's advice to consult a map, but that leads to more than paralysis. He finds the Scottish topography, the broken coast-line, "improbably intricate, like crumbling parchment. Who could memorize the shape of such a country?" he asks. The alien geography has a peculiar, vis-ceral effect on him: "I was choking. There was something too rich in the no-menclature, something that made it stick in the craw like drammach (shall we say): Pitlochry, Strath Spey, Cromarty, Dornoch, Lairg, Tongue, John o' Groats."[7] Failure to engage with the Scottish toponymy, in spite of his awed fascination with the place, is thus established via an image of ingestion; the project of ab-sorbing the imperium is shown to be physically impossible in spite of his awed fascination with Scotland.

So he abandons the Scottish setting and decides to transpose the kidnap story to the local, indeed, to map it on to the existing South African genre of Jim-comes-to-Jo'burg, but the transposition is not satisfactory: the local, the new, does not measure up to the romance of the old world.[8] A revised idea to set the story in Johannesburg just after the discovery of gold, with a Scottish hero carry-ing a copy of the newly published *Kidnapped*, is displaced by the arrival of the entry form with its list of rules, a dramatization of the circumscribed nature of postcolonial writing. The next idea exemplifies the postcolonial device of self-reflexivity: the narrator will write about an aspirant author who has been trying without success to write a story for the Kidnapped competition. "It's fairly auto-biographical, but no one need know," he says—the act of decoupling author and narrator is necessarily one of dissimulation. He has grown close to Stevenson, "to the point of beginning to affect his mannerisms."[9] The story within a story is set on the eve of the centenary of Stevenson's death, which our narrator's narrator (or author-narrator) is celebrating: "He is dressed up as the author, in grubby white flannels and a linen shirt; he half imagines, in his cups, that he *is* the author."[10] The new intertext of impersonating the canonical writer is J. M. Coetzee's *Foe,* in which Friday dresses up in the author's cloak, a moment marked both by the impossibility of reproducing the story of the colonized and by indeterminacy since Susan Barton, the narrator, fails to state categorically whether Friday's spinning in the authorial cloak reveals that he has been castrated. It is not surprising, then, that our aspirant author's strategy of impersonation does not father a text.

The idea-within-an-idea upon which our author-narrator alights is a story about Stevenson's first draft of *Kidnapped,* which is so disliked by his wife that he throws it into the fire. Again, Stevenson's biography is plundered even if the detail is kidnapped from the writing of *Dr. Jekyll and Mr. Hyde* to labor in the colonial version of "Kidnapped," and here I refer to the original late seventeenth-century meaning of the word "kidnap": to abduct children to labor on the American plantations. Ironically, this attempt to erase Stevenson's text starts with writing the word "Kidnapped" at the top of the page. But paralysis sets in once more so that "he uncorks a bottle of burgundy, to get the creative juices flowing again, fills a glass, raises it—and is felled by a stroke."[11] Friday's ambiguity is encoded in the identity of the "he" who is felled: it is of course our author-narrator but, as a representation of a representation of Stevenson, it also implies the felling of that author—who indeed died of a stroke.

The first-level narrator works on this idea of deleting *Kidnapped* from Stevenson's oeuvre, but since his plan alone far exceeds the given length of the competition—plenitude resulting perhaps from the death of the author—he puts the plan aside. More ideas are stillborn. The next one returns to an earlier idea, set in Johannesburg's gold rush, where he establishes an "appealing interplay . . . between past and present, memory and experience, Europe and Africa, fiction and fact, and so on, full of potential."[12] Again this idea is abandoned for its plenitude; it is more suitable for a novella, the narrator declares. The final idea is that staple of creative writing classes, an additional chapter at the end of the book, "Kidnapped Chapter XXXI," in other words, another form of impersonating the writer. But a Scotsman from the embassy points out that Stevenson himself had written a sequel to the novel.

After Vladislavić's narrator abandons all plans for a story, a discrete paragraph offers a final event in Stevenson's life, delivered in a curious discourse that throws into question the identity of its narrator: "At the last, when the vein of stories in his mind burst, Stevenson demanded: 'What's that?' As if a stranger had entered. There was no answer. He turned to Fanny and asked, more urgently: 'Do I look strange?' And then he fell into a coma and died."[13] This biographical text, with its insertion of Stevenson's voice, usurps the narrative discourse, and our narrator replaces the account of failed attempts at storytelling with a narration of Stevenson's life, or rather his death. It is surely the narrator that Stevenson apprehends as "the stranger," and thus genealogical filiation is at the same time evoked and shattered.

The original author is dead, and we realize that a text, the one we are reading, has been born, but before we salute Roland Barthes, note that the text at the same time and at both levels of mimesis proclaims its failure—failure to engage with the imperium, to set a story in Stevenson's Scotland, or to transpose it to South Africa. When our narrator returns to announce that there is another South African writer among the finalists, it is only to assure us that the winning stories severely lack Stevenson's storytelling skills, in other words, like Elvis, the author also continues to live.

I read "'Kidnapped,'" with its multiple embeddings, its Russian-doll structure with proposed settings that shift between South Africa and Scotland, as a meditation on the concept of author and his troubled relationships with reader, narrator, and setting. There is a first-level narrator who is an aspirant author, and who via the idea of an embedded story in the mode of autobiography is recast as simultaneously character and author. This author-narrator, who embarks on an autobiographical story about writing a story, evokes a correspondence with the actual author, Vladislavić, and his project of constructing a story about an aspirant author. And the hierarchical relationship between author and reader is deconstructed as our author-narrators are also avid readers of the original author, Stevenson (as Vladislavić himself must be). The first-level story-within-the-story fails to materialize, but the process of contemplating possibilities and strategies of course produces a story that is read by real-life readers who correctly think of Vladislavić as its author. Thus self-reflexivity that fails at the second embedding is nevertheless at the first level of mimesis dramatized as a solution to the problem of postcolonial writing. But the canonical distinction between writer and narrator, or poet and speaker, is surely in this instance deliberately blurred.

The multiple levels of authorship, or the ubiquity of the author's role, can at one level be read as a demonstration of Barthes's "author-function," but here, surely, the author is not dead, he has simply been kidnapped by the postcolonial to labor as an intertext. In Stevenson's novel the character is kidnapped in order to pack him off to the colonies; in Vladislavić, the echolalic postcolonial writer strikes back at metropolitan theory itself. There is also intertext embedded within intertext: one of the translated settings is that of our narrator dreaming that he wanders companionably through the veld with Stevenson. But untranslatability is asserted by Stevenson's implied rejection of his companion, for he is reading Hazlitt's "On Going a Journey,"[14] an essay in which that author baldly states that journeys should be undertaken on one's own. If Barthes's death of the author allows for the reader's liberation into textuality through the phenomenon of intertextuality, then Vladislavić employs the very intertextuality to resurrect the author in other guises while at the same time keeping alive a reader (without whom the notion of a story that is ultimately written cannot be realized) *and* who therefore exists in a symbiotic rather than a hierarchical relationship with the author. The dream at the same time of course asserts the colonial's desire for fraternity as well as highlighting the incivility of being rejected by metropolitan writing.

Setting is a fundamental problem for Vladislavić's aspirant author who spends a good time thinking about or consulting maps for a suitable setting. Having been sickened by the map of Scotland, he is troubled by falling short of Stevenson's faith in the inspirational effect of maps. He recalls that while *Treasure Island* grew out of a map of an invented place, *Kidnapped* was written with the aid of real maps, and imagines Stevenson (displaced) in England, "propped up in bed . . . with the maps scattered around him like another land of counterpane" so that the setting for *Kidnapped* "was a country of the memory."[15] The narrator returns to the atlas and once again feels sick when it opens "(at Hungary as it happened)."[16] This fleeting reference, complete with parentheses, is to a geographical displacement of another political order that corresponds to another level of authorship, the eastern Europe of our real author's grandfather Vladislavić who emigrated to South Africa.

Vladislavić's story is one of many postcolonial texts in which the notion of authorship and authority is examined. Critics have, for instance, been exercised by the last section of Coetzee's *Foe*, and particularly by the identity of its unnamed narrator. David Attwell gingerly suggests that the narrator "(possibly standing for Coetzee himself) dissolves the narration in an act of authorial renunciation,"[17] whereas Derek Attridge is bolder in his belief that the narrator is replaced by the author in the final section.[18] Other postcolonial instances of referencing the authorial self are found in Toni Morrison's *Jazz* and Salman Rushdie's *The Satanic Verses*.[19] In the latter, the authorial voice reveals to Gibreel that he has posed as God. Materialized into a human form sitting at the edge of the bed, he is described as the real Rushdie (whom we know from photographs of the author), able to mobilize "the traditional apparatus of divine rage . . . wind and thunder."[20] In her commentary on this phenomenon, Gayatri Spivak dismisses the orthodox postcolonial argument: "As metropolitan writing is trying to get rid of a subject that has too long been the dominant, the postcolonial writer must still foreground his traffic with the subject position? Too easy I think."[21] Instead, she distinguishes between the metropolitan decentered subject and Rushdie's *staging* of the author as a representation of decentering the subject, so that Rushdie's is "more like a self-ironic yet self-based modernism . . . than an object-coded or subject-decentred avant-garde."[22] I would like to suggest that this foregrounding of the authorial is indeed a departure from the usual traffic with subjectivity but that, instead of staging representation, such resurrection of the author is also concerned with asserting an ethics of authorial responsibility in an ostentatious coupling of author and narrator.

The enigmatic, unidentified, and unreliable narrator in Toni Morrison's *Jazz*, who says that her characters cannot save themselves without her "because—well, it's my storm, isn't it? I break lives to prove I can mend them back again," is equally ostentatious.[23] Morrison's mise-en-scène is the city, celebrated as the site of passion, of freedom of ex-slaves to love, the birthplace of jazz, and the site of black modernity. Echoes of the modernist intertexts of "Prufrock" and "The Waste Land" abound in *Jazz*, especially in the intensely private, confessional ending where the repeated reference to hands is redolent of "What the Thunder Said," but as a counterdiscourse rather than an endorsement of Eliot's unreal city of alienation and spiritual sterility.[24] Morrison's final page offers a lover's discourse in which the speaker, stepping outside the role of narrator, speaks of her own clandestine love that longs for public expression. But, ambiguously, she also seems to be addressing the reader in the act of reading, asserting a flesh and blood storyteller who insists on her own corporeality as well as that of her reader. Having disclaimed authoritative knowledge of her characters throughout the narrative, the authorial voice now identifies with them. She also delights in the reader's physical engagement with the book:

> I envy them their public love. I myself have only known it in secret, shared it in secret and longed, aw longed to show it—to be able to say out loud what they have no need to say at all: *That I have loved only you, surrendered my whole self reckless to you and nobody else. . . . That I love the way you hold me, how close you let me be to you. I like your fingers on and on, lifting, turning. I have watched your face for a long time now, and missed your eyes when you went away from me. Talking to you and hearing you answer—that's the kick.*

But I can't say that aloud; I can't tell anyone that I have been waiting for this all my life. . . . If I were able I'd say it. Say make me, remake me. You are free to do it and I am free to let you because look, look. Look where your hands are. Now.[25]

Reference to characters who originate from a photograph and now have taken on real lives of their own—"not sepia, still, losing their edges to the light of a future afternoon"[26]—also suggests that it is the voice of an author commenting on the completion of her project, the production of the text. The abandonment of her narrator at this stage foregrounds the artifice. Morrison's reader, having reached the end of the narrative, is free to interpret the story and to recycle it, as indeed she has done. In other words, the author may balk against being critically abstracted into writer, but her resurrection, far from implying a Barthesian death of the reader, proposes a more complex relationship. And through oxymoronically stating that which is claimed to be unutterable, through insisting via the use of italics on the difference between speech and writing, and between author and narrator, Morrison succeeds in rendering the very word "author" free of embarrassment precisely because the relationship between author and writer is shown to be more nuanced than metropolitan theory proposes.

This intimate relationship between author, narrator, and reader, the authorial foregrounding of her own subjectivity and of the ethics of representing her people who have come through the horror, is achieved through Morrison's curious use of deixis: the discourse refuses to provide unambiguous referents for "I," "me," "you," "this," or "now." Only "they" can be identified as the reconciled, middle-aged couple whose love story, representative of a people and of the sound of the city, has just been told with infinite tenderness.

Fortified by my detour via other texts' assertions of flesh and blood authors, I now must address my own situation as a writer living in Scotland whose fictions are set in South Africa, "another land of counterpane" perhaps with which to keep at bay the Northern chill.[27] But before doing so, let me defer once again, this time to the narratologist Mieke Bal, who sees setting as crucial to the presentation of story because of its function of "concretization and subjectification of space into place."[28] It is, she says, through proprioceptivity that abstract space becomes concrete place into which the subject, delimited by its skin, is keyed. Bal borrows the concept of proprioceptivity from Kaja Silverman, who describes it as "the apprehension of the subject of his/her ownness . . . best understood as that egoic component to which concepts like 'here,' 'there,' and 'my' are keyed. . . . The sensational ego . . . includes both physical feeling and the subject's simultaneous mental registration, on the basis of that feeling, of a 'here-ness' and 'ownness.'"[29] Distinguishable from identity that depends on the image, proprioceptivity is bound up with the body's sensation of occupying a point in space, and with the terms under which it does so.[30] For Silverman, ego and body are thus interchangeable, and subjectness is bound up with the postural, the way in which the body deploys its muscles for the purpose of fitting it smoothly within an imagined spatial envelope. Mieke Bal elaborates as follows: "By placing deixis within/on/at the body, Silverman extends the meaning and importance of Benveniste's thought that deixis, not reference, is the essence of language. . . . This proprioceptive basis for deixis comprehends the muscular basis as well as the space around the body, the space within which it 'fits' like within a skin."[31] Benveniste's thesis that the subject is constructed through language, through her ability to distinguish "I" from "you," is thus extended to spatial deixis. The consequences for narrative fiction seem unavoidable: the subjectivity of characters is bound up with their proprioceptivity, which in turn is intimately, necessarily connected to the physical settings they occupy. Morrison describes her reconciled couple with their "leaf-sigh, old-time love" in terms of the comfortable shape their bodies form under a quilt.

Echoing the narratives I have cited, I wish to foreground the corporeal author, and claim that it is out of that figure's proprioceptivity that fictional settings can be imagined. If the foreigner is marked by her visual salience and the natives' focus on her difference, the imagined envelope of space will not fit her snugly; she will necessarily have difficulty in setting her fictions in that space or in pressing her characters into ill-fitting envelopes that would render them posturally disfigured. It is proprioceptivity that will prevent her from presuming to be a writer in the foreign culture.

For the South African writer Bessie Head, who moved to Botswana, the early years in that country were not fruitful in terms of her writing. Margaret Daymond says of her work of that period that "without the representation of the located experience of belonging to a place and its people, the idea of a collectivity on which individuality must be founded cannot become a reality and . . . for Head this meant that in certain respects she could not achieve the recreation of self that she was seeking through her writing when she first arrived in Serowe."[32] I have no idea whether Bessie Head wrote in order to recreate herself, but from the abstract short pieces she produced it would seem to be the case that she had difficulties with setting fictions in her new country. All her spatial references are to a vague, nonspecific "Africa." When Head says of Robert Sobukwe, leader of the Pan African Congress, that he gave her a comfortable black skin in which to live, it is surely the implication of proprioceptivity that allows Africa to transform into a specific location, a "here" in which her novels can comfortably be set. It is also the concept of proprioceptivity that for me renders problematic Homi Bhabha's notion of the postcolonial occupying an "inbetween" space. By invoking a metaphoric field of spatial ambiguity and celebrating the interstitial, Bhabha would seem to deny corporeality to the postcolonial writer in much the same way as does the foreign culture that hosts her invisibility.

The writer's envelope of space finds a ready metaphor in the house of fiction, a structure that occupies a circumscribed place, the setting of which is literally foundational, which is to say that it can be taken for granted. It is the homeliness of that constructed space that allows fictional characters to act and interact in the context of a shared history and a common identity. Homi Bhabha finds a concomitant creativity in unhomeliness: "To live in the unhomely world, to find its ambivalences and ambiguities enacted in the house of fiction, or its sundering and splitting performed in the work of art, is also to affirm a profound desire for social solidarity."[33]

It is a brave view and one that I, speaking as a writer, ought to consider. How possible is it to build such a house of fiction in a foreign world? I fear that what comes cravenly to mind is a construction that can be none other than a folly.

16

COETZEE'S *SLOW MAN* AND THE REAL:
A LESSON IN READING AND WRITING (2009)

In J. M. Coetzee's "As a Woman Grows Older," Elizabeth Costello questions the point of her life's work as a writer. Her daughter, Helen, argues that it is of value "not because what you write contains lessons but because it *is* a lesson"—a pronouncement that I take to assert the heuristic value of reading.[1] Coetzee's *Slow Man* (2005), a novel that makes extraordinary demands on the reader, would seem to offer such a lesson. The text abounds with references to lessons, in which lessons are ostentatiously delivered by characters, present themselves in the unfolding of events, or are disparaged as in Paul Rayment's dismissal: "One can torture a lesson out of the most haphazard sequence of events."[2] This essay, in its attempt to engage with the problem of reading *Slow Man*, suggests that the novel's insistent cross-mixing of reference and phenomenalism is a heuristic device for alerting the reader to the complex relations between author, narrator, and character. It is as a lesson in reading, which is to say re-reading, that *Slow Man* demands the reader's active tracking of the relationship between representation and the real, or rather levels of the real, and offers insights into the business of writing.

I start with a moment in the text where the character Paul Rayment reads the author-character Costello's notebook and finds in it references to his own thoughts. Thus it would seem that he is not an autonomous subject but rather the product of her imagination. For Paul, "the mind threatens to buckle. . . . Is this what it is like to be translated to what at present he can only call *the other side*? . . . There is a second world that exists side by side with the first, unsuspected. One chugs along in the first for a certain length of time; then the angel of death arrives . . . one tumbles down a dark hole. Then, hey presto, one emerges into a second world *identical with the first*, where time

241

resumes and the action proceeds—flying through the air like a cat."[3] Paul's experience mirrors that of reading the novel. If the story of a man, who comes through an accident with an amputated leg, chugs along according to our expectations of verisimilitude, the entry of Costello would disrupt mimesis, and in its intimations of other levels of reality disorientate the reader. The italics of "identical with the first" alert us not only to the typography, the material aspect of writing, but also to Paul's sensation of "flying through the air like a cat" as a repetition, a representation from the opening paragraph of the novel, which we earlier read as a real event of an accident, or rather, the representation of a real event. Thus the reader, like Paul, is cut loose, as another level of reality is established within the fictional work itself. If the first were presented as a world that we as readers enter, then Paul's "reality" would turn out to be that of another world, another level into which he enters through writing.

We should not have been so surprised. Immediately after the accident, Paul's emerging consciousness is described in terms of an attempt at writing "[a] letter at a time, *clack clack clack*, a message is being typed on a rose-pink screen that trembles like water each time he blinks . . . E-R-T-Y, say the letters, then F-R-I-V-O-L, then a trembling, then E, then Q-W-E-R-T-Y, on and on."[4] We witness the physical aspect of writing, the letters arranged on a keyboard from which the writer taps out words. The letters "E-R-T-Y" are meaningful, but while sounding like a suffix, it is not the correct one, and the word "FRIVOL" remains incomplete, or followed by an "E" (*FRIVOLE*), which hints at Paul's French origins. The letters "Q-W-E-R-T-Y" constitute a shift back to the very beginning of the first line and the first consecutive letters of the keyboard, a pronounceable sequence, although arbitrary in terms of meaning. It speaks thus of beginnings, of the raw material of writing, the real thing in the world from which meaning is made, and from Paul's point of view of the difficulty of coming into being as a character through writing.

The question of *whose* writing only arises once Costello arrives, and that is when the text demands a *re*reading, one that points to an ambiguity: the character appears both to be writing himself as well as to be being written. If Paul thinks that the screen is his own inner eyelid, the word "screen" is also an early reference to photography, where a screen in the process of picture-making is the surrogate surface for framing and focusing a previewed image. It is that which interposes between the phenomenological subject and its representation, here still trembling in the process of being formed. Rereading also highlights an early comment, easily overlooked, on the text being focalized through a character who is in fact a character in a novel that is necessarily structured by temporality: "From the opening of the chapter, from the incident on Magill Road to the present, he has not behaved well, has not risen to the occasion: that much is clear to him."[5] Much later, when Costello quizzes Paul on how it felt at the time of the accident, she supplies the cliché of death as an apprehension of the whole of your life flashing before you. Paul confirms the experience as a death of sorts: "My life seemed frivolous," he replies.[6] But can we trust the duplicitous author's declared ignorance of how it felt? Does her question not confirm Paul's identity as an already written character?

We are, of course, not unfamiliar with such self-reflexivity. Every schoolgirl understands the mimetic doubling in Ted Hughes's "The Thought Fox," where the efficacy of the imagination is illustrated in terms of an unambiguous author who is at one with his creation, so that the fox "enters the dark hole of the head" and "the page is printed."[7] There the act of writing is shown to be so complete, the imagination so replete, that the text proclaims a merging of the real and the represented. Paul, however, fails to act and thus to embody characterness; his story cannot be written, and Coetzee's wary representation references a subject in the real world that is not yet fully transformed or animated into a character whose actions should drive the story; in other words, the imagination and the writing process are shown to be agonistic. The Paul who rises out of unconsciousness experiences the world as a death—"transported"; "dead air"; "encased in concrete"; "whiteness unrelieved"[8]—and only authorial labor can bring him to life. Elizabeth Costello appears at both the beginning and the end as midwife: "Push!" she says in this droll representation of the birth of a text that exists at yet another level of reality.[9] Thus she asserts the ambiguities and the lack of clear distinction between their roles. She chides Paul: "Think how well you started. What could be better calculated to engage one's attention than the incident on Magill Road. . . . What a sad decline ever since! Slower and slower, till by now you are almost at a halt."[10] Costello, the author, is also both character and midwife who assists in the birth of the text, and Paul, the character, appears at various levels of reality to be preauthored, expected at some level to be coauthor of the text, or to be self-authored, a representation of the way in which a writer finds her character taking on a life of his own, departing from the idea from which he originated.

Italo Calvino's discussion in "Levels of Reality in Literature" is helpful in making sense of the head-spinning conundrum. He speaks of the "layers of subjectivity and feigning that we can discern underneath the author's name, and the various 'I's that go to make up the 'I' who is writing. . . . The author-*cum*-character is both something less and something more than the 'I' of the individual as an empirical subject."[11] Such unpacking and refraction of authorship is of course already referenced in the hybrid genre of Coetzee's own *Boyhood* and *Youth,* where "confessing in the third person" also asserts the author's fictionality and alludes to the fluid relationship between author and character, which is to say also between author and the empirical world.[12]

In my attempt to reconnect *Slow Man* with things-in-the-world, including texts (for what else can a reader do?), and resorting once again to similitude, that which structures the reading and interpretation of texts, I alight upon another contemporary work that produces a similarly vertiginous experience: Rachel Whiteread's sculptures, her trademark architectonic cast objects, like "House" in London. What links their works is the concept of substitution, and I will go on to argue for substitution as a key device in Coetzee's articulation of the real. In "House," Whiteread substitutes for a real house on the Roman Road in London a casting of its interior, which demands that the viewer reimagine the original, real house, from its negative. For the viewer, such disclosure of normally concealed space is analogous to Coetzee substituting for a narrative the interior, normally hidden mechanisms and problems of writing a novel. Both works, as I will discuss later, find a common emblem in photography.

The following commentary on Whiteread's practice precisely captures the experience of reading *Slow Man.* Fiona Bradley, comparing casting with photography, notes that it "combines that which is present with that which is other— the residue of the original which advances and retreats in the mind of the viewer," a phenomenon also experienced by Paul as he struggles with consciousness, or with being written.[13] Whiteread does not cast objects but rather the space they occupy, the negative space inside them, so that the sculptures, occupying different kinds of relationships with the "real" object, also reference different levels of the real.[14] The condition of entropy that according to Paul Rayment rules the world[15] is experienced by the reader of *Slow Man,* where Coetzee dramatizes the real difficulties that beset the writer trying to produce a story from an initial, inchoate idea. In the process of doing so, the house of fiction, like Whiteread's architectonic cast object, is turned inside out. Coetzee's Marianna, the blind woman with whom the blindfolded Paul has sex, wears her dress "inside out, with the dry-cleaning instructions protruding like a bold little flag."[16] This I consider as emblem of *Slow Man,* which, staging the writer's problem of how to proceed with a story and with a character that necessarily arrives inchoate, turns itself inside out, leaving its scaffolding intact and laying bare its own uncertain procedures, its own construction. Thus, like the viewer of Whiteread's "House" in situ of a thing turned inside out in its casting, the reader of this novel must negotiate between the presence of the given text and absence of a narrative promised at the beginning and expected through the conventions of fiction. The real then is experienced at different levels and from different angles, demanding what Roland Barthes calls a "cubist reading" of the realistic portrait.[17] Whiteread makes material that which normally exists as structured space. If the cast replaces what is lost—for in making the cast of a house, or bed, or bookshelf, she has to destroy the real object—*Slow Man* also trades in flamboyant substitutions, offering dizzying levels of reality for the reader to negotiate. Costello's entry or eruption into the narrative voids the first level of reality, casting off the stabilizing muffler of realism. She comes as a weary deus ex machina, who, it turns out, is not up to the job, so that ultimately we are given multiple crossings over and are steered through a continuous slippage between reference and phenomenalism. And as Costello's position in the narrative shifts, fictionality turning inward asserts itself more emphatically and leaves the reader to orientate him- or herself within the various levels of reality.

The interpretation of signs is of course interwoven with the representation of reality, and in *Slow Man* we do not have to hunt for signs: they are given, but rather than referencing things in the world, they refer to the novel itself. Toward the end of the novel Costello tells Paul: "Your missing leg is just a sign or symbol or symptom, I can never remember which is which, of growing old, old and uninteresting,"[18] a dismissal that at a first reading I find reasonable and set aside as unremarkable. Events in the novel are after all bracketed by reference to signs. There is the flag of Marianna's dress label at the beginning, and at the end the substitute for a substitute, a recumbent tricycle with orange pennant, or flag, built by the nurse's son, Drago, as substitute for the prosthesis that Paul refuses.[19] These signs of signs, literally flagged in the text, would seem to indicate the infinite regress of sign reproducing the object that is represented by the sign. Or so an early reading suggests.

In this story of Paul Rayment, the amputee who develops a passion for his nurse Marijana, Costello is thus introduced as an agent to deal with the unsuitability of the passion, and thus to develop a story that threatens either to go in an unsuitable direction—or to grind to a halt. Through substituting in loud postcolonial fashion for the discreet author of European realism, Costello throws into question the very nature of mimesis. And one of the hermeneutic keys that is (paradoxically) flagged, is substitution, a concept that structures the novel and at the same time admits to a problem within substitution: Costello herself has to be narrated; as a character who interrupts a narrative, she cannot replace the narrative agent employed by Coetzee, but rather, existing as she does at another level of reality, she is at the same time supplementary, and would seem to illustrate what Derrida discusses as the "internal division within *mimesis*, a self-duplication of repetition itself, *ad infinitum.* . . . Perhaps, then, there is always more than one kind of *mimesis*; and perhaps it is in the strange mirror that reflects but also displaces and distorts one *mimesis* into the other, as though it were itself destined to mime or mask *itself*, that history—the history of literature—is lodged, along with the whole of its interpretation. Everything would then be played out in the paradoxes of the supplementary double: the paradoxes of something that, added to the simple and the single, replaces and mimes them, both like and unlike."[20]

I now list some of these substitutions in the novel, in events as well as in their emblems, and attempt to show how they relate to representation, including the connection with language itself, from textuality right down to the level of the symbol, the letter which may or may not be a phoneme.

1. Costello substitutes for an author who must solve the diegetic problems of the story as if they were events in the real world. But why? Readers are after all familiar with "unsuitable passions" and their consequences in fiction; we do not, like the naïve natives in Jane Campion's *The Piano* (1993), lunge at a character on stage to prevent him from chopping off another character's hand. Yet, here sophisticated readers who, according to Paul de Man, would not dream of trying "to grow grapes by the luminosity of the word 'day,'" are boldly confronted with the slippage between reference and phenomenalism as a given.[21] But, in a further resort to similitude, we should also remember wincing as the mute central character in *The Piano* has her fingers chopped off "for real" toward the end of that narrative.

2. The visual relationship between Costello and Coetzee's names is enigmatic and supports the first substitution; it is also a reminder of the graphic aspect of writing. The crucial role of substitution in making visible similitude in poetic parallelism, where a degree of repetition coexists with difference, is visible here at the level of the letter. The patterning in the following,

C O E T Z E E—

C O S T E LL O,

with its repetitions, substitutions, and centrally positioned chiasmus (the crossed "Es" and phonic repetition/difference between "S" and "Z") serves to foreground the author function—as well as what Calvino calls "the successive layers of subjectivity and feigning that we can discern underneath the author's name."[22] The S/Z axis reminds us of Barthes's focus on the process of reading and the crucial role assigned to intertextuality in the production of meaning, although chiasmic reversal also cautions against uncritical reading of Barthes. The final or extra "O" then could be read as supplementarity in Costello or as ellipsis in Coetzee, grammatical ellipsis itself being a form of substitution in which an item is replaced by nothing. In discourse analysis lexical substitution and ellipsis assume crucial roles in achieving textual cohesion; it is also worth noting that ellipsis leaves specific structural slots to be filled from elsewhere in a text. The character Paul, on whose cooperation the author is so abjectly dependent, would seem to be a strong candidate.

3. When Costello arrives and recites/repeats the opening paragraph of the novel—this time in italics—the disruption of mimesis is also achieved through verbal substitution. The lexical item "*tumbles*" ("*through the air*") substitutes for "flies" in plain text, and later in the same exchange, in free indirect discourse, Paul offers a further substitution of "soaring through the air."[23] Such minimal substitution indicates repetition with a difference, and italics are repeatedly used in the text to flag supplementarity.

4. Phonology alerts us to the theme of forgery in the homophonic Fauchery photographs. Drago substitutes the digitally doctored photographs for the originals. Specifically, a Jokić grandfather substitutes for one of the Irish/Cornish miners, and Ljuba substitutes for one of the children in front of the settlers' mud and wattle cabin, a scene of poverty that Paul finds particularly poignant. Through substitution Drago inserts the Croatian immigrants into the Australian national memory so that the photograph literally binds the past with the future. I will return to photography as a device in Coetzee's exploration of the real.

5. Prosthesis, or the substitution of a real leg for an artificial one, which Rayment refuses, is (like Whiteread's house) present in the story as an absence. Attention is drawn to the word as early as page 7 when Paul discusses it with the doctor: "'Prosthesis,' he says, another difficult word." Prosthesis is also a linguistic term for the addition of a letter or syllable at the beginning of a word to facilitate pronunciation, or for prosodic reasons—a supplementarity that complicates the question of reference in phonology. In addition, linguistic prosthesis is known as, or substitutes for, the word prothesis (ellipsis of the "s"), which has a second meaning that relates directly to *Slow Man* as a display text. Prothesis means setting out in public, and refers to the Eastern Orthodox Church where

elements of the Eucharist are set out at the credence table, where bread and wine substitute for the body and blood of Christ; in other words, where the real is transformed. It is then through language and wordplay that one mimesis is displaced into another, and the doubling effect of substitution serves to highlight ambiguities within the notion of the real. Transformation in the Eucharist relies of course on belief, a commodity in the shape of suspension of disbelief that is required for the successful reception of a fictional text. And for the writer, the pursuit of an inchoate idea too is an act of faith: what is required is belief that the surprising or seemingly irrational events or images that arise in the act of writing will eventually link with other elements in a meaningful way.

6. Costello's solution to Paul's unsuitable passion is to substitute Marijana with Marianna, the dejected, blind woman. The difference between speech and writing is evoked: the names sound the same, so that Costello has to specify Marianna "with two *ns*," thus drawing our attention to print and representation, rather than to the women of phenomenalism.[24] Thus through substitution the text refutes a simple relationship between the thing and its representation: the inchoate Marianna clearly does not occupy the same degree of reality as the woman she substitutes for. Her shadowy nature, her improbable behavior, as well as the bizarre blindfolding suggest a character whom the author fails to develop and thus has to abandon; her fictionality is encoded in Paul's first encounter with what he calls "the crone leading the hastily clad princess in an enchanted sleepwalk."[25]

7. The name Marianna recalls substitutions in *Measure for Measure* where Angelo, who substitutes for the Duke, pursues his illicit desire for Isabella. The Duke engineers the substitution of Isabella with the "dejected" Mariana (of one "n"), and the sexual act that takes place in the dark echoes Paul Rayment, blindfolded and manipulated by Costello, having sex with another dejected Marianna, whose name with the double "n" points to substitution that is also the supplementary double of mimesis. As the Mari(j)an(n)as displace one mimesis into another, Paul's offer of money to the Jokićs is shown to substitute for Angelo's mercy-for-sex. Angelo's callous sexual behavior is again echoed later in *Slow Man* when Paul confesses that he once took to bed an unattractive employee who had fallen in love with him: "I left a note for her: a time, a place, nothing else. She came, and I took her to bed."[26] Costello, substituting the unattractive "rugby player" for Marijana, is appalled by this story. She asks: "Your rugby player had enough love for two, you say. Do

you really think love can be *measured?* That as long as you bring a case
of it, the other party is permitted to come empty-handed—empty-
handed, empty-hearted? Thank you, Marijana (Marijana with a *j* this
time), for letting me love you. . . . Thank you for letting me give you my
money. Are you really such a dummy?"[27]

These variations on the name Mariana illustrate Barthes's point about the
proper name acting as a magnetic field for the semes, its meanings accrued
through a variety of intertexts.[28] Perhaps the most pertinent of these is the echo
of the name in Calvino's character, Marana, translator in *If on a Winter's Night
a Traveller.* If *Slow Man* does not endorse that text's desire to absorb experience
into a totalizing concept of language, or its overarching concern with the role
of the reader, it nevertheless alludes to the Marana who produces counterfeit
texts, substitutes manuscripts, and mixes works and authors. Marana believes
that "the author of every book is a fictitious character whom the existent author
invents to make him the author of his fictions."[29] The first-person narrator in *If
on a Winter's Night a Traveller,* who could be seen to be identical with Calvino,
explains that Marana is interested in him "first, because I am an author who
can be faked; and second, because he thinks I have the gifts necessary to be a
great faker, to create perfect apocrypha."[30] The question of real and fake overtly
addressed in *Slow Man* will be discussed later.

From a postcolonial perspective, intertextuality as a way of reading offers more
than an openness of the text and the productive role of the reader: it operates
also as a form of substitution aimed at re-presentation. *Slow Man's* dramatization of the problem of what to do with characters who arrive inchoate and for
whom a history has to be created is also staged via intertexts from the author's
own oeuvre—the introduction of textual echoes, images, and repetition of
strategies from, for instance, *Foe* and *Elizabeth Costello.*[31] Similarly, Rachel
Whiteread's analogous sculptures not only revise and re-present buildings or
objects; there is, as Stuart Morgan notes, "a strong sense of interplay between
separate sculptures . . . a rich dialogue ensues between one piece and the
next."[32] In other words, both artists plunder events and images from their previous works in order to revisit the questions of authorship and the ambiguous relationship between representation and the real.

For *Slow Man* on the whole, the internal, hidden mechanisms of producing
a narrative and the research that precedes writing substitute for a narrative.
Having turned itself inside out, the novel reveals its halting construction that
substitutes for the story and at the same time constitutes the story. Substitution,

then, is multifunctional: serving the interest of the real, and by definition a version of the original, it is staged in the text at a variety of levels. In its shifting relationship with language and representation, substitution insists on engagement with the real that is, however, shown to be heterogeneous, shifting, elusive, and illusionary. Again, Whiteread's house that substitutes for a real house, and that allows for the viewer's *simultaneous* apprehension of both the house of phenomenalism and the not-house work of art, is helpful here. The representation is at the same time supplementary; it supervenes upon the real; these works, while insisting upon the real at the same time, do not allow the traditional notion of the real as that which is distinct from and precedes mimesis. Instead, we see Derrida's paradox of the supplementary double, "something that, added to the simple and single, replaces and mimes them, both like and unlike."[33]

If substitution in the above instances points variously to replacement, reversal, ellipsis, trickery, ambiguity, excess, or supplementarity, it is also significantly bound up with transformation. The linguistic shift from prosthesis to prothesis references transformation, instantiated in the first place in the figure and name of Paul Rayment, the boy from Lourdes, where miracles of healing are available for believers. His very name, Paul, speaks of the conversion of Saul on the road to Damascus, and there is the promise of further transformation into a fully fledged character who will transcend the flaws of the gloomy, hesitant, and abject amputee. Costello has come to save him from himself, but this amounts to little more than nagging him to act: "This is your story, not mine. The moment you decide to take charge, I will fade away."[34] Her offer of the blind Marianna "is like a sea beating against his skull. . . . The slap of water that will in time strip his bones of the last sliver of flesh. Pearls of his eyes; coral of his bones."[35] However, the promise of Shakespearean transformation fails as the sexual act amounts to no more than manipulation by Costello, who lacks Prospero's magical omnipotence, and since Paul resists his author, Marianna too cannot be fully animated into a character, so that the event constitutes a dark cul-de-sac in the narrative. But the promise of salvation persists. In Marijana's last visit as a nurse, Paul laments the fact that he is too *labile* for her taste. That, he says, is the word she is hunting for.[36] But labile has another meaning: not only liable to lapse (as does Angelo in *Measure for Measure*) but also liable to undergo displacement in position or change in nature and form—another reference perhaps to prothesis and the Eucharist table. In other words, Paul is aware of the potential for transformation that coexists with the drive to lapse, its mechanisms achievable within language and representation. And yet, the promise of transformation is not kept: when Paul says goodbye to Costello there is no salvation,

no resolution on offer. *Slow Man*, after all, remains a novel about the failure of
an author to transform her raw material into a credible work of fiction.

The concept of reality to which every representation necessarily refers is also
overtly discussed by the characters. Costello arrives as a doubting Thomas, taking Paul's hand to establish his and also her own reality. There are numerous
occasions when Paul questions reality: "Now let me ask you straight out, Mrs
Costello: Are you real?" Her reply, "Of course I am real. As real as you," is within
the realm of fiction perfectly acceptable.[37] At the same time, it confirms the
work as fiction, that which is separated from empirical reality and is commonly
discussed in terms of a self-reflecting mirror. Not surprisingly, then, the cloth
that Paul draped over the mirror in his house has been removed by Costello;
this he discovers after she has left when he once again covers the mirror.[38] Later
he tells Marijana that everyone should be more labile: "We should shake ourselves up more often. We should also brace ourselves and take a look in the mirror,
even if we dislike what we will see there."[39] In other words, the reflection is not
congruent with what we think of as our "real" selves, thus a lesson inheres in
such an act of looking. When Costello repeatedly comments on the Jokić
house with its Japanese garden ("So real! . . . So authentic! . . . Who would have
thought it!"),[40] Paul, who exists on a different level of reality, assumes that she is
being ironic. For the reader, however, it is surely a reference to the protean nature of representations, the propensity of fiction to slip beyond the author's control, and to beget further fictions. The Jokićs as characters, who arrive via
Mrs. Putts (that is, not in Costello's original scheme),[41] have, unlike Paul, taken
off, and represent a level of reality at which even the author must marvel. The
fiction, turned in upon itself, cannot be cut adrift from referentiality; even the
illusionary must refer to the world of things, so that the simulacral nature of a
Japanese garden in an Australian suburb does not detract from its reality. Costello's problem is that she cannot achieve the same level of reality for her character
Paul: "I stay on," she says, "because I don't know what to do about you."[42]

The inherently reproductive nature of fiction is shown to have a number of
consequences. The disconcerting level of reality introduced by Costello's arrival
in the text is followed by a further disruption: the character of Drago moves
center stage to oust Costello, who has no story to tell after all other than to lament
the impossibility of advancing with Paul's story. When Paul casts her out, we
are also reminded of the first level of mimesis: Costello is only another fictional
character making mischief among characters, rather than omniscient author.
She may have arrived with a history for the Jokić family, but Miroslav, in telling
his history to Paul, adds details that Costello appears not to know. It also transpires

that she knows nothing of Paul's childhood; he had come to her "with no history attached."[43] She is a representation of an unreliable author/character, who, for instance, forgets her own story about sleeping rough. It is clearly the case that the story *does* have reference independent of Elizabeth Costello, and that there is another level of mimesis, although these levels, shifting and sliding as they do into each other, are not stable.

The scene by the riverside where she feeds the ducks (an ironic allusion perhaps to the Ugly Duckling's tale of misrecognition and misreading that passes for a tale of transformation), and where a couple in a swan-shaped pedal boat passes by, offers something of a commentary on the text and its narration. The swan is fake, and although there are indeed "real" people sailing by in a "real" pedal boat of plastic, the spectacle points to the simulacral, so that we question the nature of this reality. In this scene Costello and Rayment's self-reflexive discussion raises overtly the question of the real. She sketches out the complexity of a phenomenalist position: "Let me tell you what you see, or what you tell yourself you are seeing. An old woman by the side of the River Torrens feeding the ducks. . . . But the reality is more complicated than that, Paul. In reality you see a great deal more—see it and then block it out."[44] Here levels slide into each other as Costello attributes the text to Paul, who we remember is not only character but also focalizer, the agent who substitutes for the narrator, so that she quotes back at him the opening words of that chapter, "*He finds her by the riverside . . . ,*" this time represented in italics. In the following, she alludes to a reciprocal relationship between reality and representation. Writing does not only imitate, it animates and vitalizes the world: "It is not good enough. It does not bring me to life . . . it has the drawback of not bringing you to life either. Or the ducks, for that matter, if you prefer not to have me at the centre of the picture. Bring these humble ducks to life and they will bring you to life."[45]

Costello, in attributing the text to Paul, suggests that he as focalizer/narrator is another substitute for the author. Calvino's question "How much of the 'I' who shapes the characters is in fact an 'I' who has been shaped by the characters?" is pertinent.[46] Costello herself has not produced any of the text we read; like all the other characters, she too has to be animated through the fiction, and as representation of an author she can only be apprehended through the narration. In the process of writing, characters animate one another, and author and character are interrelated: "You were sent to me," she explains, "I was sent to you. Why that should be, God alone knows."[47] In this reciprocity, they are both versions of the author function, albeit at different levels of reality, but it is also the promise of intersubjectivity, whether Paul likes it or not, that is asserted, as well as its crucial role in the world-disclosing function of the sign—as Habermas in his argument against postmodernism would have it.

The real in *Slow Man* is bound up not only with substitution, but also with the story's exploration of photography. It is in dialogue with *Camera Lucida*, where Barthes speaks of photography as "the Real, in its indefatigable expression" precisely because it is never distinguished from its referent.[48] Contrary to the imitations of painting or discourse, Barthes states, it is "the *necessarily* real thing which has been placed before the lens, without which there would be no photograph. . . . I can never deny that *the thing has been there.*"[49] In other words, substitution of the thing by the image does not impinge on the real; rather, the photograph (as opposed to writing) tells for certain what has actually been; it has an evidential force, and "its testimony bears not on the object but on time."[50] This is echoed by Paul, who explains to Drago about the collection of Fauchery photographs that on his death will become public property, part of their historical record.[51] Moved by one of the images, Paul speaks of the way in which "this distribution of particles of silver that records the way the sunlight fell, one day in 1855, on the faces of two long-dead Irishwomen, an image in whose making he, the little boy from Lourdes, had no part and in which Drago, son of Dubrovnik, has had no part either, may, like a mystical charm—*I was here, I lived, I suffered*—have the power to draw them together."[52] What is valorized here is the real, its transformation through photography that not only recalls the actual subjects of the past, but has affective value in the present.

But Barthes himself allows for a chink in his certainty about photography as evidence of the real. There is a foreshadowing of Drago's digital trickery, when Barthes laments the "sensation of inauthenticity" in a portrait photograph where he sees himself as subject-become-object, a micro-version of death: "others . . . turn me, ferociously, into an object, they put me at their mercy, at their disposal, classified in a file, ready for the subtlest deceptions," he complains.[53] When Barthes finds the same photograph on the cover of a pamphlet he is distressed by the artifice of printing. It is similar artifice, updated by digital technique, that drives the story of *Slow Man* to its ending. Drago has doctored the Fauchery photograph, leaving Paul with the substituted forgery, and Costello takes him to the Jokićs' house, where Marijana is outraged by his demand for the original: "What is this thing, original photograph? You point camera, click, you make copy. . . . Camera is like photocopier. So what is original? Original is copy already." Paul's reply addresses the complex relationship between the real and representation: "That is nonsense, Marijana. . . . A photograph is not the thing itself. Nor is a painting. But that does not make either of them a copy. Each becomes a new thing, a new real, new in the world, a new original."[54] In linking representation with renewal, and by implication devaluing the notion of authenticity and origin, Coetzee also avoids the reductive divide between the referential, that is to say Barthes's *"necessarily* real thing," and the simulacral of poststructuralism. Instead, the real is presented as renewable, substitutable, supplementary, and characterized by slippage between reference and phenomenalism. (It is such renewal that Habermas sees as a way out of the infinite regress of the sign.)

Costello's proposal that she and Paul live together comes with further elucidation of the relationship between the real and representation: "You can tell me more stories . . . ," she says, "which I will afterwards tell back to you in a form so accelerated and improved that you will hardly recognise them."[55] This is not as preposterous as it sounds. Paul's account is already a reworking of original events, and what is writing but an endless re-production of words that takes shape also through substitution? Paul's question aptly explains the process: "Isn't the whole of writing a matter of second thoughts—second thoughts and third thoughts and further thoughts?"[56] By accelerating and improving his stories, Costello would be addressing Paul's ponderousness, the characteristic that prevents him from acting.

The final section of the novel tackles the question of writing and the relationship between author and character directly. Costello laments the burden of being "an old woman who scribbles away, page after page . . . damned if she knows why. If there is a presiding spirit . . . then it is me he stands over, with his lash."[57] Art is the tyranny that binds the author to her own creation, to a character who must be animated into action. Costello's description of the partnership— "For me alone Paul Rayment was born and I for him. His is the power of leading, mine of following; his of acting, mine of writing"[58]—contains the linguistic figures I listed earlier in my sketch of substitutions: chiasmus, parallelism, ellipsis. The absolute authority of the author is relinquished in favor of a figural reciprocity: it is the character with his origins in the real world who, once animated, takes off and cooperates in producing the diegesis of fiction; in other words, he also ideally assumes an author function. And the notion of animation that introduces a magical, irrational element into creativity is a long way from Barthes's death of the author.

But Paul Rayment cannot act in the way his author wants him to. The scene at the Jokićs' house confirms his resistance to the fiction. Marijana says of Drago's gift, the recumbent bike: "It suits you. I think you should give it a whirl."[59] Not only is Marijana's own fictionality underlined in the classical posture of thought she adopts in propping up her elbow and holding her chin, her words establish fiction's relationship with other fictions. They echo Costello's earlier urging that he should act, be less of a tortoise. She chides him: "*We only live once*, says Alonso, says Emma, *so let's give it a whirl!* Give it a whirl, Paul. See what you can come up with."[60] And in choosing Emma Bovary and Don Quixote as models, with their actual words re-presented in italics, Costello references Calvino's "Levels of Reality in Literature," where the same characters are cited. But Paul resists; he won't be a real character, the subject of a novel, just as he will never use that one-off, custom-made, original construction that is the recumbent.

Such oscillation between fiction and the real is also enacted in the forgery that turns out to be a joke. Indeed, where Paul and Costello discuss the visit to the Jokić family, the word "joke" occurs nine times, as if we were in danger of forgetting the phonological link with the Croatian family name.[61] Costello, who appeared to have foreknowledge of the trickery, now reveals that the photograph has not disappeared and thus that Drago's manipulation cannot strictly speaking be called a forgery. We may be tempted to ask whether the entire event is not fake, unreal. There are after all discrepancies such as Marijana's comment that Paul should give up the idea of being a godfather before she reads the letter in which he proposes this. But by now we know that to question whether event or character is real is meaningless in this narrative conundrum, with its multiple reflections that converge and collapse on the reader. The simple distinctions between reality and representation—as well as between the real and the simulacral—have been refracted. We can be certain only of being engaged in reading a fiction that has as its subject the plight of an author writing a fiction that cannot be fleshed out to imitate reality. What is also dramatized is the intersubjectivity between author and invented character who, following Barthes's "ready-formed dictionary," has no other origin than language itself.[62] The autonomy and omnipotence of the author is itself shown to be a fiction, which is not to say that the author is dead and that the text is constructed entirely by the reader, but rather that a complex web of relations holds between the real and the represented, between the author and the character he or she has animated.

Marijana urges Paul to live with Costello as an antidote to his gloom. She points out that in Croatian the word "glumi" means pretend, not real; the suggestion is that taking up Costello's invitation would enable entry into the "real," which is to say into fictionality. But for Paul, pretense does not pose a problem. For instance, on their return trip from the Jokićs, Costello claims to recognize Drago as one of the young men who flash by on their motorcycles. Paul knows that it is too much of a coincidence, but he does not insist on being realistic: "Let them pretend nevertheless that the one in the red helmet was Drago." Theatrically he sighs, "Ah Drago . . . ah for youth!"[63] And within this dissimulation a truth emerges: the connection between Paul's gloom and the real raises the question of youth's antithesis—the wrecked body that Costello had so cavalierly dismissed as a sign or symbol. It is hard to believe that, as reader, I had so readily and perversely accepted the dismissal. The absence of a leg, which for Paul is the real presence of a stump and which the reader encounters in all its raw physicality, could be discussed in terms of what Hal Foster calls traumatic realism, one of the conceptual shifts in contemporary art "from reality as an effect of representation to the real as a thing of trauma."[64]

Costello's final offer to Paul of joining her in Melbourne is of herself as nurse, a substitute of sorts for Marijana. Paul declines; he will not be transformed or redeemed. He chooses to remain a one-legged inchoate character, and they part with sardonic reference to the flags they could attach to their comic vehicles. Costello's flag, Paul says, would be mottoed as *malleus maleficorum,* a reference to the multiauthored fifteenth-century Counter-Reformation text that advocated the persecution of witches, and that targeted midwives in particular as the most dangerous of witches. In other words, this is a wry comment on the role of the writer, whose task it is to bring characters into being. It is also a wry inversion of the idea of art as apotropaic: how could animation into art avert evil influence or bad luck when an accident at the first level of mimesis had turned Paul Rayment's leg into an obscene stump and had tumbled him into another level of fiction, into the hands of the writer/midwife? Paul's refusal then could be read as an assertion of traumatic realism, a refusal to unite the imaginary and the symbolic against the real. In his discussion of trauma discourse, Foster cites Kristeva on the body as primary site of the abject, which she defines as a category of (non)being, of neither subject nor object, a condition that Paul the amputee claims for himself against Costello's importunities, against her insistence on textuality. Foster's description of the appropriation of art that pushes illusionism to the point of the real is pertinent to this novel turned inside out: "Here illusionism is employed not to cover up the real with simulacral surfaces, but to *un*cover it in uncanny things."[65] In contemporary art practice, Foster identifies a bipolar postmodernism in which the real, repressed in poststructuralism, returns as traumatic. Both the textual model of culture and the conventional view of reality are dismissed by artists who wish to "possess the obscene vitality of the wound and to occupy the radical nihility of the corpse."[66]

It is the fact that its referent adheres, says Barthes, that makes photography unclassifiable and thus a condition of disorder. Such entropy also inheres in the fact that no matter how long he contemplates the photograph, it teaches him nothing—there is an arrest of interpretation because of the certainty *this-has-been*.[67] Rosalind Krauss finds Barthes's comments on photography pertinent to a reading of Rachel Whiteread, whose congealing of space into a rigidly entropic condition also strips it of any means of being "like" anything. However, Krauss's words on the monochrome plaster of Whiteread's casts that "announce their own insufficiency, their status as 'ghosts,'"[68] uncannily describe *Slow Man* and its characters. Krauss, by way of commenting on Whiteread, cites Barthes on photography as a kind of death, both structured and asymbolic (and in other words paradoxical), where he is led to say: "I have no other resource than this irony: to speak of the 'nothing to say.'"[69] If photography's absence-as-presence takes me back to entropy and the concern with death in both Whiteread and *Slow Man*, it also brings me to the irony of an arrest in interpretation: *Slow Man* offers itself as prothesis, lays out on the credence table its own hermeneutic. It waves its flags; there is ultimately nothing hidden; I can only describe what-has-been-read.

Part Three

INTERVIEW

INTERTEXTUALITIES, INTERDISCOURSES, AND INTERSECTIONALITIES: AN INTERVIEW WITH ZOË WICOMB

Conducted by Andrew van der Vlies

ANDREW VAN DER VLIES: The earliest essays in this collection date from the cusp of the political transition in South Africa but offer reflections from different locations, the twin poles of your professional and creative lives, South Africa and Scotland. For the purposes of setting the scene, I wonder whether you could sketch your movements after leaving the country of your birth? I am particularly interested in your experience of going back and forth between Britain and South Africa, and how that sense of having established a life outside South Africa might have inflected your participation in the events *in* the country during that febrile, exciting period of transition.

ZOË WICOMB: The late sixties was a period of severe repression. I left South Africa in January 1970, not least because the resistance movements had been crushed. Had I known of Steve Biko's Black Consciousness Movement that soon gained ground in the Eastern Cape, I would not have felt so despondent and anxious to get away. The South African Embassy confiscated my passport, and I did not return until the 80s, traveling on a British passport. My first extended stay in South Africa was as a Jagger Fellow at the University of Cape Town for three months in 1990, after Mandela's release. I reacquired citizenship and returned to Cape Town, where I taught for three years in the English Department at the University of the Western Cape (U.W.C.) until December 1993. Thereafter I changed my contract to work for half the year, which would have allowed me to spend the other half in Glasgow, but family commitments made that arrangement impossible, so that I then reconciled myself to living in Glasgow, and applied for a full-time post at Strathclyde University in 1994. My life, however, remained immersed in South Africa in the sense that all my work, creative and critical, was centered in the place where I did not live. Pathological perhaps, but until fairly recently I didn't feel that I had established a meaningful life outside South Africa. So I managed fellowships at universities in the Cape during northern-hemisphere summer breaks and sabbaticals, and for some years was a visiting professor at Stellenbosch University.

AV: The first essay in this collection, "Tracing the Path from National to Official Culture," takes an event in Glasgow in September 1990 as its point of departure. Glasgow was, you show, a location of antiapartheid activism and of cultural work that looked forward to a particular version of the "New" South Africa. Your fiction also traces links between Scotland and South Africa: I am thinking of the Scottish interludes in *David's Story* and *Playing in the Light* and of Scotland's central place in the life of one of the protagonists of *October*, but also how many of the stories in *The One That Got Away* turn on connections between the countries, or uncover South African characters' sometimes complicated links with Scotland. Some of these stories first appeared during the period we're talking about, the early 1990s, in publications with an expressly antiapartheid organizing principle (at least one of these publications appeared in Scotland: "In the Botanic Gardens" was included in *The End of a Regime: An Anthology of Scottish–South African Writing Against Apartheid*, edited by Brian Filling and Susan Stuart and published by Aberdeen University Press in 1991).

Could you say something about the process by which Scotland came to feature in your creative work during the period? How did you come to think of Scotland as different from England, where you had also lived, in the 1970s, but which does not feature in your creative work in the same way? How might critical work and teaching in Scotland function in relation to your own creative writing?

ZW: Yes, England does not feature in my writing. *You Can't Get Lost in Cape Town* was written in Nottingham, where I lived in the mid-1980s, and the place of writing was as structured an absence as the gaps between the stories. An act of denial perhaps, but also about playing with the genre of autobiography, which, being black South African writing, was how I thought the work would be received. In Nottingham I worked for the Anti-Apartheid Movement, and I still shudder thinking of the public talks I had to do. My fear of speaking meant that I prepared meticulously, writing out every word of my talk, so that critical writing was not much of a leap from that.

In 1987 we moved to Glasgow, where I was shocked by the crude brand of racism, even at the level of language: usage long since deemed unacceptable in England, at least amongst the educated middle classes, was no problem here. Here was evidence of the hegemonic relationship with England, and at the time that seemed to be how Scots defined themselves, so that intolerance of the other fueled by relative poverty and insecurity was the order of the day. The operations of nationalism and its relationship with racism pricked my interest, as did the history of Scottish settlement in South Africa. Then Scotland was not a place where I wanted to live, but its colonial ties with South Africa guaranteed it a place in my fiction. It was here I found names that I had thought of as English to be Scottish, where the roots of our South African Calvinism as well as our education and legal systems lay, and where our nonstandard English still resonated. My first short story written in Scotland, "In the Botanic Gardens," which you mention, explores some of these aspects.

But Scottish culture in the new century underwent radical changes—indeed, changes that challenge our received views about nationalism—since it is with the rise of the Scottish National Party that the Scotland of today is a very different place. In this unprecedented version of nationalism, now all but deracinated, a public discourse of inclusivity is vigorously embraced. So, in spite of my earlier appeal to proprioceptivity to explain why Scotland is not a possible setting for my fictions, Glasgow in particular has in fact over the years become an increasingly comfortable "spatial envelope" for my characters.

AV: Would you tell us what you were teaching during the period? How did this work influence you as a commentator on South African cultural politics, as a literary critic, and as a writer of fiction?

zw: I think of teaching as the single most important factor in my intellectual development. Perhaps I go on about literacy and pedagogy because my university education in South Africa was so poor; it did not even attempt to address the cultural and linguistic deficit of its students. In England it was an equally woeful business of clever people delivering virtuoso readings of texts, with no interest in explaining how they arrived at such readings. I started teaching in secondary schools where, panic-stricken, I realized that I would have to teach myself to read in order to teach A-level students. And so the desire to read, which I had hoped to develop at university, turned into a more formal understanding of how texts work. Teaching Further and Adult Education classes allowed me to develop my interest in Women's Writing and Black Writing, and so I devised such courses alongside the staples of Eng. Lit.

But structuralism and literary theory, having entered academia after I had left university, revolutionized my thinking. I read Eagleton's *Introduction to Literary Theory*, Catherine Belsey's *Critical Practice*, and Deborah Cameron's *Feminism and Linguistic Theory*, and was drawn back into the academy—literary linguistics, the works of Barthes, Said, Spivak (to name a few), these were life-changing, and the analysis of media texts offered new pedagogical opportunities. In addition to regular English Literature classes, I taught South African Literature and also English language at U.W.C., and at Strathclyde University Ways of Reading—a course developed by Strathclyde literary linguists—as well as Postcolonial theory and writing. Latterly, as Creative Writing crept into the British academy, I devised a skills-based Masters Course taught jointly at Strathclyde and Glasgow Universities, and thereafter Creative Writing that linked with literary texts on the Strathclyde Honours English degree of which it was a component.

AV: Looking back over the past twenty-five years, your warnings about the ways tradition would come to serve attempts to valorize "official" versions of a "national" culture seem terribly prescient. "Tracing the Path" cautions that "a movement from reactive to reactionary parallels the shift from a national culture, an imaginary entity that fires our will to be free, into an official culture that is . . . an attempt to fix certain forms, to authorize and validate them as *the* desirable, correct forms." You observe, too, that "the process, of course, will continue regardless."

Were there moments over the past quarter century when you felt you might have been too pessimistic? What have the most egregious instances of this ossification been, to your mind? And might I ask you to venture some thoughts about whether what you call "the reflectionist model of cultural expression" (which is to say "that it simply mirrors what we experience"; you remind us that this simply "conceals the relationship between culture and power") has had a disproportionate effect on South African writing over the past decades?

ZW: Ah, it's been salutary reading my opinionated younger self. In the halcyon days of Nelson Mandela's presidency there was, I think, a new sense of freedom of expression, and many of the hallowed positions of the struggle period (along with many struggle poets) quietly disappeared. The validation, then, of the "reflectionist model" can be seen to be a function of resistance to apartheid, one promoted also by leftier-than-thou critics during the 80s and early 90s. But my cocky dismissal is, of course, overturned by Nadine Gordimer, whose work throughout, rather than concealing the relationship between culture and power, has always attempted to uncover it. And my questioning of Goldblatt's documentary photography too seems a foolish way of addressing his commentator's views; Goldblatt's work consistently addresses South African culture with insight, and with an independent eye. At the time I could not have imagined the work of William Kentridge rooted in the social geography of Johannesburg. Not only does it engage with political injustice, but constructed as it is from fragments, and bringing into focus what he sees as the provisionality of the post-apartheid city, it radically transforms the given material. Interesting too how he uses the elements of culture that I deride in "National . . . Official Culture," African song and dance, but renewed to serve the contemporary world continually in flux, and inviting the viewer to construct a narrative whilst at the same time dissolving the fixity of that world. And these dazzling spectacles often include the artist himself, reflexively investigating his own work.

Of course the radical writing of John Coetzee, Ivan Vladislavić, Marlene van Niekerk, Njabulo Ndebele had already been established, but Zakes Mda's, for instance, having shifted from drama to fiction, became a powerful new voice, infused with the magical. The 90s also brought new black voices like K. Sello Duiker and Mary Watson, who have no interest in "correct" forms, as well as interesting work in popular genres—I'm thinking of Lauren Beukes's speculative fiction. Then there is Masande Ntshanga, who was shortlisted for the Caine Prize in 2015 and who in his first novel, *The Reactive*, tackles the urgent issue of chemical abuse with no apparent knowledge of the old restrictions.

So whilst official culture was worryingly present during the period of resistance, the demise of apartheid put paid to such valorization. In fact, the appeals to tradition, exemplified by Zuma's polygamy, for instance, have done much to discredit the notion of tradition. If nationalism has shown its reactionary force in the shape of xenophobia towards African immigrants, it is also the case that the arts are flourishing and are by no means subject to prescriptive forms. The current unpopularity of the African National Congress and its loss of moral authority also means that what once was paraded as the official culture is of no interest at all to the born-free generation. So yes, I've been pessimistic about cultural production, but the current crisis of legitimacy, manifested also in student protests, once more shows a worrying appeal to autochthony—history repeating itself, as the dream of a rainbow nation collapses.

AV: I want to ask you about irony. Being alert to the operation of irony seems crucial for understanding your work, both critical and creative. It is central to ideas of implicature in pragmatics, which is important to you and to which I'll return shortly. As a classical rhetorical device, *eirōneía*, a feigned ignorance,

involves dissimulation through which someone in an inferior position in relation to the powerful speaks truth, offers critique, stands to the side of the stage,
and asks us to think differently about what is unfolding. Thus, as you say in
"Tracing the Path from National to Official Culture," "the branding of irony as
an elitist discourse is a misconception."

I'd like to ask you about the witty (even ironic!) observation in this essay that
"irony has had . . . a bad press in the resistance movement." I'm quoting out of
context: the observation is promised as a question that will be addressed, and it
follows a conditional statement that "even if, as Fanon so persuasively argues,
the nostalgic desire for the past is misguided, the very fact that it exists implies
its representability, if only with the deployment of irony." I wonder if you might
say whether you think irony still has a bad press in South Africa, or, putting the
question differently, if you have seen a flowering of the kind of irony you
imagined as a powerful counterdiscourse (or something with counterdiscursive
possibilities) in South Africa over the past twenty-five years?

zw: I don't think that irony nowadays has a bad press in South Africa, which is
not to say that there has been a flowering either; indeed, I am not sure if culture
is of much interest to the generation of born-free black South Africans. While
disillusionment with the A.N.C. has led to a revisiting of the political culture of
the transition, there is little being said about cultural production, which is not
to say that both visual and literary arts are not flourishing. Instead, the new black
consciousness movement addresses the persistence of racial inequality and specifically the distribution of wealth, the fact that 10 percent of the population still
owns 90 percent of all assets. There appears to be little room for irony in the
preoccupation with such concerns. These tensions are played out on university
campuses where unrest fomented in the Rhodes Must Fall and Fees Must Fall
campaigns has included the burning of artworks from university holdings. So
perhaps ironic after all as students target artworks as metonymy for white privilege and adopt the role of philistines. Language too has been an issue in universities where black students agitate against the use of Afrikaans, and instead
demand English, the language of economic advancement. To my knowledge
there are no demands for including indigenous languages in the academy.
Ironic only in the sense that the constitution guarantees the rights of all South
African languages, and that decolonization as formulated by Ngũgĩ was precisely about the hegemony of English. Then again, one ought to wonder whether
that too is a superficial reading of the situation. Are there further ironies at play?

But it is the case that irony is also fun, that there is pleasure to be found in
the cognitive activity of figuring and figuring out irony, and that in our be-

nighted world the ludic is to be treasured. Only prigs do not like to be teased. On rereading these essays I am struck by the absence of the ludic in my own thinking—that too was suppressed by a po-faced apartheid culture. And I can hardly believe that none of these essays mentions Lewis Nkosi, who was an extraordinary, iconoclastic critic of South African literary culture. Not only was he a wonderful ironist, he also lamented as early as in his *Home and Exile* the inability of white authors "to see and underline the fantastic ambiguity, the deliberate self-deception, the ever-present irony beneath the mock humility and moderation of speech" of black South Africans. In other words, he was alert to the subversive powers of irony and so spoke also scathingly about black writing's "prim disapproval" of irony. As for current practitioners, Ivan Vladislavić continues to deploy irony in both a humorous and searing manner. Interestingly, given that Johannesburg according to Brian Chikwava's brilliant novel *Harare North* could be seen as Harare South, no such Chikwavian irony can be found in South African depictions of migrants.

AV: I think you're being a little too hard on yourself! There is certainly evidence of something like the ludic in several of the essays in Part 2 of this collection. I am thinking of the final chapters in particular, your wry comment in "Setting, Intertextuality, and the Resurrection of the Postcolonial Author" that you are often asked to "speak as a writer" (I suppose I'm doing something like that here), and your extraordinary parsing of Coetzee's ludic impulses in "Coetzee's *Slow Man* and the Real." In both cases, and in fact in all cases where your own writing engages with the ludic, what is at issue for you is always the question of ethics. Irony and ironic play serve to decenter dominant discourses. In "Tracing the Path," you wonder about the usefulness of Deleuze and Guattari's use of territorialization (and deterritorialization) as descriptions of the potential of cultural practice in relation to notions of tradition and official culture. I think "deterritorializing" describes very well the operation of certain energies in your own novels (the decentering of discourses of race in *David's Story* and *Playing in the Light*, of the moral authority of the struggle in *David's Story*, of "home" itself in *October*).

Would you reflect on the role of criticism in engaging (revealing?) these operations? Can criticism (however cautiously framed) run the risk of reterritorializing? Perhaps I'm asking you to reflect on the status of *difficulty* in cultural production *and* in the discourses that might be necessary to make clear its workings (or its potential to work in particular ways).

ZW: I can't comment on my own work. But yes, "difficulty" remains a thorny issue, not least because it can't be pinned down. Besides, it doesn't seem to

operate on a clear continuum, so that cultural arbiters sometimes wrongly decide on what people may find difficult. For critics then to decide that a work is
too difficult is often condescending—never too difficult for the pronouncer
but deemed difficult for others. The classroom offers a good example of how
difficulty can be negotiated. Most students start off believing that a text is difficult, but they also discover that such works are only accessible to those who
are prepared to grapple with strangeness and complexity. That is the role, the
value, of education: we learn that instant understanding is a facile expectation;
we do not expect that problems, taken in a rather macho fashion by the horns,
can be instantly solved. Instead, the critical reader values the questions posed
in difficult works; in other words, values the operation of thought itself that the
work promotes, rather than arrival at an answer. And by grappling with such
works, they are preserved and passed on through the education system.

I also wonder if what Achille Mbembe calls the politics of patience (in relation to student unrest) is not applicable here. The kind of understanding of the
world opened up by art operates more slowly; we have to be patient, be prepared
to reread endlessly, look again and again in different ways at works of art. There
is a temporality involved, but also a certain acceptance of the epiphanic, which
is where the difficulty with difficulty lies. Which is not to say that the realm of
such understanding is wholly nonmaterial, one that will not happily submit to
an earthy metaphor. I do think that territorialization remains a viable metaphor
for the political inflection of language, but that the line between reterritorialization and deterritorialization can perhaps not be as clearly cut as its proponents wish it to be.

AV: Revealing a text's invitation to apprehend moments of potential epiphany is
a task for the critic, and one that you offer in these essays time and again. It
strikes me that your act of "Rereading Gordimer's *July's People*" (Chapter 11)
does precisely this; you write that "what *July's People* introduces into the inevitability of a new political order is the ethical and therefore the personal: face-to-
face interaction on a new footing that takes its measure from new languages and
new registers yet to be learned by interlocutors." But you are concerned, too,
with the limits of critical or intellectual work in the face of brute want, the fact
that people are hungry, that people remain in poverty in South Africa. We are
introduced to a preoccupation with this profound challenge to any discourses
presuming a claim on our attention, even writing itself, in "Nation, Race, and
Ethnicity." There is a moment at the end of this essay when you summon the
"real voices that intrude upon us as we sit down to write"; you wonder "how to

continue the activity of writing that is disturbed by the beggars beating at our doors for food: how not to think of writing in this context as a shameful activity that does little or nothing about redistributing cultural and linguistic capital."

zw: I think it is exasperation, my exhaustion with arguments about art production, that is expressed in these rhetorical questions, as well as despair of the economic situation that makes one feel so guilty about having more than enough to eat.

av: You were writing this essay in the early 1990s, and it seems to me that you might be seen here to be voicing sympathy with a version of the argument that art must be "relevant" (a debate that raged through the 1980s). "Is there really a case for privileging representational art?" you ask. "Is there a case at all for giving writing a central position in our culture?" I think you imply an answer in the affirmative, elsewhere certainly, and another answer is offered in your development of what is effectively an ethics of form in your own work (we'll talk a little later about that). Here I want to ask whether you would still pose this question in the same way today? Of course "relevance" comes to mean something different when we turn to thinking about pragmatics, but would you reflect on your attitudes to the way in which "relevance" functioned more instrumentally in debates about the literary in the 1980s, and how you sought to position yourself in relation to these debates?

zw: I would dismiss "relevance" as vehemently today as I have ever done. It is a conservative notion that seeks to keep the dog tied to its own vomit—as Beckett said of habit; it is condescending, and underestimates people's desire for something other than their daily experiences. Which is not to say that such daily experiences are not representable. There is clearly value in people seeing their life conditions represented, but "relevance" is myopically limited to what people know as opposed to the wealth of things in the world that they could conceivably get to know.

Nonetheless, I believe my question stands: the homeless and unemployed rummaging through our dustbins for food may not invalidate our reading and writing, but it surely makes us shudder with shame. I am finally reconciled to not living in South Africa, but hiding in Europe where the division between rich and poor is not quite as stark does of course not protect one against the guilt and shame. The folly of my exasperated question about whether there is a place for writing in a world where people starve lies in its hierarchization of needs.

What these essays do not engage with is the important critiques of relevance offered by Nkosi and Ndebele, well before Albie Sachs pronounced its weakness from the official A.N.C. platform.

AV: The question of the need for representational art, and of the relative privileging of different forms of cultural production (questions to which you return), suggests broader questions about your engagement with visual art. Could you tell us how you came to art? What was your introduction to visual art, South African as well as European and American? In relation to the latter, I'm thinking about your references to Martha Rosler, Carrie Mae Weems, Jan Dibbets, and so on. In relation to the former, could you tell us about your acquaintance with some of the artists you discuss, Jackson Hlungwani, Noria Mabasa, Chickenman Mkhize, Derrick Nxumalo, Tito Zungu?

ZW: I don't think that art was taught in any coloured schools in Cape Town; I barely knew what art was. (For that matter, I had never been to a theater, seen an art film, or come across any black writing before I went abroad.) Reading University is one of the few in the U.K. with an Art Practice department, and while I failed to make any friends in the English department, I did for some reason hang out with art students, and indeed moved to London to live with artists who started the first Artists Housing Association (ACME) in disused buildings in Tower Hamlets. I educated myself with regard to European and American art. Only thereafter (as was the case with literature) did I engage with South African art, notably the work of Gerard Sekoto, who lived in exile in Paris. The non-African artists I refer to in the essays interested me for their explicit concern with the problems and politics of representation. Also, their engagement with language as visual information was challenging, curiously resonating with works by nonliterate South African artists.

In the late 80s there were several survey exhibitions in Europe of antiapartheid art that seemed so much more vibrant than the writing of the time, and I was struck by the ways in which poorly educated people used materials cast off by the wealthy sector to produce works of aesthetic value. My partner, Roger Palmer, who is an artist, photographer, and educator, introduced me to difficult contemporary art that I would otherwise have given up on. In 1992 I went along on his research trip to artists in the north of South Africa. At the time, he was selecting work for an exhibition cocurated with Tessa Jackson at the Arnolfini in Bristol, and it was moving to discuss with people how their lives are enriched through expressing themselves in visual forms, how they overcome material poverty through art. In spite of living in basic conditions, none of the artists actually thought of themselves as poor; indeed, the women in particular, who adorned their mud walls and yards with beautiful hand-inscribed patterns, cared nothing about destructive weather conditions. They were happy to redo the short-lived decorative work, and thus in asserting pride in aesthetic control, undermined the definition of the homelands to which they were banished as arid and poverty-stricken.

Since my essay on orality, William Kentridge's extraordinary multimedia works have achieved world fame. It's interesting that his preferred drawing material is the printed book, tomes like dictionaries chosen for their use value, the quality of the paper, rather than content. The printed text then becomes a visual background for his charcoal drawings and their imperfect erasures, so that reading becomes a matter of assembling fragments into a narrative that dissolves before our very eyes, and further undermines the hallowed nature of the original books.

AV: Kentridge's practice in those works to which you refer reminds me of your artist figure, Drew Brown, and his remaking of an overdue library book that becomes effectively both performance art and an archival intervention in your short story "The One That Got Away." In relation to the South African artists about whom you write in the early essays, the question of literacy is crucial: visual literacy, you argue, is widespread, and it is present even where a "reader" (or "producer") is not (strictly) *textually* "literate" (in these cases, it can also involve "text"). You are here, of course, addressing the competencies that exist despite the legacy of inferior education for black South Africans, but also the longevity of other forms of archiving knowledge (and belief). I'm drawn to this observation: that "contemporary visual works in South Africa have outstripped the need for apologias on behalf of the nonliterate or poorly educated who produce art forms that in their use of writing curiously coincide with postmodernist practices in the overdeveloped West." Do you still feel this way? Do you sense that the situation has changed in any way in South Africa over the past twenty-five years, either in relation to literacy, or the need for apologias, or indeed the capitalization of the art market? Would an essay on "Reading, Writing, and Visual Production" today offer a different argument, or prognosis?

ZW: Indeed, the issues are completely different. The focus on orality proved to be a function of cultural recovery during the period of transition, and neither does the lack of literacy nowadays appear to have a central or visible role in producing art, nor is the representation of language present as a trope of desire in contemporary works. Literacy, including visual literacy, has come a long way since democratization in South Africa. Since 1994, black enrollments at schools have doubled, growing by 91 percent, although it is the case that only 12 percent go on to higher education, as opposed to 58.5 percent of white school leavers. Thus, not surprisingly, the art scene has been transformed. Many universities offer Fine Art degrees, and black South African artists generally have been through art education, so that the dominant production nowadays is a far cry from the works I cite. While the visual heuristic I describe in the essay probably continues to exist in underdeveloped rural areas, black art is now represented in all the major galleries, of which there has been a proliferation over the past decade. Furthermore, many artists have achieved international recognition and, via the successful Cape Town and Johannesburg Art Fairs, operate within the global art scene.

AV: The point of your analysis of visual art is to argue for the existence of literacies that have the potential to act as counterhegemonic force in a fledgling democracy, to keep open the capacity to hear the variety in a way that refuses hierarchy—and exoticization, or anthropologizing analysis—and that might prevent the ossification of national cultures into official culture. Encouraging recognition of these literacies, and their propagation, is part of what you call a "radical pedagogy" (in "Culture Beyond Color?"), something that has actively to be taught, capacities that have actively to be cultivated. Your essay on "Motherhood and the Surrogate Reader," it seems to me, offers perhaps your most programmatic attempt at developing this pedagogy, at proposing a mode of reading—here, reading text and image (you use Victor Burgin's term "scripto-visual" analysis)—and situating this set of strategies as a development of pragmatics.

Several questions follow. First, could you describe how you came to pragmatics? Through which thinkers and theorists, and how did pragmatics function in the teaching that you were doing in Glasgow, if at all?

ZW: I had followed in the media the dismissal of Colin MacCabe from Cambridge, allegedly for teaching alien structuralism and poststructuralist theories in the 80s. A Channel 4 program on an extraordinary course that he had set up in Glasgow, and the broadcast of their conference "Arguments Between Language and Literature," with luminaries like Derrida, Mary Louise Pratt, Jameson, and others in attendance, led me to Strathclyde University, where I did the postgraduate Literary Linguistics course and later taught in the late 1990s. Belatedly I discovered Pratt and Traugott's early textbook, *Linguistics for Students of Literature*, and Pratt's model of discourse analysis also using pragmatics that produces insightful readings of literary text, indeed readings that affirm the connection as Edward Said argued between texts and the world. I don't imagine that my teaching departed from attention to the relationship between ethics and aesthetics that gained currency at the time, but I feel as committed as ever to close reading of texts in all media and especially the ways in which imagery intersects with linguistic messages. (No doubt there all kinds of challenges posited by the new digital media, but someone who has resisted the mobile phone is not in a position to comment.)

It is shocking to find that as I write today women in universities are protesting against the sexual abuse they endure, not only perpetrated by gangs of jackrollers in South Africa as I mention in "Motherhood and the Surrogate Reader." Does this not spell a failure of our education systems? It seems urgent that young people, both male and female, should be taught even at high school about the inscription of ideological meanings, taught how to access meaning across media. Such work cannot be left to sensitive readings of literary texts alone.

AV: I agree. As 2016 turns into 2017, after the "Brexit" referendum in the U.K. and the most recent presidential election in the United States, and given ongoing political uncertainties in South Africa, such failures of education seem ungainsayable. It seems to me that pragmatics is absolutely suited to attempts to find a place for art's progressive political potential in a multilingual context (and one thought of either as unevenly literate, or indeed multiply "literate" in diverse ways); the use of common types of implicature are things one learns with one's first language, after all. Do you think pragmatics has played a significant enough role in postapartheid pedagogy and/or cultural criticism?

ZW: I don't understand postapartheid pedagogy. The closing down of teacher training colleges in the interest of more advanced postgraduate training, which has left primary education in a parlous state, makes no sense. I have no patience with the position that Western theory is inappropriate for Africa, but for those who espouse such views, pragmatics is surely an "innocuous" way forward towards questioning ideological assumptions and the ways in which they are inscribed in culture. As for cultural criticism, we have been through exciting times with or without the help of pragmatics, and in South Africa theory in the academy has, in Literary Studies at least, gone some way towards overhauling colonial thought. However, black students are currently demanding "decolonization," and having recently in the leafy suburbs of Cape Town encountered widespread claims (including Western Cape Premier Helen Zille's) for the social and economic benefits brought to South Africa by colonialism, I realize that those of us in literary studies live in an educational bubble. Not surprisingly,

then, black students' attempts at indigenizing their English—being "woke"—
are, in the interest of upholding "standards," met with derision in the academy.

AV: The discursive landscape does seem more polarized now than it has been
for some time, to be sure. In those early essays, you draw on Gricean and neo-
Gricean theories and on their outgrowth, Relevance theory, particularly in the
work of Dan Sperber and Deirdre Wilson. Relevance theory speaks to your interest in irony, of course; as you explain, it foregrounds "irony's effect of making
us question the given or shared knowledge" (as urgent today, as you imply, as
such a questioning ever was). In "Motherhood and the Surrogate Reader," however, you supplement Sperber and Wilson with the work of Michel Pêcheux on
the grammatical inscription of ideology; ideology directs those interdiscourses
that provide framing inferences with which we bridge gaps in communication.
Could you reflect on the practice of scripto-visual analysis you proposed in this
essay? Is it equal to the New South Africa twenty years on? Has your attraction to
Sperber and Wilson, and to Pêcheux, lasted? How has it influenced your thinking about representing dialogue (amongst other things) in your own fiction?

zw: I was dissatisfied with art criticism's metaphorical use of "visual language"
and I wanted to explore how pragmatic negotiation between image and text
could be more helpful in explicating such works. If Althusser's notion of inter-
pellation seemed unsatisfactory, Pêcheux's account of how grammar and in particular the relative pronoun and subordinate clauses inscribes ideology was
more convincing, although his notion of interdiscourse is too deterministic and
does not allow for resistance. Prior to this essay I had written on Jenny Holzer's
text works and by way of introduction looked closely at how visual material in
Tristram Shandy interacts with the text. Perhaps these were attempts at engaging with what I saw as unsatisfactory ways in which advertising and also film
(especially films of novels) were discussed in literary criticism, as if the visual
information were incidental. What Pêcheux and Sperber and Wilson offer is of
course close reading with a difference, and one of the sad consequences of theory has been precisely the neglect of close reading, as if the latter would mili-
tate against wider philosophical readings. I am as attached as ever to the efficacy
and also the pleasure of close reading, whether of image or text; and yes, it requires time and necessarily involves many rereadings.

As for my own use of dialogue: I am unaware of influence from theorists, although the writer is presumably influenced by everything she experiences.
What I realized at the outset was that dialogue was incredibly difficult, and that
the old advice of "listen to how people speak and then reproduce it" is nonsense,

since representation of speech is nothing like a transcript of real speech. I think certain writers have a felicitous ear for distilling the spoken into written dialogue. Was it perhaps my own weakness in this regard that drove me towards free indirect discourse? I don't know, but it remains my favored mode, and so many years later I am pleased to find Fredric Jameson in *The Antinomies of Realism* (2013) historicize and theorize *style indirect libre*, its relationship to irony and its multidimensional representation of reality.

AV: Some might say that your early essays, and here I'm thinking in particular of "To Hear the Variety of Discourses" and "Motherhood and the Surrogate Reader" (though it's clear, too, in "The Path from National to Official Culture"), display the insights of what we would now call intersectionality. Could you say something about *how* and *when*, and with what theoretical inspirations (to which you came *where*), your insights about the necessary imbrication of feminism and critical race studies took shape?

ZW: Intersectionality seems so blindingly obvious a notion, but the formalization of such ideas is useful. Its underlying insights had of course been around for some time, notably through African American theorizing of race and gender, and for me Angela Davis's *Women, Race, and Class* (1981) was an eye-opener. Then there are bell hooks, Patricia Hill Collins, the fictional works of Toni Morrison, also Gayatri Spivak and others. I had not read Kimberlé Crenshaw at the time.

In the 1980s there was so much exciting scholarship I had to catch up on: Edward Said's *Orientalism* and Johannes Fabian's *Time and the Other*, to name a couple. If colonial discourse or othering, as they show, is linguistically inscribed and has common features, then it seemed necessary to look at the ways in which sexism too could be theorized, and to examine the intersection of race and gender. It is the case that the various turns taken by critical studies—to language, ethics, and so on—invariably pointed to the imbrication of various social inequities. So, it was impossible not to be shaped by these insights.

AV: In a conversation with Homi Bhabha, John Comaroff reflected on post-apartheid South Africa's "heroic, hopeful effort," after 1994, "to build a modernist nation-state under postmodern postmortem conditions; at just the time, that is, when the contradictions of modernity were becoming inescapable."[1] In "Shame and Identity," you observe that ongoing inequalities in postapartheid South Africa illustrate "the diverging interests of postmodernism and postcoloniality, or . . . may indicate the need to revise popular definitions of the latter to include the coexistence of oppositional and complicit forms." In your readings of the works of individual authors in Part 2 of this collection, you frequently make pragmatic use of Bhabha and others, too. I wonder if you would reflect on the ongoing tensions between postmodernism and postcoloniality in contemporary South Africa, either in relation to identity politics, or cultural production, or both.

zw: Undoubtedly aspects of postmodernist thought are dismissable, such as the abandonment of enlightenment principles that remain of interest and relevance to postcolonial cultures, but I am reminded of Lewis Nkosi's wry question of whether Tutuola's *The Palm-Wine Drinkard* is a postmodernist text that does not know its own name. He also asks how indigenous African-language literature can possibly be read without passing through the grid of the current postmodernism. Which is to point as Homi Bhabha does to the contradictions of modernity. If I refer to the postmodern effacement of history in coloured people's denial of slavery, that has come full circle: the symbolic rainbow nation has run out of steam, and search for roots has unearthed coloured people's slave heritage, indeed the more-indigenous-than-thou scramble for alterity flourishes amongst some coloured communities as a riposte to black nationalism. Having embraced the orthodox postcolonial position of valorizing nationalism, South Africa has been saddled with that unwieldy monster. As I discussed elsewhere, the problem arises once the goal of liberation has been achieved when we see that the toxicity of nationalism spirals into its inherent xenophobia and intolerance of minorities that have been disguised by the notion of freedom. (Interesting here to chart the differences between South African and Scottish nationalisms.) Much of what I say has of course been superseded by Achille Mbembe's incisive analysis of identity politics, its obsession with autochthony and difference, and its very development within a racist paradigm.

av: Yes, you use that wonderfully critical formulation "scramble for alterity" in your essay on recuperations of whiteness in postapartheid writing by a number of Afrikaans-language writers (Chapter 9).

zw: I appreciate Kwame Appiah's insistence that identity should be related to the ethical. I love his quotation of John Tomasi's humorous dismissal of fetishized cultural membership, seen as "a primary good only in the same uninteresting sense as say, oxygen. . . . It's like form: you can't not have it."[2]

av: Yet the need for others and otherness is, you observe, at the heart of postmodern theory, which elevates otherness—in the guise of the minoritarian (in the work of Deleuze and Guattari, for instance)—to necessary metaphor, and yet (and this is a point you make in your engagement with Bhabha in the essay on shame and identity, too) because "otherness is clearly not a desirable condition for actual minorities, nor for the politically colonized who actively struggle for territory itself, it would seem that such an idealized view is essentially an albocentric, metropolitan one." Thus you hold to account the insights of any theory that is generative but comes up short against local conditions.

Could you say a little about your sense of the usefulness of theory in your own theoretical development (and, if I can push you, your own fiction)? Would you venture some thoughts about current debates about the need for "theory from the South"?

zw: I'm reluctant to comment on my own work, but as I mentioned earlier, writing cannot be impervious to ideas or theories that occupy you at the time, much as you wouldn't like to think of your fictional work as theory driven. It is fashionable to diss poststructuralism, and indeed I do in some of the essays question its usefulness, but at the time it was also immensely liberating. The very notion of decentering allowed one to question hegemonies, to escape orthodoxies and their strictures, so that the discovery that poststructuralism did not always chime with local conditions was itself thought provoking. And as you imply, such dissatisfaction has led to the need for theory from the South, a rejection of the West's liberal universal, which in turn is also an aspect of decentering the dominance of the West.

South-south conversations are clearly a welcome change from the old one-way exchange, but by the same recognition of the incivility of the old model, one would like to think that it does not dismiss northern thought or exclude global exchange. As its theorists say, the North *needs* our input, but populist denigration of "Western knowledge" that surfaced during the current student rebellion is alarming. In these early days discourses about theory from the South seem to be more about the need for it, rather than articulation of actual theories. If the South is as the Comaroffs claim a space of experimentation, I look forward to such experimentation, such revitalizing knowledge production. There is an encouraging optimism about their idea of conversion from revolution to revelation and of social regeneration, but the proposed quest for wisdom and redemption is as yet hard to discern in South African political culture.

As far as I know, curriculum transformation has happened largely in Literary Studies. The worrying new appeal to "relevance"—current student protests are focused on difference, the uniqueness of their African identity, and that which they recognize or demand in a curriculum as relating to them—would suggest that transformation has not been as widespread as we imagined. Of course, the economy of scarcity, as Mbembe points out, impacts on subjectivity; however, while economic inequality fuels the student movement, the vast expanses of shantytowns, failure of education at primary level, and the fact that the majority of black students study at dysfunctional historically black universities in Limpopo, Venda, and Zululand are not the focus of the protests. Having said that, I do have some sympathy nowadays for students' impatience with the status quo, their insistence on black identity in a culture that is as racially polarized as contemporary South Africa.

Nowadays legitimate disappointment and anger about A.N.C. corruption and its loss of moral authority have somehow legitimated the idea of corruption-as-black, which via current South African media has become a recognizable discursive formation, while the term "white monopoly capital" is routinely cited in scare quotes, presented as an absurd excuse for economic inequity. What is overlooked is the element of exchange that inheres in corruption. The independent Forbes List of billionaires in South Africa, published annually, shows a continuum of wealth from the apartheid regime. Inferable, then, that politicians line their pockets with lucre passed on by the already wealthy in return for lucrative state contracts that ensure continued wealth, but the reciprocity necessarily involved in money changing hands does not feature in the discourse of black corruption. The transaction of exchange is disregarded: the hands that give, in keeping with the category of whiteness, remain invisible. So theorizing the South is no doubt a laudable project, but where the South is as racialized as South Africa is, we should perhaps start with learning to read our newspapers more carefully.

av: Indeed. It seems to me, in fact, that we need the modes of reading and re-reading you prescribe (and model) now more than ever. Allow me to turn (back) to the literary as space for reading. Your essays frequently deploy examples of cultural production from many media and genres, but you frequently turn back to the literary, including in these essays that we've chosen to group together as public-political interventions (or performances). Writers who feature here in particular include Sol Plaatje, Miriam Tlali, Njabulo Ndebele, and—preeminently—Bessie Head. Could you say something about where you first read each of these writers, and what it was about them that interested you? What in particular has Bessie Head meant to you, and why?

zw: Yes, I was particularly interested in Bessie Head as the only coloured woman who, at the time that I tried to write, was a published author. Not surprisingly, I had not heard of Head until the early 70s when I came across *Maru* in the U.K.; but to my surprise I found that the Heinemann edition had a picture of me on its cover.

av: Do you have any idea how that came to pass?

zw: I later worked out that I had briefly met the photographer in a social situation at the time of publication, but I had no idea that he had taken the (unflattering) picture. Uncannily, and much as I hated the unauthorized use of the picture, I felt an affinity with her; Head's novel gave me the courage or perhaps permission to write. While I find the homophobia in *A Question of Power* repulsive, her examination of race and exposure of African discrimination against the Masarwa is extraordinary for being explored within her commitment to Africa. She shows that it is not only possible but essential to be critical of that which you love and are part of. I am also moved by the ways in which she reworked her own tragic life story into fiction, so much more creative than the label of autobiography that critics invariably attach to black women's writing.

Sol Plaatje's *Mhudi* was not only the first African novel written in English, its publication history itself is significant. Edward Said's injunction about the worldliness of texts as well as the importance of geography in the relationship between politics and culture take on a practical cast in relation to one of the more serendipitous effects of the 1976 Soweto rebellion. The Lovedale Missionary Press, fearful of student vandalism and believing that the rebellion would be confined to the North, moved their archives to Rhodes University in the Eastern Cape. In the process, the original typescript of *Mhudi* that Lovedale had earlier claimed to have lost, fell into the hands of Witwatersrand scholars Stephen Gray and Tim Couzens, who were at the time working on a reissue of the novel for the Heinemann African Writers Series. Previously dismissed by critics as a dull co-opted colonial offering, *Mhudi* turned out to have been severely bowdlerized, Lovedale Press having pressed the novel into a European realist mode. Thus Plaatje's attempts at translation of traditional African forms into a Western novel by introducing a storyteller who passes on the history to a narrator, or by incorporating various elements of orality, including folktales, had been compromised.[3] For me it was wonderful to be able to teach South African students about the translation of traditional forms and its contribution to theories of postcolonial hybridity.

av: Moving on to those writers whose work you address in the essays we have grouped together as Part 2, could you comment on how you came to Coetzee and Vladislavić in particular? What has their work meant to you? And are there other writers from South Africa or elsewhere whose work has been particularly instructive or inspiring (or useful) for you in recent years?

zw: White writing from South Africa was not hard to come by, so there were no obstacles to encountering these writers who are undoubtedly the most innovative, the most serious in exploring a new aesthetic for representing the South African crisis. How ingenious, Coetzee's sidestepping the problem, for instance, of writing about a dispossessed black character as in Michael K, or Friday (of whom of course Lewis Nkosi had written earlier)! Coetzee was one of the first to look at settler culture, and through naming take responsibility for the colonial enterprise and its violence—all brave moves in the face of the various orthodoxies of the time.

While Ivan Vladislavić too is concerned with the ethical, it is his humor and irony that endure for me. Who would have thought that literary fiction could be a laugh-out-loud experience? In his latest collection of stories he also tackles the difficult issue of writing about atrocity, the torture and suffering that bring migrants to our shores. "The Reading" gets around the problem through a narrative structure that includes narration by an English-language translator of the account of suffering. A story of horror is then embedded within another story of an event of its public reading, so that the taboo of horror and excessive feeling is shifted to the translator's response. Central to Vladislavić's story is an absence of the actual handwritten words by the subject of horror, the original writer who is present at the event. The embedded story then must remain incomplete in a number of ways. Another brilliant device for framing the horror is Vladislavić's spotlighting of various members of the audience, their hilarious thoughts and activities, so that one thinks of Breughel's Icarus, or rather, of Auden's account of Breughel's Icarus.

The topical issue of migration is represented very differently in Brian Chikwava's extraordinary 2009 novel *Harare North*, a narrative about Zimbabwean migrants in the heterotopic city of London. Here nonstandard English and an intertext of Sam Selvon's *Lonely Londoners* serve to revise the liberatory postcolonial project—now distinctly postlapsarian. Formally complex, and celebrating the rhetorical dimension of language, the novel explores the disturbing migrant life of its unreliable narrator whose identity eventually slips into that of his compatriot, an "original native" who holds out against the deracination of "lapsed Africans." It is indeed humor and irony that steer this delicately managed writing of atrocity towards the ethical.

AV: Perhaps it's worth noting that we had originally thought about including your wonderful essay on Chikwava's novel in this collection but omitted it in order to retain a more tightly focused "South Africa" focus.[4] This is a strength, I think, but it might also of course be an indictment of a tendency to that old chestnut, South African exceptionalism. Do you find yourself turning away from South Africa in what you read or write, or does its pull continue to direct your work?

ZW: Yes, I'm disappointed that the Chikwava essay didn't make it. Perhaps because I don't live there, South Africa in terms of writing remains my focus, and nowadays with history seeming to repeat itself, writing is once more a way of dealing with the distress of my visits to the Cape. Certainly my reading is not limited to South Africa; that would be unnecessarily punitive and, well, unthinkable. But exceptionalism remains a problem. There is, for instance, within the country very little foreign news in the daily newspapers, and cousin to exceptionalism is xenophobia, as seen in the horrific violence of the poor against African immigrants.

AV: Let us leave our conversation there, with this version of the beggars at our doors that you invoke for us as an emblem of ongoing injustice. Your writing and your thinking, exemplified in these essays and in your generous responses to my questions, continue to model ethical returns to these dilemmas. Thank you, Zoë.

November 2016 and March 2017
Glasgow and London

Appendix 1

TRANSCRIPT OF BOETA DICKIE IN CONVERSATION

This narrative about life in District Six in the 1960s was taped in Cape Town in 1993. A translation is given in Appendix 2. For a discussion see Chapter 12.

BOETA DICKIE: . . . because I always felt . I've got to have a reserve. I've got to have . a reserve. not to say I'm building a shell around me or anything like that but a certain limit there . I must . I must have a reserve that's my opinion my . maar hy my pêllie hy sê ok listen er you must trust her in total . in other words you must share everything . every little thing with your wife . now erm ek figure weer uit ok nei .. maar ok daai dag . toe . sit ek it amper soe . er hoe sal ek sê . op die spel . ek sit dit oppie spel due to the fact that the morning .. I knew look this thing happen the Saturday night . the Sunday I got all the news that those chaps the one that was shot . and the other one . erm two were shot . ja ja there were five er . they made a case against me . er . the police will be picking me up soon I can expect that right . so the Monday went past . nothing happen so I knew it was gonna be the Tuesday morning or the Wednesday morning early in the early hours it happen like that . in Van der Leur street that was in their area right . the DK[1] area I'm upstairs mos right . ek sê man Roli my sixth sense is is surprising me man . wat daai boere hulle voete op die onderste steppie sit and now steps mos come up and then he's in my front room er . ek het opstairs gebly . my ma het onner gebly . ek sê . when that policeman put his foot on . toe skrik . ek is wakker maar toe hou ek my nog meerdere aan die slaap ok . right nou gat ek uit er . [interruption—inaudible] hulle kom op ja . nou vra hulle is ek Sedick Anthony. ja ek ek is Sedick Anthony . hulle kom op . right up there . right ( ) waar's die er . rewolwer wat ekkie mense mee geskiet het . oh ne ek wiettie . daai mense moet wiet wat hulle . sit . kyk hier maak vir julle comfortable en ( ) listen get some coffee going give the chaps some coffee . hulle begin ook sommer te skud ook die twee vat my storie . man hulle skud so ne . ek werk . ( ) daar's daar's in my kas daai tyd gewees certain er slui- tels . daai sluitels . maar jy kan sien man you know the keys was in the process of being made and all that . and there was other things as well but soe blind is hulle hulle soek net gun right they looking for the gun die een sê nog nee dit sallie hier wees and all that ok .

ek sê nei kyk daai mense moet weet waar dit is because they wanted to rob me and that is my story . and they said ok they saw they not gonna get anywhere by me . toe sê hulle or-right ek moet hulle six o'clock by hulle kantoor kom sien daai evening en 'n statement vir hulle gee and orright dan . ek gat werk toe but before I leave that house I put that what I just said to the test . hoe ver .. kan jy jou vrou vertrou .. you know . right . because she asked me already before that and I didn't I didn't want to say . that morning she asked me . for the first time I say listen . she's pregnant now . now I tell her listen Fatima I tell her . listen don't you worry let me do the worrying and leave this in my capable hands and I'll handle it as I see fit . and you jus cool it . ok ek trek my aan en so aan before I leave she ask me again and then it it struck me hei daai buddie het gesê jy moet jou vrou in total trust now this is a case where you can put that to the test . ek sê vir haar listen it's in the fig tree er . but don't worry . né and I'll handle it the way I .. and ok I go to work . whilst I go to work she tell my sister my sister's also living there my oldest sister . er my sister ask her some-thing about it er . vroumense geselskap en daar sê sy is innie vyeboom .. my sister again thinking ok she's gonna er be some help . she's gonna chuck it away somewhere she takes it out there . she puts it in her bag . she go up to Constitution street . from Van der Leur street to Constitution street to her other friend there . a bigger woman than what she is . but that other woman apparently didn't . had a dislike for me or whatever . I don't know mos . I don't know the people. I never associated with the woman or such . but in any event . ok . so . this woman she . when she came in there . the woman tell her ja Diekie willie hoor nie ne hy's alweer innnie moeilikheid ne . then she say yes er hier het ek die gun ek gaannie gun weggooi . and the woman say ok er . listen go to the post office there in Hanover street go post these letters for me . and leave your bag here and go post the letters . en sy gaat af . sy gaat die briewe pos . wat sy trug kom toe's die Boere hiersa ( ) met haar bag . come on listen this is your bag hey . that woman in the meantime phone the police..

BOETA ROLI: to say

BOETA DICKIE: to say here's the gun . you know that . right . ok . there they got the gun I'm at work . working here in Lansdowne at ( ) en my office face die . pad en soos ek . I just happen to look up at that moment man . en ek sien . hier ry Sersant Hartnick vannie moord-en-roof van van die Skiereiland . en . agter hom nog so 'n Volkswagentjie en agter hom nog so 'n lang kar en agter hom 'n nog 'n kar . ek dink hei hier's die hele outfit jong die ouens en ek sien sommer vier vat pos hier by die er entrance die main entrance twee vat pos daar twee vat pos daar en twee kom in en daar's 'n paar wat nog bly daar by haar sy bly by die kar en hulle kom nou vir my haal .. in the meantime ek het twee stoppe ek gee dit vir 'n anner buddie . er ou Henry ok daar's daai twee stoppe . ek willie nog gaan met sulke goed op my nie because daai tyd toe's gun sake mos expensive man . you know . is mos few and far between that guys had guns that time man . . .

BOETA ROLI: it was something big

BOETA DICKIE: something big ja if you had a gun if you're a gunman . in any event ok so I er hulle kom hey die lanies skrik jong . hulle kannie believe nie . hoekom . can this guy be this guy what you're talking about . because we ..

BOETA ROLI: we don't know this man..

BOETA DICKIE: we don't know this man . like that jong . we erm . this is a collar and tie collar and tie . and you know what I mean doing a job and all that you know hey ek sê ne Boeta Ali . right hier het hulle vir my . ek sê vir die lanies ok listen this an that net shortly explain ek dit . this is jus er 'n incident happened there . they wanted to rob me an ok there's the gun but it's er dingis and ok I'll go an straighten things out an see . ( ) lanie sê ook vir my . jong . er if you found guilty you not going to have a job but if I'm innocent then my job will be open right ek is daar weg right police stasie toe . hei toe's die boere kwaad want die boere wat die oggend daar gewees het . ek het hulle mos geswitch man . nou die middag se boere dis hulle weer en nou daar's Brok ook . nie Brok nie er Van Rensburg . nou hy't nie vir my gelyk at all nie because we gave'm a run around a lot that time we were mos young man . slim getrek met hulle want er . ( ) jy so sê en weet wies jy man jy . you know .. colours en daai right . in any event hy's ook daar hy sê no . they mus tie me up like and all that . orright ek dink fuck jou ek gee nie antwoord ook nie ok ek los hom net so ok I must now just scheme now . the first thing I'm scheming is . once once you get me to that books my sister must be out of here . en ek kry dit reg you see once they got me to the books . out is my sister . ek is gecharge .. jy weet . sy's nie eens gecharge met found found in possession of a gun niks nie . als is nou net ek . right ( ) 'n ek sê nou's dit drie sake . is erm unlicensed firearm . ammunition . en is nou attempted murder . hei ek sien die saak loop . soos die saak loop jong .. die goose moet geboorte gee . daar . daar . daar . . die alle ietse wat te doen het daarmee . die familie . die uitkring van die van die een iets wat gebeur het . you know ok right . in any event it happened also a couple of times . now they . hulle drinkplek is oorkant onse huis die DK's in other words that time we moved into their territory . you know when this thing transpired . nou so so soos wat ek hoor . net so oorkant . is iemand . die grootste er er merchants . wine merchants . Baai . that's correct . ou Baai . en toe kô kry jy nou hulle hulle hou mos van daar voor . net soes die ouens hier sit man . sit so daar . now I had to go to the shop . now I had to keep my cool the moment I show the sign of weakness er er ..

BOETA ROLI: then they'll be on to you

BOETA DIEKIE: er not just me . my family's gonna suffer . you know mos how it was that time man . I had to be that guy otherwise . you know . en ek vat dit so ok my sisters het 'n netball club . dis girls wat kom daar by die huis . hulle sal almal gemolesteer word almal daai so a lot was hanging on it so I had to be a strong face . right . hulle sit daar een Saterdag middag . ek gaan oor . that was the day they were planning on like but the case was still going but they trying to sort of . weet jy hoe simple sit ek vir hulle . as I'm walking . die een skree . hei jy gunman . ek loop nog ek hoor die anner een sê ook ja . iets van gunman er toe draai ek . daai ding wat julle in gedagte het hy't 'n voël in sy hol . because why as jy 'n man is dan staan jy uit dan praat jy met my soes 'n man . moenie wag tot julle 'n klomp is daar dan wil julle skuil agter my rug nie man . julle vlag is geskeer and there I go I mean there I tore their flag so to speak in a manner of speaking . where their way of talk en daai is concerned ek was dan alleen . julle was vyf man . wat kan julle my gewys het hoekom het julle boere toe gehardloop . daar's hulle vlag geskeer because in the district the code was . ja . thou shalt not squeal er right Boeta Ali that was the code . you . thou shalt not squeal . we settle settle our differences ourselves our way . reg . ek sal jou either weer gekry het of jy moet vir my weer gekry het or one of the two maar jy gaan nie die boere se nie die ding die dingis nie ..

BOETA ROLI: ja ja he's out of the picture boere is die laastse een . target number one ..

BOETA DICKIE: you know when the case come in front now there they also switch the case from the one regional to another regional and eventually when it er came to the last of it . I'll never forget that day . ja. Fatima was still a baby then . she was born . hulle ja vir Farieda uit die hof uit moet Farieda want Fatima huil innie hof while this thing is happening here . now imagine jy jy staan innie dock you fighting for your life now here . I mean for a couple of years of your life . instead of giving them the benefit of the years of your life I mean and you hear your daughter crying outside in the chambers . jy weet mos man hoe was dit daar innie Caledon straat man . now that echo almost like it give me extra power to sort of think like hey fuck yous man now its on with me and yous . en waar maak hy sy mistake wat ek mos die lawyer uitgesmyt het toe handle ek hulle mos nou nou . toe handle ek hulle the woman tell her *ja* mos so my way . laat hulle praat ek hou my net . mister jy weet in suiwerde Afrikaans en so aan ek het mos klaar establish ek het my werk statement en so aan .. daais mos als al gepraat al .. en so aan die soorte mense right ek condemn hulle sommer hoekom hulle wil boere toe gehardloop het eerste . ek sê nei hulle wil geskiet het man . en dis hulle dinge.

Appendix 2

TRANSLATED TRANSCRIPT OF BOETA DICKIE
IN CONVERSATION

The original narrative, transcribed in Appendix 1 and translated here, was taped in Cape Town in 1993. For a discussion see Chapter 12.

BOETA DICKIE: . . . because I always felt . I've got to have a reserve. I've got to have . a reserve. not to say I'm building a shell around me or anything like that but a certain limit there . I must . I must have a reserve that's my opinion my . but he my pal says ok listen er you must trust her in total . in other words you must share everything . every little thing with your wife . now erm but I figure ok no . but ok that day . then . I almost put it so . er how shall I say . to the test . I put it to the test due to the fact that the morning . I knew look this thing happen the Saturday night . the Sunday I got all the news that those chaps the one that was shot . and the other one . erm two were shot . ja ja there were five er . they made a case against me . er . the police will be picking me up soon I can expect that right . so the Monday went past . nothing happen so I knew it was gonna be the Tuesday morning or the Wednesday morning early in the early hours it happen like that . in Van der Leur street that was in their area right . the DK[1] area I'm upstairs mos right . I say man Roli my sixth sense is is surprising me man . when those boers put their feet on the first step . and now steps mos come up and then he's in my front room er . I lived upstairs . my ma lived below . I say . when that policeman put his foot on . then I started . I'm awake but then I pretended to be more asleep ok . right now I go out er . [interruption—inaudible] they come up ja . now they ask am I Sedick Anthony . ja I'm Sedick Anthony . they come up . right up there. right ( ) where's the er . revolver with which I shot the people . oh but I dunno . those people must know what they . sit . look here make your-selves comfortable and ( ) listen get some coffee going give the chaps some coffee . they begin to shake up the place . also the two accept my story . man how they shake it hey . I work . ( ) there's there's in my cupboard at that time there was certain er keys . those keys . but you can see man you know the keys was in the process of being made and all that . and there was other things as well but so blind are they they search just for the gun right they looking for the gun . the one still say no it won't be here and all that . ok . I say no

287

look those people must know where it is because they wanted to rob me and that is my story . and they said ok they saw they not gonna get anywhere by me . so they say orright I must come see them at six o'clock by their office that evening and give them a statement and orright then . I go to work but before I leave that house I put that what I just said to the test . how far .. can you trust your wife .. you know . right . because she asked me already before that and I didn't I didn't want to say . that morning she asked me . for the first time I say listen . she's pregnant now . now I tell her listen Fatima I tell her . listen don't you worry let me do the worrying and leave this in my capable hands and I'll handle it as I see fit . and you jus cool it . ok I dress and so on before I leave she ask me again and then it it struck me hey that buddy he said you must trust your wife in total now this is a case where you can put that to the test . I said to her listen it's in the fig tree er . but don't worry . ok and I'll handle it the way I .. and ok I go to work . whilst I go to work she tell my sister my sister's also living there my oldest sister . er my sister ask her something about it er . women's talk and there she says it's in the fig tree .. my sister again thinking ok she's gonna er be some help . she's gonna chuck it away somewhere she takes it out there . she puts it in her bag . she go up to Constitution street . from Van der Leur street to Constitution street to her other friend there . a bigger woman than what she is . but that other woman apparently didn't . had a dislike for me or whatever . I don't know mos . I don't know the people . I never associated with the woman or such . but in any event . ok . so . this woman she . when she came in there . the woman tell her ja Diekie won't listen hey he's again in trouble hey . then she say yes er here I've got the gun I'm gonna chuck it away . and the woman say ok er . listen go to the post office there in Hanover street go post these letters for me . and leave your bag here and go post the letters . and she goes off . she goes to post the letters . when she got back then the boers were here ( ) with her bag . come on listen this is your bag hey . that woman in the meantime phone the police..

BOETA ROLI: to say

BOETA DICKIE: to say here's the gun . you know that . right . ok . there they got the gun I'm at work . working here in Lansdowne at ( ) and my office face the . road and as I . I just happen to look up at that moment man . and I see . driving up is Sergeant Hartnick of the murder-and-theft of of the Peninsula . and . and behind him also a little Volkswagen and behind him such a long car and behind him another car . I think hey here's the whole outfit man the guys and I see four take post here by the er entrance the main entrance two take post here two take post there and two come in and there's a pair that stay out there with her she stays in the car and they now are coming to get me .. in the meantime I have two joints I give to another buddy . er . old Henry ok that's the two joints . I don't wanna go with such stuff on me because those days gun cases were expensive man . you know . is mos few and far between that guys had guns that time man . . .

BOETA ROLI: it was something big

BOETA DICKIE: something big ja if you had a gun if you're a gunman . in any event ok so I er they come hey man the boers[2] take fright . they can't believe it . why . can this guy be this guy what you're talking about . because we ..

BOETA ROLI: we don't know this man..

BOETA DICKIE: we don't know this man . like that man . we erm . this is a collar and tie collar and tie . and you know what I mean doing a job and all that you know hey I say hey Boeta Ali . right here they've got me . I say to the boers ok listen this an that just shortly I explain it . this is jus er an incident happened there . they wanted to rob me and ok there's the gun but it's er thingy and ok I'll go and straighten things out and see . ( ) the boer also says to me . man . er if you found guilty you not going to have a job but if I'm innocent then my job will be open right I leave there right to the police station . hey so then the boers were furious because the boers who were there in the morning . well I switched them [managed to fool them] man . now that afternoon's boers that was now them and now there was also Brok . no not Brok er Van Rensburg . now he didn't like me at all because we gave'm a run around a lot that time we were mos young man . pulled wool over their eyes because er . ( ) you say so and know who you are man you . you know .. colors and that right . in any event he's also there he says no . they must tie me up like and all that . orright I think fuck you I don't answer ok I leave him just like that ok I must now just scheme now . the first thing I'm scheming is . once once you get me to that books my sister must be out of here . and I get it right you see once they got me to the books . out is my sister . I'm charged .. you know . she's not even charged with found found in posses-sion of a gun no nothing . everything is now me . right ( ) and I say now it's three cases . is erm unlicensed firearm . ammunition . and it's now attempted murder . hey I see how the case goes . as the case goes man .. the goose[3] must give birth . there . there . there .. all the things that go with that . the family . the fall out . from the one thing that hap-pened . you know ok right . in any event it happened also a couple of times . now they . their drinking place is opposite our house the DK's in other words that time we moved into their territory . you know when this thing transpired . now from from what I can hear . just across . there's someone . the biggest er er merchants . wine merchants . Baai . that's correct . old Baai . and so so you get them they mos keep themselves there. Just as the guys sit there man . sit so there . now I had to go to the shop . now I had to keep my cool the moment I show the sign of weakness er er ..

BOETA ROLI: then they'll be on to you

BOETA DIEKIE: er not just me . my family's gonna suffer . you know mos how it was that time man . I had to be that guy otherwise . you know . and I take it like this ok my sisters have a netball club . its girls who come to the house . they'll all be molested all that so a lot was hanging on it so I had to be a strong face . right . they sit there one Saturday after-noon . I go over . that was the day they were planning on like but the case was still going but they trying to sort of . do you know how simple I put it to them . as I'm walking . one of them shouts . hey you gunman . I carry on walking I hear the other one also say ja . something about gunman er so I turned round . that thing you have in mind that thing has a dick in its arse . because why if you're a man then stand up and speak to me like a man . don't wait until there's a group of you and then want to take shelter behind my back man . your flag is torn and there I go I mean there I tore their flag so to speak in a manner of speaking . where their way of talk and so on is concerned then I was alone .

you were five of you man . what could you show me why did you run to the boers . there their flag is torn because in the district the code was . ja . thou shalt not squeal er right Boeta Ali that was the code . you . thou shalt not squeal . we settle settle our differences ourselves our way . right . either I would have got at you or you would have got back at me or one of the two but you don't speak to the boers the thing the thing is not ..

BOETA ROLI: ja ja he's out of the picture the boer is the last one . target number one ..

BOETA DICKIE: you know when the case come up now there they also switch the case from the one regional to another regional and eventually when it er came to the last of it . I'll never forget that day . ja . Fatima was still a baby then . she was born . they chase Farieda out of court Farieda must get out because Fatima cries in court while this thing is happening here . now imagine you you standing in the dock you fighting for your life now here . I mean for a couple of years of your life . instead of giving them the benefit of the years of your life I mean and you hear your daughter crying outside in the chambers . you mos know man how things were in the Caledon street man. now that echo almost like it give me extra power to sort of think like hey fuck yous man now its on with me and yous . and where he makes his mistake when I mos chuck the lawyer out then I handle them mos now . then I handle them mos my way . let them talk I just keep myself . mister you know in pure Afrikaans and so on I mos already established I have my work statement and so on ..all that has mos already been said ..and so on these kinda people right I just condemn them why because they first wanna run to the boers . I say no man they wanted to shoot . and that's their doings.

NOTES

ZOË WICOMB'S SOUTH AFRICAN ESSAYS

1. Carol Sicherman, "Literary Afterword," in Zoë Wicomb, *You Can't Get Lost in Cape Town* (1987; New York: Feminist Press at the City University of New York, 2000), 187–208; at 194.
2. Ezekiel (Es'kia) Mphahlele, *The African Image* (New York: Praeger, 1962); Lewis Nkosi, *Home and Exile* (London: Longman, 1965).
3. Nadine Gordimer, *The Essential Gesture: Writing, Politics and Places*, ed. Stephen Clingman (New York: Knopf, 1988).
4. J. M. Coetzee, *White Writing: On the Culture of Letters in South Africa* (New Haven: Yale University Press, 1988), *Doubling the Point: Essays and Interviews*, ed. David Attwell (Cambridge, MA: Harvard University Press, 1992), *Giving Offense: Essays on Censorship* (Chicago: University of Chicago Press, 1996), *Stranger Shores: Essays, 1986–1999* (New York: Viking, 2001), *Inner Workings: Literary Essays 2000–2005* (New York: Viking, 2007), *Late Essays: 2006–2017* (New York: Viking, 2018).
5. Njabulo S. Ndebele, *South African Literature and Culture: Rediscovery of the Ordinary*, ed. Graham Pechey (Manchester: Manchester University Press, 1994), *Fine Lines from the Box: Further Thoughts About Our Country* (Cape Town: Umuzi, 2007). See also his more recent essays and op-ed journalism, including, on the Marikana massacre (in August 2012), "Liberation Betrayed by Bloodshed," *Social Dynamics: A Journal of African Studies* 39.1 (2013), 111–14.
6. Ndebele, "The Rediscovery of the Ordinary: Some New Writings in South Africa," in *South African Literature and Culture: Rediscovery of the Ordinary*, ed. Graham Pechey (Manchester: Manchester University Press, 1994), 37–57; at 55.
7. Njabulo S. Ndebele, "The Rediscovery of the Ordinary: Some New Writings in South Africa," *Journal of Southern African Studies*, 12.2 (April 1986), 143–57.
8. Saikat Majumdar, for example, suggests that *You Can't Get Lost in Cape Town* "exemplifies [an] important alternative narrative where the minute textures of the ordinary are foregrounded in a striking gesture of critique of the grand and dramatic

narratives of colonial domination and its public resistance." See his *"You Can't Get Lost in Cape Town* and the Counter-Ethnography of the Banal," *Genre* 39 (Summer 2006), 301–28; at 304.

9. Sicherman, "Literary Afterword," 197. Similarly, Judith Raiskin, in a study of "creole" writing, notes that it was "unsettling" both for undermining "traditional genres of novel, short story, and autobiography," while also not fitting "comfortably with the body of overtly political fiction and poetry called 'resistance literature' by Barbara Harlow and others." Judith L. Raiskin, *Snow on the Cane Fields: Women's Writing and Creole Subjectivity* (Minneapolis: Minnesota University Press, 1996), 215.

10. See Rita Barnard, "Rewriting the Nation," in *The Cambridge History of South African Literature,* ed. David Attwell and Derek Attridge (Cambridge: Cambridge University Press, 2012), 652–75; at 652. Barnard cites Loren Kruger, "'Black Atlantics,' 'White Indians,' and 'Jews': Locations, Locutions, and Syncretic Identities in the Fiction of Achmat Dangor and Others," *Scrutiny2* 7.2 (2002), 34–50; at 35.

11. Edward W. Said, *Humanism and Democratic Criticism* (New York: Columbia University Press, 2004), 140.

12. I discuss this structure of feeling more fully elsewhere; see Andrew van der Vlies, *Present Imperfect: Contemporary South African Writing* (Oxford: Oxford University Press, 2017), viii–ix, 8–10, 18–19, 24.

13. Zoë Wicomb, *October* (New York: New Press, 2014), 16.

14. On the development of the idea of a South African state and citizenship, Saul Dubow notes that the coalescing of the idea of "South Africa" from a mere geographical description, which referred more broadly to the subcontinent south of the Zambezi, to a collective term for the four polities that would combine as the Union of South Africa (a dominion within the British Empire) in 1910 (the British colonies of the Cape and Natal and the former "Dutch," "Boer" (farmer), or proto-Afrikaner republics of the Orange Free State and Transvaal (South African Republic)), was aided by accounts of travel by the writers James Froude (who toured 1875–85) and Anthony Trollope (1877), and by plans floated by a series of colonial officials (Grey, Carnarvon, Frere) earlier in the century for political federation. See further Saul Dubow, "South Africa and South Africans: Nationality, Belonging, Citizenship," in *The Cambridge History of South Africa, Volume 2: 1885–1994,* ed. Robert Ross, Anne Kelk Mager, and Bill Nasson (Cambridge: Cambridge University Press, 2011), 17–65.

15. Activism against the Act galvanized the newly formed South African Native National Congress, Africa's oldest liberation movement, which had been founded the year before (in 1912). It was renamed the African National Congress in 1923.

16. Deborah Posel, "The Apartheid Project, 1948–1970," in *The Cambridge History of South Africa, Volume 2: 1885–1994,* ed. Robert Ross, Anne Kelk Mager, and Bill Nasson (Cambridge: Cambridge University Press, 2011), 319–68; at 319. Posel continues: "The symbolic condensation of apartheid as the global signifier of racism risks conferring an apparent—and misleading—transparency on the system of apartheid, as if comprehensible simply as the extremity of racism. This renders its historical unevenness and complexity irrelevant and/or uninteresting" (ibid.).

17. Ibid., 320. See also Saul Dubow, *Apartheid: 1948–1994* (Oxford: Oxford University Press, 2014).

18. Zoë Wicomb, *You Can't Get Lost in Cape Town* (1987; New York: Feminist Press at the City University of New York, 2000), 9.

19. Ibid., 14, 26.

20. Dorothy Driver, "Transformation Through Art: Writing, Representation, and Subjectivity in Recent South African Fiction," *World Literature Today* 70.1 (Winter 1996), 45–52; at 47.

21. Derek Attridge, "Zoë Wicomb's Home Truths," *Journal of Postcolonial Writing* 41.2 (2005), 156–65; at 159.

22. "Zoë Wicomb Interviewed by Eva Hunter—Cape Town, 5 June 1990," in *Between the Lines II: Interviews with Nadine Gordimer, Menán du Plessis, Zoë Wicomb, Lauretta Ngcobo*, ed. Eva Hunter and Craig MacKenzie (Grahamstown: NELM, 1993), 79–96; at 81.

23. "The novel acknowledges, both in its content and the very fact of its emergence from Wicomb's pen, the compulsion to seek for a historical and genealogical grounding for one's sense of identity, even as it offers a telling critique of such enterprises," Attridge notes. He observes too that such an "exploration of genealogy has become a common feature of post-apartheid South African novels, no doubt reflecting a need to complicate the myths of purity, linearity, and separation on which apartheid was founded." Attridge, "Zoë Wicomb's Home Truths," 159.

24. Barnard, "Rewriting the Nation," 665–66.

25. Zoë Wicomb, *Playing in the Light* (New York: New Press, 2006), 120–21.

26. Ibid., 121.

27. On race, "passing," and the question of the archive in *Playing in the Light*, see variously: Maria Olaussen, "Generation and Complicity in Zoë Wicomb's *Playing in the Light*," *Social Dynamics* 35.1 (2009), 149–61; Andrew van der Vlies, "The Archive, the Spectral, and Narrative Responsibility in Zoë Wicomb's *Playing in the Light*," *Journal of Southern African Studies* 36.3 (2010), 583–98; Stéphane Robolin, "Properties of Whiteness: (Post)Apartheid Geographies in Zoë Wicomb's *Playing in the Light*," *Safundi: The Journal of South African and American Studies* 12.3–4 (2011), 349–71.

28. Zoë Wicomb, "10 Questions: Zoe Wicomb," by Anna James, *The Bookseller*, June 3, 2017, http://www.welovethisbook.com/features/10-questions-zoe-wicomb.

29. David Robinson, "Under the Skin of Lies," *Scotsman*, 27 May 2006 (Saturday Critique), 20.

30. See Sicherman, "Literary Afterword," 194.

31. Zoë Wicomb, *David's Story* (2000; New York: Feminist Press at the City University of New York, 2001), 188.

32. Zoë Wicomb, *October* (Cape Town: Umuzi, 2014), 158–59; the American edition, published by the New Press, (incorrectly) uses the spelling "colored" (138). The New Press's edition of *Playing in the Light* (referenced above), by contrast, uses the South African spelling "coloured" throughout.

33. Marcia Wright provides useful information to contextualize issues of respectability and shame for the coloured community; see her "Historical Introduction," in Zoë

Wicomb, *You Can't Get Lost in Cape Town* (New York: Feminist Press at the City University of New York, 2000), vii–xxiv; at xvii–xxi. See also J. U. Jacobs, "Playing in the Dark/Playing in the Light: Coloured Identity in the Novels of Zoë Wicomb," *Current Writing* 20.1 (2008), 1–15.

34. Originally published in *Writing South Africa: Literature, Apartheid, and Democracy, 1970–1995*, ed. Derek Attridge and Rosemary Jolly (Cambridge: Cambridge University Press, 1998), 91–107; at 92.

35. Wright, "Historical Introduction," xvii.

36. Wicomb, "Shame and Identity," quoting Homi Bhabha's *The Location of Culture* (London: Routledge, 1994), 13.

37. Wicomb, "Shame and Identity."

38. Bharati Mukherjee, "They Never Wanted to Be Themselves," *New York Times*, Sunday, 24 May 1987 (Late City Final Edition), section 7, 7. The inference about postmodernism and the political is Mukherjee's.

39. Sue Marais, "Getting Lost in Cape Town: Spatial and Temporal Dislocation in the South African Short Fiction Cycle," *English in Africa* 22.2 (October 1995), 29–43; at 33.

40. Aryn Bartley, "The Violence of the Present: *David's Story* and the Truth and Reconciliation Commission," *Comparative Literature Studies* 46.1 (2009), 103–24; at 117. For further discussion of the engagement *David's Story* offers with rape and sexual violence, including cases committed by members of the African National Congress's armed wing, see Meg Samuelson, "The Disfigured Body of the Female Guerilla: (De) Militarization, Sexual Violence, and Redomestication in Zoë Wicomb's *David's Story*," *Signs: Journal of Women in Culture and Society* 32.4 (2007), 833–56. On gender, narrative, and the T.R.C., see Fiona Ross, *Bearing Witness: Women and the Truth and Reconciliation Commission in South Africa* (London: Pluto Press, 2003), and Mark Sanders, *Ambiguities of Witnessing: Law and Literature in the Time of a Truth Commission* (Stanford: Stanford University Press, 2007).

41. Carli Coetzee, "'The One That Got Away': Zoë Wicomb in the Archives," *Journal of Southern African Studies* 36.3 (2010), 559–69; at 569.

42. Stéphane Robolin, "Loose Memory in Toni Morrison's *Paradise* and Zoë Wicomb's *David's Story*," *MFS: Modern Fiction Studies* 52.2 (2006), 297–320; at 312.

43. "Zoë Wicomb Interviewed by Eva Hunter," 80, 92.

44. Zoë Wicomb, "Translations in the Yard of Africa," *Journal of Literary Studies* 18.3 (2002), 209–23; at 218.

45. For discussion of nature of Wicomb's intertextuality in relation to cosmopolitanism and sexuality, see Andrew van der Vlies, "Zoë Wicomb's Queer Cosmopolitanisms," *Safundi: The Journal of South African and American Studies* 12.3–4 (July–October 2011), 425–44. On Wicomb's conversation with (and rewriting of) Millin, see Mark Sanders, "Cape Impudence," *Current Writing* 23.2 (2011), 118–26.

46. On the status of Paton's novel, see Rita Barnard, "Oprah's Paton, or South Africa and the Globalization of Suffering," *English Studies in Africa* 47.1 (2004), 85–107; and Andrew van der Vlies, "Whose *Beloved Country*? Alan Paton and the Hypercanonical," *South African Textual Cultures* (Manchester: Manchester University Press, 2007),

71–105. On *Disgrace's* reputation, see Andrew van der Vlies, "The Novel's Reception," in *J. M. Coetzee's Disgrace* (London: Continuum, 2010), 71–80. For analysis of the early reception of Coetzee's work, see Clive Barnett, "Constructions of Apartheid in the International Reception of the Novels of J. M. Coetzee," *Journal of Southern African Studies* 25.2 (1999), 287–301.

47. The tension between autobiographical and fictional strands in Head's creative work (particularly in her 1973 novel, *A Question of Power*), as much as the negotiation and performance of authority in biographical work on Head (and in critical work that has recourse to biographical sources), has been much discussed. See, for instance, Susan Gardner, "'Don't Ask for the True Story': A Memoir of Bessie Head," *Hecate* 12.1–2 (1986), 110–29; Teresa Dovey, "A Question of Power: Susan Gardner's Biography Versus Bessie Head's *Autobiography*," *English in Africa* 16.1 (1989), 29–38; Dorothy Driver, "Reconstructing the Past, Shaping the Future: Bessie Head and the Question of Feminism in a New South Africa," in *Black Women's Writing*, ed. Gina Wisker (New York: St. Martin's Press, 1993), 160–87; Gillian Stead Eilerson, *Bessie Head: Thunder Behind Her Ears* (1995; Portsmouth, NH: Heinemann, 1996).

48. Stephan Meyer and Thomas Olver, "Zoë Wicomb Interviewed on Writing and Nation," *Journal of Literary Studies* 18.1 (2002), 182–98; at 189.

49. On Wicomb, the archive, culture, and syncretism, see: Dorothy Driver, "The Struggle over the Sign: Writing and History in Zoë Wicomb's Art," *Journal of South African Studies* 36.3 (2010), 523–42; Carli Coetzee, "'The One That Got Away'"; and Van der Vlies, "The Archive, the Spectral, and Narrative Responsibility." On Wicomb and the history of the Griqua people in particular, see: Wright, "Historical Introduction," viii–xi; and Driver, "Transformation Through Art," 47.

50. Zoë Wicomb, "Interview: Zoë Wicomb in Conversation with Hein Willemse," *Research in African Literatures* 33.1 (2002), 144–52; at 147, 145.

51. A European Union–sponsored designation awarded to a different city every year.

52. Albie Sachs, "Preparing Ourselves for Freedom," in *Spring Is Rebellious: Arguments About Cultural Freedom*, ed. Ingrid de Kok and Karen Press (Cape Town: Buchu Books, 1990), 19–29. This influential position paper was first delivered at an A.N.C. seminar on culture in Lusaka, Zambia, where it was read on Sachs's behalf. It then appeared in print in the left-wing *Weekly Mail* newspaper in Johannesburg in February 1990, generating much debate. Peter D. McDonald gives a valuable summary of the impact of Sachs's intervention, in *The Literature Police: Apartheid Censorship and Its Cultural Consequences* (Oxford: Oxford University Press, 2009), 343–46.

53. Bhekizizwe Peterson, "Modernist at Large: The Aesthetics of *Native Life in South Africa*," in *Sol Plaatje's Native Life in South Africa: Past and Present*, ed. Janet Remmington, Brian Willan, and Bhekizizwe Peterson (Johannesburg: Wits University Press, 2016), 18–36; at 32–33. Peterson lists the National Arts Council, Pan South African Language Board, South African Heritage Resources Agency, National Heritage Council, and the National Film and Video Foundation.

54. For instance, "Tributaries," an exhibition at Museum-Afrika in Johannesburg in 1985, and "Art from South Africa," an exhibition at the Museum of Modern Art, Oxford, in

association with the Zabalaza Festival, London. The catalogue for the former appeared as *Tributaries: A View of Contemporary South African Art*, ed. Ricky Burnett (Johannesburg: BMW [South Africa] Communication Department, 1985; see also *Jackson Hlungwani: An Exhibition*, ed. Ricky Burnett [Johannesburg: BMW (South Africa) Communication Department, 1989]). The catalogue for the latter was published as *Art from South Africa* (Oxford: Museum of Modern Art, 1990). On the impact of these exhibitions, see Anitra Nettleton, "Home Is Where the Art Is: Six South African Rural Artists," *African Arts* 33.4 (2000), 26–39, 93–94. See also Gavin Younge, *Art of the South African Townships* (London: Thames and Hudson, 1988), and *Art in South Africa: The Future Present*, ed. Sue Williamson and Ashraf Jamal (Cape Town: David Philip, 1996).

55. See Rosalie Finlayson, "Women's Language of Respect: Isihlonipho sabafazi," in *Language in South Africa*, ed. Rajend Mesthrie (Cambridge: Cambridge University Press, 2002), 279–96.

56. On Baartman, see Clifton Crais and Pamela Scully, *Sara Baartman and the Hottentot Venus: A Ghost Story and a Biography* (Princeton: Princeton University Press, 2009), and on Wicomb's engagement with Baartman, see Kai Easton, "Travelling Through History, 'New' South African Icons: The Narratives of Saartje Baartman and Krotoä-Eva in Zoë Wicomb's *David's Story*," *Kunapipi* 24.1–2 (2002), 237–66, and, in general, Meg Samuelson, *Remembering the Nation, Dismembering Women? Stories of the South African Transition* (Scottsville: University of KwaZulu-Natal Press, 2007).

57. I am grateful to Rita Barnard for this observation. For critics who have engaged with shame in relation to South African writing and culture, see Neville Hoad's reading of the dynamics of sexual shame in Thabo Mbeki's stance on HIV-AIDS in his *African Intimacies: Race, Homosexuality, and Globalization* (Minneapolis: University of Minnesota Press, 2007), chapter 5 ("The Intellectual, the Archive, and the Pandemic"), as well as Timothy Bewes, *The Event of Postcolonial Shame* (Princeton: Princeton University Press, 2011).

58. Abu Bakr Effendi's *Uiteensetting van die Godsdiens*; see Andrew van der Vlies, "The History of the Book in Sub-Saharan Africa," in *The Oxford Companion to the Book*, vol. 1, ed. Michael F. Suarez and Henry Woudhuysen (Oxford: Oxford University Press, 2010), 313–20; at 318. See also Archie L. Dick, *The Hidden History of South Africa's Book and Reading Cultures* (Toronto: University of Toronto Press, 2012), especially chapter 1, "Early Readers at the Cape, 1658–1800," and chapter 2, "Literacy, Class, and Regulating Reading, 1800–1850" (12–53).

59. First delivered at the "Short Fiction 2" conference, Nice, France, in March 1997, and published in *Telling Stories: Postcolonial Short Fiction in English*, ed. Jacqueline Bardolph (Amsterdam: Rodopi, 2001), 157–70. We have chosen not to republish the essay in this collection given that its treatment of Coetzee's texts as short fictions was superseded by their incorporation into book-length texts. "What Is Realism?" was delivered as a lecture at Bennington College, thereafter published in *Salmagundi*, and later included as the first "lesson" in Coetzee's *Elizabeth Costello* in 2003; a piece in the Canadian journal *West Coast Line* turned out to be an excerpt from a chapter of Coetzee's *Boyhood* (1997), the first in what became the *autre*biographical trilogy *Scenes from Provincial Life* (2011).

60. J. M. Coetzee, *Disgrace* (London: Secker and Warburg, 1999), 71.
61. Leon de Kock, "'A Change of Tongue': Questions of Translation," in *The Cambridge History of South African Literature*, ed. David Attwell and Derek Attridge (Cambridge: Cambridge University Press, 2012), 739–56; at 743.
62. Ibid., 744. See, for instance, Leon de Kock, "South Africa in the Global Imaginary: An Introduction," *Poetics Today* 22.2 (2001), 263–98.
63. See, for example, Nicholas Visser, "Beyond the Interregnum: A Note on the Ending of *July's People*," in *Rendering Things Visible: Essays on South African Literary Culture*, ed. Martin Trump (Johannesburg: Ravan, 1990), 61–67; Michael Green, "Nadine Gordimer's 'Future Histories': Two Senses of an Ending," *Wasafiri* 19 (1994), 14–18; and André Brink, "Complications of Birth: Interfaces of Gender, Race and Class in *July's People*," *English in Africa* 21.1–2 (1994), 157–80.
64. Posel, "The Apartheid Project, 1948–1970," 329.
65. Vladislavić's work to date includes short-story collections (*Missing Persons, Propaganda by Monuments, 101 Detectives*), novels (*The Folly, The Restless Supermarket, Double Negative*), linked stories (*The Exploded View*), and creative nonfiction (*Portrait with Keys*). There is now a growing body of academic work on Vladislavić's oeuvre. See, for example, *Marginal Spaces: Reading Ivan Vladislavić*, ed. Gerald Gaylard (Johannesburg: Wits University Press, 2011). See also my own chapter on Vladislavić in *Present Imperfect*.
66. David Goldblatt, *TJ* (Rome: Contrasto, 2010). See further Tamar Garb and David Goldblatt, "David Goldblatt" (268–73), and "Interviews and Artists' Statements" (263–99), in Tamar Garb, *Figures and Fictions: Contemporary South Africa Photography*, ed Tamar Gard (London: V&A Publishing, 2011). See also David Goldblatt, *fifty-one years* (Barcelona: Museu d'Art Contemporani de Barcelona, 2001).
67. Wicomb, *October*, 171, 8, 142.
68. Wicomb indicates that the 1971 Heinemann African Writers Series edition of *Maru* featured on its cover a photograph of herself, taken by George Hallett at a party and, Wicomb asserts, used without her permission. It is an extraordinary conflation of Head's work and Wicomb's life, and stages uncomfortably, too, questions of the unauthorized rendering as spectacle of the body of the woman of color, and of the conflation of the autobiographical and the exemplary.
69. One is reminded here of J. M. Coetzee's various statements of this observation, including that all writing is autobiographical, and all autobiography involves the writing of the life of the other that one was in the past (that it is *autre*biography): see variously J. M. Coetzee, *Truth in Autobiography* (Cape Town: University of Cape Town Press, 1984), 5; Coetzee, *Doubling the Point*, 391; J. M. Coetzee, "All Autobiography Is *Autre*-biography" (Interview), in *Selves in Question: Interviews on Southern African Auto/Biography*, ed. Judith Lütge Coullie, Stephan Meyer, Thengani Ngwenya, and Thomas Olver (Honolulu: University of Hawai'i Press, 2006), 214–15; J. M. Coetzee and Arabella Kurtz, *The Good Story: Exchanges on Truth, Fiction and Psychotherapy* (London: Harvill Secker, 2015), 3.

1. TRACING THE PATH FROM NATIONAL TO OFFICIAL CULTURE

1. Anne McClintock points out that for the Black Consciousness Movement "the question of cultural values took centre stage as literacy campaigns, black theatre, and poetry readings were fostered in the belief that cultural nationalism was the road to political nationalism." See "'Azikwelwa' (We Will Not Ride): Politics and Value in Black South African Poetry," *Critical Inquiry* 13.3 (1987), 597–623; at 611.

2. "Sechaba, Glasgow 1990," staged in Glasgow's City Halls from Sunday 23 through Thursday 27 September, was formally billed as the International Conference of Cultural Resistance to Apartheid. According to its publicity materials, it was organized by the Scottish Committee of the Anti-Apartheid Movement in association with the Scottish Trades Union Congress, and in consultation with the African National Congress. [Ed.]

3. Hugh Trevor-Roper, "The Invention of Tradition: The Highland Tradition of Scotland," in *The Invention of Tradition*, ed. Eric Hobsbawm and Terence Ranger (Cambridge: Cambridge University Press, 1983), 15–42.

4. Raymond Williams, *Culture* (Glasgow: Fontana, 1981), 184.

5. Frantz Fanon, *The Wretched of the Earth* [orig. *Les damnés de la terre*, 1961], trans. Constance Farrington (1963; London: Penguin, 1967, 2001), 178.

6. See "To Hear the Variety of Discourses," Chapter 5 in this volume. [Ed.]

7. See "Motherhood and the Surrogate Reader," Chapter 6 in this volume. [Ed.]

8. Johannes Fabian, *Time and the Other: How Anthropology Makes Its Object* (New York: Columbia University Press, 1983), 31.

9. Williams, *Culture*, 187.

10. Fanon, *Wretched of the Earth*, 180.

11. Brenda Cooper, in discussing J. M. Coetzee's distaste for the "colonisation of creative fiction by the discourse of history," refers to the political stratum that "in the name of returning culture to 'the people,' dictates a particular *political* role, strategy, content, and even appropriate form to writers." Brenda Cooper, "New Criteria for an 'Abnormal Mutation'? An Evaluation of Gordimer's *A Sport of Nature*," in *Rendering Things Visible*, ed. Martin Trump (Johannesburg: Ravan, 1990), 68–93; at 92.

12. Francis Mulhern, *Culture/Metaculture* (London: Routledge, 2000), 3–7.

13. Dan Sperber and Deirdre Wilson, *Relevance: Communication and Cognition*, 2nd ed. (1986; Oxford: Blackwell, 1995), 237–43.

14. Ibid., 242. In the first edition of the work cited, Sperber and Wilson ascribed these lines to Voltaire's *Candide*. In a note in the second edition (ibid., 294), they note their discovery, while preparing a French translation of the first edition of their work, that the phrasing was the work of Voltaire's translator into English.

15. Sperber and Wilson, *Relevance*, 242.

16. Mark Twain, *The Adventures of Huckleberry Finn* (1884; London: Penguin, 2012), 101.

17. Ibid., 98.

18. Sperber and Wilson, *Relevance*, 224

19. Edward Said, *The World, the Text, and the Critic* (Cambridge, MA: Harvard University Press, 1983), 169.

20. Williams, *Culture*, 13.

21. Benedict Anderson, *Imagined Communities* (1983; London: Verso, 2006), 6.

22. "Nkosi Sikelele i'Afrika," meaning "Lord, bless Africa," a prayer in Xhosa written by Enoch Sontonga in 1897 and set to a tune based on a Methodist hymn, came to be used at meetings of the South African Native National Congress after 1912 and was later adopted by its successor organization, the African National Congress (after 1925). Additional stanzas were added by Xhosa poet Samuel Mqhayi in 1927. Used, in translation, as the national anthem of postindependence Zambia between 1964 and 1973, and of Zimbabwe from 1980 to 1994, it currently serves as national anthem of Tanzania (sung in Swahili). Under the terms of the 1996 constitution, it forms part of the new National Anthem of South Africa (combined with part of "Die Stem"/"The Call of South Africa," the apartheid-era anthem). [Ed.]

23. Said, *The World, the Text, and the Critic*, 11.

24. Jeff Guy, "Gender Oppression in Southern Africa's Precapitalist Societies," in *Women and Gender in Southern Africa to 1945*, ed. Cherryl Walker (Cape Town: David Philip, 1990), 33–47; 44. See also Sandra Burman, "Fighting a Two-Pronged Attack: The Changing Legal Status of Women in Cape-Ruled Basutoland, 1872–1884," in the same collection (48–75).

25. Neville Dubow, "Photography in South Africa: The New Dilemmas Facing Apartheid's Chroniclers," *Creative Camera* 36 (1990), 36–38.

26. David Goldblatt, *The Transported of KwaNdebele: A South African Odyssey* (New York: Aperture, 1989).

27. Craig Owens, "The Discourse of Others: Feminists and Postmodernism," in *Postmodern Culture*, ed. Hal Foster (1983; London: Pluto Press, 1987), 57–82; at 69.

28. Ibid., 70.

29. Gilles Deleuze and Félix Guattari, *Kafka: Toward a Minor Literature* [orig. *Kafka: Pour une littérature mineure*, 1975], trans. Dana Polan (Minneapolis: University of Minnesota Press, 1986), 27.

30. Ibid., 19.

31. Ibid., 26.

32. Michael Vaughan, "Storytelling and Politics in Fiction," in *Rendering Things Visible: Essays on South African Literary Culture*, ed. Martin Trump (Johannesburg: Ravan, 1990), 186–204; at 194.

33. Ibid., 196.

34. Njabulo S. Ndebele, *Fools and Other Stories* (Harlow: Longman, 1985), 30–52. Vaughan's support of a narrow political agenda in writing can be found in an earlier essay, "Literature and Politics: Currents in South African Writing," *Journal of Southern African Studies* 9.1 (1982), 118–38. In this essay, Vaughan critiques Matshoba's work as follows: "Despite the richness of its imagery of township life, Matshoba's stories don't make a very positive connection with forms of social struggle of industrial society. Matshoba's semi-petty bourgeois status manifests itself in the centrality of the image of the traveller-storyteller, and in the relative poverty of concrete images of collective struggle" (138).

35. Ndebele, *Fools and Other Stories*, 34.
36. Ibid., 46.
37. Ibid., 47.
38. Ibid., 32.
39. Ibid., 40, 43, 44.
40. Njabulo S. Ndebele, *South African Literature and Culture: Rediscovery of the Ordinary* (1991; Manchester: Manchester University Press, 1994), 69.
41. Ndebele, *Fools and Other Stories*, 33.
42. Ndebele, *South African Literature and Culture*, 37.
43. Ibid., 49
44. Ibid., 67.

2. NATION, RACE, AND ETHNICITY

A version of this essay was delivered at the New Nation Writers Conference, held in Johannesburg in December 1991, in the panel entitled "Nation, Race, and Ethnicity: Beyond the Legacy of Victims."

1. The work was first published in 1930 by Lovedale Press, in bowdlerized form; a version attempting to recuperate Plaatje's original text appeared in 1978. [For more on the publication history of the text, see Tim Couzens, "Printers' and Other Devils: The Texts of Sol T. Plaatje's *Mhudi*," *Research in African Literatures* 9.2 (1978), 198–215. For a reassessment, see: Brian Willan, "What 'Other Devils'? The Texts of Sol T. Plaatje's *Mhudi* Revisited," *Journal of Southern African Studies* 41.6 (2015), 1331–47. (Ed.)]
2. Sol T. Plaatje, *Mhudi* (1930; London: Heinemann, 1978), 174.
3. Ibid., 175. [Lobola, bride wealth; see Chapter 2. (Ed.)]
4. Robert Miles, *Racism* (London: Routledge, 1989), 107.
5. Ibid., 71.
6. Bessie Head, *Maru* (London: Heinemann 1971), 11.
7. Ibid. [The term in more common use in Botswana today is Basarwa (collective), Mosarwa (singular), with Masarwa considered offensive. (Ed.)]
8. Head, *Maru*, 11.
9. Ibid., 24. [The term "Coloured" has a complex history in South Africa, where it served as a term of racial classification under the country's apartheid laws to refer to people with mixed-race ancestry, who descended from slaves brought to the region from present-day Indonesia and from elsewhere along the Indian Ocean rim during the period of Dutch East India Company rule, and also to those aboriginal or autochthonous peoples not regarded historically as black Africans and known at different times as Hottentot or Bushman, now collectively as Khoisan or Khoesan (this would include the Masarwa about whom Head writes). See further the introduction to this volume. (Ed.)]
10. See "Tracing the Path from National to Official Culture," Chapter 1 in this volume.
11. Quoted in Craig Owens, "The Discourse of Others: Feminists and Postmodernism," in *Postmodern Culture*, ed. Hal Foster (London: Pluto Press, 1985), 57–82; at 68.

3. CULTURE BEYOND COLOR?

1. Bessie Head, *A Question of Power* (1973; Rosebank: Penguin South Africa, 2011), 79, 79–80.
2. Omar Badsha et al., *Submission to CODESA from the Federation of South African Cultural Organisations: Towards a National Cultural Policy for the Development of Arts and Culture in a Democratic South Africa*, 2 March 1992 (Wynberg: n.p., 1992).
3. FOSACO was a politically nonaligned, civil-society initiative that grew from a national consultative conference of cultural workers in Johannesburg in 1990 and campaigned for the democratic transformation of parastatal cultural organizations during the transition to democracy. It collapsed after the rise of the National Arts Policy Plenary, later the National Arts Coalition, in 1992 (see n. 5 below). Some of its most important policy documents are archived at the Africa South Art Initiative website, http://asai.co.za/peoplesculture/federation-south-african-cultural-organisations/. [Ed.]
4. This prize, named for two of Southern Africa's leading antiapartheid writers, both recently deceased, was established by the Congress of South African Writers (COSAW) in 1988. [Ed.]
5. The National Arts Policy Plenary, held over two days in December 1992 and attended by more than a thousand delegates, grew from the "Arts for All" campaign, launched by a range of cultural organizations sympathetic to the Left seeking to influence future national arts policy in the expectation of a negotiated settlement in the country. See Kenneth W. Grundy, "Art as a Political Weapon: South Africa's Cultural Workers Debate Their Role in the Struggle," in *Ngũgĩ Wa Thiong'o: Text and Contexts*, ed. Charles Cantalupo (Trenton, NJ: Africa World Press, 1995), 137–64; at 157–61. [Ed.]
6. Schooling for black South Africans was administered by the Department of Bantu Education between 1953 and 1978, and thereafter by the Department of Education and Training. Education was focused on vocational training and spending per schoolchild was far less than per capita on white children's education. See further *The History of Education Under Apartheid, 1948–1994: The Doors of Education and Learning Shall Be Opened*, ed. Peter Kallaway (Cape Town: Maskew Miller Longman, 2002). [Ed.]
7. Vusumuzi Derek (or Derrick) Nxumalo, born 1962 in Umzinto, KwaZulu-Natal, lives and works as an artist in KwaDumisa. His work has been included in a number of exhibitions in South Africa and abroad (including in Oxford and London). Fanozi (Chickenman) Mkhize, born 1959 in Richmond in southern KwaZulu-Natal, lived in Edendale (near Pietermaritzburg) for most of his life; died 1995. Deton (Tito) Zungu, born 1946 in Mapumulo district, present-day KwaZulu-Natal, worked in a dairy in Pinetown after 1966 and later as domestic worker (gardener and cook) in Durban. His work was introduced to the African Art Centre in Durban by his employer, Mary Clarke, in 1970, and has been exhibited in shows in South Africa. [Ed.]
8. See also Wicomb's discussion of Mkhize in the next chapter, "Reading, Writing, and Visual Production in the New South Africa" [Ed.]

9. Rian Malan, *My Traitor's Heart* (1990; London: Vintage, 2015), 152, 157.

10. See George Steiner, *After Babel: Aspects of Language and Translation*, 3rd ed. (1975; Oxford: Oxford University Press, 1998); chapter 6 is entitled "Topologies of Culture."

4. READING, WRITING, AND VISUAL PRODUCTION IN THE NEW SOUTH AFRICA

A version of this essay was first delivered as the Arthur Ravenscroft Memorial Lecture at the University of Leeds, on 26 January 1995.

1. Ruth Finnegan, *Literacy and Orality* (Oxford: Blackwell, 1988).

2. See Walter J. Ong, *Orality and Literacy: The Technologizing of the Word* (London: Methuen, 1982).

3. Brian Street, *Literacy in Theory and Practice* (Cambridge: Cambridge University Press, 1984), 27.

4. Ibid.

5. Patrick Harries, "The Roots of Ethnicity: Discourse and the Politics of Language Construction in South-East Africa," *African Affairs* 87.346 (January 1988), 25–52; at 26.

6. On Plaatje, see Brian Willan, *Sol Plaatje: A Biography* (Johannesburg: Ravan Press, 1984).

7. Ong, *Orality and Literacy*, 179

8. Sachs's intervention, a position paper entitled "Preparing Ourselves for Freedom," was delivered at an A.N.C. seminar in Lusaka in 1989 and published in South Africa in the *Weekly Mail* on 2 February 1990, the same day F. W. De Klerk announced the unbanning of proscribed liberation organizations and the release of political prisoners (including Nelson Mandela). Sachs's essay was republished, with more than twenty responses, in *Spring Is Rebellious: Arguments About Cultural Freedom*, edited by Ingrid de Kok and Karen Press (Cape Town: Buchu Books, 1990). [Ed.]

9. Njabulo S. Ndebele, *Rediscovery of the Ordinary* (Johannesburg: COSAW, 1991), 65.

10. Ibid., 130.

11. Nadine Gordimer, "The Concept of a People's Literature," *Staffrider* 9.1 (1990), 41.

12. The Lovedale Mission Station was established by the Glasgow Missionary Society in the Eastern Cape in late 1823. Its press was in large measure responsible for the vibrant Christian Xhosa print culture that developed in the area from the early 1820s. In the 1920s and 1930s, Lovedale Press published important work, such as the first edition of Sol Plaatje's *Mhudi*. The mission school—out of which grew the South African Native College, subsequently the University of Fort Hare—was closed by the apartheid government in 1955, after the Bantu Education Act restricted educational opportunities for black South Africans. [Ed.]

13. Colin Richards, "desperately seeking 'africa,'" in *Art from South Africa* (Oxford: Museum of Modern Art, 1990), 40.

14. Muafangejo, born 1943 in Angola, died 1987 in Windhoek (in present-day Namibia), is highly regarded as a visionary printmaker. He moved to an Anglican mission in

what is now Namibia (South African–ruled South West Africa) in 1956, and later trained at the Fine Art School at Rorke's Drift in present-day KwaZulu-Natal (South Africa), where he served a period as artist-in-residence in the mid 1970s. His work was widely exhibited internationally (inter alia in Britain, Sweden, Brazil, Canada, the United States, and [West] Germany), as well as in South Africa, during his lifetime. Muafangejo was nominated as Guest Artist by the National Arts Festival in Grahamstown in 1987, shortly before his sudden death. [Ed.]

15. Roland Barthes, *Image—Music—Text*, trans. Stephen Heath (London: Fontana, 1977), 41.

16. For notes on Nxumalo, Mkhize, and Zungu, see the previous essay, "Culture Beyond Color?" [Ed.]

17. *Sunday Times*, April 1989.

18. Noria Muelwa Mabasa, born 1938 in Xigalo, Venda (South Africa), is well known as a ceramicist and sculptor and runs her own art school in the Vuwani area of present-day Limpopo Province, South Africa. [Ed.]

19. I visited these artists in 1993 with Roger Palmer, who was researching work for the Arnolfini exhibition "Earth and Everything," cocurated with Tessa Jackson in 1996.

20. Jackson Mbhazima Hlungwani, born 1923, died 2010, worked for a tea and coffee merchant in Johannesburg after 1941 and later was employed in Pietersburg (Polokwane), ordained as a minister in the African Zionist Church in 1946, and subsequently established his own church, Yesu Galeliya One Aposto in Sayoni Alt and Omega. He lived and worked latterly in Mbhokota, a rural village near Elim in present-day Limpopo Province, until his death. [Ed.]

21. Ivan Illich "A Plea for Research on Lay Literacy" in *Literacy and Orality*, ed. David R. Olson and Nancy Torrance (Cambridge: Cambridge University Press, 1991), 28–46; at 28.

22. Claude Lévi-Strauss, *Tristes tropiques* (1955), trans. John and Doreen Weightman (1973; New York: Penguin, 1992), 296.

23. Jacques Derrida, *Of Grammatology* (1967), trans. Gayatri Chakravorty Spivak (Baltimore: Johns Hopkins University Press, 1976), 109.

24. Gcina Mhlope, "The Toilet," in *Being There*, ed. Robin Malan (Cape Town: David Philip, 1994), 117–23; at 119.

25. Ibid., 123.

26. Ibid., 119.

27. Ibid., 123.

28. Ibid., 117.

29. Bessie Head, *The Cardinals* (Oxford: Heinemann Educational, 1995), 76.

30. Ibid, 10.

31. Ibid., 5.

32. Ibid., 7.

33. Ibid., 10.

5. TO HEAR THE VARIETY OF DISCOURSES

1. See, for instance, Nadine Gordimer in conversation with Stephen Clingman in "The Future Is Another Country," *Transition* 56 (1990), 132–52. "To me, so much of this feminist writing is therapy," Gordimer declared; "in my political activity, it's always been the freedom of the individual within the good of the whole that has mattered" (140).
2. See Alice Walker, *In Search of Our Mothers' Gardens: Womanist Prose* (London: Women's Press, 1984). Chikwenye Okonjo Ogunyemi, "Womanism: The Dynamics of the Contemporary Black Female Novel in English," *Signs* 11.1 (1985), 63–80; at 68.
3. Cecily Lockett, "Feminism(s) and Writing in English in South Africa," in *South African Feminisms: Writing, Theory, and Criticism 1990–1994*, ed. M. J. Daymond (New York: Garland, 1996), 3–26; at 20.
4. Sachs lost his right arm to a bomb planted by apartheid security agents in Mozambique in 1988. See also Chapter 4, n. 8. [Ed.]
5. Ogunyemi, "Womanism," 68.
6. Ibid.
7. Michel Foucault, *Language, Counter-Memory, Practice* (Oxford: Blackwell, 1977), 199.
8. See Jo Beall, Shireen Hassim, and Alison Todes, "'A Bit on the Side'?: Gender Struggles in the Politics of Transformation in South Africa," *Feminist Review* 33 (1989), 30–56.
9. Lockett, "Feminism(s) and Writing in English in South Africa," 16.
10. Ibid., 14, quoting from D. Nkululeko, "The Right to Self-determination in Research: Azanian Women," in *Women in Southern Africa*, ed. C. Qunta (Braamfontein: Skotaville, 1987).
11. Hazel Carby, *Reconstructing Womanhood: The Emergence of the Afro-American Woman Novelist* (New York: Oxford University Press, 1987), 18.
12. Lockett, "Feminism(s) and Writing in English in South Africa," 12.
13. Toni Morrison, *Beloved* (London: Chatto and Windus, 1987), 273.
14. Lockett, "Feminism(s) and Writing in English in South Africa," 20.
15. Boitumelo Mofokeng, in "Breaking the Silence," in *Buang Basadi: Khulumani Makhosikazi: Women Speak* (Johannesburg: COSAW, Transvaal Region, 1988), 11–18; at 17.
16. Nise Malange, in "Breaking the Silence," 13.
17. Ogunyemi, "Womanism," 68.
18. Ingrid Obery, ed., *Vukani Makhosikazi: South African Women Speak* (London: Catholic Institute for International Relations, 1985), 106.
19. Roseline Naapo, in "Breaking the Silence," 10.
20. For example, Elsa Joubert's *The Long Journey of Poppie Nongena* (Johannesburg: Jonathan Ball, 1985), first published as *Die swerfjare van Poppie Nongena* (1978).
21. Miriam Tlali, "'Fud-u-u—a!'" in *Footprints in the Quag* (Cape Town: David Philip, 1989), 27–42; at 42.
22. Mofokeng, in "Breaking the Silence," 9.
23. Lockett, "Feminism(s) and Writing in English in South Africa," 22.

24. Henry Louis Gates, Jr., ed., *Black Literature and Literary Theory* (New York: Methuen, 1984), 5.
25. Ibid.
26. Miriam Tlali, "Devil at a Dead End," in *Footprints in the Quag*, 102–18.
27. Ogunyemi, "Womanism," 76. See Bessie Head, *Maru* (London: Heinemann, 1971).
28. Head, *Maru*, 11. [Compare Wicomb's discussion in Chapter 2. (Ed.)]

6. MOTHERHOOD AND THE SURROGATE READER

1. See further Joanna Thornborrow, "The Woman, the Man and the Filofax: Gender Positions in Advertising" (128–51), and Chris Christie, "Theories of Textual Determination and Audience Agency: An Empirical Contribution to the Debate" (47–66), in *Gendering the Reader*, ed. Sara Mills (London: Harvester Wheatsheaf, 1994).
2. J. L. Austin, *How to Do Things with Words* (Oxford: Clarendon Press, 1962); J. R. Searle, *Speech Acts: An Essay in the Philosophy of Language* (Cambridge: Cambridge University Press, 1969). Performing a speech act involves performing a locutionary act, which is to produce a grammatical utterance. Austin uses the extraordinary example of *"Shoot her!"* to explain how such an utterance could have the illocutionary force of ordering, advising, or urging an addressee to perform the act of shooting. See, in general, Stephen C. Levinson, *Pragmatics* (Cambridge: Cambridge University Press, 1983), chapter 5.
3. The perlocutionary effect of the utterance *"Shoot her!"* is to force, persuade, or frighten the addressee into shooting a person. Such an effect could, however, only take place if certain conditions of appropriateness, or felicity conditions, hold. For instance, the utterance can have the required perlocutionary effect only if the addressee is holding a gun.
4. H. P. Grice's theory of implicatures is about how people use language. Grice identifies maxims such as clarity, relevance, and sincerity, which encompass a general cooperative principle to ensure efficient conversation. If we fail to understand an utterance according to one of the maxims, we make inferences or implicatures that restore a cooperative principle at a deeper level. Implicatures involve an addressee in bridging the gap between the actual utterance and what she might have expected, so that a bridging assumption is added in order to make sense of the utterance. See H. P. Grice, "Logic and Conversation," in *Syntax and Semantics, Volume 3: Speech Acts*, ed. Peter Cole and Jerry L. Morgan (New York: Academic Press, 1975), 41–58. In general see Grice, *Studies in the Way of Words* (Cambridge, MA: Harvard University Press, 1989).
5. Norman Fairclough, *Language and Power* (London: Longman, 1989), 10.
6. Michel Pêcheux, *Language, Semantics and Ideology* (Basingstoke: Macmillan, 1982).
7. Roland Barthes, *Image—Music—Text*, trans. Stephen Heath (London: Fontana, 1977), 39.
8. Judith Williamson, *Decoding Advertisements: Ideology and Meaning in Advertising* (London: Boyars, 1978), 43.

9. Trevor Pateman, "How Is Understanding an Advertisement Possible?" in *Language, Image, Media*, ed. Howard Davis and Paul Walton (Oxford: Blackwell, 1983), 187–204; at 204.

10. Ibid.

11. Dan Sperber and Deirdre Wilson, *Relevance: Communication and Cognition*, 2nd ed. (1986; Oxford: Blackwell, 1995).

12. Victor Burgin, "Seeing Sense," in *Language, Image, Media*, ed. Howard Davis and Paul Walton (Oxford: Blackwell, 1983), 226–44; at 232.

13. Burgin describes the "popular preconscious" as containing the "ever-shifting contents which we might reasonably suppose can be called to mind by the majority of individuals in a given society at a particular moment in its history; that which is common knowledge." Victor Burgin, "Photography, Phantasy, Function" (1980), in *Situational Aesthetics: Selected Writings by Victor Burgin*, ed. Alexander Streitberger (Leuven: Leuven University Press, 2009), 111–48; at 129. Such common knowledge or ideas are transmitted through various cultural media and become inscribed in the popular preconscious to serve as an advertisement's pre-text. Thus the actual verbal text interacts with the pre-text, the preconstituted fragments in a field of discourse.

14. According to the code model, communication is achieved by encoding and decoding messages so that the linguistic message at source is equivalent to that at destination. The existence, however, of a gap between semantic representations of sentences and the thoughts of a speaker renders such a model invalid, since it is a process of inference rather than further decoding that fills the gap.

15. Grice discusses the discrepancies between what a speaker means by an utterance and the meaning of a sentence. In the case of ironic utterances, what the speaker means, or nonnatural meaning (meaning-nn), will be in conflict with the natural or sentence meaning. We process meaning-nn as an inference, which is openly intended to be communicated as opposed to the incidental transfer of information. See Levinson, *Pragmatics*, 16.

16. Levinson, *Pragmatics*, chapter 2.

17. Kathy Myers, "Understanding Advertisers," in *Language, Image, Media*, ed. Howard Davis and Paul Walton (Oxford: Blackwell, 1983), 205–23; 205.

18. Pêcheux, *Language, Semantics and Ideology*, 111–12.

19. Ibid., 63–64.

20. Ibid., 117.

21. Textual cohesion depends on relationships within and between sentences. Endophoric relations in a text show how the meaning of pronominal expressions like *it* can be recovered by referring (a) back to a previous sentence or earlier part of a sentence, or (b) forward to find the referent later in the sentence or text. Endophora is distinguished from exophora, where interpretation lies outside the text—in the context of the situation. See M. A. K. Halliday and Ruqaiya Hassan, *Cohesion in English* (London: Longman, 1976), 33.

22. The Population Development Programme, incorporated by South Africa's Department of National Health, has, since 1989, taken over most of the advertising for birth

control. Its advertising generally dispenses with the image, occupies a full newspage in upper case, and directly addresses people to take responsibility for educating others in population reduction. One such advertisement, "Helping Women to Help Themselves," appeals to white women to become involved in the self-help program for black women. Others target farmers to encourage their workers to limit reproduction.

23. Annette Kuhn, *Women's Pictures: Feminism and Cinema* (London: Routledge and Kegan Paul, 1982), 53.

24. In a patriarchal society, where manhood is invested in the number of offspring, advertising must be careful not to exclude or alienate men. *Drum* magazine of the same date as *True Love* carries an advertisement of an overdressed man awkwardly balancing a young child on his knees. The child utters an improbable text in celebration of its carefully planned existence. While targeting men and offering a revised construction of fatherhood through the image, the text ensures that the father retains his distance from the business of reproduction and child rearing. But a current leaflet (1991) issued by the Department of National Health and Population Development and displayed in municipal offices is headed "Information for Men." The text starts as follows: "The man is the head of the family and has the responsibility to make important decisions about his family."

25. Levinson, *Pragmatics*, 279.

26. Kate Linker, "Representation and Sexuality," in *Art After Modernism: Rethinking Representation*, ed. Brian Wallis (New York: Museum of Contemporary Art, 1984), 391–416; at 392.

27. Sara Mills, "Introduction," in *Gendering the Reader*, ed. Sara Mills (London: Harvester Wheatsheaf, 1994), 1–22.

28. *Weekly Mail*, 25 October 1991.

29. *Sunday Times*, 27 October 1991.

7. SHAME AND IDENTITY

A version of this essay was first delivered as an address at the African Literature Association Conference in Columbus, Ohio, in March 1995, and subsequently at the annual conference of the Association of University English Teachers of South Africa (AUETSA) at the University of the Western Cape, Cape Town, in July 1996.

Epigraph. Ludwig Wittgenstein, *Remarks on Colour*, ed. G. E. M. Anscombe, trans. Linda L. McAlister and Margaret Schättle (Berkeley: University of California Press, 1977), 25e/29.3, paras. 60–61.

1. Sander L. Gilman, "Black Bodies, White Bodies: Toward an Iconography of Female Sexuality in Late Nineteenth Century Art, Medicine and Literature," *Critical Inquiry* 12.1 (1985), 204–42. [See further Chapter 2, n. 9. (Ed.)]

2. Baartman's remains were in fact returned to South Africa in 2002 and buried with full state honors near Hankey, in the Eastern Cape province, on 9 August. The first published version of this essay reflected the then current (late 1990s) view that

Baartman had been born in the Western Cape. Wicomb has amended that in this version. [Ed.]

3. Salman Rushdie, *Shame* (London: Picador, 1984), 16, 69.

4. Ibid., 39.

5. Ibid., 122.

6. I locate the meaning of the term "postcolonial" not in etymology but rather in discursive fields where it has been shaped through usage and has acquired a variety of meanings, including, for instance, oppositionality, resistance, the practice of radical readings, and neocolonialism, as well as the interrogation of the very term.

7. Stuart Hall, "What Is This Black in Popular Culture?" in *Black Popular Culture*, ed. Michelle Wallace and Gina Dent (New York: New Press, 1998), 21–33; at 30.

8. An astounding number of so-called cultural workers adopt District Six as their place of birth; CVs for foreign circulation even append to the privileged Harold Cressy High School in the city of Cape Town the barely justifiable address of District Six.

9. Fredric Jameson, "Postmodernism, or The Cultural Logic of Late Capitalism," in *Postmodernism: A Reader*, ed. Thomas Docherty (Hemel Hempstead: Harvester Wheatsheaf, 1993), 62–92; at 74.

10. Richard Rive, *"Buckingham Palace," District Six* (Cape Town: David Philip, 1986), 4.

11. Ibid., 6.

12. Bessie Head, *The Cardinals* (Cape Town: David Philip, 1993), 16.

13. Ibid., 121, emphasis added.

14. Bessie Head, *A Woman Alone: Autobiographical Writings* (Oxford: Heinemann, 1990), 97.

15. Hein Willemse, "Die Skrille Sonbesies: Emergent Black Afrikaans Poets in Search of Authority," in *Rendering Things Visible*, ed. Martin Trump (Johannesburg: Ravan, 1990), 367–401; at 380.

16. Mtutuzeli Matshoba, "A Son of the First Generation," in *Call Me Not a Man* (Harlow: Longman, 1979), 65–91; at 91.

17. Don Mattera, "Die Bushie is dood . . . ," in *Being Here: Modern Short Stories from Southern Africa*, ed. Robin Malan (Cape Town: David Philip, 1994), 138–42.

18. Max Ozinsky and Ibrahim Rasool, "Developing a Strategic Perspective for the Coloured Areas in the Western Cape," *African Communist* 133 (Second Quarter 1993), 39–47.

19. Mahmood Mamdani, "Reconciliation Without Justice," *Southern African Review of Books* 46 (Nov./Dec. 1996), 3–5.

20. Robert Ross, *Cape of Torments: Slavery and Resistance in South Africa* (London: Routledge and Kegan Paul, 1983), 76.

21. See J. M. Coetzee, *White Writing: On the Culture of Letters in South Africa* (New Haven: Yale University Press, 1988), 136–62.

22. Sol Plaatje, *Mhudi* (Oxford: Heinemann, 1978), 175.

23. Liz Gunner, "You, the Lioness," *Southern African Review of Books* 6.2 (1994), 15.

24. Dick Hebdige, *Hiding in the Light: On Images and Things* (London: Comedia, 1988), 193.

25. Nadine Gordimer, *My Son's Story* (London: Penguin, 1990), 21.
26. Homi K. Bhabha, *The Location of Culture* (London: Routledge, 1994), 13.
27. Ibid.
28. Ibid., 111.
29. Robert Young's *Colonial Desire: Hybridity in Theory, Culture and Race* (London: Routledge, 1995), published since I delivered an earlier version of this essay in March 1995, dismisses the postcolonial concept of hybridity as one that "assumes . . . the prior existence of pure, fixed and separate antecedents," and that is "still repeating its own cultural origins." Thus Young claims that "the threat of degeneration and decay incipient upon a 'raceless chaos' has not yet been fully redeployed and re-inflected" (25). This claim is summarily dismissed by Stuart Hall as a simple coincidence of using the same terminology that bears different meanings in "When Was 'the Post-Colonial'? Thinking at the Limit," in *The Post-Colonial Question*, ed. Iain Chambers and Lidia Curti (London: Routledge, 1996), 242–59.
30. The Kleurling Weerstandsbeweging vir die Vooruitgang van Bruinmense (literally, the Coloured Resistance Movement for the Advancement of Brown People) was founded in early 1995 by Mervyn King, a former trade union activist and erstwhile member of the A.N.C. Observers at the time noted the name's likely echo of that of the far-right A.W.B. (Afrikaner Resistance Movement), established in 1973 and led, until his death in 2010, by Eugene Terre'Blanche. [Ed.]
31. See David Bunn, "'Some Alien Land': Arthur Nortje, Literary History, and the Body in Exile," *World Literature Today* 70.1 (Winter 1996), 33–44, for an account of Arthur Nortje's problematic relationship with the A.N.C. This is suggestive in relation to the explicit, self-loathing references to miscegenation and colouredness in Nortje's poems. The vagrant K appears in Coetzee's 1983 novel *Life & Times of Michael K*.
32. Gordimer, *My Son's Story*, 23–24. [A stoep is a veranda; *moer* is beat up; *lanies* is a derogatory colloquialism for wealthy people, suggesting affectation. (Ed.)]
33. Bhabha, *Location of Culture*, 5.
34. Aijaz Ahmad, *In Theory: Classes, Nations, Literatures* (London: Verso, 1992), 129.
35. Carrie Mae Weems, *Then What? Photographs and Folklore* (Buffalo: CEPA Gallery Publications, 1990).

8. REMEMBERING NELSON MANDELA

1. Margaret Thatcher, prime minister of the United Kingdom from 1979 to 1990, died on April 8, 2013, and her death was greeted by an impromptu celebration on George Square in central Glasgow. Many Glaswegians revile Thatcher's Conservative government for its introduction of a hated poll tax, in 1989, and for its neoliberal economic policies, which many blame for the demise of heavy industries that had long been central to the economy of cities like Glasgow. [Ed.]
2. An Nguni word meaning something like "humanity," "human-ness," or "human kindness," *ubuntu* has come—in Southern Africa and more widely—to stand for a humanist ethics of restorative justice, an ethics of altruism and community mindedness,

and a recognition of human interconnectedness, all of which are suggested in the Zulu expression "Umuntu ngumuntu ngabantu," "a person is a person through other people." [Ed.]

3. See Amina Cachalia, *When Hope and History Rhyme: An Autobiography* (Johannesburg: Picador Africa, 2013). [Ed.]

4. A traditional Afrikaner treat, sweet plaited pastries, deep-fried and soaked in syrup. [Ed.]

9. FIVE AFRIKANER TEXTS AND THE REHABILITATION OF WHITENESS

A version of this essay was delivered at the "Culture dell'Alterita: Il territorio africano e le sue rappresentazione" conference held at the University of Bergamo, Italy, in October 1997.

1. A.W.B.: The Afrikaner Weerstandsbeweging (which translates as the Afrikaner Resistance Movement) was a white-supremacist, paramilitary organization on the far Right, founded in 1973 and led by the charismatic Eugene Terre'Blanche (died 2010), which agitated for a separate (white) Afrikaner state. The A.W.B. achieved notoriety with its actions in attempt to disrupt the negotiations that led to South Africa's constitutional settlement, in particular its abortive attempt to prop up the dictatorial leader of Bophuthatswana, Lucas Mangope, during March 1994, in advance of that erstwhile homeland's scheduled incorporation into a unitary South African state. [Ed.]

2. South Africa's Truth and Reconciliation Commission (T.R.C.) was established under the terms of the Promotion of National Unity and Reconciliation Act (no. 34 of 1995, as amended), in the words of the Act, "to provide for the investigation and the establishment of as complete a picture as possible of the nature, causes and extent of gross violations of human rights committed during the period from 1 March 1960 to the cut-off date contemplated in the Constitution" (about which there was some debate; it was eventually moved, in December 1996, to 10 May 1994), "within or outside the Republic, emanating from the conflicts of the past, and the fate or whereabouts of the victims of such violations" (p. 1 of the Act, which can be found online at http://www.justice.gov.za/legislation/acts/1995–034.pdf). It allowed for amnesty in return for "full disclosure of all the relevant facts relating to acts associated with a political objective committed in the course of the conflicts of the past," made possible the recording of violations suffered by victims, and envisaged reparations for victims. The first hearings of the Human Rights Violations Committee took place on 16 April 1996. The Amnesty Committee considered 7,116 applications, rejecting up to five thousand; up to thirteen thousand were granted indemnity from prosecution under the terms of the Act. The T.R.C. report, published in 1998, is archived online on the Department of Justice website (http://www.justice.gov.za/trc/). [Ed.]

3. Vladimir Tretchikoff (1913–2006), self-taught Russian-born artist long resident in Cape Town. Born in Petropavlovsk (Petropavl) to a wealthy family who fled to China in 1917, Tretchikoff later lived in Singapore and was interned in a P.O.W. camp in present-day Indonesia during World War II. In 1946, he joined his wife and family

in South Africa, to which they had been evacuated, and here he lived for the remainder of his life. Tretchikoff's painting *Chinese Girl* (1950) became one of the best-selling prints of the twentieth century. Although his work was widely disseminated through affordable prints, it was not critically well regarded, his name becoming a byword for kitsch in South African colloquial speech. In 2011, the Iziko National Gallery of South Africa in Cape Town mounted an unprecedented and controversial special retrospective of his career under the title "The People's Painter."

Alan Paton (1903–88), South African author best known for his 1948 novel *Cry, the Beloved Country*, almost certainly the best-selling work of fiction by a South African in the twentieth century. Paton was a critic of apartheid, though many on the left regarded his writing as patronizing. Lionel Rogosin's 1959 film *Come Back, Africa*, for example, includes a scene in which black characters dismiss liberal positions about race and politics, citing Paton's novel as chief example. [Ed.]

4. Antjie Krog, "Cry, Beloved Country," *Guardian*, 18 January 1997, A6.
5. Ibid. See also Antjie Krog, *Country of My Skull*, new ed. (London: Vintage, 1999), 72ff.
6. Pippa Skotnes's postmodern ethnographic artwork/exhibition at the South African National Gallery in Cape Town, called *Miscast: Negotiating the Presence of the Bushmen*—like the accompanying publication edited by Skotnes (University of Cape Town Press, 1996)—is a case in point. The controversial exhibition attempted to represent and challenge colonial othering of the Bushman, a spectacle that in turn was protested against by many self-identifying Bushman descendants.
7. Hal Foster, *The Return of the Real: The Avant-Garde at the End of the Century* (Cambridge, MA: MIT Press, 1996), 173.
8. Gilles Deleuze and Felix Guattari, *A Thousand Plateaus*, trans Brian Massumi (London: Athlone Press, 1988), 291.
9. Sipho Sepamla, "The Land," in *The Soweto I Love* (London: Rex Collings, 1977), 17.
10. The Pan Africanist Congress (P.A.C.), founded in 1959 by A.N.C. members breaking with their organization's expanded nonracial platform, was the leading black nationalist and pan-Africanist movement among the country's antiapartheid groupings. It is now known as the Pan Africanist Congress of Azania. The slogan "Kill the Boer, kill the farmer" is, in fact, understood to have originated not with the P.A.C. but with Peter Mokaba, erstwhile president of the A.N.C. Youth League, according to some reports at a memorial rally in 1993 for assassinated A.N.C. and South African Communist Party leader Chris Hani. Wicomb may have had in mind the slogan "One settler, one bullet," in use by the Azanian People's Liberation Army, the armed wing of the P.A.C., particularly during the 1980s; it was intended as a parody of the A.N.C. slogan "One person, one vote." After the chant "Kill the Boer, kill the farmer" resurfaced in the early 2000s, in particular after its use at Mokaba's own funeral in 2002, a white Afrikaner organization, the Freedom Front, lodged a complaint with the South African Human Rights Commission, which ruled in 2003 that the slogan was hate speech and thus not protected under the South African constitution's guarantee of free speech. This was confirmed by a 2010 decision in the South Gauteng High Court. [Ed.]

11. Neil Smith, *Uneven Development* (Oxford: Blackwell, 1984), 77.
12. Serton in S. J. N. Gie, *Geskiedenis van Suid-Afrika* (Stellenbosch: Pro Ecclesia, 1942), 265, my translation.
13. Ibid., 268.
14. Ibid., 269.
15. The first Dutch who moved out of the Cape Peninsula and Stellenbosch called themselves *trekboere*.
16. Op U Almag vas vertrouend het ons vadere gebou:
    Skenk ook ons die krag, o Here, om te handhaaf en te hou—
    Dat die erwe van ons vaad're vir ons kinders erwe bly:
    Knegte van die Allerhoogste, teen die hele wêreld vry.

    C. J. Langenhoven, "Die Stem van Suid-Afrika," in *Junior Verseboek*, ed. D. J. Opperman (Cape Town: Tafelberg, 1973), 66.
17. Edward Said, *The World, the Text, and the Critic* (Cambridge, MA: Harvard University Press, 1983), 18–20.
18. C. J. Langenhoven, "Die Onteiening," in *Junior Verseboek*, ed. D. J. Opperman (Cape Town: Tafelberg, 1973), 64–65; at 64.
19. Krog, "Cry, Beloved Country," A6. [See Krog, *Country of My Skull*, 73, where *kamferolie* becomes *kanferfoelie* (honeysuckle). (Ed.)]
20. Hein Willemse, "Die Skrille Sonbesies," in *Rendering Things Visible*, ed. Martin Trump (Johannesburg: Ravan Press, 1990), 367–401.
21. For a comprehensive account and a provocative argument, see Kenneth Parker, "Gendering a Language, Liberating a People: Women Writing in Afrikaans and the 'New' South Africa," *Social Identities* 2.2 (1996), 199–220.
22. J. M. Coetzee, *White Writing: On the Culture of Letters in South Africa* (New Haven: Yale University Press, 1988), 118.
23. Contemporary theorists of whiteness include Richard Dyer, "White," *Screen* 9.4 (1988), 44–64; Ruth Frankenberg, ed., *Displacing Whiteness: Essays in Social and Cultural Criticism* (Durham, NC: Duke University Press, 1993); Mike Hill, *Whiteness: A Critical Reader* (New York: New York University Press, 1997); and Toni Morrison, *Playing in the Dark: Whiteness and the Literary Imagination* (New York: Vintage Books, 1993).
24. Dyer, "White," 46.
25. Coetzee, *White Writing*, 11.
26. Ibid., 110.
27. Jacques Derrida, "Des Tours de Babel," in *A Derrida Reader*, ed. Peggy Kamuf (Hemel Hempstead: Harvester, 1991), 244–253; at 251.
28. Coetzee, *White Writing*, 95.
29. Etienne van Heerden, *Ancestral Voices*, trans. Malcolm Hacksley (1989; London: Allison and Busby, 1993), 14.
30. Krog, "Cry, Beloved Country," A6.
31. Van Heerden, *Ancestral Voices*, 250.
32. Marlene van Niekerk, *Triomf* (Cape Town: Queillerie, 1994), 5. See also *Triomf*, trans. Leon de Kock (London: Abacus Books, 2000), 6.

33. Marlene van Niekerk, "Kanonbaai," in *Die vrou wat haar verkyker vergeet het* (Pretoria: HAUM-Literêr, 1992), 16–35; at 30.
34. Breyten Breytenbach uses the word in titles such as *Return to Paradise* to refer to the entire country and to encode the exile's desire.
35. Krog, "Cry, Beloved Country," A6.
36. Antjie Krog, "land," *World Literature Today* 70.1 (Winter 1996), 119.
37. Chris Barnard, *Moerland* (Cape Town: Tafelberg, 1992), 24.
38. Ibid., 23. My translation.
39. Ibid., 52. Dialogue in English in the original.
40. Ibid., 28. My translation
41. Homi Bhabha, *The Location of Culture* (London: Routledge, 1994), 141.

10. J. M. COETZEE'S *DISGRACE*

1. J. M. Coetzee, *White Writing: On the Culture of Letters in South Africa* (New Haven: Yale University Press, 1988), 122.
2. Andrew Benjamin, "Translating Origins: Psychoanalysis and Philosophy," in *Rethinking Translation: Discourse, Subjectivity, Ideology*, ed. Lawrence Venuti (London: Routledge, 1992), 18–41.
3. Lawrence Venuti, *The Translator's Invisibility: A History of Translation*, 3rd ed. (New York: Routledge, 2018), 255.
4. Ibid., 256, 263.
5. Homi K. Bhabha, *The Location of Culture* (London: Routledge, 1994), 224.
6. Ibid., 225.
7. George Steiner, *After Babel: Aspects of Language and Translation*, 3rd ed. (Oxford: Oxford University Press, 1998), 316–17.
8. Gayatri Chakravorty Spivak, *Outside in the Teaching Machine* (London: Routledge, 1993), 183.
9. Steiner, *After Babel*, 3rd ed., 319.
10. Fanon paraphrased by Bhabha, *Location of Culture*, 38.
11. Jan—or Johan Anthoniszoon—van Riebeeck (1619–77), employee of the Dutch East India Company (V.O.C.), which he served variously as surgeon, trader, and colonial administrator, volunteered to serve as commander of a proposed refreshment station at the Cape of Good Hope, intended to service the V.O.C.'s trading fleet on its routes to Indochina, Batavia, and Japan. His fleet (three ships, eighty-two men, eight women) departed the Netherlands on 24 December 1651 and made landfall on 6 April 1652. Construction had begun on a fort within a week, and while the V.O.C. had no plans to colonize the region, wars between the Dutch Republic and England made substantial fortifications desirable. During Van Riebeeck's tenure as commander of the Cape settlement (to 1662), expeditions were mounted into the interior, former company employees (the so-called Free Burghers), having agitated to be released from their contracts, were permitted to establish independent farms, and slaves were imported from present-day Indonesia and Madagascar (after 1657). The date of Van

Riebeeck's arrival was marked as a public holiday between 1952 (the occasion of a tercentenary celebration) and 1994. [Ed.]

12. H. B. Thom, ed., *Journal of Jan van Riebeeck*, vol. 2 (Cape Town: Balkema, 1952), 343.

13. Richard Elphick, *Khoikhoi and the Founding of White South Africa* (Johannesburg: Ravan, 1985), 108.

14. R. H. Du Prè, *Separate but Unequal* (Johannesburg: Jonathan Ball, 1993), 14.

15. Thom, *Journal of Jan van Riebeeck*, 266.

16. Carli Coetzee, "Krotoa Remembered: A Mother of Unity, a Mother of Sorrows?" in *Negotiating the Past: The Making of Memory in South Africa*, ed. Sarah Nuttall and Carli Coetzee (Cape Town: Oxford University Press, 1998), 112–19.

17. Elphick, *Khoikhoi and the Founding of White South Africa*, 202.

18. John L. Comaroff, "Reflections on the Colonial State in South Africa and Elsewhere: Factions, Fragments, Facts and Fiction," *Social Identities* 4.3 (October 1998), 321–61; at 330.

19. Bhabha, *Location of Culture*, 226.

20. Andrew Benjamin, *Translation and the Nature of Philosophy: A New Theory of Words* (London: Routledge, 1989), 148.

21. Benjamin, "Translating Origins," 21.

22. J. M. Coetzee, *Disgrace* (London: Secker and Warburg, 1999), 21.

23. Ibid., 23.

24. Ibid., 214.

25. Ibid., 199.

26. Ibid., 194.

27. Ibid., 25.

28. Ibid., 53, 50.

29. Steiner, *After Babel*, 3rd ed., 484–85.

30. One of the most brutal methods of punishing suspected informants, as practiced in some South African townships during the 1980s, victims had tires filled with gasoline forced over their heads and arms, before being set alight. See chapter 3. [Ed.]

31. Roland Barthes, *Image—Music—Text*, trans. Stephen Heath (London: Fontana, 1977), 155–64.

32. Mikhail Bakhtin, "From the Pre-History of Novelistic Discourse," in *Modern Criticism and Theory*, ed. David Lodge (Longman: Harlow, 1988), 125–57; at 125, 156.

33. Julia Kristeva, *Desire in Language* (Oxford: Blackwell, 1987), 37.

34. Coetzee, *Disgrace*, 146.

35. Ibid., 145.

36. Frances Yates, *The Art of Memory* (London: Routledge and Kegan Paul, 1966), 1–2.

37. Coetzee, *Disgrace*, 60.

38. Ibid., 62.

39. Walter Benjamin, "The Task of the Translator," in *Illuminations* (London: Fontana, 1973), 69–82; at 75.

40. Benjamin, *Translation and the Nature of Philosophy*, 22.

41. Coetzee, *Disgrace*, 71.

11. REREADING GORDIMER'S *JULY'S PEOPLE*

An early version of this essay was delivered as a seminar paper at the University of Stellenbosch in about 2005, and another version at the University of Michigan, Ann Arbor, on 14 February 2007. It has not previously been published.

1. Stephen Clingman, *The Novels of Nadine Gordimer: History from the Inside* (London: Bloomsbury, 1993), 203.

2. Nancy Bailey, "Living Without the Future: Nadine Gordimer's *July's People*," *World Literature Written in English* 24.2 (1984), 215–24; at 222.

3. Nicholas Visser, "Beyond the Interregnum: A Note on the Ending of *July's People*," in *Rendering Things Visible*, ed. Martin Trump (Johannesburg: Ravan, 1990), 61–67; at 65–66.

4. Elleke Boehmer, "Endings and New Beginnings: South Africa Fiction in Transition," in *Writing South Africa: Literature, Apartheid, and Democracy, 1970–1995*, ed. Derek Attridge and Rosemary Jolly (Cambridge: Cambridge University Press, 1998), 43–56; at 50, 45.

5. Ibid., 51

6. Nadine Gordimer, "Living in the Interregnum," in *The Essential Gesture*, ed. Stephen Clingman (1988; London: Penguin, 1989), 261–84; at 269–70.

7. Mikhail Bakhtin, "Discourse in the Novel," in *The Dialogic Imagination*, ed. Michael Holquist, trans. Caryl Emerson and Michael Holquist (Austin: University of Texas Press, 1981), 259–422; at 364.

8. G. F. van L. Froneman, a former apartheid-era deputy minister of justice, mines, and planning, quoted in Jacklyn Cock, *Maids and Madams: A Study in the Politics of Exploitation* (Johannesburg: Ravan Press, 1980), 359.

9. The strip, by Stephen Francis and Rico Schacherl, first appeared in July 1992 in two formats—weekly, in black and white, in the *Weekly Mail* (the forerunner of the *Mail and Guardian* newspaper, where it currently appears); and monthly, in color, in *Living* magazine. Five weekday black-and-white strips were added the following year. [Ed.]

10. Michel Foucault, "The Order of Discourse," in *Untying the Text: A Post-Structuralist Reader*, ed. Robert Young (London: Routledge and Kegan Paul, 1981), 48–78; at 69.

11. Michel Foucault, "My Body, This Paper, This Fire," trans. Geoff Bennington, *Oxford Literary Review* 4.1 (Autumn 1979), 9–28; at 27.

12. Nadine Gordimer, *July's People* (1981; London: Penguin, 1982), 1.

13. Ibid., 70.

14. Ibid., 95 (ellipses in the original).

15. Ibid.

16. Ibid., 97.

17. Ibid.

18. Ibid., 100.

19. Ibid.

20. Ibid., 72.

21. Johannes Fabian, *Time and the Other: How Anthropology Makes Its Object* (New York: Columbia University Press, 1983), 31.

22. Es'kia Mphahlele, "Mrs Plum," in *Modern African Stories, ed. Charles R. Larson* (London: Fontana, 1971), 155–92.

23. Gordimer, *July's People*, 45.

24. Ibid., 96.

25. Ibid., 97.

26. Ibid., 86.

27. Ibid., 85.

28. Gordimer, "Living in the Interregnum," 266.

29. Richard Rorty, *Truth and Progress: Philosophical Papers, Volume 3* (Cambridge: Cambridge University Press, 1998), 180.

30. Gordimer, *July's People*, 117.

31. Jacques Derrida, "From 'Des Tours de Babel,'" in *A Derrida Reader*, ed. Peggy Kamuf (Hemel Hempstead: Harvester, 1991), 244–53; 244–45.

32. Gordimer, *July's People*, 151.

33. Ibid., 152.

34. Bakhtin, "Discourse in the Novel," 365.

35. Gordimer, *July's People*, 152.

36. Ibid., 132.

37. J. M. Coetzee, *White Writing: On the Culture of Letters in South Africa* (New Haven: Yale University Press, 1988), 116–17. [Coetzee goes on to elaborate Smith's practice: "Whether we look at Smith as a novelist working with foreign material or as a translator of Afrikaans culture, her enterprise—preserving (or sometimes in fact creating) marks of origin for her material—is therefore an unusual one. For this process I will reserve the name *transfer*, which I will define as the rendering of (imagined) foreign speech in an English stylistically marked to remind the reader of the (imagined) foreign original." (Ibid., 177.) (Ed.)]

38. Gordimer, *July's People*, 134.

39. Nadine Gordimer, "Blinder," in *Something Out There* (Johannesburg: Ravan, 1984), 79–88; at 85.

40. Richard Rorty, "Human Rights, Rationality and Sentimentality," in *Wronging Rights? Philosophical Challenges for Human Rights*, ed. Aakash Singh Rathore and Alex Cistelecan (Abingdon: Routledge, 2012), 107–31; at 127–28.

41. See Richard Rorty, "Pragmatism, Davidson and Truth," in *Truth and Interpretation: Perspectives on the Philosophy of Donald Davidson*, ed. Ernest LePore (Oxford: Blackwell, 1986), 333–55.

42. Jürgen Habermas, *Postmetaphysical Thinking*, trans. William Mark Hohengarten (Cambridge, MA: MIT Press, 1992), 38.

43. Gordimer, *July's People*, 160.

12. NATURAL NARRATIVE AND TALL TALES

This essay was first delivered as a lecture with the same title at Emory University in Atlanta, in November 2006, and at Nelson Mandela Metropolitan University in Port Elizabeth, South Africa, in 2012. It is published here for the first time, in revised form.

1. The student in question was Roland Jethro (Boeta Roli), and I am grateful to him for taping the evening's storytelling.

2. The language project involved studying a local variety of working-class coloured speech that typically uses code-switching between nonstandard varieties of English and Afrikaans. It aimed to (i) mobilize students' passive knowledge of language; (ii) dispel myths about "chaotic" language; and thus (iii) to counter the educationally damaging concept of semilingualism.

3. Working with material that is the cultural activity of other people necessarily places the investigator in a hierarchical relationship to what becomes the object of her inquiry. The fact that they had given me permission to use the material could be seen as faux naïveté by the first-world subject of knowledge who would not allow herself to be the object of someone else's inquiry. The ethics of publishing the stories of the other has been widely debated in relation to works of fiction. Elsa Joubert's *The Long Journey of Poppie Nongena* (1980) was based on the oral account of the eponymous dispossessed black woman's life, Pamela Jooste's novel about a coloured family's forced removal from District Six, *Dance with a Poor Man's Daughter* (1998), acknowledges the debate in her preface, where she offers justification on the basis of intimate knowledge of the life of a family servant. Richard Rive's condemnation of white fictional accounts of District Six relies on a converse argument of lack of experience, knowledge, and authenticity. See Shamil Jeppie and Crain Soudien, eds., *The Struggle for District Six: Past and Present* (Cape Town: Buchu Books, 1990).

4. See Suzanne Romaine, *Bilingualism* (Oxford: Blackwell, 1989), 149.

5. Other pragmatic functions cited by Romaine (ibid.) are: to qualify a message; to distinguish between topic and comment; to mark personalization from objectivization; and to mark shifts in style, all of which are exemplified in the transcript in Appendix 1.

6. Bill Nasson, "Oral History and the Reconstruction of District Six," in *The Struggle for District Six: Past and Present*, ed. Shamil Jeppie and Crain Soudien (Cape Town: Buchu Books, 1990), 44–66; at 49.

7. Anne McClintock, *Imperial Leather: Race, Gender and Sexuality in the Colonial Contest* (New York: Routledge, 1995), 311.

8. Hofmeyr laments the fact that investigation of oral history is not informed by the culturalist thrust of oral narratives and that attention to the "facts" has dominated over form. See Isabel Hofmeyr, *"We Spend Our Years as a Tale That Is Told"—Oral Historical Narrative in a South African Chiefdom* (Johannesburg: Wits University Press, 1993). Elizabeth Tonkin dismisses the distinction between oral history and oral literature: "An oral testimony cannot be treated only as a repository of facts and errors of facts"; it is rather in the rhetorical skills of speakers that meaning is to be found, thus "facts and opinions do not exist as freestanding objects, but are reproduced through grammar and larger conventions of discourse"; *Narrating Our Pasts: The Social Construction of Oral History* (Cambridge: Cambridge University Press, 1992), 2–14.

9. See Martin Kreiswirth, "Merely Telling Stories? Narrative and Knowledge in the Human Sciences," *Poetics Today* 21.2 (Summer 2000), 294–318.

10. Peggy Delport, "Signposts for Retrieval: A Visual Framework for Enabling Memory of Place and Time," in *Recalling Community in Cape Town*, ed. Ciraj Rasool and Sandra Prosalendis (Cape Town: District Six Museum, 2001), 31–46; at 36.

11. See Deborah Cameron, *Feminism and Linguistic Theory* (London: Macmillan, 1985), 31–44, on folk-linguistic beliefs about women's language.

12. Hofmeyr, *We Spend Our Years*, 7. In her study of gender and storytelling, Hofmeyr found that women mostly told fictional stories (associated with the hut area), while men's narratives were "true" historical stories (told in the courtyards).

13. Mary Louise Pratt, "Linguistic Utopias," in *The Linguistics of Writing: Arguments Between Language and Literature*, ed. Nigel Fabb, Derek Attridge, Alan Durant, and Colin MacCabe (Manchester: Manchester University Press, 1987), 48–66; at 60.

14. Kay McCormick, "The Vernacular of District Six," in *The Struggle for District Six: Past and Present*, ed. Shamil Jeppie and Crain Soudien (Cape Town: Buchu Books, 1990), 88–109; at 88. Significantly, speakers in McCormick's linguistic study in District Six are anxious to differentiate their variety of Afrikaans from the "suiwer" (pure) Afrikaans spoken by white Afrikaners, while they do not perceive their English to differ from the standard dialect (ibid.).

15. Square brackets contain a translation of the original. See the full transcript in Appendix 1, translated in full in Appendix 2.

16. Boeta Dickie's language shows his distance from the revolutionary movement, and the implied appeal to the culture of resistance is rendered spurious by his reference to "darkies."

17. Kreiswirth, "Merely Telling Stories?" 302.

18. Mary Louise Pratt, *Towards a Speech Act Theory of Literary Discourse* (Bloomington: Indiana University Press, 1977), 73.

19. Steven Seidman, ed., *Jürgen Habermas on Society and Politics: A Reader* (Boston: Beacon Books, 1989), 72.

20. Jean-François Lyotard, *The Postmodern Condition: A Report on Knowledge*, trans. Geoffrey Bennington and Brian Massumi (Manchester: Manchester University Press, 1984), 19.

21. Ibid., 10.

22. Walter J. Ong, *Orality and Literacy: The Technologizing of the Word* (London: Methuen, 1982), 44.

23. Lyotard, *The Postmodern Condition*, 20.

24. Jean-François Lyotard, *The Postmodern Explained to Children: Correspondence, 1982–1985* (Sydney: Power Publications, 1992), 31–32.

25. See for example: Adam Zachary Newton, *Narrative Ethics* (Cambridge, MA: Harvard University Press, 1997); Martha Nussbaum, *Love's Knowledge: Essays on Philosophy and Literature* (New York: Oxford University Press, 1990); and Martha Nussbaum, *Poetic Justice: The Literary Imagination and Public Life* (Boston: Beacon Press, 1997).

26. It was through the circulation of oral accounts that the curators came to hear of the original street signs that were kept by one of the apartheid bureaucrats who had supervised the demolition of District Six. These were reclaimed from him for the first exhibition, and the story is itself presented alongside the signs in the museum.

27. See Hofmeyr's *We Live Our Life*, Chapter 8, "History as Farce?"
28. Arthur Danto, *Narration and Knowledge* (New York: Columbia University Press, 1985), 340.
29. Richard Cohen, *Face to Face with Levinas* (New York: SUNY Press, 1984), 20.
30. M. A. K. Halliday, "Language and the Order of Nature," in *The Linguistics of Writing: Arguments Between Language and Literature*, ed. Nigel Fabb, Derek Attridge, Alan Durant, and Colin MacCabe (Manchester: Manchester University Press, 1987), 135–54; at 145.
31. Ibid., 144. Halliday compares the following sentences:

    (i) He also credits his former big size with much of his career success.
    (ii) He also believes that he succeeded in his career mainly because he used to be big.

32. Annie E. Coombes, *History After Apartheid: Visual Culture and Public Memory in a Democratic South Africa* (Durham, NC: Duke University Press, 2003), 125–26.
33. Michel Foucault, *The Order of Things*, trans. A. M. Sheridan Smith (London: Tavistock, 1970), 327.

13. "GOOD RELIABLE FICTIONS"

A version of this essay was first delivered as a paper at "Nostalgia, Narration, and Nationhoods: Third Apartheid Archive Conference" at the University of the Witwatersrand in Johannesburg in July 2011. It has not previously been published.

1. Richard Rorty, *Truth and Progress: Philosophical Papers, Volume 3* (Cambridge: Cambridge University Press, 1998), 183.
2. Svetlana Boym, *The Future of Nostalgia* (New York: Basic Books, 2001), xv.
3. Jacob Dlamini, *Native Nostalgia* (Auckland Park: Jacana, 2009), 3.
4. Ibid., 4. ["Influx control" was a euphemism for the restrictions placed on black South Africans' travel to and residence in "white" cities, for which the hated pass books served as internal passport, visa, and identity document. (Ed.)]
5. Boym, *The Future of Nostalgia*, xviii.
6. Ibid., xvi.
7. Ivan Vladislavić, *Double Negative* (Rome: Contrasto, 2010), 191. The novel was published in South Africa by Umuzi in 2011; the Contrasto edition paired the novel with Goldblatt's *TJ*.
8. Julia Kristeva, *Strangers to Ourselves*, trans. Leon S. Roudiez (New York: Columbia University Press, 1991), 9.
9. Ibid., 153.
10. Ibid., 154.
11. Ibid., 182.
12. Quoted in *Postmodernism: A Reader*, ed. Thomas Docherty (Hemel Hempstead: Harvester Wheatsheaf, 1993), 77.
13. Vladislavić, *Double Negative*, 37.

14. Boym, *The Future of Nostalgia*, 29.

15. Roland Barthes, *Camera Lucida*, trans. Richard Howard (London: Vintage, 1993), 71.

16. Walter Benjamin, "Theses on the Philosophy of History," in *Illuminations*, trans. Harry Zohn (1968; New York: Schocken, 1969), 253–64; at 259.

17. Ibid.

18. Vladislavić, *Double Negative*, 78.

19. Ibid., 78.

20. Ibid., 79.

21. Jacques Derrida, "From 'Psyche: Inventions of the Other,'" in *A Derrida Reader: Between the Blinds*, ed. Peggy Kamuf (Hemel Hempstead: Harvester Wheatsheaf, 1991), 200–221; at 203.

22. Dennis Walder, *Postcolonial Nostalgias* (London: Routledge, 2011), 128.

23. Ibid., 136–37, emphasis added.

24. Linda Hutcheon, "Irony, Nostalgia, and the Postmodern," *University of Toronto English Library*, http://www.library.utoronto.ca/utel/criticism/hutchinp.html.

25. See the discussion of irony, using Sperber and Wilson, and referring to *The Adventures of Huckleberry Finn*, in the first essay in this collection, "Tracing the Path from National to Official Culture." [Ed.]

26. Elaine Scarry, *On Beauty and Being Just* (1999; London: Duckworth, 2006), 5; see 3–5.

27. Ibid., 4 (Scarry's subtitle); 111 (citing Simone Weil).

28. Scarry, *On Beauty and Being Just*, 113.

29. Barthes, *Camera Lucida*, 8.

30. Ibid., 9.

31. Ibid., 21.

32. Ibid.

33. Ibid., 91.

34. Ibid., 85. See Boym, *The Future of Nostalgia*, 263.

35. If Landsberg's "prosthetic memory" is cast as a healthy ethical device in the age of mass culture because it "enables the transmission of memories to people who have no 'natural' or biological claim to them," Nev's observation shows that mass culture can also produce the photographic evidence. See Alison Landsberg, *Prosthetic Memory: The Transformation of American Remembrance in the Age of Mass Culture* (New York: Columbia University Press, 2004), 18.

36. Vladislavić, *Double Negative*, 198.

37. Benjamin, "Theses on the Philosophy of History," 73.

38. Vladislavić, *Double Negative*, 87.

39. Ibid., 76.

40. Ibid., 78.

41. Ibid., 77.

42. Ibid., 83.

43. Ibid., 87.

44. Ibid., 148.

45. Ibid., 99. Joe Slovo (1926–95), South African politician. Long-time general secretary of the South African Communist Party, Slovo served in exile as a commander of the A.N.C.'s armed wing, uMkhonto we Sizwe. He served in Nelson Mandela's cabinet as minister for housing before his death, from cancer, aged sixty-eight. Slovo's first wife was the lawyer and activist Ruth First. [Ed.]

46. Herman Melville, "Bartleby," in *Billy Budd, Sailor and Other Stories* (1967; Harmondsworth: Penguin, 1985), 57–99; 68–94, 97.

47. Vladislavić, *Double Negative*, 130.

48. Ibid., 131.

49. Ibid.

50. Ibid.

51. Melville, "Bartleby," 99.

52. Vladislavić, *Double Negative*, 196.

53. Ibid., 174.

54. Ibid., 203.

55. Paul de Man, *Blindness and Insight: Essays in the Rhetoric of Contemporary Criticism* (London: Routledge, 1983), 207.

56. Vladislavić, *Double Negative*, 222.

14. IDENTITY, WRITING, AND AUTOBIOGRAPHY

A version of this essay was first given as an address at the School of Oriental and African Studies at the University of London in 1994, under the title "Not-Autobiography, the Law and Prohibition in Bessie Head's Fiction."

1. See variously Craig Mackenzie and Cherry Clayton, eds., *Between the Lines: Interviews with Bessie Head, Sheila Roberts, Ellen Kuzwayo, Miriam Tlali* (Grahamstown: National English Literary Museum, 1989), 5–29; Cecil Abrahams, ed., *The Tragic Life: Bessie Head and Literature of Southern Africa*, (Trenton, NJ: Africa World Press, 1990); Michael Chapman, *Southern African Literatures* (London: Longman, 1996), 380–82; Gillian Stead Eilersen, *Bessie Head: Thunder Behind Her Ears* (Cape Town: David Philip, 1995); Huma Ebrahim, ed., *Emerging Perspectives on Bessie Head* (Asmara: Africa World Press, 2004).

2. Bessie Head, *A Woman Alone: Autobiographical Writings*, ed. Craig MacKenzie (Oxford: Heinemann, 1990), 3.

3. Ibid., 4.

4. M. J. Daymond, "On Retaining and on Recognising Changes in the Genre 'Autobiography,'" *Current Writing* 3 (1991), 31–41; at 33.

5. Henry Louis Gates Jr., "Criticism in the Jungle," in *Black Literature and Literary Theory*, ed. Henry Louis Gates Jr. and Sunday Ogbonna Anozie (New York: Methuen, 1984), 1–27; at 5–6.

6. J. M. Coetzee, *Doubling the Point: Essays and Interviews*, ed. David Attwell (Cambridge, MA: Harvard University Press, 1992), 17.

7. bell hooks, "Postmodern Blackness," in *Colonial Discourse and Post-Colonial Theory*, ed. Patrick Williams and Laura Chrisman (Hemel Hempstead: Harvester, 1993), 421–27; at 425.

8. Randolph Vigne, ed. *A Gesture of Belonging: Letters from Bessie Head, 1965–1979* (London: Heinemann, 1991), 17. [See also Wicomb's discussion of *The Cardinals* in Chapter 4. Head's correspondence with the Cullinans, published in 2005 as *Imaginative Trespasser: Letters Between Bessie Head and Patrick and Wendy Cullinan, 1963–1977* (Trenton, NJ: Africa World Press), had not yet been published when Wicomb wrote this essay. (Ed.)]

9. Jacques Derrida, "How to Avoid Speaking: Denials," in *Languages of the Unsayable: The Play of Negativity in Literature and literary Theory*, ed. Sanford Budick and Wolfgang Iser (New York: Columbia University Press, 1989), 3–70; 57.

10. The Immorality Act (No. 5 of 1927) prohibited sexual intercourse outside marriage between white and "native" South Africans. The Prohibition of Mixed Marriages Act (No. 55 of 1949) prohibited marriages between South Africans of different races, eliminating the exception allowed under the 1927 legislation, and an Immorality Amendment Act (No. 21 of 1950) expanded the prohibition of sexual relations between whites and people of any other racial group. These prohibitions were consolidated under the Immorality Act (No. 23 of 1957), later renamed the Sexual Offences Act; several related pieces of legislation sought to police sexual relations during the apartheid period. [Ed.]

11. Bessie Head, *The Cardinals: With Meditations and Stories* (Oxford: Heinemann Educational, 1995), 6.

12. Ibid., 7.

13. Gayatri Chakravorty Spivak, "Acting Bits/Identity Talk," *Critical Inquiry* 18.4 (Summer 1992), 770–803; at 790.

14. Head, *Cardinals*, 8.

15. Ibid., 8.

16. Ibid., 9.

17. Ibid., 10.

18. Julia Kristeva, *Language the Unknown* (Hemel Hempstead: Harvester, 1989), 274–75.

19. Head, *Cardinals*, 10.

20. Ibid., 11.

21. See Spivak, "Acting Bits/Identity Talk," 785, 984–95, and passim.

22. Bessie Head, *Maru* (London: Heinemann, 1971), 11. [See Chapter 2. (Ed.)]

23. Head, *Cardinals*, 16.

24. Ibid., 70.

25. Spivak, "Acting Bits/Identity Talk," 791.

26. Head, *Cardinals*, 70.

27. Derrida, "How to Avoid Speaking: Denials," 29.

28. Wolfgang Iser, "The Play of the Text," in *Languages of the Unsayable: The Play of Negativity in Literature and Literary Theory*, ed. Sanford Budick and Wolfgang Iser (New York: Columbia University Press, 1989), 325–39; at 336–38.

29. Head, *Cardinals*, 33.

30. Ibid., 37.

31. Ibid.

32. Ibid., 56.

33. Umberto Eco, in Stefano Rosso and Carolyn Springer, "A Correspondence with Umberto Eco [Genova-Bologna-Binghamton-Bloomington, August–September, 1982 March–April, 1983]," *boundary 2* 12.1 (Autumn 1983), 1–13; at 2–3.

34. Head, *Cardinals*, 62.

35. Robert Mangaliso Sobukwe (1924–78), once a member of the African National Congress, led a faction of Africanists out of the organization and founded the Pan Africanist Congress in 1959. Sobukwe led demonstrations against the pass system, and it was largely P.A.C. supporters who were shot by police at Sharpeville on 21 March 1960. Imprisoned for three years in May 1960, he was detained for a further six years under extraordinary powers granted the minister of justice by the apartheid legislature. On his release, Sobukwe's movements were severely restricted. [Ed.]

36. Head, *Cardinals*, 76.

15. SETTING, INTERTEXTUALITY, AND THE RESURRECTION OF THE POSTCOLONIAL AUTHOR

A version of this essay was first delivered as the keynote address at the Third Conference of the Associazione Italiana di Studi sulle Letterature in Inglese, Rome, Italy, in September 2004.

1. Edward Said, *The World, the Text, and the Critic* (Cambridge, MA: Harvard University Press, 1983), 7, 8.

2. J. M. Coetzee, *Youth* (London: Secker and Warburg, 2002), 116. Lewis Nkosi too speaks of the South African writer as being constructed out of a historical wound (private communication).

3. Shlomith Rimmon-Kenan, *Narrative Fiction* (London: Routledge, 1983), 66.

4. Roland Barthes, "The Death of the Author," in *Image—Music—Text*, trans. Stephen Heath (London: Fontana, 1977), 142–148.

5. See Nadine Gordimer, "Blinder," in *Something Out There* (London: Jonathan Cape, 1984), 79–88. [See also Chapter 11. [Ed.])

6. Jacques Derrida, "From 'Des Tours de Babel,'" in *A Derrida Reader: Between the Blinds*, ed. Peggy Kamuf (Hemel Hempstead: Harvester, 1991), 243–53; at 249.

7. Ivan Vladislavić, "'Kidnapped,'" *Propaganda by Monuments* (Cape Town: David Philip, 1996), 157–73; 161. [Drammach is a Scottish mixture of cold water and oatmeal. (Ed.)]

8. In the Jim-comes-to-Jo'burg genre, an innocent man from the country arrives in the big, potentially corrupting, city. Often such narratives reinforced white liberal preconceptions about the supposed purity of "tribal" life. [Ed.]

9. Vladislavić, "'Kidnapped,'" 168

10. Ibid.

11. Ibid.

12. Ibid., 169.

13. Ibid., 172.

14. Could it be, I wonder, that Vladislavić at his white school in the Transvaal studied the same set text as I did? In *Harrap's English Essays*, Hazlitt's "On Going a Journey" is followed by the only Scottish contribution in the anthology, Stevenson's "Old Scots Gardener." See J. B. Skinner and D. Rintoul, eds., *English Essays* (London: George Harrap, 1961).

15. Vladislavić, "'Kidnapped,'" 163.

16. Ibid.

17. David Attwell, *J. M. Coetzee: South Africa and the Politics of Writing* (Berkeley: University of California Press, 1993), 104.

18. Derek Attridge, "Oppressive Silence: J. M. Coetzee's *Foe* and the Politics of the Canon," in *Decolonizing the Tradition: New Views of Twentieth Century "British" Literary Canons*, ed. Karen Lawrence (Urbana: University of Illinois Press, 1992), 212–38; at 230.

19. In an interview with Sean French on *The Satanic Verses*, Rushdie says: "I wanted to write about a thing that I find difficult to admit even to myself, which is the fact that I left home." See Lisa Appignanesi and Sara Maitland, eds., *The Rushdie File* (London: Fourth Estate, 1989), 6–8; at 7.

20. Salman Rushdie, *The Satanic Verses* (London: Viking, 1988), 319.

21. Gayatri Chakravorty Spivak, *Outside in the Teaching Machine* (New York: Routledge, 1993), 225.

22. Ibid.

23. Toni Morrison, *Jazz* (New York: Penguin, 1992), 219.

24. See T. S. Eliot, "The Waste Land," *T. S. Eliot: The Complete Poems and Plays* (London: Faber and Faber, 1969), 59–80; at 74, lines 419–24.

25. Morrison, *Jazz*, 229.

26. Ibid., 226.

27. Vladislavić's narrator is interested in the promise to entrants of a Bank of Scotland commemorative note with Stevenson's image, rather than in the prize money. My short story about a South African in Scotland searching for her lost son was inspired by a Scottish banknote commemorating Livingstone, with a puzzling image of smiling, shackled slaves on the reverse.

28. Mieke Bal, *Looking In—The Art of Viewing* (Amsterdam: Overseas Publishers Association, 2001), 214.

29. Kaja Silverman, *The Threshold of the Visible World* (London: Routledge, 1996), 16–17.

30. Significantly, Spivak refers to her residence in the United States in terms of "the ghostliness in the figure of the long-term Resident Alien"; see Gayatri Chakravorty Spivak, "Resident Alien," in *Relocating Postcolonialism*, ed. David Theo Goldberg and Ato Quayson (Oxford: Blackwell, 2002), 47–65; at 47.

31. Bal, *Looking In*, 214.

32. Margaret Daymond, "Finding a Safe House of Fiction," in *Telling Stories: Postcolonial Short Fiction in English*, ed. Jacqueline Bardolph (Amsterdam: Rodopi, 2001), 183–96; at 185.

33. Homi K. Bhabha, *The Location of Culture* (London: Routledge, 1994), 18.

16. COETZEE'S *SLOW MAN* AND THE REAL

1. J. M. Coetzee, "As a Woman Grows Older," *New York Review of Books* 51.1 (2004), 11–14; at 12.
2. J. M. Coetzee, *Slow Man* (London: Secker and Warburg, 2005), 198.
3. Ibid., 122.
4. Ibid., 3.
5. Ibid., 14–15.
6. Ibid., 83.
7. Ted Hughes, "The Thought Fox" (1957), in *The Norton Anthology of Poetry*, ed. Margaret Ferguson, Mary Jo Salter, and John Stallworthy (New York: W. W. Norton, 2014), 1810.
8. Coetzee, *Slow Man*, 3.
9. Ibid., 83, 204.
10. Ibid., 100.
11. Italo Calvino, "Levels of Reality in Literature," in *The Uses of Literature*, trans. Patrick Creagh (New York: Harcourt, Brace, 1986), 101–24; at 111.
12. The phrase is from Derek Attridge's description of the autrebiographies; see *J. M. Coetzee and the Ethics of Reading: Literature in the Event* (Chicago: University of Chicago Press, 2004), 138–61.
13. Fiona Bradley, "Introduction," in *Rachel Whiteread: Shedding Life* (Liverpool: Tate Gallery, 1997), 8–17; at 11.
14. A subsequent Whiteread work, the Holocaust Memorial in Vienna's Judenplatz, is derived from a cast of the interior of a library. The resulting monolithic cube is an impenetrable structure of shelves turned inside out so that the spines of the books face inward, and what is normally concealed on the bookshelf forms the surface of the sculpture. The sculptural conundrum is that of a bookshelf turned inside out, but in terms of a library the structure is one of outside in, a reversal of "House."
15. Coetzee, *Slow Man*, 119.
16. Ibid., 36.
17. Roland Barthes, *S/Z*, trans. Richard Miller (New York: Hill and Wang, 1975), 61.
18. Coetzee, *Slow Man*, 229.
19. Ibid., 255.
20. Jacques Derrida, "The Double Session," in *A Derrida Reader: Between the Blinds*, ed. Peggy Kamuf (Hemel Hempstead: Harvester Wheatsheaf, 1991), 171–99; at 176–77.
21. Paul de Man, *The Resistance to Theory* (Minneapolis: University of Minnesota Press, 1986), 11.
22. Calvino, "Levels of Reality in Literature," 111.
23. Coetzee, *Slow Man*, 81, 1, 83.
24. Ibid., 98.
25. Ibid., 36.
26. Ibid., 200.
27. Ibid., 202, emphases added.
28. Barthes, *S/Z*, 67.

29. Italo Calvino, *If on a Winter's Night a Traveller*, trans. William Weaver (London: Picador, 1982), 142.

30. Ibid.

31. *Elizabeth Costello* was preceded by a real performance in 1996, when Coetzee on invitation by P.E.N. International in London delivered what promised to be a talk on the subject "What Is Realism?" On that occasion, Coetzee, the real author/speaker, substituted the genre of the lecture with a story about a fictional Australian writer, Elizabeth Costello, who delivers an acceptance speech on the subject of realism.

32. Stuart Morgan, "Rachel Whiteread," in *Rachel Whiteread: Shedding Life* (Liverpool: Tate Gallery, 1997), 19–28; at 23.

33. Derrida, "The Double Session," 177.

34. Coetzee, *Slow Man*, 100.

35. Ibid.

36. Ibid., 209.

37. Ibid., 233,

38. Ibid., 164.

39. Ibid., 210.

40. Ibid., 242.

41. Ibid., 99.

42. Ibid., 155.

43. Ibid., 195.

44. Ibid., 158.

45. Ibid., 159.

46. Calvino, "Levels of Reality in Literature," 113.

47. Coetzee, *Slow Man*, 161.

48. Roland Barthes, *Camera Lucida*, trans. Richard Howard (London: Vintage, 1993), 4.

49. Ibid., 76.

50. Ibid., 89.

51. Coetzee, *Slow Man*, 177.

52. Ibid.

53. Barthes, *Camera Lucida*, 13, 14.

54. Coetzee, *Slow Man*, 245.

55. Ibid., 232.

56. Ibid., 228.

57. Ibid., 233.

58. Ibid.

59. Ibid., 257.

60. Ibid., 229.

61. Ibid., 259.

62. Barthes, "The Death of the Author," in *Image—Music—Text*, trans. Stephen Heath (London: Fontana Press, 1977), 142–48; at 146.

63. Coetzee, *Slow Man*, 262.

64. Hal Foster, *The Return of the Real: The Avant-Garde at the End of the Century* (Cambridge, MA: MIT Press, 1996), 146.

65. Ibid., 152.
66. Ibid., 166.
67. Barthes, *Camera Lucida*, 6.
68. Rosalind Krauss, "X Marks the Spot," in *Rachel Whiteread: Shedding Life* (Liverpool: Tate Gallery, 1997), 74–81; at 81.
69. Ibid., 76.

INTERTEXTUALITIES, INTERDISCOURSES, AND INTERSECTIONALITIES

1. John Comaroff in Comaroff and Homi K. Bhabha, "Speaking of Postcoloniality, in the Continuous Present: A Conversation," in *Relocating Postcolonialism*, ed. David Theo Goldberg and Ato Quayson (Oxford: Blackwell, 2002), 15–46; at 32.
2. Kwame Anthony Appiah, *The Ethics of Identity* (Princeton: Princeton University Press, 2005), 124, quoting John Tomasi, "Kymlicka, Liberalism, and Respect for Cultural Minorities," *Ethics* 105.3 (April 1995), 580–603; at 589.
3. See further note 1 to Chapter 2 in this volume. [Ed.]
4. The essay referenced is "Heterotopia and Placelessness in Brian Chikwava's *Harare North*," in *The Globalization of Space: Foucault and Heterotopia*, ed. Mariangela Palladino and John Miller (2015; London: Routledge, 2016), 49–64. [Ed.]

APPENDIX 1: TRANSCRIPT

1. The name of a gang.

APPENDIX 2: TRANSLATED TRANSCRIPT

1. The name of a gang.
2. While "lanies" (in the original) translates as "toffs," here used for the police because they are white, I've used "boers," as Boeta Dickie calls them earlier.
3. His woman or wife

BIBLIOGRAPHY

Abrahams, Cecil, ed. *The Tragic Life: Bessie Head and Literature of Southern Africa*. Trenton, NJ: Africa World Press, 1990.

Africa South Art Initiative. http://asai.co.za.

Ahmad, Aijaz. *In Theory: Classes, Nations, Literatures*. London: Verso, 1992.

Anderson, Benedict. *Imagined Communities*. 1983. London: Verso, 2006.

Appiah, Kwame Anthony. *The Ethics of Identity*. Princeton: Princeton University Press, 2005.

Appignanesi, Lisa, and Sara Maitland, eds. *The Rushdie File*. London: Fourth Estate, 1989.

Art from South Africa. Oxford: Museum of Modern Art, 1990.

Attridge, Derek. "Oppressive Silence: J. M. Coetzee's *Foe* and the Politics of the Canon." In *Decolonizing the Tradition: New Views of Twentieth Century "British" Literary Canons*. Ed. Karen Lawrence. Urbana: University of Illinois Press, 1992. 212–38.

———. *J. M. Coetzee and the Ethics of Reading: Literature in the Event*. Chicago: University of Chicago Press, 2004.

———. "Zoë Wicomb's Home Truths." *Journal of Postcolonial Writing* 41.2 (2005), 156–65.

Attwell, David. *J. M. Coetzee: South Africa and the Politics of Writing*. Berkeley: University of California Press, 1993.

Austin, J. L. *How to Do Things with Words*. Oxford: Clarendon Press, 1962.

Badsha, Omar, et al. *Submission to CODESA from the Federation of South African Cultural Organisations: Towards a National Cultural Policy for the Development of Arts and Culture in a Democratic South Africa*, 2 March 1992.

Bailey, Nancy. "Living Without the Future: Nadine Gordimer's *July's People*." *World Literature Written in English* 24.2 (1984), 215–24.

Bakhtin, Mikhail. "Discourse in the Novel." In *The Dialogic Imagination*. Ed. Michael Holquist, Trans. Caryl Emerson and Michael Holquist. Austin: University of Texas Press, 1984. 259–422.

———. "From the Pre-History of Novelistic Discourse." In *Modern Criticism and Theory*. Ed. David Lodge. Longman: Harlow, 1988. 125–157.

Bal, Mieke. *Looking In—The Art of Viewing*. Amsterdam: Overseas Publishers Association, 2001.

Barnard, Chris. *Moerland*. Cape Town: Tafelberg, 1992.

Barnard, Rita. "Oprah's Paton, or South Africa and the Globalization of Suffering." *English Studies in Africa* 47.1 (2004), 85–107.

———. "Rewriting the Nation." In *The Cambridge History of South African Literature*. Ed. David Attwell and Derek Attridge. Cambridge: Cambridge University Press, 2012. 652–75.

Barnett, Clive. "Constructions of Apartheid in the International Reception of the Novels of J. M. Coetzee." *Journal of Southern African Studies* 25.2 (1999), 287–301.

Barthes, Roland. *S/Z*. Trans. Richard Miller. New York: Hill and Wang, 1975.

———. *Image—Music—Text*. Trans. Stephen Heath. London: Fontana, 1977.

———. *Camera Lucida*. Trans. Richard Howard. London: Vintage, 1993.

Bartley, Aryn. "The Violence of the Present: *David's Story* and the Truth and Reconciliation Commission." *Comparative Literature Studies* 46.1 (2009), 103–24.

Beall, Jo, Shireen Hassim, and Alison Todes. "'A Bit on the Side'? Gender Struggles in the Politics of Transformation in South Africa." *Feminist Review* 33 (1989), 30–56.

Benjamin, Andrew. *Translation and the Nature of Philosophy: A New Theory of Words*. London: Routledge, 1989.

———. "Translating Origins: Psychoanalysis and Philosophy." In *Rethinking Translation: Discourse, Subjectivity, Ideology*. Ed. Lawrence Venuti. London and New York: Routledge, 1992. 18–41.

Benjamin, Walter. "Theses on the Philosophy of History." *Illuminations*. Trans. Harry Zohn. 1968. New York: Schocken, 1969. 253–64.

———. "The Task of the Translator." *Illuminations*. Trans. Harry Zohn. 1968. London: Fontana, 1973. 69–82.

Bewes, Timothy. *The Event of Postcolonial Shame*. Princeton: Princeton University Press, 2011.

Bhabha, Homi. *The Location of Culture*. London: Routledge, 1994.

Boehmer, Elleke. "Endings and New Beginnings: South Africa Fiction in Transition." In *Writing South Africa: Literature, Apartheid, and Democracy, 1970–1995*. Ed. Derek Attridge and Rosemary Jolly. Cambridge: Cambridge University Press, 1998. 43–56.

Boym, Svetlana. *The Future of Nostalgia*. New York: Basic Books, 2001.

Bradley, Fiona. "Introduction." *Rachel Whiteread: Shedding Life*. Liverpool: Tate Gallery, 1997. 8–17.

"Breaking the Silence." In *Buang Basadi: Khulumani Makhosikazi: Women Speak*. Johannesburg: COSAW, Transvaal Region, 1988. 11–18.

Brink, André. "Complications of Birth: Interfaces of Gender, Race and Class in *July's People*." *English in Africa* 21.1–2 (1994), 157–80.

Bunn, David. "'Some Alien Land': Arthur Nortje, Literary History, and the Body in Exile." *World Literature Today* 70.1 (Winter 1996), 33–44.

Burgin, Victor. "Seeing Sense." In *Language, Image, Media*. Ed. Howard Davis and Paul Walton. Oxford: Blackwell, 1983. 226–44.

———. "Photography, Phantasy, Function [1980]." *Situational Aesthetics: Selected Writings by Victor Burgin*. Ed. Alexander Streitberger. Leuven: Leuven University Press, 2009. 111–48.

Burman, Sandra. "Fighting a Two-Pronged Attack: The Changing Legal Status of Women in Cape-Ruled Basutoland, 1872–1884." In *Women and Gender in Southern Africa to 1945.* Ed. Cherryl Walker. Cape Town: David Philip, 1990. 48–75.

Burnett, Ricky, ed. *Tributaries: A View of Contemporary South African Art.* Johannesburg: BMW Communication Department, 1985.

——, ed. *Jackson Hlungwani: An Exhibition.* Johannesburg: BMW Communication Department, 1989.

Cachalia, Amina. *When Hope and History Rhyme: An Autobiography.* Johannesburg: Picador Africa, 2013.

Calvino, Italo. *If on a Winter's Night a Traveller.* Trans. William Weaver. London: Picador, 1982.

——. "Levels of Reality in Literature." *The Uses of Literature.* Trans. Patrick Creagh. New York: Harcourt, Brace, 1986. 101–24.

Cameron, Deborah. *Feminism and Linguistic Theory.* London: Macmillan, 1985.

Chapman, Michael. *Southern African Literatures.* London: Longman, 1996.

Christie, Chris. "Theories of Textual Determination and Audience Agency: An Empirical Contribution to the Debate." In *Gendering the Reader.* Ed. Sara Mills. London: Harvester Wheatsheaf, 1994. 47–66.

Clingman, Stephen. *The Novels of Nadine Gordimer: History from the Inside.* London: Bloomsbury, 1993.

Cock, Jacklyn. *Maids and Madams: A Study in the Politics of Exploitation.* Johannesburg: Ravan Press, 1980.

Coetzee, Carli. "Krotoa Remembered: A Mother of Unity, a Mother of Sorrows?" In *Negotiating the Past: The Making of Memory in South Africa.* Ed. Sarah Nuttall and Carli Coetzee. Cape Town: Oxford University Press, 1998. 112–19.

——. "'The One That Got Away': Zoë Wicomb in the Archives." *Journal of Southern African Studies* 36.3 (2010), 559–69.

Coetzee, J. M. *Life & Times of Michael K.* London: Secker and Warburg, 1983.

——. *Truth in Autobiography.* Cape Town: University of Cape Town Press, 1984.

——. *White Writing: On the Culture of Letters in South Africa.* New Haven: Yale University Press, 1988.

——. *Doubling the Point: Essays and Interviews.* Ed. David Attwell. Cambridge, MA: Harvard University Press, 1992.

——. *Giving Offense: Essays on Censorship.* Chicago: University of Chicago Press, 1996.

——. *Disgrace.* London: Secker & Warburg, 1999.

——. *Stranger Shores: Essays, 1986–1999.* New York: Viking, 2001.

——. *Youth.* London: Secker and Warburg, 2002.

——. "As a Woman Grows Older." *New York Review of Books* 51.1 (2004), 11–14.

——. *Slow Man.* London: Secker and Warburg, 2005.

——. "All Autobiography Is *Autre*-biography." In *Selves in Question: Interviews on Southern African Auto/Biography.* Ed. Judith Lütge Coullie, Stephan Meyer, Thengani Ngwenya, and Thomas Olver. Honolulu: University of Hawai'i Press, 2006. 214–15.

——. *Inner Workings: Literary Essays 2000–2005.* New York: Viking, 2007.

——. *Late Essays: 2006–2017.* New York: Viking, 2018.

Coetzee, J. M., and Arabella Kurtz. *The Good Story: Exchanges on Truth, Fiction and Psychotherapy*. London: Harvill Secker, 2015.

Cohen, Richard. *Face to Face with Levinas*. New York: SUNY Press, 1984.

Comaroff, John L. "Reflections on the Colonial State in South Africa and Elsewhere: Factions, Fragments, Facts and Fiction." *Social Identities* 4.3 (October 1998), 321–61.

Comaroff, John, and Homi K. Bhabha. "Speaking of Postcoloniality, in the Continuous Present: A Conversation." In *Relocating Postcolonialism*. Ed. David Theo Goldberg and Ato Quayson. Oxford: Blackwell, 2002. 15–46.

Coombes, Annie E. *History After Apartheid: Visual Culture and Public Memory in a Democratic South Africa*. Durham, NC: Duke University Press, 2003.

Cooper, Brenda. "New Criteria for an 'Abnormal Mutation'? An Evaluation of Gordimer's *A Sport of Nature*." In *Rendering Things Visible: Essays on South African Literary Culture*. Ed. Martin Trump. Johannesburg: Ravan, 1990. 68–93.

Couzens, Tim. "'Printers' and Other Devils: The Texts of Sol T. Plaatje's *Mhudi*." *Research in African Literatures* 9.2 (1978), 198–215.

Crais, Clifton, and Pamela Scully. *Sara Baartman and the Hottentot Venus: A Ghost Story and a Biography*. Princeton: Princeton University Press, 2009.

Danto, Arthur. *Narration and Knowledge*. New York: Columbia University Press, 1985.

Daymond, Margaret J. "On Retaining and on Recognising Changes in the Genre 'Autobiography.'" *Current Writing* 3 (1991), 31–41.

———. "Finding a Safe House of Fiction." In *Telling Stories: Postcolonial Short Fiction in English*. Ed. Jacqueline Bardolph. Amsterdam: Rodopi, 2001. 183–96.

de Kock, Leon. "'A Change of Tongue': Questions of Translation." In *The Cambridge History of South African Literature*. Ed. David Attwell and Derek Attridge. Cambridge: Cambridge University Press, 2012. 739–56.

Deleuze, Gilles, and Félix Guattari. *Kafka: Toward a Minor Literature*. Trans. Dana Polan. Minneapois: University of Minnesota Press, 1986.

———. *A Thousand Plateaus: Capitalism and Schizophrenia*. Translated by Brian Massumi. London: Athlone Press, 1988.

Delport, Peggy. "Signposts for Retrieval: A Visual Framework for Enabling Memory of Place and Time." In *Recalling Community in Cape Town*. Ed. Ciraj Rasool and Sandra Prosalendis. Cape Town: District Six Museum, 2001. 31–46.

de Man, Paul. *Blindness and Insight: Essays in the Rhetoric of Contemporary Criticism*. London: Routledge, 1983.

———. *The Resistance to Theory*. Minneapolis: University of Minnesota Press, 1986.

Derrida, Jacques. *Of Grammatology*. Trans. Gayatri Chakravorty Spivak. Baltimore: Johns Hopkins University Press, 1976.

———. "How to Avoid Speaking: Denials." In *Languages of the Unsayable: The Play of Negativity in Literature and Literary Theory*. Ed. Sanford Budick and Wolfgang Iser. New York: Columbia University Press, 1989. 3–70.

———. "From 'Des Tours de Babel.'" In *A Derrida Reader: Between the Blinds*. Ed. Peggy Kamuf. Hemel Hempstead: Harvester, 1991. 244–53.

———. "The Double Session." In *A Derrida Reader: Between the Blinds*. Ed. Peggy Kamuf. Hemel Hempstead: Harvester, 1991. 171–99.

———. "From "Psyche: Inventions of the Other.'" In *A Derrida Reader: Between the Blinds*. Ed. Peggy Kamuf. Hemel Hempstead: Harvester, 1991. 200–221.

Dick, Archie L. *The Hidden History of South Africa's Book and Reading Cultures*. Toronto: University of Toronto Press, 2012.

Dlamini, Jacob. *Native Nostalgia*. Auckland Park: Jacana, 2009.

Docherty, Thomas, ed. *Postmodernism: A Reader*. Hemel Hempstead: Harvester Wheatsheaf, 1993.

Dovey, Teresa. "A Question of Power: Susan Gardner's Biography Versus Bessie Head's Autobiography." *English in Africa* 16.1 (1989), 29–38.

Driver, Dorothy. "Reconstructing the Past, Shaping the Future: Bessie Head and the Question of Feminism in a New South Africa." In *Black Women's Writing*. Ed. Gina Wisker. New York: St. Martin's Press, 1993. 160–87.

———. "Transformation Through Art: Writing, Representation, and Subjectivity in Recent South African Fiction." *World Literature Today* 70.1 (Winter 1996), 45–52.

———. "The Struggle over the Sign: Writing and History in Zoë Wicomb's Art." *Journal of South African Studies* 36.3 (2010), 523–42.

Dubow, Neville. "Photography in South Africa: The New Dilemmas Facing Apartheid's Chroniclers." *Creative Camera* 36 (1990), 36–38.

Dubow, Saul. "South Africa and South Africans: Nationality, Belonging, Citizenship." In *The Cambridge History of South Africa, Volume 2: 1885–1994*. Ed. Robert Ross, Anne Kelk Mager, and Bill Nasson. Cambridge: Cambridge University Press, 2011. 17–65.

———. *Apartheid: 1948–1994*. Oxford: Oxford University Press, 2014.

Du Prè, R. H. *Separate but Unequal*. Johannesburg: Jonathan Ball, 1993.

Dyer, Richard. "White." *Screen* 9.4 (1988), 44–64.

Easton, Kai. "Travelling Through History, 'New' South African Icons: The Narratives of Saartje Baartman and Krotoä-Eva in Zoë Wicomb's *David's Story*." *Kunapipi* 24.1–2 (2002), 237–66.

Ebrahim, Huma, ed. *Emerging Perspectives on Bessie Head*. Asmara: Africa World Press, 2004.

Eilerson, Gillian Stead. *Bessie Head: Thunder Behind Her Ears*. 1995. Portsmouth, NH: Heinemann, 1996.

Eliot, T. S. *T. S. Eliot: The Complete Poems and Plays*. London: Faber and Faber, 1969.

Elphick, Richard. *Khoikhoi and the Founding of White South Africa*. Johannesburg: Ravan, 1985.

Fabian, Johannes. *Time and the Other: How Anthropology Makes Its Object*. New York: Columbia University Press, 1983.

Fairclough, Norman. *Language and Power*. London: Longman, 1989.

Fanon, Frantz. *The Wretched of the Earth*. Trans. Constance Farrington. 1963. London: Penguin, 1967, 2001.

Finlayson, Rosalie. "Women's Language of Respect: Isihlonipho sabafazi." In *Language in South Africa*. Ed. Rajend Mesthrie. Cambridge: Cambridge University Press, 2002. 279–96.

Finnegan, Ruth. *Literacy and Orality*. Oxford: Blackwell, 1988.

Foster, Hal. *The Return of the Real: The Avant-Garde at the End of the Century.* Cambridge, MA: MIT Press, 1996.

Foucault, Michel. *The Order of Things.* Trans. A. M. Sheridan Smith. London: Tavistock, 1970.

———. *Language, Counter-Memory, Practice.* Oxford: Blackwell, 1977.

———. "My Body, This Paper, This Fire." Trans. Geoff Bennington. *Oxford Literary Review* 4.1 (Autumn 1979), 9–28.

———. "The Order of Discourse." In *Untying the Text: A Post-Structuralist Reader.* Ed. Robert Young. London: Routledge and Kegan Paul, 1981. 48–78.

Frankenberg, Ruth, ed. *Displacing Whiteness: Essays in Social and Cultural Criticism.* Durham, NC: Duke University Press, 1993.

Garb, Tamar, ed. *Figures and Fictions: Contemporary South Africa Photography.* London: V&A Publishing, 2011.

Gardner, Susan. "'Don't Ask for the True Story': A Memoir of Bessie Head." *Hecate* 12.1–2 (1986), 110–29.

Gates, Henry Louis, Jr. "Criticism in the Jungle." In *Black Literature and Literary Theory.* Ed. Henry Louis Gates Jr. and Sunday Ogbonna Anozie. New York: Methuen, 1984. 1–27.

———, ed. *Black Literature and Literary Theory.* New York: Methuen, 1984.

Gaylard, Gerald, ed. *Marginal Spaces: Reading Ivan Vladislavić.* Johannesburg: Wits University Press, 2011.

Gie, S. J. N. *Geskiedenis van Suid Afrika.* Stellenbosch: Pro Ecclesia, 1942.

Gilman, Sander L. "Black Bodies, White Bodies: Toward an Iconography of Female Sexuality in Late Nineteenth Century Art, Medicine and Literature." *Critical Inquiry* 12.1 (1985), 204–42.

Goldblatt, David. *The Transported of KwaNdebele: A South African Odyssey.* New York: Aperture, 1989.

———. *fifty-one years.* Barcelona: Museu d'Art Contemporani de Barcelona, 2001.

———. *TJ.* Rome: Contrasto, 2010.

Gordimer, Nadine. *July's People.* 1981. London: Penguin, 1982.

———. *Something out There.* Johannesburg: Ravan, 1984.

———. *The Essential Gesture: Writing, Politics and Places.* Ed. Stephen Clingman. New York: Knopf, 1988.

———. "The Concept of a People's Literature." *Staffrider* 9.1 (1990), 41.

———. *My Son's Story.* London: Penguin, 1990.

Gordimer, Nadine, in conversation with Stephen Clingman. "The Future Is Another Country." *Transition* 56 (1990), 132–52.

Green, Michael. "Nadine Gordimer's 'Future Histories': Two Senses of an Ending." *Wasafiri* 19 (1994), 14–18.

Grice, H. P. "Logic and Conversation." In *Syntax and Semantics, 3: Speech Acts.* Ed. Peter Cole and Jerry L. Morgan. New York: Academic Press, 1975. 41–58.

———. *Studies in the Way of Words.* Cambridge, MA: Harvard University Press, 1989.

Grundy, Kenneth W. "Art as a Political Weapon: South Africa's Cultural Workers Debate Their Role in the Struggle." In *Ngũgĩ Wa Thiong'o: Text and Contexts.* Ed. Charles Cantalupo. Trenton, NJ: Africa World Press, 1995. 137–64.

Gunner, Liz. "You, the Lioness." *Southern African Review of Books* 6.2 (1994), 15.

Guy, Jeff. "Gender Oppression in Southern Africa's Precapitalist Societies." In *Women and Gender in Southern Africa to 1945*. Ed. Cherryl Walker. Cape Town: David Philip, 1990. 33–47.

Habermas, Jürgen. *Postmetaphysical Thinking*. Trans. William Mark Hohengarten. Cambridge, MA: MIT Press, 1992.

Hall, Stuart. "What Is This Black in Popular Culture?" In *Black Popular Culture*. Ed. Michelle Wallace and Gina Dent. New York: New Press, 1998. 21–33.

———. "When Was 'the Post-Colonial'? Thinking at the Limit." In *The Post-Colonial Question*. Ed. Iain Chambers and Lidia Curti. London: Routledge, 1996. 242–59.

Halliday, M. A. K. "Language and the Order of Nature." In *The Linguistics of Writing: Arguments Between Language and Literature*. Ed. Nigel Fabb, Derek Attrdige, Alan Durant, and Colin MacCabe. Manchester: Manchester University Press, 1987. 135–54.

Halliday, M. A. K., and Ruqaiya Hassan. *Cohesion in English*. London: Longman, 1976.

Harries, Patrick. "The Roots of Ethnicity: Discourse and the Politics of Language Construction in South-East Africa." *African Affairs* 87.346 (January 1988), 25–52.

Head, Bessie. *Maru*. London: Heinemann, 1971.

———. *A Woman Alone: Autobiographical Writings*. Ed. Craig MacKenzie. Oxford: Heinemann Educational, 1990.

———. *The Cardinals*. Cape Town: David Philip, 1993.

———. *The Cardinals: With Meditations and Stories*. Oxford: Heinemann Educational, 1995.

———. *A Question of Power*. 1973. Johannesburg: Penguin South Africa, 2011.

Hebdige, Dick. *Hiding in the Light: On Images and Things*. London: Comedia, 1988.

Hill, Mike. *Whiteness: A Critical Reader*. New York: New York University Press, 1997.

Hoad, Neville. *African Intimacies: Race, Homosexuality, and Globalization*. Minneapolis: University of Minnesota Press, 2007.

Hofmeyr, Isabel. *"We Spend Our Years as a Tale That Is Told"—Oral Historical Narrative in a South African Chiefdom*. Johannesburg: Wits University Press, 1993.

hooks, bell. "Postmodern Blackness." In *Colonial Discourse and Post-Colonial Theory*. Ed. Patrick Williams and Laura Chrisman. Hemel Hempstead: Harvester, 1993. 421–27.

Hughes, Ted. "The Thought Fox [1957]." In *The Norton Anthology of Poetry*. Ed. Margaret Ferguson, Mary Jo Salter, and John Stallworthy. New York: W. W. Norton, 2014. 1810.

Hutcheon, Linda. "Irony, Nostalgia, and the Postmodern." *University of Toronto English Library*, http://www.library.utoronto.ca/utel/criticism/hutchinp.html.

Illich, Ivan. "A Plea for Research on Lay Literacy." In *Literacy and Orality*. Ed. David R. Olson and Nancy Torrance. Cambridge: Cambridge University Press, 1991. 28–46.

Iser, Wolfgang. "The Play of the Text." In *Languages of the Unsayable: The Play of Negativity in Literature and Literary Theory*. Ed. Sanford Budick and Wolfgang Iser. New York: Columbia University Press, 1989. 325–39.

Jacobs, J. U. "Playing in the Dark/Playing in the Light: Coloured Identity in the Novels of Zoë Wicomb." *Current Writing* 20.1 (2008), 1–15.

Jameson, Fredric. "Postmodernism, or The Cultural Logic of Late Capitalism." In *Postmodernism: A Reader*. Ed. Thomas Docherty. Hemel Hempstead: Harvester Wheatsheaf, 1993. 62–92.

Jeppie, Shamil, and Crain Soudien, eds. *The Struggle for District Six: Past and Present.* Cape Town: Buchu Books, 1990.

Joubert, Elsa. *The Long Journey of Poppie Nongena.* 1980. Johannesburg: Jonathan Ball, 1985.

Kallaway, Peter, ed. *The History of Education Under Apartheid, 1948–1994: The Doors of Education and Learning Shall Be Opened.* Cape Town: Maskew Miller Longman, 2002.

Krauss, Rosalind. "X Marks the Spot." In *Rachel Whiteread: Shedding Life.* Liverpool: Tate Gallery, 1997. 74–81.

Kreiswirth, Martin. "Merely Telling Stories? Narrative and Knowledge in the Human Sciences." *Poetics Today* 21.2 (Summer 2000), 294–318.

Kristeva, Julia. *Desire in Language.* Oxford: Blackwell, 1987.

——. *Language the Unknown.* Hemel Hempstead: Harvester, 1989.

——. *Strangers to Ourselves.* Trans. Leon S. Roudiez. New York: Columbia University Press, 1991.

Krog, Antjie. "land." *World Literature Today* 70.1 (Winter 1996), 119.

——. "Cry, Beloved Country." *Guardian,* 18 January 1997, A6.

——. *Country of My Skull.* New ed. London: Vintage, 1999.

Kruger, Loren. "'Black Atlantics,' 'White Indians,' and 'Jews': Locations, Locutions, and Syncretic Identities in the Fiction of Achmat Dangor and Others." *Scrutiny2* 7.2 (2002), 34–50.

Kuhn, Annette. *Women's Pictures: Feminism and Cinema.* London: Routledge and Kegan Paul, 1982.

Landsberg, Alison. *Prosthetic Memory: The Transformation of American Remembrance in the Age of Mass Culture.* New York: Columbia University Press, 2004.

Langenhoven, C. J. "Die Stem van Suid-Afrika." In *Junior Verseboek.* Ed. D. J. Opperman. Cape Town: Tafelberg, 1973. 66.

——. "Die Onteiening." In *Junior Verseboek.* Ed. D. J. Opperman. Cape Town: Tafelberg, 1973. 64–65.

Levinson, Stephen C. *Pragmatics.* Cambridge: Cambridge University Press, 1983.

Lévi-Strauss, Claude. *Tristes tropiques.* 1955. Trans. John and Doreen Weightman. 1973. New York: Penguin, 1992.

Linker, Kate. "Representation and Sexuality." In *Art After Modernism: Rethinking Representation.* Ed. Brian Wallis. New York: Museum of Contemporary Art, 1984. 391–416.

Lockett, Cecily. "Feminism(s) and Writing in English in South Africa." In *South African Feminisms: Writing, Theory, and Criticism 1990–1994.* Ed. M. J. Daymond. New York: Garland, 1996. 3–26.

Lyotard, Jean-François. *The Postmodern Condition: A Report on Knowledge.* Trans Geoffrey Bennington and Brian Massumi. Manchester: Manchester University Press, 1984.

——. *The Postmodern Explained to Children: Correspondence, 1982–1985.* Sydney: Power Publications, 1992.

MacKenzie, Craig, and Cherry Clayton, eds. *Between the Lines: Interviews with Bessie Head, Sheila Roberts, Ellen Kuzwayo, Miriam Tlali.* Grahamstown: National English Literary Museum, 1989. 5–29.

Majumdar, Saikat. "*You Can't Get Lost in Cape Town* and the Counter-Ethnography of the Banal." *Genre* 39 (Summer 2006), 301–28.

Malan, Rian. *My Traitor's Heart.* 1990. London: Vintage, 2015.

Mamdani, Mahmood. "Reconciliation Without Justice." *Southern African Review of Books* 46 (Nov./Dec. 1996), 3–5.

Marais, Sue. "Getting Lost in Cape Town: Spatial and Temporal Dislocation in the South African Short Fiction Cycle." *English in Africa* 22.2 (October 1995), 29–43.

Matshoba, Mtutuzeli. *Call Me Not a Man.* Harlow: Longman, 1979.

Mattera, Don. "Die Bushie is dood . . ." In *Being Here: Modern Short Stories from Southern Africa.* Ed. Robin Malan. Cape Town: David Philip, 1994. 138–42.

McClintock, Anne. "'Azikwelwa' (We Will Not Ride): Politics and Value in Black South African Poetry." *Critical Inquiry* 13.3 (1987), 597–623.

——. *Imperial Leather: Race, Gender and Sexuality in the Colonial Contest.* New York: Routledge, 1995.

McCormick, Kay. "The Vernacular of District Six." In *The Struggle for District Six: Past and Present.* Ed. Shamil Jeppie and Crain Soudien. Cape Town: Buchu Books, 1990. 88–109.

McDonald, Peter D. *The Literature Police: Apartheid Censorship and Its Cultural Consequences.* Oxford: Oxford University Press, 2009.

Melville, Herman. *Billy Budd, Sailor and Other Stories.* 1967. Harmondsworth: Penguin, 1985.

Meyer, Stephan, and Thomas Olver. "Zoë Wicomb Interviewed on Writing and Nation." *Journal of Literary Studies* 18.1 (2002), 182–98.

Mhlope, Gcina. "The Toilet." In *Being Here: Modern Short Stories from Southern Africa.* Ed. Robin Malan. Cape Town: David Philip, 1994. 117–23

Miles, Robert. *Racism.* London: Routledge, 1989.

Mills, Sara, ed. "Introduction." *Gendering the Reader.* London: Harvester Wheatsheaf, 1994. 1–22.

Morgan, Stuart. "Rachel Whiteread." In *Rachel Whiteread: Shedding Life.* Liverpool: Tate Gallery, 1997. 19–28.

Morrison, Toni. *Beloved.* London: Chatto and Windus, 1987.

——. *Jazz.* New York: Penguin, 1992.

——. *Playing in the Dark: Whiteness and the Literary Imagination.* New York: Vintage Books, 1993.

Mphahlele, Ezekiel (Es'kia). *The African Image.* New York: Praeger, 1962.

Mphahlele, Es'kia. "Mrs Plum." In *Modern African Stories.* Ed. Charles R. Larson. London: Fontana, 1971. 155–92.

Mukherjee, Bharati. "They Never Wanted to Be Themselves." *New York Times.* Sunday, 24 May 1987 (Late City Final Edition), section 7, 7.

Mulhern, Francis. *Culture/Metaculture.* London: Routledge, 2000.

Myers, Kathy. "Uderstanding Advertisers." In *Language, Image, Media.* Ed. Howard Davis and Paul Walton. Oxford: Blackwell, 1983. 205–23.

Nasson, Bill. "Oral History and the Reconstruction of District Six." In *The Struggle for District Six: Past and Present.* Ed. Shamil Jeppie and Crain Soudien. Cape Town: Buchu Books, 1990. 44–66.

Ndebele, Njabulo S. *Fools and Other Stories*. Harlow: Longman, 1985.

———. "The Rediscovery of the Ordinary: Some New Writings in South Africa." *Journal of Southern African Studies*, 12.2 (April 1986), 143–57.

———. *Rediscovery of the Ordinary*. Johannesburg: COSAW, 1991.

———. *South African Literature and Culture: Rediscovery of the Ordinary*. Ed. Graham Pechey. Manchester: Manchester University Press, 1994.

———. *Fine Lines from the Box: Further Thoughts About Our Country*. Cape Town: Umuzi, 2007.

———. "Liberation Betrayed by Bloodshed." *Social Dynamics: A Journal of African Studies* 39.1 (2013), 111–14.

Nettleton, Anitra. "Home Is Where the Art Is: Six South African Rural Artists." *African Arts* 33.4 (2000), 26–39.

Newton, Adam Zachary. *Narrative Ethics*. Cambridge, MA: Harvard University Press, 1997.

Nkosi, Lewis. *Home and Exile*. London: Longman, 1965.

Nkululeko, D. "The Right to Self-determination in Research: Azanian Women." *Women in Southern Africa*. Ed. C. Qunta. Braamfontein: Skotaville, 1987.

Nussbaum, Martha. *Love's Knowledge: Essays on Philosophy and Literature*. New York: Oxford University Press, 1990.

———. *Poetic Justice: The Literary Imagination and Public Life*. Boston: Beacon Press, 1997.

Obery, Ingrid, ed. *Vukani Makhosikazi: South African Women Speak*. London: Catholic Institute for International Relations, 1985.

Ogunyemi, Chikwenye Okonjo. "Womanism: The Dynamics of the Contemporary Black Female Novel in English." *Signs* 11.1 (1985), 63–80.

Olaussen, Maria. "Generation and Complicity in Zoë Wicomb's *Playing in the Light*." *Social Dynamics* 35.1 (2009), 149–61.

Ong, Walter J. *Orality and Literacy: The Technologizing of the Word*. London: Methuen, 1982.

Owens, Craig. "The Discourse of Others: Feminists and Postmodernism." In *Postmodern Culture*. Ed. Hal Foster. 1983. London: Pluto Press, 1987. 57–82.

Ozinsky, Max, and Ibrahim Rasool. "Developing a Strategic Perspective for the Coloured Areas in the Western Cape." *African Communist* 133 (Second Quarter 1993), 39–47.

Parker, Kenneth. "Gendering a Language, Liberating a People: Women Writing in Afrikaans and the 'New' South Africa." *Social Identities* 2.2 (1996), 199–220.

Pateman, Trevor. "How Is Understanding an Advertisement Possible?" In *Language, Image, Media*. Ed. Howard Davis and Paul Walton. Oxford: Blackwell, 1983. 187–204.

Paton, Alan. *Cry, the Beloved Country*. London: Jonathan Cape, 1948.

Pêcheux, Michel. *Language, Semantics and Ideology*. Basingstoke: Macmillan, 1982.

Peterson, Bhekizizwe. "Modernist at Large: The Aesthetics of *Native Life in South Africa*." In *Sol Plaatje's* Native Life in South Africa: *Past and Present*. Ed. Janet Remmington, Brian Willan, and Bhekizizwe Peterson. Johannesburg: Wits University Press, 2016. 18–36.

Plaatje, Sol T. *Mhudi*. 1930. London: Heinemann, 1978.

Posel, Deborah. "The Apartheid Project, 1948–1970." In *The Cambridge History of South Africa, Volume 2: 1885–1994*. Ed. Robert Ross, Anne Kelk Mager, and Bill Nasson. Cambridge: Cambridge University Press, 2011. 319–68.

Pratt, Mary Louise. *Towards a Speech Act Theory of Literary Discourse*. Bloomington: Indiana University Press, 1977.

———. "Linguistic Utopias." In *The Linguistics of Writing: Arguments Between Language and Literature*. Ed. Nigel Fabb, Derek Attridge, Alan Durant, and Colin MacCabe. Manchester: Manchester University Press, 1987. 48–66.

Promotion of National Unity and Reconciliation Act (No. 34 of 1995, as amended), http://www.justice.gov.za/legislation/acts/1995-034.pdf.

Raiskin, Judith L. *Snow on the Cane Fields: Women's Writing and Creole Subjectivity*. Minneapolis: Minnesota University Press, 1996.

Richards, Colin. "desperately seeking 'africa.'" In *Art from South Africa*. Oxford: Museum of Modern Art, 1990. 40.

Rimmon-Kenan, Shlomith. *Narrative Fiction*. London: Routledge, 1983.

Rive, Richard. *"Buckingham Palace," District Six*. Cape Town: David Philip, 1986.

Robinson, David. "Under the Skin of Lies." *Scotsman*, 27 May 2006 (Saturday Critique), 20.

Robolin, Stéphane. "Loose Memory in Toni Morrison's *Paradise* and Zoë Wicomb's *David's Story*," *MFS: Modern Fiction Studies* 52.2 (2006), 297–320.

———. "Properties of Whiteness: (Post)Apartheid Geographies in Zoë Wicomb's *Playing in the Light*." *Safundi: The Journal of South African and American Studies* 12.3–4 (2011), 349–71.

Romaine, Suzanne. *Bilingualism*. Oxford: Blackwell, 1989.

Rorty, Richard. "Pragmatism, Davidson and Truth." In *Truth and Interpretation: Perspectives on the Philosophy of Donald Davidson*. Ed. Ernest LePore. Oxford: Blackwell, 1986. 333–55.

———. *Truth and Progress: Philosophical Papers, Volume 3*. Cambridge: Cambridge University Press, 1998.

———. "Human Rights, Rationality and Sentimentality." In *Wronging Rights? Philosophical Challenges for Human Rights*. Ed. Aakash Singh Rathore and Alex Cistelecan. Abingdon: Routledge, 2012. 107–31.

Ross, Fiona. *Bearing Witness: Women and the Truth and Reconciliation Commission in South Africa*. London: Pluto Press, 2003.

Ross, Robert. *Cape of Torments: Slavery and Resistance in South Africa*. London: Routledge and Kegan Paul, 1983.

Rosso, Stefano, and Carolyn Springer. "A Correspondence with Umberto Eco [Genova-Bologna-Binghamton-Bloomington, August–September, 1982, March–April, 1983]." *boundary 2* 12.1 (Autumn 1983), 1–13.

Rushdie, Salman. *Shame*. London: Picador, 1984.

———. *The Satanic Verses*. London: Viking, 1988.

Sachs, Albie. "Preparing Ourselves for Freedom." In *Spring Is Rebellious: Arguments About Cultural Freedom*. Ed. Ingrid de Kok and Karen Press. Cape Town: Buchu Books, 1990. 19–29.

Said, Edward W. *Humanism and Democratic Criticism.* New York: Columbia University Press, 2004.

——. *The World, the Text, and the Critic.* Cambridge, MA: Harvard University Press, 1983.

Samuelson, Meg. "The Disfigured Body of the Female Guerilla: (De)Militarization, Sexual Violence, and Redomestication in Zoë Wicomb's *David's Story." Signs: Journal of Women in Culture and Society* 32.4 (2007), 833–56.

——. *Remembering the Nation, Dismembering Women? Stories of the South African Transition.* Scottsville: University of KwaZulu-Natal Press, 2007.

Sanders, Mark. *Ambiguities of Witnessing: Law and Literature in the Time of a Truth Commission.* Stanford: Stanford University Press, 2007.

——. "Cape Impudence." *Current Writing* 23.2 (2011), 118–26.

Scarry, Elaine. *On Beauty and Being Just.* 1999. London: Duckworth, 2006.

Searle, J. R. *Speech Acts: An Essay in the Philosophy of Language.* Cambridge: Cambridge University Press, 1969.

Seidman, Steven, ed. *Jürgen Habermas on Society and Politics: A Reader.* Boston: Beacon Books, 1989.

Sepamla, Sipho. "The Land." *The Soweto I Love.* London: Rex Collings, 1977.

Sicherman, Carol. "Literary Afterword." In Zoë Wicomb, *You Can't Get Lost in Cape Town.* 1987. New York: Feminist Press at the City University of New York, 2000. 187–208.

Silverman, Kaja. *The Threshold of the Visible World.* London: Routledge, 1996.

Skinner, J. B., and D. Rintoul, eds. *English Essays.* London: George Harrap, 1961.

Skotnes, Pippa, ed. *Miscast: Negotiating the Presence of the Bushmen.* Cape Town: University of Cape Town Press, 1996.

Smith, Neil. *Uneven Development.* Oxford: Blackwell, 1984.

Sperber, Dan, and Deirdre Wilson. *Relevance: Communication and Cognition.* 2nd ed. Oxford: Blackwell, 1995.

Spivak, Gayatri Chakravorty. *Outside in the Teaching Machine.* London: Routledge, 1993.

——. "Acting Bits/Identity Talk." *Critical Inquiry* 18.4 (Summer 1992), 770–803.

——. "Resident Alien." In *Relocating Postcolonialism.* Ed. David Theo Goldberg and Ato Quayson. Oxford: Blackwell, 2002. 47–65.

Steiner, George. *After Babel: Aspects of Language and Translation.* New York: Oxford University Press, 1975.

——. *After Babel: Aspects of Language and Translation.* 3rd ed. Oxford: Oxford University Press, 1998.

Street, Brian. *Literacy in Theory and Practice.* Cambridge: Cambridge University Press, 1984.

Thom, H. B., ed. *Journal of Jan van Riebeeck.* Cape Town: Balkema, 1952.

Thornborrow, Joanna. "The Woman, the Man and the Filofax: Gender Positions in Advertising." In *Gendering the Reader.* Ed. Sara Mills. London: Harvester Wheatsheaf, 1994. 128–51.

Tlali, Miriam. *Footprints in the Quag.* Cape Town: David Philip, 1989.

Tomasi, John. "Kymlicka, Liberalism, and Respect for Cultural Minorities." *Ethics* 105.3 (April 1995), 580–603.

Tonkin, Elizabeth. *Narrating Our Pasts: The Social Construction of Oral History.* Cambridge: Cambridge University Press, 1992.

Trevor-Roper, Hugh. "The Invention of Tradition: The Highland Tradition of Scotland." In *The Invention of Tradition.* Ed. Eric Hobsbawm and Terence Ranger. Cambridge: Cambridge University Press, 1983. 15–42.

Truth and Reconciliation Commission Report, 1998, http://www.justice.gov.za/trc/.

Twain, Mark. *The Adventures of Huckleberry Finn.* 1884. London: Penguin, 2012.

van der Vlies, Andrew. *South African Textual Cultures: Black, White, Read All Over.* Manchester: Manchester University Press, 2007.

———. "The Archive, the Spectral, and Narrative Responsibility in Zoë Wicomb's *Playing in the Light.*" *Journal of Southern African Studies* 36.3 (2010), 583–98.

———. "The History of the Book in Sub-Saharan Africa." In *The Oxford Companion to the Book.* Ed. Michael F. Suarez and Henry Woudhuysen. Volume 1. Oxford: Oxford University Press, 2010. 313–20.

———. "The Novel's Reception." *J. M. Coetzee's* Disgrace. London: Continuum, 2010. 71–80.

———. "Zoë Wicomb's Queer Cosmopolitanisms." *Safundi: The Journal of South African and American Studies* 12.3–4 (July–October 2011), 425–44.

———. *Present Imperfect: Contemporary South African Writing.* Oxford: Oxford University Press, 2017.

van Heerden, Etienne. *Toorberg.* Cape Town: Tafelberg, 1986.

———. *Ancestral Voices.* Trans. Malcolm Hacksley. 1989. London: Alison and Busby, 1993.

van Niekerk, Marlene. "Kanonbaai." In *Die vrou wat haar verkyker vergeet het.* Pretoria: HAUM-Literêr, 1992. 16–35.

———. *Triomf.* Cape Town: Queillerie, 1994.

———. *Triomf.* Trans. Leon de Kock. London: Abacus Books, 2000.

Vaughan, Michael. "Literature and Politics: Currents in South African writing." *Journal of Southern African Studies* 9.1 (1982), 118–38.

———. "Storytelling and Politics in Fiction." In *Rendering Things Visible: Essays on South African Literary Culture.* Ed. Martin Trump. Johannesburg: Ravan, 1990. 186–204.

Venuti, Lawrence. *The Translator's Invisibility: A History of Translation.* 3rd ed. New York: Routledge, 2018.

Vigne, Randolph, ed. *A Gesture of Belonging: Letters from Bessie Head, 1965–1979.* London: Heinemann, 1991.

Visser, Nicholas. "Beyond the Interregnum: A Note on the Ending of *July's People.*" In *Rendering Things Visible: Essays on South African Literary Culture.* Ed. Martin Trump. Johannesburg: Ravan, 1990. 61–67.

Vladislavić, Ivan. *Propaganda by Monuments.* Cape Town: David Philip, 1996.

———. *Double Negative.* Rome: Contrasto, 2010.

Walder, Dennis. *Postcolonial Nostalgias.* London: Routledge, 2011.

Walker, Alice. *In Search of Our Mothers' Gardens: Womanist Prose.* London: Women's Press, 1984.

Weems, Carrie Mae. *Then What? Photographs and Folklore.* Buffalo: CEPA Gallery Publications, 1990.

Wicomb, Zoë. *You Can't Get Lost in Cape Town.* 1987. New York: Feminist Press at the City University of New York, 2000.

———. "Zoë Wicomb Interviewed by Eva Hunter—Cape Town, 5 June 1990." In *Between the Lines II: Interviews with Nadine Gordimer, Menán du Plessis, Zoë Wicomb, Lauretta Ngcobo.* Ed. Eva Hunter and Craig MacKenzie. Grahamstown: NELM, 1993. 79–96.

———. "Shame and Identity: The Case of the Coloured in South Africa." In *Writing South Africa: Literature, Apartheid, and Democracy, 1970–1995.* Ed. Derek Attridge and Rosemary Jolly. Cambridge: Cambridge University Press, 1998. 91–107.

———. *David's Story.* 2000. New York: Feminist Press at the City University of New York, 2001.

———. "Interview: Zoë Wicomb in Conversation with Hein Willemse." *Research in African Literatures* 33.1 (2002), 144–52.

———. "Translations in the Yard of Africa." *Journal of Literary Studies* 18.3 (2002), 209–23.

———. *Playing in the Light.* New York: New Press, 2006.

———. "10 Questions: Zoe Wicomb." By Anna James. *The Bookseller,* June 3, 2014. http://www.welovethisbook.com/features/10-questions-zoe-wicomb.

———. *October.* Cape Town: Umuzi, 2014.

———. *October.* New York: New Press, 2014.

———. "Heterotopia and Placelessness in Brian Chikwava's *Harare North.*" In *The Globalization of Space: Foucault and Heterotopia.* Ed. Mariangela Palladino and John Miller. 2015. London: Routledge, 2016. 49–64.

Willan, Brian. *Sol Plaatje: A Biography.* Johannesburg: Ravan Press, 1984.

———. "What 'Other Devils'? The Texts of Sol T. Plaatje's *Mhudi* Revisited." *Journal of Southern African Studies* 41.6 (2015), 1331–47.

Willemse, Hein. "Die Skrille Sonbesies: Emergent Black Afrikaans Poets in Search of Authority." In *Rendering Things Visible: Essays on South African Literary Culture.* Ed. Martin Trump. Johannesburg: Ravan, 1990. 367–401.

Williams, Raymond. *Culture.* Glasgow: Fontana, 1981.

Williamson, Judith. *Decoding Advertisements: Ideology and Meaning in Advertising.* London: Boyars, 1978.

Williamson, Sue, and Ashraf Jamal, eds. *Art in South Africa: The Future Present.* Cape Town: David Philip, 1996.

Wittgenstein, Ludwig. *Remarks on Colour.* Ed. G. E. M. Anscombe. Trans. Linda L. McAlister and Margaret Schättle. Berkeley: University of California Press, 1977.

Wright, Marcia. "Historical Introduction." In Zoë Wicomb, *You Can't Get Lost in Cape Town.* New York: Feminist Press at the City University of New York, 2000. vii–xxiv.

Yates, Frances. *The Art of Memory.* London: Routledge and Kegan Paul, 1966.

Young, Robert. *Colonial Desire: Hybridity in Theory, Culture and Race.* London: Routledge, 1995.

Younge, Gavin. *Art of the South African Townships.* London: Thames and Hudson, 1988.

INDEX

!Kun, 13
!Xam, 13

Africa, personified as mother, 92–93, 101, 152
African National Congress (A.N.C.), 6–7, 18–19, 22, 37–39, 45, 53, 60, 68, 82, 116, 118, 120–21, 124–25, 127, 128–29, 135, 265, 266, 270, 278, 299n22; Women's League, 127; Youth League, 127
Afrikaans, 9–10, 64, 121, 129, 135, 145, 149, 157, 173, 184, 194–95, 266, 286, 290; and accent, 153; and Afrikaner-hood, 133–34, 141–43; as creole, 9, 10, 25, 142; as language of oppressor, 119, 129, 142, 266; literature in, 25, 119–20, 124, 140, 144, 152, 266; local, non-standard, and racialized varieties of, 118–20, 124, 142, 146, 148, 153, 188–90, 193–95; and National Party, 121; printing in, 24–25; syntax, 126, 190; as Wicomb's family's first language, 12, 24. *See also* Afrikaner(s); *Kaaps*
Afrikaner(s), 129, 157, 181; as barbaric, 135; Black, and blackness, 135, 142, 144, 148, 152–54; British oppression of, 135, 140; Brown, 124–25, 145–47; and Calvinism, 142–43, 148, 154; culture, writing, and

the land, 24–25, 136–42, 144–55; food, 64–65, 129; as Israelites, trope of, 140, 142, 146; Krotoa-Eva as ancestor of, 160–61; and language, 141–43, 153, 157; revision of identity of, 24–25, 133–37, 154–56; and whiteness, 24–25, 121, 142–44, 147, 156. *See also* Afrikaans: and Afrikanerhood; *Afrikaner Weer-standsbeweging*; boer (*Boer*): as racial term; National Party; Orania
Afrikaner Weerstandsbeweging (A.W.B.), 125, 133, 309n30, 310n1
Ahmad, Aijaz, 126
Althusser, Louis, 274
Anderson, Benedict, 44, 49, 56
antiapartheid movement (Anti-Apartheid Movement), 12, 142, 262
apartheid, 3–6, 9–10, 12, 18, 20, 23–24, 26–30, 37–39, 43, 48, 54, 56–60, 63, 68–69, 76–77, 81, 84, 86, 88–90, 95, 101, 112, 115–17, 119, 121–22, 126, 128–29, 133, 136–39, 143, 148, 150, 152, 155–56, 159, 162, 164, 167–69, 171–73, 180–81, 187, 188–92, 196, 200–202, 204, 206–7, 212–14, 217–18, 221, 226, 229, 264, 267, 278; banality of, 129; geography of, 138–39, 145, 149, 231–32; as hubristic, 146; as spectacle, 5. *See also* Group